Torn Sprockets

Torn Sprockets

The Uncertain Projection of the Canadian Film

Gerald Pratley

An Ontario Film Institute Book
Newark: University of Delaware Press
London and Toronto: Associated University Presses

Associated University Presses
440 Forsgate Drive
Cranbury, NJ 08512

Associated University Presses
25 Sicilian Avenue
London WC1A 2QH, England

Associated University Presses
2133 Royal Windsor Drive
Unit 1
Mississauga, Ontario
Canada L5J 1K5

Library of Congress Cataloging in Publication Data

Pratley, Gerald.
  Torn sprockets.

  Bibliography: p.
  Filmography: p.
  Includes index.
    1. Moving-picture industry—Canada—History.
  2. Moving-pictures—Canada—Catalogs. I. Title.
  PN1993.5.C2P7 1987   384′.8′0971   83-40110
  ISBN 0-87413-194-4

Printed in the United States of America

Contents

Acknowledgments

The author thanks Peter Cowie (editor, *International Film Guide,* London), Robert Landry (Editor Emeritus), *Variety,* New York), Patricia Thompson (editor, *Canadian Film Digest YEARBOOK,* Toronto), Robert Weaver (producer, Canadian Broadcasting Corporation, Toronto), Sherie Brehtour (Ontario Film Institute, Toronto), and the National Film Board of Canada, Montreal and Toronto, for their services and assistance, and with fond reference to Risa Shuman for her support and encouragement. I must also thank my editor, Beth Gianfagna, for her skill and patience, her helpfulness and understanding during the production of this book. Film historians Peter Morris and the late Hyman Bossin deserve a special mention for their pioneering work in researching and writing the history of Canadian motion picture production and exhibition. Without it, much of what is in this book would never have been known.

All illustrations are from the Stills Collection of the Ontario Film Institute and Archive and are used by courtesy of the copyright owners. Particular thanks are due to the National Film Board for providing additional photographs from its films.

Torn Sprockets

Part 1
Early Canadian Film-making 1900–1939

1
Cinema in Canada
An Introduction

Canada's early work in film-making is not important, and there is little point in trying to pretend otherwise. Between the years 1886, when films as we know them were first projected in a musée on Toronto's Yonge Street, and 1939, when the National Film Board was formed, the production of motion pictures in Canada was often interesting, determined, usually well-intentioned, always with high hopes, but in the end sadly insignificant, with little impact on audiences and containing little value for present-day study. What remains in the care of the National Film, Television, and Sound Archives of Canada in Ottawa is simple, sometimes nostalgic, and revealing in its depiction of people, places, and events. It offers tantalizing glimpses of the way Canada was, with newsreel and documentary footage far surpassing in interest, realism, and excitement the romantic fictions of the feature-length accomplishments of producers and directors, who, most often, were forced by the pressures of financiers to create the most palatable pictures for immediate profits.

Throughout this entire period, not one Canadian director, star, or picture came to find recognition either at home or abroad or to find a permanent place in the country's cinema history. This is not to say that talented individuals did not exist. The famous Canadians Mary Pickford, Walter Huston, Marie Dressler, and Walter Pidgeon, all accomplished artists and performers with little prior experience in Canada, found fame in Hollywood at the time of its greatest influence on the world.

In this situation Canada was like many other countries. The Hollywood studios' influence on the world worked in two directions: its films monopolized the world's cinemas, and the film-makers in all European countries knew, no matter how successful they were at home, that international recognition and large salaries came only from working at the studios of the Hollywood companies. So they either traveled westward in anticipation of being hired or heeded the call to accept engagements there.

Great Britain settled many lands that began as colonies and developed into nations, all entirely or predominantly English-speaking, among them Australia, Canada, South Africa, New Zealand—and the thirteen American colonies that grew into the world's greatest nation. The language that united these countries also served to work against them, so far as the verbal arts were concerned. The people of the empire, as it was then known, tended to devote their energies to the work of industrial and agricultural development and leave the arts to the mother country. Literature, in particular, whether written in the form of history, biography, education, the novel, play, or screenplay (then considered the lowliest of them all), and later the radio, usually came from Britain, or in Canada's case, with two languages, from France as well. The writers in the new lands, together with other artists, found the climate for their work uncertain and recognition hard to achieve in their lifetimes, largely because the public and the press, brought up to look toward London and Paris, and later New York, as the source of all achievement, failed to support many of their own artists ·because they believed them to be too local and limited. Not until the late 1960s and the early 1970s, with the emergence of what is now called Canadian "nationalism," did this attitude change.

Only in the United States, which changed its outward manifestations of official and political ties with its mother country, did the popular arts flourish with a wildness and abandon that led to the development of that country into one proficient in all the arts. The reason for this development was simply the vision of freedom in all aspects of life that the United States held out to the peoples of the Old World. Before the first world war, during the time of unrestricted immigration, the world's poor and persecuted, the victims of rigid social systems, religious domination, and of suffocating class distinctions, poured into the United States, knowing that they were free to start again, with none of the orders that had repressed them in the past reaching out to dominate and restrict them on the new continent. This mass movement led to the creation of a nation with an enormous population, a society free-to-all within a free-for-all existence, which brought about living conditions often just as terrible as those left behind but made tolerable by the knowledge that every man was free to go out, improve his lot, and pursue his wildest dreams without ridicule and restraint. What all this meant was that America benefitted from the hopes, dreams, aspirations, and ideas of thousands of talented people, many from Britain, who created a distinctive world of literature and art, music and theater that appealed first to the English-speaking nations of which it had once been a simple colony, and then, with the rapid growth of the cinema, to the entire world.

The brash, rough-and-ready Americans did not create the cinema single-handedly. Inventors in many lands were working on the principle of making a succession of still images come to life by their rapid projection through a machine. But the Americans, with their lack of conservative habits and willingness to try anything new and to invest money in enterprises that they hoped would make more money, saw the immediate possibilities in moving pictures as a rewarding novelty entertainment—even if it died out after a few years. So Edison's Kinetescope and later the nickelodeons thrived largely on short films made in Europe. When the supply of films for the public in Britain, France, and Italy came to a near halt during the First World War, the Americans, whose economy was unaffected by the war and who remained outside the conflict until 1917, forged ahead in film-making, captured existing overseas markets where audiences were desperate for diversions, and through sheer efficiency, resourcefulness, its own immense and wealthy home market, and by strong-arm methods monopolized the world's cinema for the next sixty-five years.

They were able to do this because Hollywood's films appealed to mass audiences everywhere. They depicted, often wrongly, a society fresh and vigorous, young and challenging, where virtue was rewarded, happiness could be bought, and where America was a land of freedom and opportunity. Many of the thousands of people who emigrated to the United States during this period did so because of the life they saw on the silver screens of their own depressed communities. Among the monopolized countries, none was more dominated by Hollywood than Canada. And the more proficient the Hollywood studios became with recording sound, developing color, discovering stars, and telling stories, the less likely it seemed that film makers anywhere else could ever hope to do as well.

Not realizing that they were being subtly influenced by the American way of life, which they saw week after week in their cinemas, the public everywhere flocked to see American films. What other nations did with armies, the Americans did with motion pictures: they conquered the world. In non-English-speaking countries, intertitles were printed in the language of the country, and later, with sound, actors' voices were removed and "dubbed" with other voices speaking the language of the country. Some nations, however, with the means to make films and with their own strong artistic traditions, resisted the Hollywood invasion somewhat by means of government subsidies and quotas. In this way Sweden, France, Great Britain, Italy, and Russia, for example, assisted native producers and created distinctive national cinemas. Economics played a large part in the worldwide distribution and exhibition of American films: no other developed countries had an audience as great as the United States, where most of its films (and today, its television programs) paid for themselves at home, making them cheap to sell abroad.

But in Canada, neither the public nor its politicians seemed to think that they should have a cinema of their own, partly because, in the public's opinion, they lived so close to the Americans that their life might not seem to be separate; and, particularly not, in the opinion of the politicians, if the production of films required assistance from the treasury. Some individuals viewed with concern the constant depiction of American life on Canadian screens, but their voices were weak; many film-makers wanted to resist the tide with movies of Canadian life, but their resources were meager.

When Canadians did manage to make a film, who would show it? The major cinemas were owned by the Americans, who had no wish to displace one of their own money-making movies for a Canadian picture. The public on the whole was quite happy to see American films. It was generally assumed that anything glamorous and exciting took place south of the border. The Americans had all the heroes and the history, won all the victories and flew their flag high. They had the stars, the cowboys, the gangsters and comedians, the songs and dances. What would Canadian films consist of? Life there was quiet, respectable, orderly, and dull—not likely to be transformed into cinema. The fact that many Canadian performers and directors were succeeding in London and Hollywood was, it was thought, only because of the superior technical knowledge of film-making that existed abroad and was most unlikely to be duplicated at home. Canadian politicians, who were mostly "above" movies and seldom deigned to attend any, seemed to be content to see the public happy at the picture palaces. Perhaps it never occurred to most of them to be concerned about the indoctrination of the Canadian public by American behavior, speech, and attitudes. In official circles, film was not considered a respected form of endeavor. Anything American in the arts or popular entertainment was considered vulgar and trite, and the cinema was the world of cigar-smoking producers and over-sexed stars getting drunk at parties and divorced in Reno. This was not an enterprise to be emulated by decent Canadians. Suggestions were made, from time to time during the thirties, by members of both the House of Commons and the Ontario legislature, that a quota be introduced in theaters, not for Canadian films, but for British films, as a means of "preserving our heritage," and to counter the flood of Americanism on the screens. But these suggestions were never acted on. Most newspaper editorials spoke out against such a move, largely on the grounds that a quota was "against free enterprise," and that British pictures (also fighting for their place at home against the power of Hollywood) were sometimes poor. No one thought to mention that there should be a quota for Canadian films. There were at this time several Canadians distributing films who believed that British films deserved to be shown and who worked hard on their behalf. In Quebec, films from France also found themselves limited by the strength of the American companies.

Year after year the Canadian public went by the thousands to American-owned cinemas—sold to them, then as now, by financially beleaguered or profit-minded Canadian businessmen—and paid out millions of dollars in admission charges that went back to the United States, to strengthen their film-making capacities. For this, they hardly ever saw anything genuinely Canadian on the screen. Quebec was satisfied with films from France, but enjoyed American movies as much as any audiences elsewhere. There was not even a genuinely Canadian newsreel. Had it not been for a minor piece of legislation in 1933 by the Ontario government that required the inclusion in the American newsreels of some Canadian or British events, au-

diences in pretelevision days would probably never have seen a Canadian public figure, national event, tragedy, or disaster on their screens. Everything of interest happened elsewhere. The newsreels, which were far from being neutral in reporting the news, blared their American point of view throughout Canadian cinemas and were strongly influential in forming public opinion. A Montreal company, Associated Screen News (now defunct) made short subjects under a series name, *Canadian Cameo,* directed by Gordon Sparling, and they alone battled for their place on the screen and reminded Canadians that they did have a country and that it did have some attractions and many interesting people. Even Australia did better during this period and now has a interesting film history replete with several motion pictures that can be called classics.

While other nations saw the necessity of establishing film-making as an artistic and creative way to project their country's people, life, and history, Canada did nothing to stem the tide of American motion pictures and soon became part of Hollywood's domestic marketplace, controlled from Los Angeles and New York. Canadian audiences were considered to be no different from those in Texas or Michigan, Oregon or Dakota, and the same advertising campaigns were used in Canada as in the United States, American reviewers were quoted at large, and no allowances were made on the grounds that Canada was not the United States. For this reason, Canada's cinema past is slight indeed, both in the number of films made and in written accounts of it, and of this small output even less has been saved.

The youth of today, who grew up with the television set from the day they first crawled across the living room carpet, who have become film-oriented from toddlerhood and now use 8mm or 16mm cameras in school in a way their parents would never have dreamed possible, now ask why there are no books available on the history of the Canadian cinema and why dramatic films made in the past are not available as a source of historical and sociological study. The early films they look at are all American.

As so little was achieved, anyone who attempted to write about the subject was faced with a negative and cheerless task that always ended with the wishful hope for a better future. That future is with us now, and it has brought about some positive results, but not until 1967 did this promise, so devoutly wished by many people over the past fifty years, begin to materialize.

The history of the cinema usually embraces the three parts that make motion pictures possible. First, the making of the films; second, their distribution to cinemas; and third, their exhibition in the cinemas. It is surprising how few people who talk about the difficulties of Canadian film-makers know the difference between production, distribution, and exhibition. The first, within which is contained the *réalisation* (the direction), is the creative part of film-making, the remaining two being the trade or business part of motion pictures. In Canada, unfortunately, this three-part system has never existed.

In American terms, this system once meant studios in Hollywood; distributing offices in all major cities in the United States and around the world; and cinemas everywhere, at home and overseas, owned and controlled for the most part by Paramount, MGM (Loew's Theatres), Twentieth Century–Fox, Warner Brothers, RKO Radio Pictures, and, to a lesser degree, Columbia, Universal, and United Artists—the latter being the only company during this time to distribute the films of producers independent of other studios and films made by producers abroad. The men who controlled these companies controlled the showings of films throughout the world, except in the USSR, and, after 1945, those countries that became part of the Soviet system. Since they had no competition other than that which took place between themselves, it was frequently of a titanic and ferocious nature. With their financial power they simply crushed all companies and individuals who refused to sell out to them. As the making of films was, and remains, such an expensive enterprise, few individuals could hope to raise sufficient money to make films without the backing of the studios.

The system they created was awesomely powerful and efficient and tolerated no interference. Without distribution and exhibition, a producer had no chance at all to recover the money he had spent in making his film. This meant that since the films were made in Hollywood, they would be American. Not until governments intervened in other countries and established quotas for native films in theaters and not until they financially assisted producers was the American monopoly challenged. Even then the major companies still retained a certain degree of control since they financed film-making in these countries (the U.K., France, and Italy, among them) and produced films known as "quota quickies," which nevertheless resulted in the production and exhibition of some native films with American backing and at the same time gave

work and experience to aspiring film-makers. But the American companies, even though they had financed these pictures, saw to it that they never made their way into mass exhibition in the United States. Their rich home market remained inviolable, and in this way they were helped by their patriotic American audiences who disliked anything foreign, and in particular British films that they considered slow and that had hard-to-understand dialogue. Oddly, these same audiences had no aversion to British actors in British stories filmed in Hollywood.

Not until between 1949 and 1951, when the Supreme Court of the United States decreed that the ownership of studios, distributing companies, and cinemas by companies owning all three constituted a monopoly practice and ordered the studios to sell their theater holdings to interests not engaged in film production, was the power of Hollywood broken. With the coming of television, which kept people at home, movie attendance dropped drastically, the studios floundered under immense overhead costs, and film production, largely inspired by a new generation of film-makers from television studios and film schools, went back on location and into the streets and countryside where it was born. Independent film-makers, no longer in the shadows of the studios, worked in association with the old studio companies, which soon passed into the hands of industrial conglomerates, with the studios used mostly for the production of television programs. The distribution companies, much-reduced in staff and the number of offices from which they worked, have remained fairly intact, are still a force to be reckoned with, and still represent the American film around the world. Now, however, distribution companies will finance independent producers, not only in the United States but in Europe. These producers are more likely to get their films shown today, unless cinema owners resist them (as they often do) on the grounds that certain movies have no appeal to audiences. Sometimes they are right, but often they are wrong, and when this happens, the distributors, whose studio companies no longer own the theaters, cannot force the owners to use the film and, probably being of a like mind about the picture's "lack of appeal," quietly leave it on the shelf and turn their efforts to promoting more profitable pictures.

2
Cinema Pioneers

An interesting pattern of movement developed in which Canadians went to the United States and Americans came to Canada. Canadians in the United States contributed to the mainstream of whatever developments they were a part of, particularly the motion picture. In Canada, the newly arrived Americans, largely due to the kindness and acquiescence of Canadians, took control of whatever they became involved with.

Thomas Alva Edison, who made some of the most important contributions to the invention of the motion picture, had strong family links with Canada. His father was born in Digby, Nova Scotia, in 1804, but fled to the United States after the rebellion of 1837 became a lost cause, since he was a supporter of its leader, William Lyon Mackenzie. Thomas was born in Milan, Ohio, on February 11, 1847. As a youth he learned to become one of the new telegraph operators and traveled between the United States and Canada. At the age of sixteen, in 1863, while he was working as a night operator for the Grand Trunk Railway in Stratford, Ontario (now famous for its annual Shakespearian Festival and former International Film Festival), he realized his first invention, an automatic report signal that made it unnecessary for him to disturb his own private studies by making periodic calls in person, which was expected of him as part of his job. Moviegoers will remember this scene in *Young Tom Edison* (1940), with Edison portrayed in a most unlikely way by Mickey Rooney. Thirty-one years later, on April 14, 1894, at 1155 Broadway, New York City, the first commercial exhibition took place of Edison's Kinetescope, a boxlike machine into which a person who had inserted ten cents looked and saw primitive

moving pictures. But it was not Edison who had arranged this showing. Several years prior to this he had left the machine neglected in his laboratory at Orange, New Jersey. Others saw its commercial possibilities as a peepshow novelty in amusement arcades and induced Edison to let them manufacture and display it. The two men who became the eastern agents for the Kinetescope Company were the Holland brothers of Ottawa, Ontario, who traveled down to New York by train to carry out this new enterprise. How they learned of it is not known, but since they were publishers and booksellers in Ottawa (34 Elgin Street), senate reporters and stenographers, and agents for the Smith premier typewriter, the Sorley storage battery, and Edison's phonograph, they presumably heard about it through these interests. And Canadians, then as now, never missed an opportunity to visit New York City.

A letter that Edison wrote to the Holland brothers thanking them for introducing his Kinetescope to the public is now in the Public Archives of Canada. It was originally given by one of the Holland sons to Colonel John Cooper, founder of the Canadian Club and former editor of the *Canadian Magazine,* when he was chairman of the Canadian Motion Picture Distributors Association. Mr. Cooper carried out the first research into the history of Canadian cinema at a time when, as Hye Bossin, editor and historian, said, "few were interested in it." Almost two years to the day since the Kinetescope had appeared, Edison's Vitascope, which utilized the invention of Thomas Armat and projected pictures on a screen, was shown to the public at Koster and Bial's Music Hall on 34th Street on April 23,

1896. But Edison had lost the race to the Lumière brothers, Louis and Auguste, who had invented a camera-projector they called the Cinematographe, and who showed short films for the first time at the Grand Café, Paris, on December 28, 1895.

In Canada, the beginnings are obscured by conflicting dates and stories. An earlier model of Lumière's Cinématographe licensed to Mr. Percy Hill of Toronto was said to be showing films on Yonge Street, in the Bijou Theatre at Robinson's Musée (on the east side of Yonge Street, at number 81, near King Street), on Monday, August 31, 1896, "Edison's Wonderful Vitascope" shared the bill with "Prof. Roentgen's Wonderful X Rays." Also in June 1896, two Frenchmen from Paris, Auguste Guay and André Vermet, demonstrated the Cinématographe in Montreal. An Edison projector was reported to be at work, in June 1896, at West End Park, Ottawa, under the auspices of O'Hearn and Soper of the Ottawa Street Railway Company. Vancouver apparently had to wait until 1898 before seeing the Edison machine.

An interesting indication of how the film immediately projected an image of the countries in which they originated is given by the programs for these two inventions, one French, the other American: the Lumière machine showed to Toronto audiences "Mr. Lumière and his family eating lunch in the garden of their home in Fontainbleau; passengers landing from a steamer at a French port; a boy playing tricks on a gardener with a hose; a train entering a station; workers leaving a factory; and several Parisien street scenes." The Edison machine showed to Ottawa audiences "two colored boys eating watermelon; the New York Central Railway's Black Diamond Express running at 80 mph; a bathing scene at Atlantic City; and LaLoie Fuller doing the Butterfly Dance." At the Ottawa premiere, the Governor-General's Foot Guards Band played the music—a role that, symbolically speaking, Canadians played in the cinema for years to come.

From this point on, motion picture exhibitions swept across Canada, fascinating the public. Every vacant store in every town and city with benches or kitchen chairs became a five- or ten-cent show. Every butcher, baker, and candlestick maker became a so-called exhibitor and in the next few years short films were shown in warehouses, empty shops, variety theaters, fairs, and amusements parks. During the Canadian National Exhibition of 1897 (then called the Toronto Industrial Exhibition) two New Yorkers showed the Bob Fitzsimmons-James J. Corbett heavyweight boxing championship in an empty store at the southwest corner of Richmond and Yonge streets. "Admission 25¢, hours 10 am to 11 pm," the sign read. They were the first, it seems, of many Americans who later were to find Canada a waiting and lucrative market, a happy-

hunting-ground for great financial returns. George Mehl came from New York with a 1,000-foot picture by George Melies of France called *Cinderella*. He found a lively film city and a year later organized the first Canadian projectionists union and became its president. Later, this union was to become part of the American union, IATSE, and remains so today.

There is no evidence to show that during these early, hectic years, any of the short primitive silent films shown so widely to unbelieving audiences were filmed in Canada. Therefore there were no Canadian scenes or subjects, places or people—only American, British, and French, the three influences that have dominated Canadian film-making ever since.

By the early 1900s, movies were longer, from 200 to 1,000 feet, and were telling stories and involving audiences in drama and excitement. *The Great Train Robbery,* for example, was a breath-taking success, and the showman John C. Green recalled that he "wore out three prints in one summer." Audiences were also scandalized by *The First Kiss,* one of the first short movies to be shown in Toronto, and by a Canadian actress at that, who, like hundreds of other Canadians to come after her, was working in New York. Her name was May Irwin. Born in Whitby, Ontario, in 1862, she became a popular stage star. On Broadway, May Irwin and John C. Rice were appearing in *The Widow Jones,* a play much criticized because it contained what was considered to be a much-too-prolonged kissing scene for those days. A Vitascope producer felt that it would be "sensational" on the screen and asked May Irwin and John Rice to come to the Edison Black Maria studio to be filmed. The result, entitled *The Kiss,* had the effect of "an earthquake." Moralists thundered and editors of newspapers were flooded with indignant letters. Cinema has been subject to similar outbursts of public wrath ever since. Seen today, *The Kiss* is still a film of exquisite beauty and feeling.

The exhibitors, who were more showmen than exhibitors as we know them today, bought their films outright from producers such as Biograph (New York), Pathé (Paris), Bioscope (London), and from many others. Distributors working on percentage charges had not yet appeared, but as the showmen made more money from their exhibitions, so producers increased the price of their films, particularly as running times of the films were lengthening all the time. The exhibitor, then as now, is the first to get his money and the least likely to lose any.

The public wanted better facilities; producers wanted to make more ambitious films; the showmen, tired of traveling and working out of makeshift premises, wanted better establishments. So permanent cinemas came into being. But again, who was first? Hye Bossin (see chapter 6) believed that John A.

Schulberg, after traveling as Johnny Nash, showing films between Vancouver and Winnipeg, opened the Edison Electric Theatre on Cordova Street, Vancouver, in the fall of 1902. (The Americans base the beginning of permanent motion picture exhibition on the opening of a theater in Los Angeles that same year.) Montreal's first permanent cinema was the Ouimetoscope, opened by L. Ernest Ouimet, at Saint Catherine and Montcalm streets on January 11, 1906. In October 1907, business being so good, Ouimet replaced the building with "the first de-luxe cinema in America," containing 1,000 seats, a cloakroom, reserved seats, advance ticket sales for the two performances a day, intermissions, singers on stage, and a six-piece orchestra to accompany the films. Toronto's first permanent cinema, the Theatorium (later the Red Mill) opened with *The Train Wreckers* (5¢ admission) in March 1906, at Yonge Street near Queen (probably near to where the present Loews-Elgin theater now stands). Owned by John Griffin, a former circus showman, it became the first cinema of what was to become the first circuit of fifteen Canadian cinemas. In a move that was to become a trend, the circuit was soon sold to Americans, who were coming into Canada to take advantage of the growing public interest in "the movies."

The first of these American entrepreneurs were the Allens. Jule Allen came to Brantford, Ontario, in the early part of 1906 from Bradford, Pennsylvania, with his father, Bernard, and his brother, Jay. They opened a Theatorium in a store with 150 kitchen chairs. This was the beginning of the Allen theater chain of fifty luxury cinemas valued at over 20 million dollars which (in a considerably reduced condition) is still operating today as Premier Theatres under Barry Allen, grandson of Jule.

Other cinema pioneers were the Bennett brothers of London and Hamilton and F. G. Spencer, who developed a chain of cinemas in the Maritimes. It became an accepted fact that they would show American films, and with the limited success of the few Canadian films that had been made, it was easier to forget about domestic productions and just sit back and take the American films as they flooded in. The men in charge of booking films into cinemas today have much the same attitude, which has become ingrown over the years.

Next came N. L. Nathanson, an American from Minneapolis, and with his entry into Canadian theater operations began the most contentious chapter of motion picture exhibition in this country, leading to the almost complete domination of our theaters by American interests. Nathanson was not to know this when he arrived at Toronto's Union Station. In fact, films were far from his mind, and he had never heard of the Allens, who by 1915 had become the major cinema circuit in Canada. They left Brantford, where they owned several cinemas, and opened a film exchange in Calgary, making that city their head office in 1911. After building many film theaters out west, they returned to Toronto in 1915 because it was in this city that all film activities took place, money was raised, deals entered into, films bought and sold. At this time, a film exchange, later to become the offices of distributors, was a place where exhibitors either bought films from producers or their agents, and exchanged films with those of other exhibitors.

The Allens looked around the downtown area of Toronto and found that although Robinson's Musée and its Bijou Theatre had been destroyed by fire in 1897, it was rebuilt and reopened as Shea's by the American vaudeville showman Jerry Shea, who had come to Toronto from New York. In 1910, he opened Shea's Victoria (twice-a-day vaudeville performances, at Adelaide and Victoria streets) and in 1914, Shea's Hippodrome (at Bay and Queen streets), both of which later became cinemas and both now demolished. From Shea's the Bijou had become the Strand, which was purchased by the Allens, probably the first of its many Toronto theaters. Their manager was Leon Schlesinger, an American who became an exhibitor and distributor, and who later returned to the United States and started the *Merrie Melodies* cartoons at Warner Brothers studios.

N. L. Nathanson originally had come to Toronto to take charge of the food concession held by an American company at the now-vanished East End Amusement Park at Scarborough Beach. When the park closed for the winter, Nathanson obtained work with the E. L. Ruddy Company, selling outdoor advertising. Motion picture advertising was becoming more frequent, and Nathanson met Jule Allen when he tried to persuade him to buy more advertising materials from Ruddy. Allen frequently gave Nathanson a ride downtown, and it was on one of these occasions that Nathanson expressed an interest in becoming part of the cinema trade. He had noticed that the Majestic Theatre (formerly the Toronto Opera House) on Adelaide Street, near Bay Street, was empty. Allen suggested that Nathanson arrange for financing and enter into "a management agreement" with the Allen circuit. The agreement finally drawn up by Nathanson was not acceptable to the Allens, who let the matter drop. In all probability, Jule Allen later came to regret that day. Nathanson, a determined and ambitious man, did not let the matter end there. He brought together a group of powerful men with money, including Ruddy, J. P. Bickell, a mining magnate, W. J. Sheppard, J. B. Tudhope, and others, and formed Regent Theatres Ltd. They then bought and refurbished the Majestic as Toronto's first deluxe motion picture theater and renamed it the Regent. This was in 1916, the second year of the First Great War.

The Regent had 1,475 seats and an orchestra under Jack Arthur, who also produced stage shows there, and later, at the Uptown Theatre. The Allens, surprised at what Nathanson had done, accepted the challenge and built the Allen Theatre at Adelaide and Victoria streets (later renamed the Tivoli, now demolished) as Toronto's first "super deluxe" motion picture theater, with music played by a young organist, Horace Lapp. (Today, Mr. Lapp, now in his eighties, still plays for silent pictures at the Ontario Film Theatre in Toronto.)

There was no stopping Nathanson, however. His company proceeded to buy up existing theaters and to build new ones in Toronto, Montreal, Ottawa, and Vancouver. In 1918, Regent Theatres became the Paramount Theatre Company, and while it had nothing to do with the Hollywood studio of the same name, it was an ominous portent of an ownership to come. While theater expansion was fast proceeding and audiences growing larger each week, theater owners raced in a mad scramble to obtain the best films from the Hollywood studios, whose movies were now running ninety minutes to two hours and were holding the bill without vaudeville and stage shows—which were dying quickly. In 1920, the Allens lost the franchise for Adolph Zukor's Famous Players–Lasky (Paramount) films. Zukor came to Toronto, and, no doubt with much behind-the-scenes double-dealing, formed an alliance with Nathanson's company, which then changed its name to Famous Players Canadian Corporation.

Famous Players–Lasky was the leading film producer in Hollywood at this time. With this fierce competition from the new Famous Players theater company, reinforced with American money, the Allens were soon in financial difficulties. They had built the Parkdale, Beach, Century, Saint Clair, College, and Bloor theaters in Toronto, and many others in various cities, but to no avail. They found it difficult to get popular films, and finally, with their backs to the wall, sold out to Famous Players. Nathanson's sense of victory can well be imagined! Magnanimously he allowed them to continue in business as an "affiliate," and, much reduced in theater holdings, they remain active as Premier Theatres. Little remains of their original confrontation with Nathanson but memories, as both the Majestic (Regent) and Allen (Tivoli) theaters, together with the Victoria and Shea's, all of which became Famous Players cinemas, have long since been demolished.

By 1930, Paramount-Publix, the trading name of Paramount Pictures (as Famous Players–Lasky had become) had bought control of Famous Players Canadian Corporation. It was, apparently, a dirty deal, a bitterly long fought-out battle, the full story of which has never been told. It came about due to the manipulations of Adolph Zukor, aided by J. P. Bickell, against the wishes of N. L. Nathanson, who later resigned, together with Sir Herbert Holt and the Hon. W. O. Ross. Bickell claimed that selling out to Famous was preferable to being taken over by other competitors, who were never named. There was a public outcry; minority shareholders said they were betrayed; editorials appeared in the press over foreign control of a vital "entertainment" medium, and questions were asked in Parliament. But the Americans and their Canadian confreres knew, then as now, that nothing would stop them, and nothing did. Very soon Famous bought up every important first-run cinema across Canada, and most second runs, and began its hold on Canadian screens that persists to this day. From 1930 on, nearly all independent circuits, including Bloom and Fine and the Twentieth-Century Theatres, started by N. A. Taylor and his associates in 1935, all existed by the grace of Famous Players as "affiliates."

Another American, who was later to play a decisive role in keeping Famous Players under American control, arrived quietly in Toronto in 1931. He was John J. Fitzgibbons, Paramount's man at Famous, and for the next ten years he worked and waited for his ascendancy to power. Canadians in the film trade, who, as in sports, education, and business, always seem anxious to sacrifice themselves on the altar of American control, were soon speaking approvingly of their great partnership with the Americans and of the great benefit this friendship brings to "our industry." References to our "great cousins" and to "love and brotherhood" flourished over the years, with continued references to "our great history" and the expression of the ever-present hope that we were on the threshold of new developments in feature film production. From then on, all celebrations relating to the historical development of the motion picture were all pale reflections of what had taken place in the United States, and all of our "great stars" had become stars in Hollywood.

The Famous Players takeover not only significantly affected film making in Canada, it also, unbelievable though it seems, adversely affected the development of the stage and the public's knowledge and appreciation of "live" theater. Nearly every theater, from burlesque to opera, had turned to showing motion pictures, but most were still available for traveling stage shows and the occasional local production. But when Paramount took over Famous, Zukor decreed that no stage shows would be permitted to break into the regular run of current movies. That would mean less money for the Hollywood studios. As only Montreal, Toronto, and Vancouver had theaters still presenting stage works, it meant that audiences living in other cities would be denied Sir John Martin Harvey, George Robey, the D'Oyley Carte, Stratford-upon-Avon Shakespeare Festival, and dozens of other touring companies. The existence of such Canadian entertainers as the Dumbells (reported James Cowan in Macleans, May 1930) "would become impossible"—and time proved him right. There was a row about this too, in the press, since theater was considered to be more important than movies; but, as usual, the public soon forgot, and it was years before Famous relented (when business slumped in the sixties) and allowed stage shows to be presented in some of its theaters, such as the Capitol, Ottawa. The rentals charged were often more than the theaters would make from showing movies—a late victory for the stage.

After his company was taken over by Paramount, N. L. Nathanson became involved in an immense gamble with William Fox, an American film producer and exhibitor who was on the point of buying control of Loew's Incorporated (which owned the MGM studios and hundreds of Loew's theaters). He had already purchased control of 300 Gaumont-British cinemas in the United Kingdom, and, with Nathanson in Canada, was about to buy up Canadian cinemas and create a circuit in competition with Paramount's Famous Players. High drama ensued, and William Fox was about to achieve this huge empire when the stock market collapsed, heralding the Great Depression and crushing him under the weight of 70 million dollars in short-term notes. He was defeated everywhere, his studio merged with Twentieth Century to become Twentieth Century–Fox, and William Fox went into retirement. This left Famous Players the clear winner in Canada. With a huge supply of films guaranteed by Famous Players–Lasky (Paramount), and with a new franchise to show the films of the fast-rising Warner Brothers studios, which, at last, had introduced sound on film as a commercial reality, Famous Players was preeminent. By 1939, the company was in a position of major control.

After the collapse of William Fox's plans, Nathanson, in spite of many differences of opinion with his new masters, stayed with Famous until 1941, when either because he was tired of them or they of him, he resigned. It was then that John J. Fitzgibbons took over. He ran Famous with a quiet and rigid efficiency. Although his company sported a maple leaf as its emblem, Fitzgibbons was an American first and last and was dedicated to Paramount, the parent company. Unlike Nathanson and the Allens, who, although Americans, controlled their own operations within Canada, Fitzgibbons was working for a head office in New York, and he kept the company American, never permitting the intrusion of anything Canadian on the screen unless forced to do so during the war as an example of patriotic "good citizenship." He persuaded the government to stay out of production of dramatic films and to have nothing to do with quotas for Canadian films. He never made statements about these matters—it was all done behind the scenes. It was common knowledge that he would have liked to have seen the elimination of the National Film Board when the war ended. He was awarded a CBE in 1945.

When N. L. Nathanson left Famous Players, however, he was far from being a spent force. Still in a fiercely competitive mood, he started a small circuit with his son Paul called Odeon Theatres. Unlike other circuits, which had begun in Toronto, the first Odeon was the Vogue in Vancouver, and opened in 1941. Nathanson's Odeon had no connection with the powerful Odeon Theatres of Britain, purchased and enlarged by J. Arthur Rank in his struggle against American control of British cinemas. But just as Nathanson's creation of the Paramount Theatre circuit in 1918 had foreshadowed control by the American company of the same name, so the use of the Odeon name foreshadowed similar and ultimate control of Nathanson's Odeon by the British company. It was the second year of the Second Great War.

Nathanson, whose story would make a film in itself, was also actively involved in distribution. While most of the big American distributing companies opened their own offices, some worked through Canadian companies. Columbia's films were distributed by the Allens (with shares owned by Nathanson). His own company, Empire Films, distributed Universal, Republic, and Disney films, among others. N. A. Taylor, who ran the Twentieth Century–Twinex Theatres (no connection with the production and distribution company of Twentieth Century–Fox) opened IFD (International Film Distributors) to bring to Canada the films of many independent producers in Britain and Europe. He sold the company to an American distribution company, NTA (National Telefilm Associates) in 1972. Today, with the changes that continue to take place, there are more small independent Canadian distributors than during the past fifty years. Most of the large American companies still have their own distributing offices in Canada, but in the interests of economy, some, like Twentieth Century–Fox and Columbia, have closed their own premises and moved in with Astral, a Canadian company.

N. L. Nathanson died in 1943. In 1944, John Davis (now Sir John Davis), then managing director of the J. Arthur Rank Organization, came to Toronto to see if he could improve the showings of British films in the Dominion. The Rank Organization in England, controlling both Odeon and Gaumont-British theater circuits, was then actively engaged in film-making at the Denham, Pinewood, and Gaumont-British studios, which it also owned, and distributed its pictures through its own distribution companies, among them General Film Distributors and Eagle-Lion. Davis found himself up against John J. Fitzgibbons, who was just as determined that no films that did not come through regular American distribution channels would find their way into Famous Players theaters. Never a man to be slighted, Davis made a deal with Paul Nathanson and purchased fifty percent of his Odeon theaters. As the power and popularity of Odeon in Canada grew, Rank took over full control in 1948. It added to the existing circuit by going into partnership with several independent theater owners (the Mortons of Winnipeg among them) and by building some fifty cinemas of an architectural design and a standard of comfort not found in the older picture palaces. The Odeon Carlton was one of the greatest of them, seating over 2,000 people. Opened in 1948, with David Lean's *Oliver Twist,* it was regrettably demolished in 1974 and marked the demise of the large cinemas.

The coming of Odeon broke the monopoly that Famous Players had held for some forty years, and apart from making British films more freely available, it also gave American distributors an alternative to Famous when it came to negotiating exhibition contracts. Paul Nathanson resigned shortly after his company was sold to Rank, and he was succeeded by J. Earl Lawson, a lawyer. That year, 1948, following a visit by J. Arthur Rank to Toronto, the Rank Organization of Canada was formed. Mr. Lawson was succeeded by Leonard Brockington, a distinguished lawyer, speaker, and public figure, and with Frank Fisher, David Griesdorf, and Christopher Salmon (who came from England) they made Odeon a highly successful venture, with a character and personality quite different from that of Famous Players. While the latter company remained rigidly American under Fitzgibbons, Odeon, largely because of its exhibition agreement with Columbia Pictures, did give wide showings to National Film Board (NFB) short subjects, distributed by Columbia. Odeon also entered into community projects and made its theaters available at low rentals to film societies, such as A-G-E and the Toronto Film Society, and to other groups interested in special showings. Although Odeon did not improve conditions for Canadian film-makers (Davis did not consider it within his company's field of endeavor to encourage production in Canada by giving financial assistance to producers), Odeon did give first showings in the early sixties of *Drylanders, The Merry World of Leopold Z* (both by the NFB), Sidney Furie's films, and David Secter's *The Offering* at a time when Famous Players preferred not to know of the existence of any Canadian-made movies. In 1978, the Rank Organization sold Odeon to a small company, Canadian Cinemas. Now called Canadian Odeon Cinemas, it is more American-oriented than was Rank.

Not until George Destounis, who was born in Montreal, took over as president of Famous Players in 1970, did the company's alien image change. Under pressure from the film-makers and the many associations formed to advance the cause of Canadian film-making, first in Montreal, then Toronto and Vancouver, and with the demand to establish a quota being heard more persistently, Destounis slowly involved Famous Players not only in the showing of Canadian-made films but also in financing them. Even so, many Canadian-made films still do not get bookings in second-run cinemas and in smaller centers. Too many are judged to be failures before they have been given the opportunity to prove themselves. Odeon has never invested money in film production. There is still considerable unrest and understandable dissatisfaction over the state of exhibition of Canadian films. The exhibitors' trite answer in reply to requests for a quota law is that people cannot be legislated into going into cinemas. That may be so, but for all these years, Famous Players, the independent cinema owners, and Odeon seldom gave the public the opportunity to see what Canadian film-makers were capable of doing.

3

Early Production

The years when men fought to build, control, divide, and conquer in the field of theater construction and ownership were marked by a bewildering procession of new companies, ruined individuals, theaters changing hands, companies bought, merged, and renamed, and culminated in 1939 with Famous Players in control of the most lucrative aspects of exhibition. During these years the battles being waged over the acquisition of motion pictures and overall efforts devoted to their greater exhibition related entirely to American films, and, to a much lesser degree, British pictures. Attempts to have British films shown during the thirties and forties presaged exactly those efforts made during the late sixties and early seventies to get Canadian pictures shown. Canadian films were seldom an issue in theaters because there were so few of them, and there is little evidence available to suggest that those involved in exhibition and distribution, who were mostly transplanted Americans, considered it in any way essential that the films they showed should include domestic productions. Their reasoning had little to do with patriotism. The Americans in Canada looked to Hollywood and showed American films because most of them made money easily and quickly. Nevertheless, there was also that special attraction to them as a result of nationality. Native Canadians in the trade seemed to believe it was natural that the films they dealt with should be American, as the Americans were best at making pictures and Canadians were not. Producers of movies inside Canada then found themselves outside a system they should have been a part of, fighting to raise money, fighting to improve their standards, fighting to find a place on the screen, with each succeeding failure, whether artistic or simply commercial, making it even harder to try again.

The Canadian Broadcasting Corporation (CBC)'s television series *The National Dream* was based on the books by Pierre Berton about the history of the Canadian Pacific Railway. A national dream for film-making in Canada also began with the CPR, almost eighty-five years ago, but it was not fulfilled and is little remembered. Although the Massey-Harris company commissioned Thomas Edison's company to make a film—Canada's first industrial film, it is said—of its new binder at work on Ontario farms for showing at the Toronto Industrial Exhibition in 1898 and later in other countries, film-making in Canada in the "epic sense" dates from 1900 when the CPR's "colonial agent" commissioned Charles Urban of London to photograph Canada. The films were to be shown throughout the United Kingdom in town halls, libraries, corn exchanges, and theaters, with a qualified lecturer, not to promote the CPR as such, but to show the British a beautiful land and thus induce them to immigrate and populate its vast open spaces. (In those days, CPR needed passengers!)

Charles Urban was an American who had gone to London from New York City to manage a British branch of a company manufacturing the Edison projector and to sell Edison films. He soon went into business for himself and was too busy to come to Canada in person to carry out the CPR assignment. He sent his English partner, F. Guy Bradford, Bradford's brother-in-law, Clifford Denham, and their chief cameraman, Joseph Rosenthal. The colonization agent for the CPR, a Mr. Armstrong, met them in Montreal and mapped out a program. It included Quebec, Northern Ontario, the prairies, scenes around Banff, Kicking Horse Pass, Fraser Canyon, the Rocky Mountains, and "others too numerous to mention," as Denham later wrote to Hye Bossin. They filmed from a flat car pushed by a locomotive and included scenes of lumbering, milling, harvesting, salmon fishing, cattle-raising and manufacturing plants. It took the three film-makers about two years to finish this "first travelogue" of Canada. They had instructions from the CPR not to photograph any winter scenes since they wanted to "dispel from the Englishmen's minds that Canada was a land of ice and snow." Not until the middle sixties, when skiing and skating and other winter sports became fashionable, were film-makers to ignore this dictum. *Living Canada,* as this series was called, was listed in the Urban catalogue in 1903. Over the years, thousands of travelogues have been made, many not as good, and in 1959, Buster Keaton came to Canada to make a short comedy for the NFB called *The Railrodder,* which saw him leave London and go across the country in eighteen minutes on a railway "hand" car, past scenery that has changed very little since the Denham-Bradford-Rosenthal trip.

Rosenthal returned to England, but Bradford and Denham, seeing at first hand the opportunities offered by Canada, remained here. Their first enterprise was to take the films they made across Canada to the thousands of Canadians who had never seen what other parts of the Dominion (as it was then affectionately called) were like. Their first engagement was at the Windsor Hall in Montreal. They gave a two-and-a-half-hour show with admission prices at $1.00 and $1.50 (the average motion picture show was 10¢) and it ran for weeks to capacity business. (Today, photographers still find it profitable to tour Canada—*World Adventure Tours* and the like—showing pictures with commentary of other countries.) Bradford and Denham then came to Massey Hall in Toronto, toured Ontario, and moved on across the countryside they had photographed until they reached Vancouver and Victoria. They made four complete trips from coast to coast, always changing the program.

Guy Bradford, although he never became one of the many exhibitors who started building and buying cinemas, was nevertheless one of the most far-sighted and energetic men in the trade until the Gaumont Company of France made him their representative in New York in the early 1920s. During his years in Canada he traveled widely and brought the first exhibition of motion pictures to many communities of all sizes. He worked mostly in Quebec and the Maritimes and developed "nickel" cinemas in Montreal (one was formerly an old church at Bleury and Saint Catherine, close to the present Alouette Cinema), Saint John, New Brunswick, Quebec City, and Saint John's, New-

foundland. Believing in the future of the motion picture, Bradford attempted to establish permanent cinemas wherever he went, but it seems he never became a theater owner himself, nor a film producer or distributor.

The company he had formed in England was the London Bioscope Company. In 1913, a company called the Canadian Bioscope Company, with the cooperation of the CPR, made what is now regarded as Canada's first feature-length dramatic film, *Evangeline.* There is no reference to Guy Bradford being involved, yet it is possible that he was a moving force behind the enterprise. *Evangeline* was produced and directed by E. P. Sullivan and W. H. Cavanaugh, both of whom appeared in the film with Laura Lyman and John F. Carleton. Based on Longfellow's poem and shot in Annapolis Valley, it was fifty minutes long and received good notices after opening at the Empire Theatre, Halifax, in 1914.

From then on, as Peter Morris notes in his *Canadian Feature Film Index* (published by the Canadian Film Institute in 1970), film production was dominated by stories about the Mounties, bears, hunters, pioneers, and adventures in the snow. It was also a "happy hunting ground" for unscrupulous promoters, who brought about high hopes, which often resulted in unfinished films and bankruptcy proceedings. Oddly enough, Canadians with money to invest in films frequently turned down talented Canadian film-makers because they had no faith in their own people, in favor of backing fly-by-night promoters from the United States, who were thought to be more knowledgeable because they were Americans. Canadians have continued to fall for these schemes until recent years. Newspaper files are filled with clippings announcing the formation of companies and the imminent production of "important" pictures, most of which never saw a cinema projector.

The Canadian Bioscope Company is also credited with *The Mariner's Compass* (1914), which may also have been called *In the Enemy's Power,* and that seems to be the end of their activities in producing films. *The Great Unknown* (1913), produced by Eclair, was set against a background of Canada's gold fields, and *The Dollar Mark* (1914), produced by George Broadhurst's World Film Company, was filmed near Coburg, Ontario. Also in 1914 a company was formed with a name that was to typify the Canadian dilemma for years to come: the Anglo-American Film Company. Its great adventure film was *Dollard des ormeaux* (the Battle of the Long Sault).

The next important development came during wartime, in 1917, with the building of a studio at Trenton, Ontario, by the Adanac Production Company, a patriotic group whose leading principal, George Brownridge, spelled "Canada" backwards to get the company's name. Although there were small studios in 1913 on the Humber River, outside Toronto, owned by an American firm called Coness and Till, they either were not available or were not used by Brownridge because he wanted to have his own studios and embark on a sustained program of production, which, after all, was and still remains every film-makers' hope. Once again the CPR, which certainly believed in the cinema in those days, helped to finance their first picture, *The Great Shadow,* which also proved to be their last. A war film "dealing with the threat of Bolshevism" and starring an American actor, Tyrone Power senior, its release was delayed two years due to a long and costly litigation. The film finally opened at the Grand Opera House in Toronto in March 1920. Like most films with delayed openings, it found no great success.

Meanwhile, the principals of Adanac quarreled, the company broke up, and the Ontario government, which in 1917 established a Motion Picture Bureau for news and educational films (later to be known as "documentary"), took over the studios at Trenton, from which its producers and cameramen then worked. (This building is still standing, although no longer used as film studios.) George Brownridge's dream of creating a Canadian Hollywood vanished. Described as a strong, good-looking man, "love's young dream" by some and "a fast promoter" by others, he vanished in 1947.

In 1918, Frank O'Byrne, who remained in production up until the early 1960s, and Charles Quick, who went on to become a veteran newsreel cameraman, worked at the CNE during the fall on *Polly At The Circus* for an American named Harold Binnie, who had come up from Hollywood to set up Canadian Photoplay Productions. Binnie started to build a studio in New Toronto, on the Lakeshore, but he ran out of money and left the building unfinished.

Whether or not it was the same company Binnie had started, Canadian Photoplay Productions Ltd. produced a film in Calgary in 1919. Entitled *Back To God's Country,* it introduced into Canadian limited film history a man who made more films in this period than any other. His name was Ernest Shipman, and as so often happens in history, little is known about him. Like a romantic melodrama, he and his pretty young wife, Nell, who was a writer and actress, appeared from out of the west, dazzled the doubters who decried Canadian production, and faded out in the east, having established a continuity of production resulting in six films (perhaps more)—few compared to the Hollywood studios, but a fine achievement for a lone Canadian producer and not surpassed by many even today. But then some say that he too was an American.

Shipmans' *Back To God's Country* (1919), based on James Oliver Curwood's "Wapi the Walrus," and *Blue*

Waters (1922) with Norma Shearer were both directed by David M. Hartford, who came from Hollywood. *Cameron of the Royal Mounted* (1921), *God's Crucible* (1921), *The Critical Age* (1922)—also known as *Glengarry School Days*—and *The Man from Glengarry* (1922) were based on the novels of Ralph Conner and were all directed by Henry MacRae, who was born in Stayner, Ontario, in 1878, and had been a member of the Royal Canadian Mounted Police before entering motion pictures in 1913. He was known as the king of the serial makers and chief of Universal City studios in Los Angeles. He died in 1944. As for Ernest Shipman, who produced these films, he simply disappeared. As with all the films made during this time, it is now impossible to know how many of Shipman's actors and technicians were Canadian or were brought from Hollywood. They are but names in a catalogue, almost all of their work having disappeared forever.

By 1920, Roy Tash, who became one of Canada's best-known newsreel cameramen, produced, directed, and photographed *Satan's Paradise* in and around Weston and Toronto, and in Loew's Winter Garden Theatre. (This is the upstairs theater in the giant Loew's Theatre, closed in 1918 due to its lack of fire exits, and which has remained a ghost theater ever since. Graham Gordon filmed scenes for his unfinished picture, *Roses In December,* in the Winter Garden in the autumn of 1963, and the theater scenes in the CBC's *Jalna* series were also filmed there in 1971.) *Satan's Paradise* opened at the Tivoli theatre in 1921. Tash recalls that the subject was spiritualism, the cast and technicians were all Canadian, and that they made the film for around $2,000. It was not successful with audiences, being somewhat ahead of its time.

Apart from Ernest Shipman's production, there was little else of importance until the filming of *Carry On Sergeant* in 1928. Titles such as *Under Northern Lights, The Vow, Campbell of the Mounted, Latin Love* (credited to Shipman, but little is known of it), *Snowblind, The Valley of the Missing, Proof of Innocence,* and *The Rapids* with Mary Astor, made in Sault Ste. Marie, were filmed mostly in Ontario between 1920 and 1922. While Canadian films were few, none were made in Quebec in either French or English at that time.

From 1923 to 1927, no Canadian films appear to have been produced, although several Grade B American outdoor adventures were shot on location. In 1927 the completion of A. D. "Cowboy" Kean's *Policing the Plains* took place, a documentary history of the Royal Canadian Mounted Police, which Kean made over several years, traveling across the country. It was said at the time that the film made realistic use of exteriors, but it received few showings. Appearing before a government committee inquiring into the workings of the film trade in 1931, Kean told them what most Canadian

Churchill's Island ("World in Action" series, 1941). (NFB)

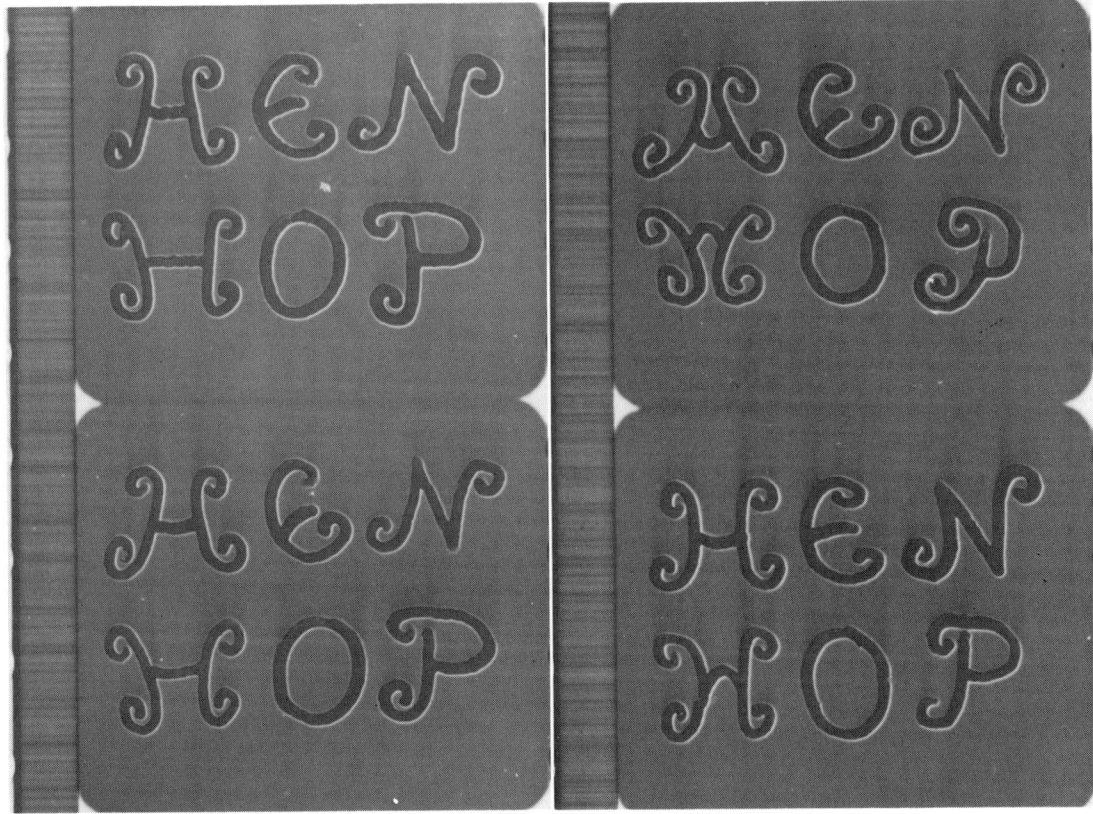

Hen Hop (1942). (NFB)

Chants populaires (1944). (NFB)

Meuniers tu dors (1944). (NFB)

This Is Our Canada (1945). (NFB)

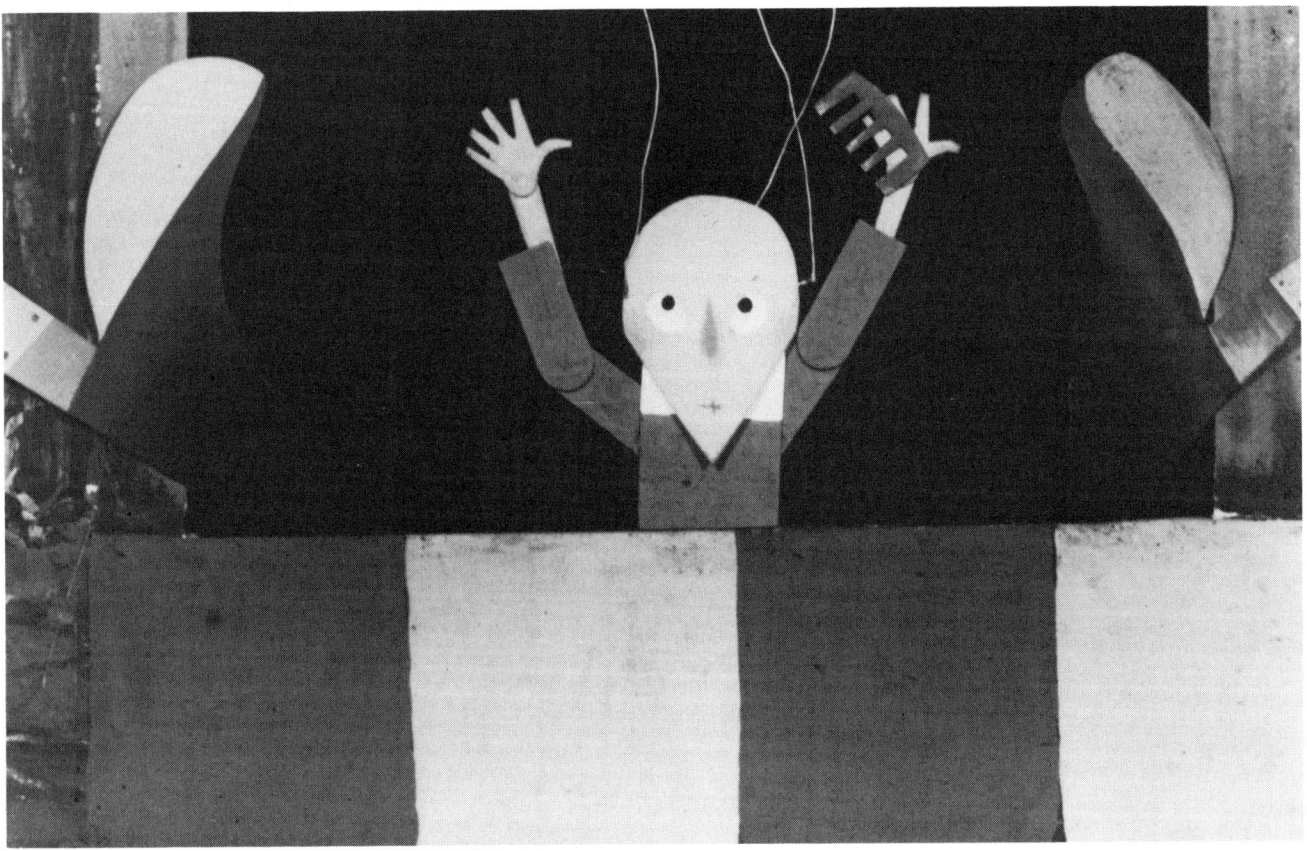

Cadet Rousselle (1946). (NFB)

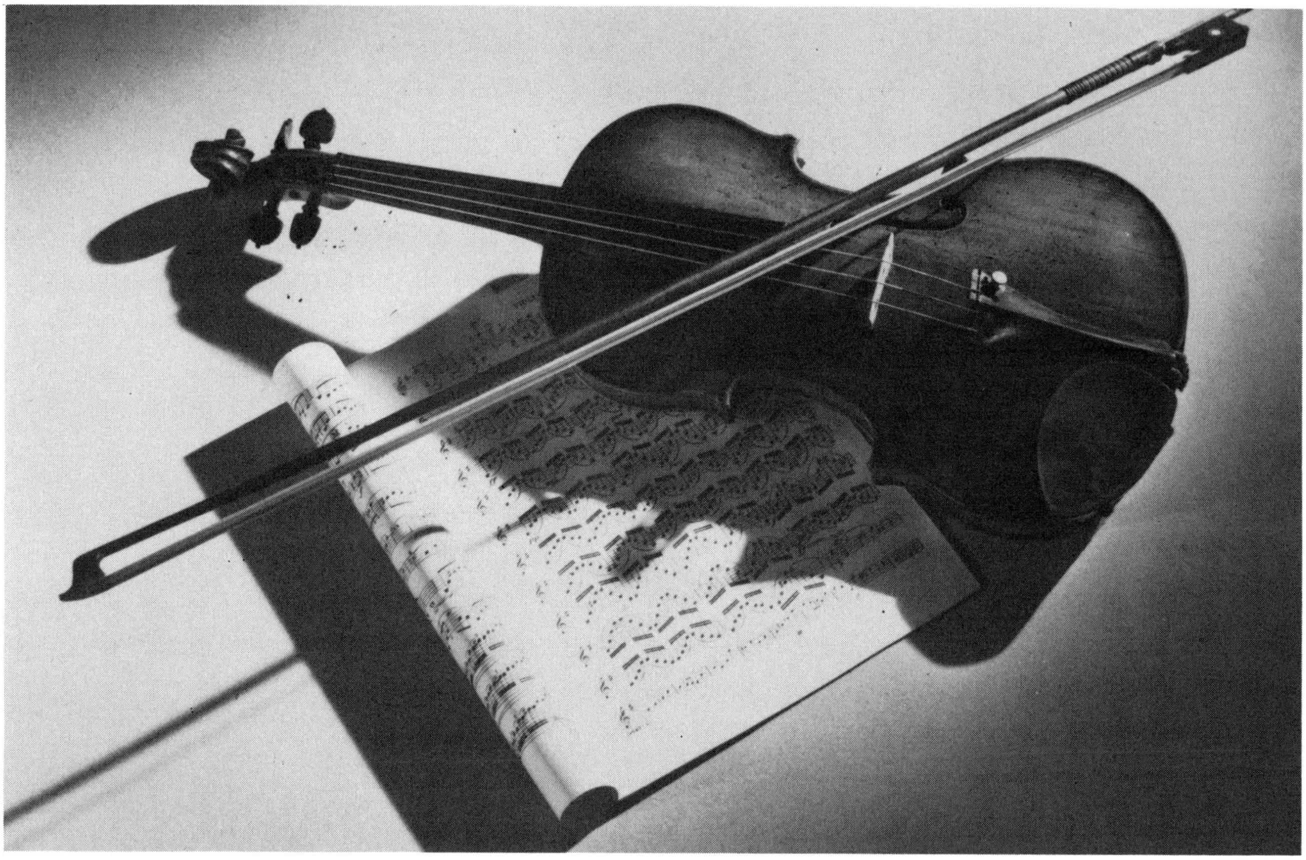

Story of a Violin (1947). (NFB)

Art for Everyone (1948). (NFB)

Valley of Gold **(1949). (NFB)**

Trees Are a Crop **(1950). (NFB)**

Now Is the Time (1951). (NFB)

Beyond the Frontier (1952). (NFB)

Land of the Long Day (1952). **(NFB)**

producers knew about their own movies: that his film was not shown because of "obstruction" from the cinema owners, meaning the circuits.

A book could have been written about Canada's most spectacular attempt to make its name in the cinema, an attempt that failed only in the sense that the film, *Carry On Sergeant,* was started in 1927, when sound was thought to be a fad, and finished in 1928, when the public had accepted sound and overnight it seemed, silent films were rendered obsolete. *Carry On Sergeant* was a World War I drama about Canadian soldiers in France, a subject never filmed previously— and never since, in spite of Canadian forces having fought in more wars. W. F. Clarke of London, England, organized British Empire Films of Canada and a subsidiary company, Canadian International Pictures, to make this film. Thirty-five shareholders invested $500,000 and the Trenton studios were leased from the Ontario government for five years. Bruce Bairnsfather, the famous British cartoonist of the day, was engaged as screenwriter and director. Trenton finally became, for a year or more, the little Hollywood George Brownridge had dreamed of. The newspapers an-

nounced that once again "Trenton was the centre of the motion picture industry of Canada" and that the film would "assist the trade of the country by showing Canada in its true light rather than in the popular concept of a land of ice and snow."

To make sure Bairnsfather directed competently (since it was his first and only film), a technical crew was brought up from Hollywood. A Paris street and an authentic-looking French village were built (which stood for fifteen years), the western front was re-created, and troops marched and clashed in big battle scenes spectacularly staged. The details were perfect, and the cast included Jimmy Savo, Hugh Buckley, Neil Watson, and Nancy Ann Hargreaves. The $500,000 budget, a huge sum for those days, was spent before the film was completed, and Bairnsfather was reported to have used his own money to finish it. The excitement and anticipation of the first weeks of filming turned to gloom and despair when, a year later, it came to an end, because now theaters were installing sound equipment and *Carry On Sergeant* had no sound. A big première was arranged at the Regent Theatre in Toronto. A huge banner across Adelaide

Street read, "Canada's First Mammoth Motion Picture." Technicians created sound effects backstage, Ernest Dainty conducted his own score, and they almost succeeded in creating a genuine Canadian motion picture event. Audiences were large enough to make the showings profitable but backstage quarrels between the producers and the theater owners over rental charges brought the engagement to an early end. After a few more unsuccessful showings elsewhere, the film was withdrawn by its discouraged producers, and the money invested was totally lost. The film passed into the custody of the Ontario government, which, with the coming of sound and the Depression, closed the Trenton studios and disbanded the Motion Picture Bureau under orders from Premier Mitchell Hepburn. The prints of *Carry On Sergeant* would no doubt have been lost too, had it not been for Gordon Sparling (assistant director on the film and later director of the short subjects in the *Canadian Cameo* series), who rescued a copy and stored it in his office at Associated Screen News (a Canadian company formed in 1932 to make short subjects and industrial films), never thinking of the historic act he had performed. In 1954, ASN donated this copy to the newly formed Canadian Film Archives (now the National Film, Television, and Sound Archives), which came into being as a result of talks between Hye Bossin and Dr. Kaye Lamb, the Dominion archivist. The fate of *Carry On Sergeant* served to reinforce public and trade opinion that Canadian films would never be successful, and investors were now even more reluctant to put their money into film-making.

Then came the "quota quickies," as they were known. In Britain, the government decreed that a certain percentage of British-made films must be shown in cinemas each year in order to assist film-makers in the United Kingdom. As in Canada, British theaters were mainly American-controlled at that time, and most British audiences scoffed at the idea of a quota, because, like Canadian and other English-speaking audiences, they thought that only Hollywood knew how to film—with its considerable number of British actors, writers, directors, and technicians, who, like Canadians, might flourish there, but not at home. They said the quota law would result in many quickly made and inferior movies, and it did. But from the continuity of production made possible because of the quota law came trained and experienced film people who, over the years, have created one of the most effective national schools of film-making anywhere in the world.

In the late twenties and up until the late thirties, a British film meant any film made in the Dominions. As Paramount had extensive theater holdings in England and had quota obligations to meet, it formed a company in Canada called British Canadian Pictures, and made three films in 1928–29: *His Destiny* in Alberta, *The Wilderness Patrol* in North Vancouver, and *North of 49* in Jasper Park, the latter being one of the first sound films made in this country. Paramount later found it easier to make quota films in England.

In the field of unrealized ambitions, Vancouver claims a special distinction. From the earliest days, its climate, scenery, and similarity to California excited would-be movie producers, both foreign and domestic, who announced that another Hollywood could be built there. Dozens appeared to have tried, right up to the present, running out when plans did not work out, and draining willing investors of millions of dollars. The studios that were built and the films made in them usually failed because the promoters were motivated largely by thought of financial gain and were interested only in films that would "make money." This meant they had to look like American films, and as a result, they never did succeed. This is a lesson that even today many Canadian producers have never learned. Among the losers were Canadian National Cinema Studios, Pacific Pictures Ltd., and the Lion's Gate Studios. The Hollywood promoters of the latter company bought up the old Haddon Hall estate in 1927 and

Angotee (1953). (NFB)

33

Germany—Key to Europe (1953). (NFB)

sold investors on the idea of making Canadian films with British actors. As the need for more money grew desperate, battles for control began in which everyone lost and the backers went to jail—one of the few times that fraudulent speculators, who constantly went into bankruptcy, were brought before the courts. A similar venture collapsed about this time in Calgary, with a leading civic official involved in the scandal.

We are accustomed today to hearing how Canada's magnificent scenery is an advantage to film-makers. They knew this in the twenties. Already, the diversity of backgrounds and places against which films were made is apparent. The years 1929 and 1930 brought *The Devil's Bear* (Fort William), *Race for Time, Spirit of the Wilderness,* and *Fatal Flower* (Thunder Bay). In Toronto, George Thorne Booth organized "the first all-Canadian company," the Ontario Film Company, later known as Booth Canadian Film Co. Ltd. In 1929 he wrote, produced, and directed *The White Road,* which he claimed was the "first all-Canadian feature picture

to be made." It disappeared after he failed to obtain theater showings. He is reported to have made in 1932 the "first all-Canadian talking picture," *The Bells,* but no record of this achievement is available.

In 1931 a motion picture came to the screen that might never have been shown at all had it not been for the disaster that marred its production. *The Viking* was made by Varick Frissell for the Newfoundland-Labrador Film Co., Inc., formed by the Maritime exhibitor and distributor J. D. Williams, on location in Newfoundland. Frissell had made *The Swilin' Racket* in 1927, a documentary on seal hunting, and had photographed more scenes of seal hunting for *The Viking,* to be included in the fictional material in which Charles Starrett, a well-known Hollywood actor, was involved in a rivalry for the hand of the leading lady, played by Louise Huntingdon. *The Viking* was the lead ship of the sealing fleet under its real-life captain, Bob Bartlett. After the first version of the film was edited in Hollywood, Frissell decided to "improve the documentary footage of the scenes on the ice and around the ship with a shot of an iceberg turning over," and so he and the crew set sail once again in *The Viking*. On March 15, 1931, around 9:00 in the evening, the ship exploded and Frissell and twenty-seven men died. One man lived, but the cause of the explosion was never known. The film was finished by Hollywood director George Melford, and an introduction spoken by Sir Wilfred Grenfell, the Newfoundland missionary, was added in which he refers to the disaster that took place. *The Viking* had some fairly successful showings based on an advertising campaign carrying the announcement that "27 men died to make this film."

Like so many Canadian motion pictures of this period, *The Viking* soon slipped into obscurity and was lost for years until 1960 when Ralph Ellis (who now owns Keg Films, Toronto, and produces and distributes television programs), as a National Film Board representative, went to Newfoundland, and quite by accident found the tins of film in a fish storage plant.

The cold had preserved *The Viking*. Like *Carry On Sergeant*, it was donated to the former Canadian Film Archives of the Canadian Film Institute and is now preserved in the National Film, Television, and Sound Archives.

The Viking, unlike *Carry On Sergeant*, was a sound film. It brought the shaky and uncertain production of Canadian films into the thirties and the era of talking pictures. At Trenton, Canadian Productions Ltd. was organized to make films for the quota market, but production never began. Other projects, announced with enthusiasm, also died out in despair. A company called Northern Films shot *Crimson Paradise* in three weeks in Vancouver in 1932 at Hadley Park Castle, the home of the Dunsmuir family. Possibly Northern Films followed it with *The Black Robe*, with Dorothy Dunsmuir, who was instrumental in providing finances. Also in 1932 Northern made *The Secrets of Chinatown*. The producer, Kenneth J. Bishop, used Hollywood directors for both pictures: Robert Hill, an

Shyness (1953). (NFB)

Corral (1954). (NFB)

Rythmetic (1956). (NFB)

Carnival in Quebec **(1957). (NFB)**

were a hybrid collection of Anglo-Canadian-American cast, crew, and stories, all filmed mostly in Victoria and having very slight claim to being called Canadian: *Lucky Fugitives* and *Lucky Corrigan* (directed by Lewis D. Collins, with William Gargan), *Secret Patrol* and *Stampede* (both directed by Ford Beebe, with Charles Starrett); *Tugboat Princess* (from a story by Dalton Trumbo, with Valerie Hobson); *Death Goes North* directed by Frank McDonald; and *Manhattan Shakedown, Vengeance, Murder Is News, Woman Against the World, Convicted,* and *Special Inspector,* the latter two starring the then-unknown Rita Hayworth, and all but two directed by Leon Barsha. Production of these B pictures came to an end when the British government excluded such films from quota benefits on the grounds that while they were made in the Dominion, they could not be considered as either Canadian or British pictures.

The period ended in 1939 on an amateur yet purely Canadian note, as Melburn Turner, a member of the

The Living Stone **(1958). (NFB)**

Englishman, for *Crimson Paradise,* and Fred Newmeyer (who had directed Harold Lloyd's *Safety Last*) for *The Secrets of Chinatown.* That same year, another of Hollywood's many B directors to work in Canadian films, D. Ross Lederman, filmed *McKenna of the Mounties* in British Columbia, with Buck Jones, the popular cowboy star.

Production by Canadian companies lapsed yet again for three years, then two United States–Canadian films, *The King's Plate* and *Undercover,* both directed by James Newfield from Hollywood, were filmed in Toronto in 1935, the first at Woodbine race track, with Toby Wing, the second at Ravenna Rink, with Charles Starrett. Montreal, which appears to have been neglected during the period, became the setting for a jewel robbery tale, *From Nine to Nine,* produced by ASN but largely Hollywood-created with director Edgar G. Ulmer (later a cult figure for a short time) and actress Ruth Roland.

In 1935 Kenneth J. Bishop entered the scene again, this time with an agreement with Columbia Pictures to make films for the British quota market. Between 1935 and 1938, under the name of Central Films, Bishop produced twelve B pictures, mainly western and crime melodramas, and seems to have been the only producer at work during this time. The pictures he made

La Canne à pêche (1959). (NFB)

London (Ontario) Little Theatre and the Ontario Dramatic League, filmed a 16mm version of a play, *Talbot of Canada,* staged by the Little Theatre Company and based on Hilda Smith's "Here Will I Nest," a story about the exploits of Thomas Talbot, eccentric founder of the Talbot Settlements. The film was never commercially shown.

Although Canada was not to be recognized abroad (or at home) for its documentary film production until after the National Film Board had begun to make films of distinction, the three most famous films of this period, which found wide audiences, were all documentaries. Two of them were made by the NFB's forerunner, the Canadian Government Motion Picture Bureau, formed in 1927: *Lest We Forget,* a powerful and moving compilation of Canada at war during 1914–18, and *Royal Visit,* a complete record of the Royal Tour of Their Majesties King George VI and Queen Elizabeth across Canada in 1939. The third documentary was the classic, *Nanook of the North* (1922).

While not actually a Canadian-inspired production (it was paid for by the fur trade company Revillon Freres, Paris, and made by the Irish-American documentarian, Robert Flaherty), it was filmed entirely in the Canadian Arctic at a time when few people thought very much about the Eskimo, and still less of these people as Canadians. Flaherty did much of his processing and editing in Toronto. He made the film twice. The footage for his first version went up in flames in Toronto during the printing. He returned to the Arctic and shot Nanook's life story over again, and said that it was a better film than the first.

From 1914 to 1939, over fifty American films were shot on location, in whole or in part in Canada. Many of them seem to have been written by James Oliver Curwood or based on Laurie York Erskine's "Renfrew of the Royal Mounted." Most of them were B pictures about the RCMP, lumberjacks, stampedes, and wolf dogs; some were made by American directors who later became recognized as distinguished film-makers:

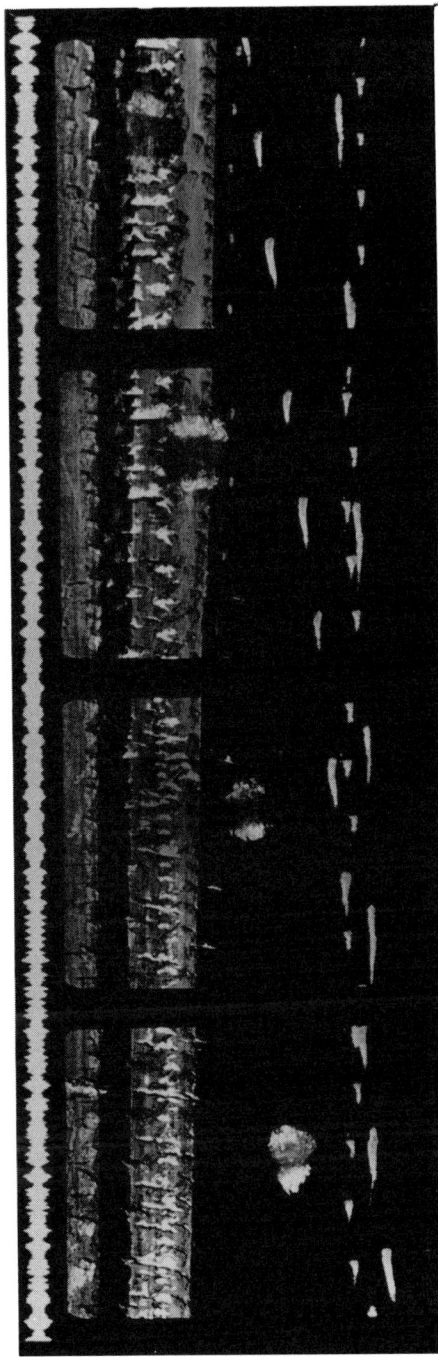
Serenal (1959). (NFB)

and *Five of a Kind* (1938) by Herbert L. Leeds; *Susannah of the Mounties* (1939) directed by William A. Seiter, with Shirley Temple, Randolph Scott, and Margaret Lockwood; and Cecil B. De Mille's *North West Mounted Police* (1940).

A few well-known Canadian books made likable American films: L. M. Montgomery's *Anne of Green Gables* (filmed twice, in 1919 with Mary Miles Minter and in 1934 with Anne Shirley), the same author's *Anne of Windy Poplars* (1939), also with Anne Shirley, and Mazo de la Roche's *Jalna,* directed by John Cromwell in 1935, with Kay Johnson, Ian Hunter, C. Aubrey Smith, and Nigel Bruce. All these had some location photography. Julien Duvivier came from France in 1934 to direct the exterior scenes for *Maria Chapdelaine,* in the Lac St. Jean region, with Madeleine Renaud, Jean Gabin, and Jean Pierre Aumont, based on Louis Hemon's novel. Pierre Berton has written a fully detailed, always fascinating, and often very funny book, "Hollywood's Canada" (McClelland and Stewart, Toronto, 1975), which describes the films made in Hollywood with supposedly Canadian backgrounds and stories and provides considerable insight about how American film-makers perceived this country.

A history of this entire period, from 1896 to 1939, is the subject of a ninety-minute documentary film called *Dreamland,* made for the National Film Board in 1975 by historians Peter Morris and Kirwan Cox. The director, Donald Brittain *(Memorandum, Paperland—The Bureaucrat Observed, Never a Backward Step),* narrates the commentary, and the film closes with this somewhat despairing yet oddly moving statement:

> The Second World War was about to break out and Canada, with the establishment of the National Film Board, and a new group of small private companies, was about to become the world's most prolific and respected maker of documentary films. But in 1939, motion picture production in Canada was a wasteland, inhabited by but a very few brave and lonely souls. The pioneers in this Dreamland—Gordon Sparling, Ernest Shipman, Roy Tash, Frank Badgely, Bill Oliver, Jack Chisholm, were a very small company of men. In many respects this was a bleak and somewhat shabby world, beset by cheap politicians, pompous bureaucrats and greedy promoters, and by an indifferent Canadian public, which seemed more interested in watching the Americans than they were in watching themselves. All of which lent a certain nobility to those few Canadian movie people who endured and refused to surrender the dream.

Dreamland was followed by a second hard-hitting installment of Canadian film history, *Has Anyone Here Seen Canada?* (1978, ninety minutes), also made by Morris and Cox, directed by John Kramer. These films could afford to be critical of those who failed to support film production. The politicians and businessmen

King Vidor's *Sky Pilot* (1920) with Colleen Moore and *Northwest Passage* (1939) with Spencer Tracy; Frank Lloyd's *The Wings of Chance* (1925); William Beaudine's *The Canadian* (1926) with Thomas Meighan; Irving Cummings's *The Country Beyond* (1926); Victor Fleming's *Man Trap* (1926) with Clara Bow; Clarence Brown's *The Trail of '98* (1928) with Dolores del Rio; three stories about the Dionne quintuplets with Jean Hersholt: *The Country Doctor* (1936) by Henry King, *Reunion* (1937) by Norman Taurog,

Between Two Wars **(1960). (NFB)**

who did nothing then or now, are either dead or are immune from criticism; they never see motion pictures and never read what is written about Canadian cinema. A third film, *The Image Makers* (1981, ninety minutes), directed by Albert Kish, is a brief but informative history of the National Film Board's first forty years. Together with the NFB's *The Eye Hears, the Ear Sees* (directed by Gavin Miller) about the work of Norman McLaren, and *Norman Jewison, Filmmaker* (directed by Douglas Jackson), these five films are indispensable in the study of Canadian film history.

An ironic footnote to the silent period came about in 1978 when five hundred reels of silent film, including newsreels, serials and features, were discovered buried beneath the permafrost in an old skating rink in historic Dawson City in the Yukon Territory. All were American.

General Vanier **(1960). (NFB)**

4

The Beginning of Canadian Documentaries

Throughout the years, successive governments, both federal and provincial, have maintained a one-sided support of motion picture production that has brought about a certain distinction for Canada in the form of film-making known as the "documentary." While the making of fictional entertainment movies with popular actors was looked upon as a free-enterprise activity, of no great educational benefit to the country, and thus was given no support by governments, the photographing of the vast outdoors with its timber, wheat, and game, and of the oceans and lakes with their harvest of fish, was considered to be a legitimate interest of governments and an entirely proper way to spend the taxpayers' money. More than education for the people, the use of film in this way was a valuable means to "publicise Canada and Canadian products abroad" and a "valuable aid to tourism." Nothing was said about making individual Canadians known to each other or to people abroad until very much later. Since the earliest days and right up until the present, few Canadian politicians ever considered the film medium as anything other than propaganda to lure travelers with the promise of bigger fish to catch, larger animals to shoot, taller mountains to climb and ski, and, on

through the years, to the doubtful thrills of waterskiing and snowmobiling.

With the outbreak of war in 1914, the two departments within the federal government most interested in the results of the CPR's immigration films were Trade and Commerce and the Department of the Interior. The Minister of Trade and Commerce, Sir George Foster, was intrigued by motion pictures and saw how valuable they could be in publicizing Canada's natural resources and production capabilities. He wanted the government to become involved in the making of film either directly or in association with private enterprise, and he might well have brought to Canada the distinction of being the first country in the world to have a government film unit had he not been anticipated and beaten to the post by another Canadian, working in England. In London in 1916, Lord Beaverbrook formed the British War Office Cinematographic Committee, in response to requests from companies and individuals asking permission to film the Great War in France. This appears to be the first known instance of significant government participation in film-making and distribution. However,

Roughnecks **(1960). (NFB)**

41

Away from It All (1961). (NFB)

Canada's Department of Trade and Commerce was not far behind and, in 1917, formed a departmental film unit, not to photograph the war in Europe, but to show life at home. Lord Beaverbrook's enterprise and Sir George Foster's initiative were inspired by different objectives; for Beaverbrook it was the temporary urgency of war, for Sir George it was the need to start a permanent program of films about Canadian life and achievement.

This was the beginning of the Dominion government's involvement in film-making, the forerunner of the Canadian Government Motion Picture Bureau. The Department of Trade and Commerce was, and still is, responsible for Canada's participation in fairs and exhibitions abroad and could see quite clearly what an added attraction films would be to these demonstrations of Canadian activity. (Fifty-five years later the same Department of Trade and Commerce contributed largely to Canada's first major participation at the Cannes Film Festival—a far cry from the fairs of 1916, with their simple, short subjects.)

The moving force behind the department's continued participation in film-making was Deputy Minis-

ter F. C. T. O'Hara, who urged Sir George Foster to establish control over all government motion picture production—to make it government policy to order all departments to have their films made by one government body in order to avoid duplication of costs and materials. This sensible proposition, to be advocated years later in the setting up of the bureau's final successor, the National Film Board, has never been completely realized, and the first dissenter was the Department of Agriculture, which insisted on making its own films.

Deputy Minister O'Hara, who fought for the bureau in all the difficult years that lay ahead until he retired in 1931, chose a draftsman, Benjamin Norrish, from the Water Power Branch of the Department of the Interior, to take charge of the Trade and Commerce's film unit. Norrish, a Canadian, had worked with the Essanay Company of Chicago while one of its units was in Canada making a film (about the Dominion's grain harvest and water power) for the United States Bureau of Commercial Economics. He was keenly interested in film-making and was an aggressive and energetic man whose interest in putting Canada on the screen was commendable. Unfortunately, in later years he became a hand-maiden to American interests in Canada—a role taken by many Canadians who took the easy way to success by throwing in, if not selling out, their lot with the Americans.

The film unit officially became the Exhibits and Publicity Bureau of the Department of Trade and Commerce on September 19, 1918. All members of Parliament and the senate were invited to a special showing of industrial and travel films made by the unit a few months before its official birth, which was the beginning of a publicity campaign to "make Canada known, as she really is, at home and abroad." How many times were Canadians to hear this phrase in the years to come! The minister envisioned the showings of these films abroad by Canadian high commissions and embassies. To a limited extent this worked, but the number of people reached was insignificant compared to those attending commercial cinemas with their Hollywood adventures and romances. In 1919, the first major exhibition of Canadian government short subjects took place at the Lyons Trade Fair in France. Fore-shadowing the Expos and Ontario Places of today, the bureau projected more than 14,000 feet of film in a specially constructed theater.

Ben Norrish remained with the film unit until June 1920, when he left Ottawa to take charge of Canada's first private film company, the Associated Screen News Corporation of Montreal (ASN), founded by the Canadian Pacific Railway Company. Norrish was succeeded in July 1920 by Raymond Peck, formerly a film editor with the bureau. He expanded production still further and developed distribution and exhibition overseas and in domestic cinemas. He was plagued by opposition from private companies who wanted government work and by the government's failure to pay attractive salaries to its bureau employees. Facilities were poor and working conditions unbearable. But he, like Norrish, received considerable support from O'Hara and the minister, both of whom were "keenly alive to the potentialities of the screen as a national advertising medium." Peck also disliked the name "Exhibits and Publicity," which sounded like outright commercialism. Finally, on April 1, 1923, the minister,

Golden Gloves (1961). (NFB)

43

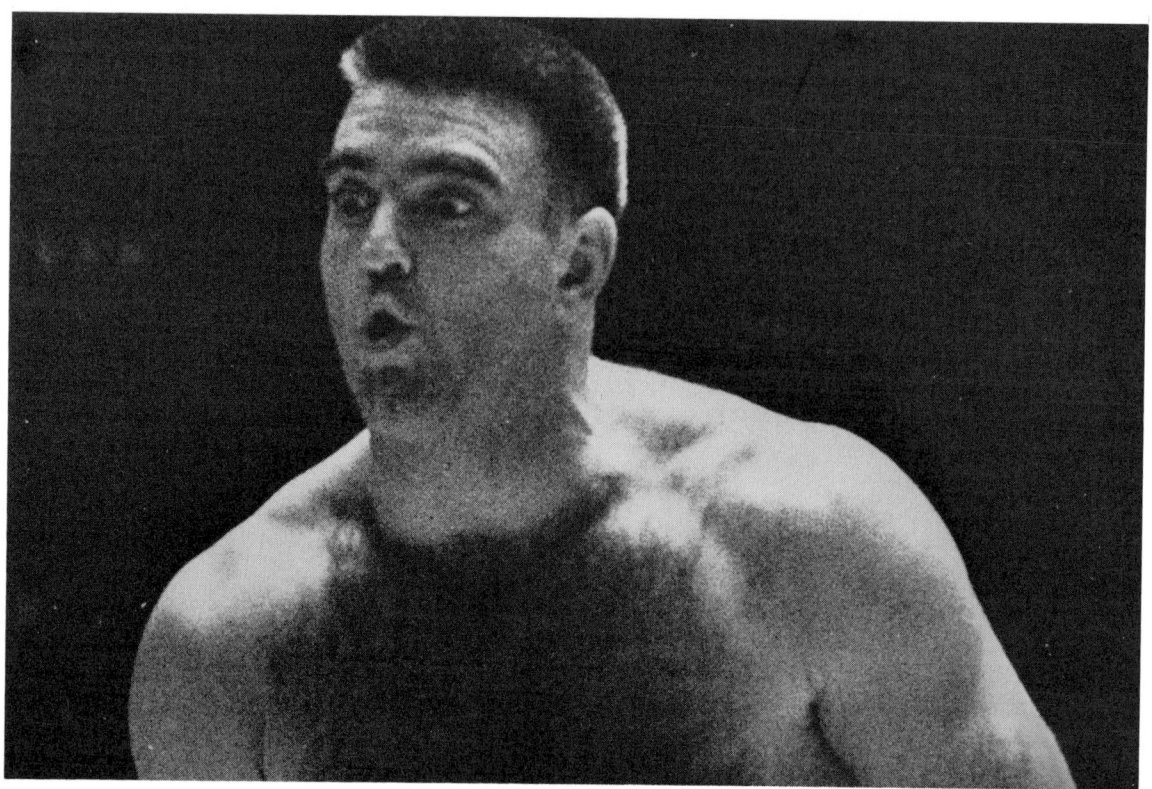

La Lutte (Wrestling) **(1961). (NFB)**

Lord Elgin: Voice of the People **(1961). (NFB)**

now the Honorable J. A. Robb, agreed to change the name of the film unit to the Canadian Government Motion Picture Bureau. Now it was described as "a valuable educational medium by which one part of Canada is enabled to know the other." Films were made on 35mm stock (as well as 16mm) and the bureau's production included *Canadian National Pictorial,* a weekly news magazine, and the *Seeing Canada* series, "extolling the nation's scenic attractions and industrial output."

Getting these short movies shown in cinemas, however, was hard going, due to increasing competition from the Hollywood studios, which had their own short films, cartoons, and newsreels, to show with their feature-length productions. Mr. Peck, however, was one of many Canadians who showed little concern over the growing American stranglehold on the distribution and exhibition of all kinds of films. In fact, several visits to Hollywood seem to have convinced him that the development of indigenous feature films in Canada was impossible. His attitude was in keeping with official government policy towards the making of commercial films, and although some loyal theater owners tried holding "All Canadian Weeks," they didn't have much to show and the government was not inclined to improve the situation. Peck believed that the government should persuade American producers to come to Canada to make "Canadian content" films, "using our natural backgrounds and scenic wonders," and politicians agreed. This notion, still harbored by many provincial politicians, reached its greatest heights of absurdity during the aftermath of the Second World War when Canada, like many nations, suffered a critical dollar shortage (see pages 83–84).

Raymond Peck died in May 1927, and his place was taken by Captain Frank Badgely. A handsome man with a distinguished army record, Badgely had played bit parts in Hollywood films and worked with D. W. Griffith as technical assistant. He had returned to his birthplace, Ottawa, in 1921 to join the bureau as an editor and, inspired by his experience in Hollywood, to make Canadian films. Badgely was to rule through difficult and painful years that included the Great Depression. His personal problems and administrative difficulties with the bureau during its most important years, what happened to the bureau before he took over and until it was superseded by the National Film Board is told in fascinating detail by Charles Backhouse in his well-researched CFI publication, "Canadian Government Motion Picture Bureau 1917–1941," which is available from the Canadian Film Institute, Ottawa. In spite of continuing support from Deputy Minister O'Hara, who retired in 1931, to be succeeded by Major J. G. Parmelee, another civil servant sympathetic to the aims and needs of the bureau, the embattled film unit suffered from the continuing severe economic situation. This resulted in lack of finances at the time when sound came to the movies. The purchase of the equipment necessary to convert to making sound films was beyond the government's resources. It was felt that the public, millions of whom were out of work and on a starvation diet, would not think kindly of a government spending tax dollars at this time on the frivolous occupation of film-making.

The thirties passed, and soon came the Second World War. The bureau, born at the end of the last great war, was to cease to function in its present form by the beginning of the next world conflict. It had been slowly suffocated by the Treasury and the Civil Service Commission, which stifled its initiative and creativity. During its existence, not one complete catalogue was printed listing all the films made by the bureau, and there does not appear to exist a complete set of the annual catalogues. Few of the films remain, and those that were saved are at long last with the National Film, Television, and Sound Archives in Ottawa, which, after years of government indecision, was created as part of the Dominion Public Archives in 1970. Added to them are several hundred short films made by the Ontario Government Motion Picture Bureau, which existed under George Patton, a dedicated English film-maker, during the years 1922 to 1934. The Ontario Bureau made films similar to those of the federal bureau, but more specifically in provincial matters such as road building, the use of mechanized farm equipment, and the providing of hot meals in schools. The Ontario Bureau was started in Toronto by Premier Hearst and thrown out by Premier Hepburn a few days after he had assured Patton that the Depression would not affect the film unit. Hepburn also ordered the destruction of the prints, but fortunately Patton saved many of them. Titles of some of the surviving Canadian Government Motion Picture Bureau films indicate their nature: *Big Timber, The Seasons of Canada, The Story of Nickel, Falling Waters,* and *Canada's Queen City,* which made use of an early split-screen effect.

Outside of this government activity, the only major private company producing short films for cinemas and advertising film for sponsors on a continuing basis during this period was Associated Screen News under Ben Norrish. ASN printed most of the release prints of the American distributors for use in Canada. The negatives were sent from the studios in Los Angeles and the prints made at ASN. It would have been extremely costly to send the required number of finished prints to Canada, although it is possible that had there not been high customs duties on the importation of films, the American companies would no doubt have thought twice about getting the work done in Canada. Norrish considered that any move on ASN's part to enter feature-film production, as the company was fre-

Pour quelques arpents de niege (1961). (NFB)

quently urged to do, would displease his American clients, so he refrained from doing so. ASN would most likely never have made short films for cinemas had it not been for the persistence of Gordon Sparling, who, working with little money and limited equipment, started the *Canadian Cameo Series* (1932 to 1953). Mr. Sparling, who had worked on *Carry On Sergeant,* managed to capture something of the social events of the time by making shorts on everybody and anything newsworthy and considered fit and simple entertainment for the masses attending the cinemas. Among his subjects were the Dionne quintuplets, Grey Owl, and Montreal nightlife, the last captured in the extravaganza *Rhapsody in Two Languages.*

The attitude of the trade to anything Canadian is well summed up by Gordon Sparling's encounter with the Palace Theatre in Montreal, where *Rhapsody in Two Languages* hardly played at all because the manager did not think that Montrealers wanted to see life in Montreal, so he replaced it with a short about nightlife in Chicago instead. Thus was the country sold out over the years, little by little, here and there, to the idea that everything happening elsewhere was of more interest to audiences than events that happened at home.

It is hard to assess the effect on society of all the short films the Canadian Motion Picture Bureau made, some 10,000 probably, over its thirty-odd years of existence. No complete record remains. On the positive side, it would be encouraging to think that these films were widely seen and did play a large part in contributing to a public awareness of a Canadian sense of identity. Regretfully, government efforts and the dreams, struggles, and ambitions of individual film-makers to further short films on education and tourism were all but swamped by American feature films. Many of these came later to be considered classic works still seen today, their directors honored artists, while the Canadian shorts produced not one recorded classic, not one distinguished film-maker, and mostly have passed into oblivion. The few that remain are superficial records of animal life, industrial activity, social events, and conferences—historically interesting but emotionally flat and without character. Yet

Canadian productions managed to hold their own in what they set out to do. But the effect on the public of nothing else but years of short films convinced it that Canadian film-makers were somehow unsuited to make full-length dramas and comedies. They were to be forever trapped in the making of "fillers," which, in cinemas, provided audiences with the excuse to leave for the washrooms or refreshment counters and occupied the screen while latecomers drifted in and wandered around looking for seats before the main attraction began. The public, whether in the cinema or the school hall, church basement, or library reading room, where government films were shown, learned little from shorts and cared even less.

The government ignored the difficulties of film-makers who wanted to produce full-length films in order to depict a greater reality. An attempt to discover the truth of life, no matter how inept and distorted it sometimes can seem on the screen, comes about in the depiction of recognizable human dealing with life in one form or another. The reality that the short films showed in the amiable, quiet Canadian way was often dull, and unconvincing. Hollywood studios, meanwhile, were turning out fast-paced, loud, jingoistic glorifications of sporting events, travel in God's Country, the might of industry, the superiority of the U.S. armed forces, its happy schools and colleges, all accompanied by boastful commentaries. The modest Canadian counterpart, more honest perhaps in its restraint, was smothered by the sheer technical virtuosity and expensive production of the American short films. The public came to believe that this was the way all films should be, and anything different, whether Canadian, British, French, was inferior. To the American film-makers, nothing was sacred and all kinds of individuals and their activities were fair game for their cameras. Many Canadians still thought that film-making was an indecent activity and that people who appeared before the cameras except on state or ceremonial occasions were somehow rather vulgar.

As 1938 came to a close, a new and promising chapter in Canadian film-making was about to begin under a man soon to become world-famous. He was John Grierson, a Scotsman who had revolutionized short

Boulevard St. Laurent **(1962). (NFB)**

Climates of North America (1962). (NFB)

Je (1962). (NFB)

film-making in Britain and contributed largely to the creation of the documentary film movement. When he was invited to Canada to study the possibilities of reorganizing the Canadian Motion Picture Bureau, Grierson told *The Ottawa Citizen* that a friend of his had remarked that to judge by Canadian short films, "if life in the Dominion is as these films represent, we might expect Canadians to be engaged only in fishing, golf and the observation of wild animals. There are practically no industries, very little work, and no working people."

Some of this negative feeling about Canadian short films had become apparent to a good many Canadians living abroad in London. The good impression created by some bureau films was flawed by many indifferent and badly worn pictures made for individual departments of the government, all loosely described as "government films," as though they had been made by the bureau but whose ownership was in doubt.

The Canadian high commissioner in London in the late thirties was the distinguished man of arts and letters, Vincent Massey. It is doubtful that he knew much about the cinema or cared greatly for it, although his brother, Raymond, a well-known stage actor, had distinguished himself in British and American motion pictures *(The Scarlet Pimpernel, Abe Lincoln in Illinois, Prince of Players)*. But Vincent Massey was not unaware of the power and place of film in society, even as being just a means of common entertainment. For this reason, when he received a report on the condition of Canadian motion picture production from his private secretary, Ross McLean (not the CBC producer), he gave it sympathetic consideration before sending it, with his approval, on to the secretary of state for External Affairs in Ottawa.

Without Ross McLean, the National Film Board of Canada might never have been created. Mr. McLean was a "rare bird" in those days, a civil servant in the overseas service who realized how influential well-made films could be in showing a nation's way of life to other countries of the world. An early film enthusiast, he had spent his spare time in London visiting film societies and looking at the films of the famous General Post Office (GPO) Film Unit. There he met John Grierson, under whose supervision these films were made. He fell under Grierson's magnetism and dynamic force and became inspired by what Grierson was doing and the possibility he held out in the development of film as a vital social force in the lives of people. McLean had also been reading Roger Manvell's Penguin book entitled *Film,* the first serious consideration of film as an art to be published in English. McLean went to work and wrote for many weeks,

finally handing in his report to Vincent Massey on November 19, 1937. In it McLean pointed out that while there were over 500 prints of bureau and government films available for showing in the United Kingdom, he was appalled at the lack of genuinely interesting material on Canada, saying that "the distribution of indifferent films is the worst kind of publicity."

He suggested sweeping changes in policy and staff in Ottawa and London and that an independent and exhaustive survey of Canadian "publicity" film activities be carried out at once. He not unexpectedly put forward Grierson's name as the most experienced person to carry out the investigation and to make recommendations for improvements.

Changes seldom happen at once in the administration of government, yet surprisingly enough, before the year was out, the Dominion government had invited John Grierson to carry out the task. He agreed to come to Canada the following spring.

He arrived in May 1938, presenting himself in Ottawa before the letter announcing his departure from London had been delivered. Grierson was throughout his life one of those tireless individuals who worked with undiminished energy day and night. A man of

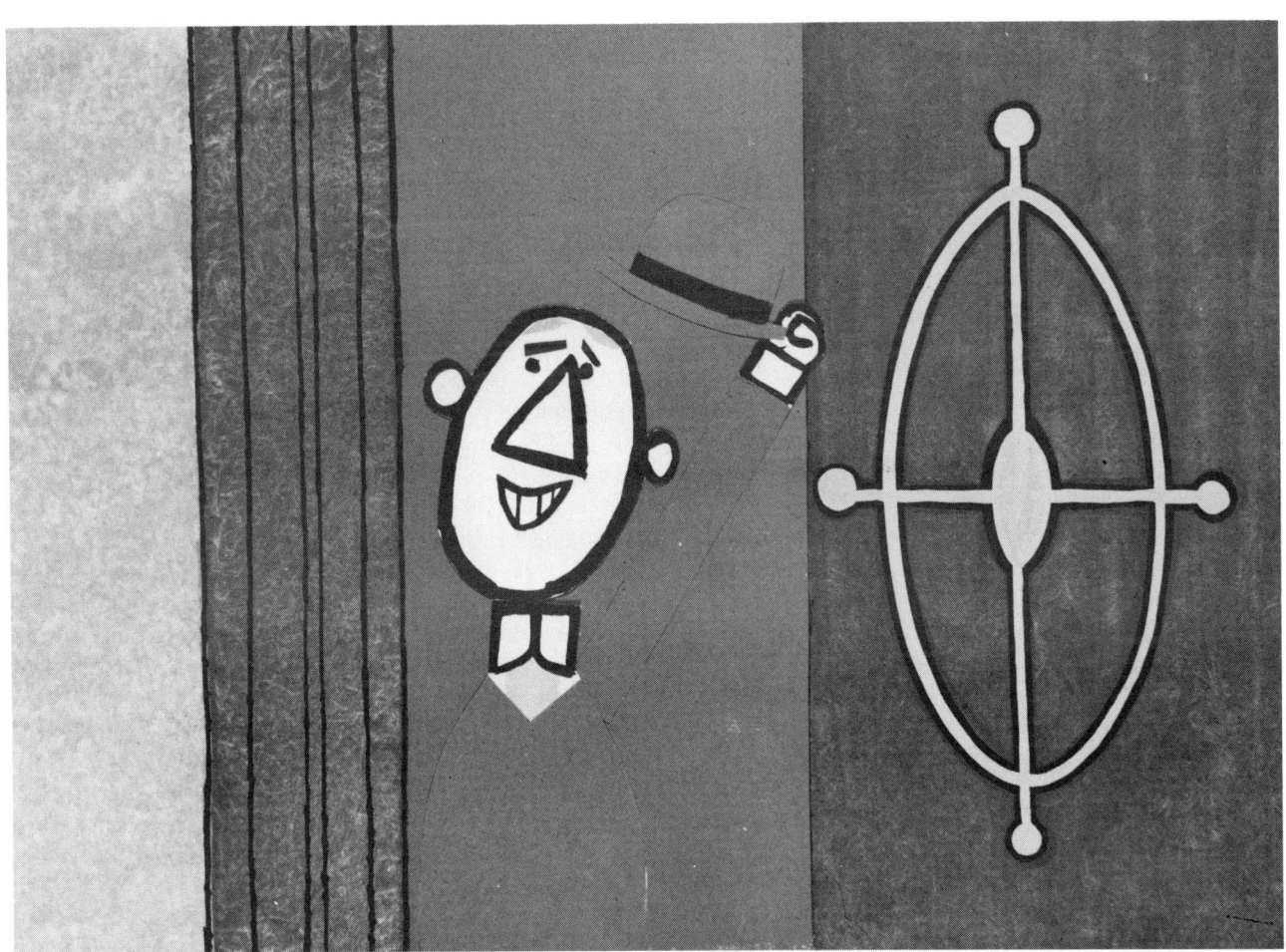

My Financial Career (1962). (NFB)

Le Vieil Age (1962). (NFB)

keen insight and intellect, a brilliant, perceptive, and forceful writer, a man who spoke his mind at all times and believed emphatically in his work, he was even then a genius who startled Ottawa's politicians in a way they had never before experienced. It is worth remembering, looking back to this time, that Grierson's original visit was not to set up the National Film Board, which was not even envisaged then. His task was to report on how the government's Motion Picture Bureau and its film activities could be improved. Both Parmalee and Badgely welcomed Grierson, for they saw in him their hope for the future: a better-equipped and financed motion picture bureau. That was all Grierson intended to do. The fates, however, particularly the gods of war, were planning differently.

Grierson's report on the bureau, its manner of work, the nature of its films, its treatment by government departments, was scathing. He recommended the creation of a strong, creative film unit, independent of any government department, with a continuing committee to guide, review, and criticize the work of the bureau,

and that a film commissioner be appointed to carry out the policy of the committee. Further, all government film-making should be centralized through the bureau. He called for the release of the bureau "from its inferiority complex" and suggested that it be developed "as a powerful institution of government propaganda policy." (As this was before the war, the word *propaganda* was not the hateful term it later became. Today it is never used in official circles lest the public think the government is attempting to indoctrinate them with fascist ideals.) Grierson then took the train for Montreal, and thence by ocean liner back to England.

It took Ottawa some time to recover from Grierson's rapid yet thorough inquiry, but by November the government agreed to his proposals and invited him back, for the sum of $2,250, to implement the report and "to develop a plan for the co-ordination of the film production and distribution activities of Departments of the Dominion Government." Grierson returned on November 22, 1938. One of his chief tasks was to pacify private producers who saw themselves without government contracts. Grierson then assured them that under his plan there would be work for all if it was carried out as he conceived it. And there was.

Because ministers and their departments were so slow in seeing him and arriving at any conclusions about their part in the board, Grierson drafted the entire bill himself, in three weeks. He recommended Badgely as commissioner and returned to London. In the bill was the first reference to a proposed National Film Board of Canada. It should be borne in mind that the proposed board was not to be a production unit, but an administrative body.

The bill went slowly through Parliament, much-discussed by the press, with most editorials against it. "The government should keep out of the arts and have nothing to do with film, a commercial enterprise for public entertainment," was the sentiment of the day. Famous Players, naturally, was highly suspicious. Assurances were given to head offices in New York and studios in Hollywood that "interpreting Canada to Canadians" was to be carried out only in shorts and educational documentaries. However, throughout the debate, the bill was strongly supported by individuals in the arts and by various organizations, including James Cowan, the National Film Society (as the Canadian Film Institute was then known), the Canadian Association for Adult Education, and others. Their favorable opinions might possibly have saved the bill from defeat caused by private enterprise lobbying. This was not Canadian private enterprise, but American vested interests.

Four months later, Parmalee sent a telegram to John Grierson reading "BILL PASSED FINAL READING IN HOUSE LAST NIGHT WITHOUT DISCUSSION." The date was March 17, 1939.

The National Film Act was seen as the salvation of the Motion Picture Bureau, which during this time had continued to make the usual short films. It had received considerable recognition for two long documentaries, *Salute To Valour*, the story of the dedication of the Canadian National Memorial at Vimy Ridge, with King Edward VIII playing a prominent part in the ceremonies; and earlier, *Lest We Forget*, made up of newsreel footage about the First World War. The Bureau was now preparing *Royal Visit*, the famous cross-Canada journey by King George VI and Queen Elizabeth, which was also to be well received.

Everyone at the bureau, including Parmalee and Badgely, prepared for a better future. The strengthening of the bureau, however, was not to be realized. At first the new National Film Board was set up as an independent advisory committee of eight members, three from the government, three from the public sector, the minister of Trade and Commerce as chairman, and the film commissioner. The NFB was to direct the policy of centralized government film production and distribution; the bureau, still under Frank Badgely, was to make the films and to be the depository for government films. (There was no film archive, and the Dominion archivist had no mandate to accept motion pictures.)

The government did not immediately appoint a commissioner, realizing that the position was a difficult one to fill and that the wrong man would destroy the concept. Then, like a bombshell, the threatening war that everyone had hoped would go away broke out on September 3, 1939. Within a few days, Canada also entered World War II. The government, in spite of the lessons of the First World War, did not think at first that films would have much to do with the war effort, and having more urgent matters on its mind, had no desire to spend too much time and money on the infant National Film Board. Prime Minister Mackenzie King, who got along well with the spirited John Grierson, decided to settle the matter of the board by inviting Grierson back yet again to "put his concept to work."

With the outbreak of war, Grierson was torn three ways: he felt he should remain in London; he had

Arctic Circle (1963). (NFB)

51

agreed to go to Australia to set up a similar film board there; and he also wanted to guide what was essentially his creation, the NFB, into a useful life in Canada. Events worked out in Canada's favor. The British government, like the Canadian one, did not at first think of films (other than training films) as playing an important role in the affairs of war; Australia, also now at war, told Grierson to come when he had finished in Canada. Grierson sailed once again for Montreal, arriving back in Ottawa, and to all intents and purposes filled the vacant position of commissioner of the National Film Board.

Grierson, active, visionary, and creative, could hardly be expected to remain still in an advisory capacity. Probably, had work at the bureau gone well, the differences that arose between him and Badgely might have been avoided. However, soon tension and resentment marked the working relationship between the two men. Badgely accused Grierson of meddling in areas of film production. Grierson was bringing in new, young men with imagination and zest. The older employees of the bureau, confirmed civil servants who had grown up with films about fishing, lumbering, and animal life, had no idea of the importance of films in modern warfare, and when they saw the first Nazi propaganda films they were overcome by the startling use of visuals, sound, and editing.

Grierson was not a man to waste time waiting around for requests to be filled through official channels. He cut through red tape and bypassed time-consuming procedures. He had brought Stuart Legg, a brilliant young film editor, with him from London, and under Legg the bureau began producing in 1940 the *Canada Carries On* series, which was inspired by the war and designed to encourage a feeling of pride

Christmas Cracker (1963). (NFB)

among Canadians of their country's considerable contribution to the war effort.

These films were made in English and French and were probably the first bureau films to be made in the French language.

The *Canada Carries On* series was narrated by Lorne Greene, then the CBC's leading reader of the national news on the Trans-Canada radio network. He had the appropriate "voice of doom" considered effective in shocking the public into an understanding of the seriousness of warfare. He still recalls very clearly his first job in film and his first encounter with John Grierson. He took the crowded night train from Toronto to Ottawa, and in the early dawn arrived at the old saw mill on Bank Street where the film makers worked under the most appallingly primitive conditions:

The Prime Minister, at that time Mackenzie King, said, "Build a centre which will produce propaganda films. We need them." Grierson did in a very short time. He got together a crew of people who were some of the finest documentary makers in the world and brought them together in one place and built a studio out of nothing. Within four months the first film was in the theatres. I remember receiving a call from Montreal. It was in April of 1940, and . . . as I had just finished a news broadcast I thought "My God, somebody's calling to complain from Montreal!" [Stuart Legg] said, "I am connected with the National Film Board—I'm a producer of docu-

National Film Board's original headquarters on John Street, Ottawa (1949).

mentary films under John Grierson." Which meant absolutely nothing to me at all! He said, "We are just completing a 10-minute film which will be one of a series—the first of a series called *Canada Carries On,* and we would like you to read the commentary for it. Would you be interested?"

I'd never even dreamed of a thing like this and I just said, "Yes. I've never done it before so I don't know how to do it." "We'll show you," he said. "Fine," I replied, "when do you want this?" "Next week. It must be in the theatres the week after, you see." I said, "Oh. Oh! Well, I don't know whether I can get some time off. Where's it going to be done? In Montreal?" He said, "No, in Ottawa." I said, "Well, you know I have my schedule here." He said, "We'll arrange it." So they got hold of Gladstone Murray, who was then the General Manager of the CBC, and they made arrangements for me to have a day-and-a-half off, and I took the train to Ottawa overnight.

In those days they didn't have tape, so everything was done on film. The effects were on film, the film was there, the music track was there, and then they made a voice track. The technicians had to mix the music, the effects, the film with the voice, live, all at the same time. The poor sound engineer was like a one-armed paper-hanger! I mean, he was going absolutely out of his mind! It took us from nine in the morning until about 10:30 at night to complete the 10-minute film. Today, I can do four half-hour films in about three hours. But then it was impossible. If the effects track was right, the music track was too

loud. If the music track was right, the effects track was too loud. If they were both right, I made some kind of error! But we finally completed it, I came back to Toronto, and I think I received the great sum of $50 for doing the narration.

About two weeks later I went to the theatre on a Saturday night to see a motion picture. I sat down and saw the title coming up for a short, *Canada Carries On.* The music seemed familiar, I couldn't recall why it sounded familiar to me, and then I heard a voice saying, "The vast Atlantic." Those are the first three words I ever spoke in a documentary, and I've done maybe seven or eight hundred of them since them. "The vast Atlantic"—and suddenly I realised it was me! It was at the Imperial Theatre in Toronto, and it was packed with people, and I felt they were all looking at me! Of course, nobody knew I was in the theatre, for God's sake! They didn't know whose voice it was—they didn't know anything—but I just felt that they were all looking at me. I didn't see the end of the film—I just leaped out of the theatre. I did! It sounded strange to me, it was so different . I'll never forget that night. From then on I did them all, under contract. I narrated all of the *Canada Carries On* and the *World in Action* series, working with Grierson.

My first meeting with Grierson came, I think, during the third film, produced by Stanley Hawes, who later became the Australian Film Commissioner. Stanley had, in the commentary, written in part of "The Mariner's Prayer," because the whole film was about a freighter called the *Manchester Progress,*

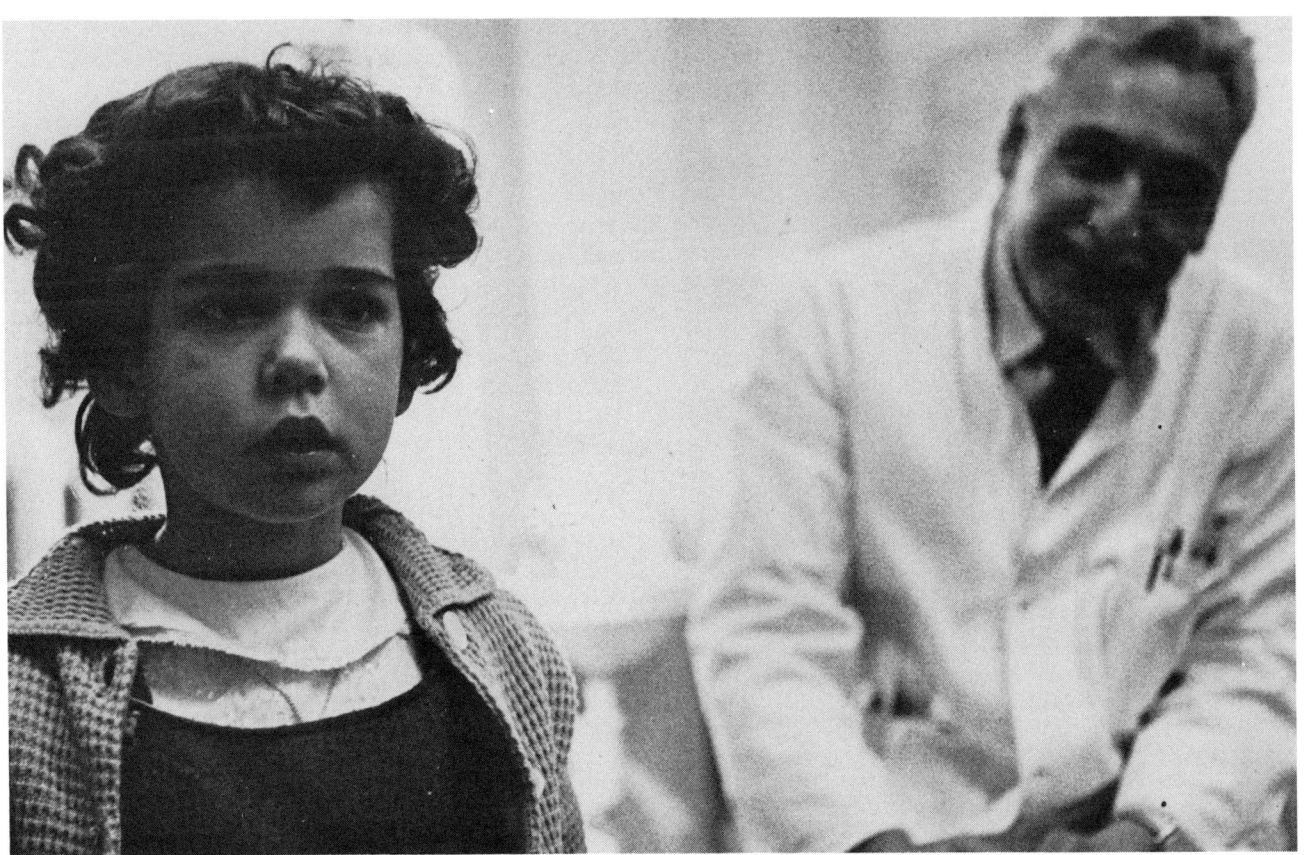

Les Enfants du silence (1963). (NFB)

Jour apres jour (Day after Day) **(1963). (NFB)**

which was torpedoed at sea. The commentary spoke to the freighter: *"Come into your berth, Manchester Progress. That's it, snug up alongside"* and so forth, talking to the ship. When the freighter sank after being torpedoed on the ocean, part of "The Mariner's prayer" again came into the commentary. We were rehearsing this and when we came to it I heard a faint roar outside the recording studio, a sound of strangled anguish! I thought somebody had tripped over something and hurt their leg. It kept on going, and suddenly the door to this little booth was flung open, torn off its hinges practically, and a short man, with glasses, whose hair seemed to be standing on end, burst in. His eyes, which were blue, were boring through me, and all he said in a broad Scots accent was, "Who told you you could read that?" I didn't know this was Grierson. He said, "You get out there and listen." So I went into the theatre, he shut the door and he read "The Mariner's Prayer." I started making marks on my script. He said, "You could do it this way" and he read it. Then he said, "Or you could do it this way" and he read again. "And you could do it this way"—twenty-seven different interpretations of "The Mariner's prayer." It taught me a tremendous lesson, which I had forgotten, which is, of course, there are an infinite number of ways to read verse. He said, "Now you come on back in here and do it." Now my knees were trembling. He wasn't a big man, but I thought he was going to kill me! So I walked back, the door was flung open again, and he walked out. We were in narrow quarters as I walked by him, and he said to me, "Bill Auden could have done it." W. H. Auden, the great English poet, had read commentaries for him in England. *Bill Auden could have done it.* That was the worst thing he could have said to me. Because Auden was a poet—not even a speaker—but *he could have done it.* That was my first meeting with Grierson. Then we became very close friends.

I saw him in London in 1955 and we spent a whole day together. He told me one of the strangest stories which I suppose, is common knowledge now. All the time he was in Ottawa, he was head of M.I.6. At the outbreak of war he was on his way back from Australia to London, stopping off in Ottawa, when Mackenzie King offered him the NFB job. Grierson cabled his superiors in London to seek their advice and they said, by all means, take the job, it's a great blind. It's a marvellous position for you to be in.

Grierson was a brilliant man, a very brilliant man! I think his testimony at the Gouzenko trials if put together would make a marvellous document, a fascianting compendium of all the political philosophies of the world. When he was asked questions by the Supreme Court Judges—most of them were his friends, they all belonged to the same club—he

Kindergarten (1963). (NFB)

would never reply to the question, but would always give a learned dissertation on Communism, Marxism, the doctrine of Socialism, Fascism, and religions of every kind. Today if students of political systems wanted to study the subject, they could get a really marvellous insight by just reading his testimony. At the Rideau Club, after the day's hearings, the Supreme Court Judges would meet him over drinks and say, "John, for God's sake, when are you going to start answering our questions?" He'd reply, "When you ask me a question I can answer." They didn't know what he meant, because they didn't know that he was Head of M.I.6. He was head of British Military Intelligence in Canada, and he couldn't answer their questions. (Lorne Greene, interview with author, 1974.)

Grierson recognized that the urgency of wartime film production made his original concept of bureau and board unworkable. He suggested that they be drawn together into one body. He was also concerned over the attitudes of other government departments that still considered the bureau as an adjunct to Trade and Commerce, and refused to cooperate with the bureau's film-makers. Grierson suggested, in June 1940, that the amalgamation take place. Nothing was done until May 1941. Then Grierson announced that he would not renew his contract, which expired in

August, and once again asked that for the good of Canadian films, the bureau and the board be made into one efficient organization.

This time the committee met and by a vote of 4 to 3 decided in favor of the move. An order in council on June 11, 1941, made the decision official and transferred the control of the Motion Picture Bureau from the Department of Trade and Commerce to the National Film Board. Thus was the NFB created, more-or-less as we know it today. Frank Badgely, a deeply disappointed man, transferred to the Department of Veterans Affairs. Some of his workers remained, others moved to different government departments. In the past two years of the bureau's life, Badgely, pushed and cajoled by Grierson, had in spite of frustrations, irritations, and conflicts, produced some forty short films, many in French, forced reluctant American-owned distributors and theaters to show the popular *Canada Carries On* and *World in Action* series, provided material for newsreels, made clips to promote savings bonds, succeeded in getting more short subjects shown in cinemas abroad, particularly in the United States, which had not yet entered the war, and begun revising nontheatrical distribution in Canada.

Early in 1941, Grierson hired a young commercial artist from Toronto to join the board and work in the cutting rooms, splicing film. His name was Sydney Newman. After rising through the ranks to become producer, he left to join CBC-TV in 1952, then later leaving CBC for British television. After ten years in London, he returned to Canada and became commissioner of the board, where he had started his career some twenty years earlier. Norman McLaren arrived three weeks after Newman and was to remain with the board permanently. He went to work immediately, experimenting with his technique of drawing directly on film with *Mail Early for Christmas,* a one-minute promotional film for the post office.

Sydney Newman recalls that when he joined the board, the production staff totaled no more than fifteen people, several of whom—Stuart Legg, Stanley Hawes, J. D. Davidson, and others—were from England. "We used to get visits from Arthur Elton, Edgar Anstey, Basil Wright, Cavalcanti, Joris Ivens, Boris Kaufman, and others, several of whom made films for us. Through Grierson, we came, in a sense, to be in touch with the film world, which had never happened before."

By the end of the summer of 1941 the Canadian Motion Picture Bureau ceased to exist in name, but what it had achieved in the history of Canadian government film-making made possible the creation of the NFB. It became a new body with a new name and a new life instilled into it by a courageous man who inspired those who came to work for him, and who was to make Canada the world's foremost nation in the production of documentary films.

John Grierson became known as the father of documentary, but he would disclaim the title and say that it properly belonged to Robert Flaherty, who perhaps started the genre with *Nanook of the North,* which still remains the definitive masterpiece on the life of the Canadian Eskimo, although it hardly qualifies as a Canadian film. Grierson himself, never a man to sail under false colors, also knew that documentary came about quite naturally with the birth of the cinema when pioneers such as the Lumière Brothers, Edwin S. Porter, and Cecil Hepworth, not knowing what at first could be done with film, excitedly photographed all forms of life around them from workers leaving the factory to the funerals of statesmen. This form of reporting became known as the newsreel, and it has left us with valuable records of the way places looked, how people dressed, and what methods of transport and communications were like. The newsreel told us almost nothing about the way people behaved and why, because the camera only photographed a surface

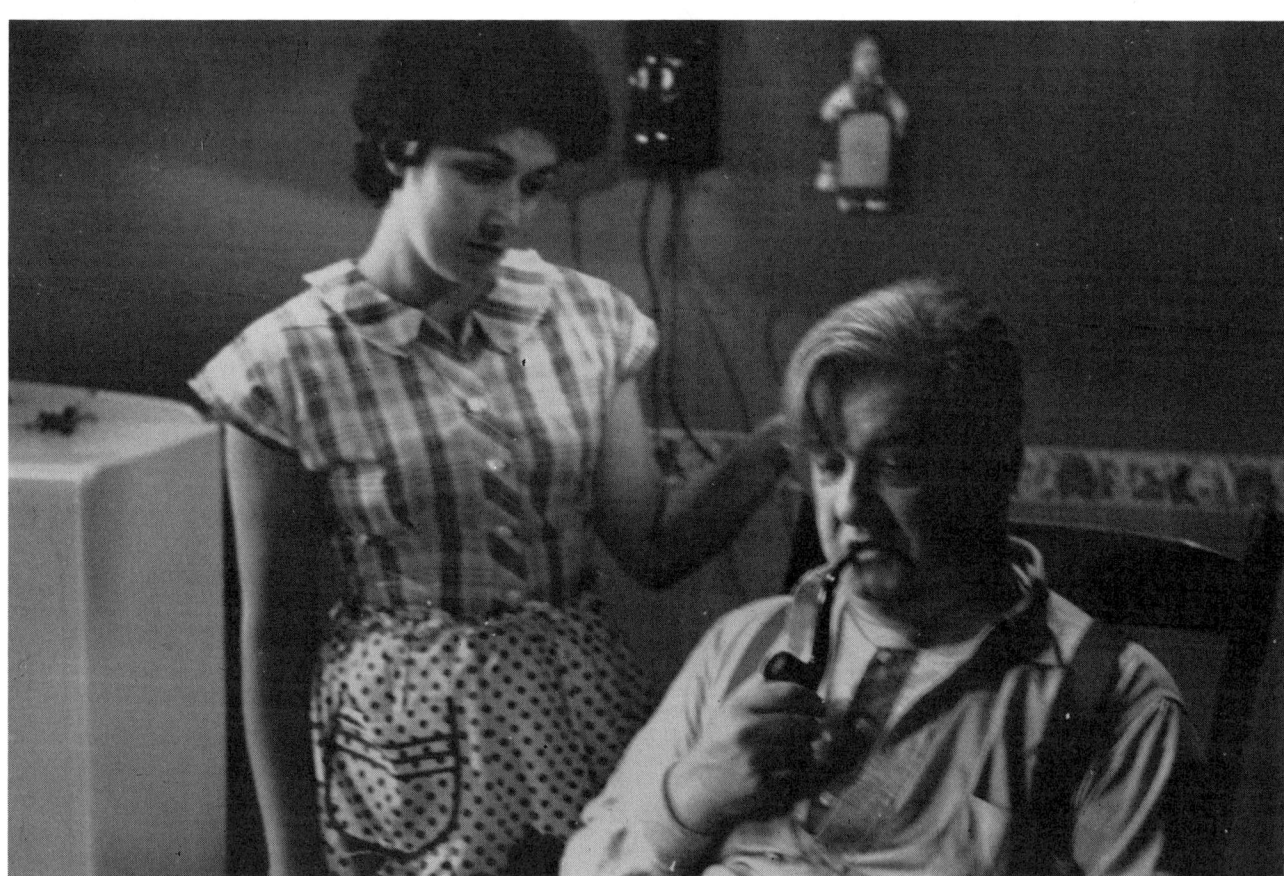

Nomades de l'ouest (Stampede) **(1963). (NFB)**

Petit Discours de la methode **(1963). (NFB)**

reality. It was this one-dimensional aspect to motion pictures that brought out the artist in the early camera-men, who then became writers and directors, notably Edwin S. Porter in the United States and Cecil Hep-worth in England. Men such as these, and often those who names may not have found their place in film history, perceived that while it was not possible to wait around and intrude into people's lives to film their emotional and dramatic responses and encounters dur-ing their everyday existence, all forms of life could be recreated by using people who would either play them-selves on the screen or who would pass in the roles of ordinary people, or by employing actors from the thea-ter to portray these characters. Stage actors looked down on the cinema as a lowly medium, and those who did appear before the cameras could not tone down their larger-than-life theatrical posturing to the quiet realism of the camera. This was why many people without acting experience who went into films became stars. They played themselves, skillfully or not, and became personalities. Since films were silent, dialogue was not important, but the power of description was vital, both visually and in the intertitles. Together they told audiences what situations were developing. This brought about hundreds of short social films, among

them Porter's *The Life of an American Fireman* and Hepworth's *Rescued by Rover.* Although no one ever called them documentaries, the term not yet having come into use, these early films were the forerunners of the documentary as it was to become known.

The early cinema, particularly in the United States, was a tremendous form of social revelation that ex-posed child labor in factories, the wretched working conditions of men and women, deplorable housing conditions, grasping landlords, and corruption in poli-tics and business. It was a positive force, however, always attempting to show the way to a better world with a possible resolution and with a happy ending for the individuals concerned, even if such endings were far-fetched. But when the film-makers discovered their power of re-creation also included those forms of anti-social behavior that the public read about daily in the newspapers, such as murder, the rackets, and robbery, cinema began to move away from the reality of everyday life and into the controversial reality of ex-citement, glamor, and romance. Porter's *The Great Train Robbery,* while completely honest in its depic-tion of the event, set the stage for thousands of rob-bery films to follow. Many of the nameless people who

Les Petits Arpents **(1963). (NFB)**

had started in movies looking like real people found themselves personalities and became so well known and liked that their presence over the years destroyed much of the reality the original narratives might have possessed.

As we have seen, Hollywood became the center of world film-making, and while the studios made enormous profits American films paid for their popularity with the mass audience in other ways, notably by a lack of respect on the part of intelligent audiences who were disappointed by compromises made with controversial material, and by massive forms of censorship, both state and religious, which watched every move made by the film-makers. Films had to be polite to the establishment, and the audiences they had created became a monster that required constant feeding of the celluloid reality they came to represent. Audiences no longer wanted social reality, they wanted a world of beautiful, wealthy people, and even if they were gangsters and thugs they were expected to move against a glamorous background of nightclubs and mansions. The western avoided these requirements, but most of

them were unreal portraits of pioneer life, of impossible heroes and falsely heroic people that glorified the U.S. Calvalry and villified the Indians.

It is always easy to generalize about the years of Hollywood's great power and influence, so easy, in fact, that it is not hard to overlook the many honest films that were made of all genres, some without stars, some of which were successful financially in the theaters, many of which were not, but have lived on through the years to become classics of the cinema. In the matter of Canadian identity, it is fitting to mention just one, *The Canadian* (1926), an American film by director William Beaudine, with Thomas Meighan, and filmed partly in Alberta. This film honestly and movingly told of the hardship of pioneer life on the prairies. Yet Mackenzie King is reported not to have liked it because Canada seemed like a hard and difficult country that would frighten away tourists and future immigrants. He wanted it retitled *The Pioneer Canadian.*

The dislike, by the establishments of most countries, of any honest portrayal of life in its less-than-

"everything is beautiful here" condition, was forcefully expressed to the studios, to the detriment of many Hollywood films, and was the despair of many documentary film-makers. Those producers, however, who believed that films were only an entertainment—meaning that they should bear little relationship to life as we know it—were greatly assisted in their endeavors by a vast public that was also not much interested in life "as we know it" on the screen. They were anxious to get away from it, which led to the general assumption by critics, producers, and psychologists that movies were an "escapist" medium.

The great strength of all the Hollywood films, however, and the reason for their appeal to world audiences, were their stars and the characters they represented. Audiences have always identified with other people. Just as theater-goers would no more attend a play, an opera, or a ballet were there not actors, singers, and dancers on the stage, so moviegoers have always resisted films that were not about people as individuals, portrayed by persons whom they knew, and who brought to life on the screen as a very definite personality or character. Audiences needed, and sometimes still do, individuals to whom they could

Pipers and A' (1963). (NFB)

respond, feel close, love, hate, or admire, people with whom they could identify in their endeavors, trials, and successes.

There have always been exceptions, of course. Films sometimes happen to coincide with a public issue or a passing fad, such as *Chariots of the Gods,* but movies without people as recognizable personalities or with people who appear only as figures whose thoughts and feelings are described off-screen by a narrator have never been popular and are generally considered to be documentaries.

It was against this background that John Grierson came to work in Ottawa in 1939. He knew very well that documentary as he and Flaherty, Louis de Rochemont, Willard Van Dyke, and Pare Lorentz knew it was not new and not particularly popular with audiences. When asked to define a documentary he described it, at its best as "the creative interpretation of reality." At that time, in the forties, it made sense, since few movies were coming from the studios in Los Angeles or anywhere else that could be described in these terms. Had Grierson really been permitted to make films that were "the creative interpretation of reality," he would have made full-length dramas about people in different walks of life, using screenplays, actors, and directors (as he did in England ten years later with his Group Three production unit). Grierson knew only too well, as he said in his popular Montreal lectures in 1970, that the only way a reality is created is to break down the situation and its people and re-create them with insight, feeling, and passion through the writer, actor, and director. Life is going on all around us, but filming what is happening in the streets, homes, offices, and factories is only an observation of it, not a revelation of character and situation. On some occasions people from ordinary walks of life with no acting ability or experience can be used tellingly by artists such as De Sica, who knew that the faces and mannerisms of good but familiar actors can weaken the reality of the life being created. The mark of a truly great actor is in giving a performance in which he disassociates himself from his previous roles and presents himself as an entirely different character to audiences. This, however, has nothing to do with being a "star."

Grierson was not an intellectual snob who considered his form of film-making superior to any other type or better than Hollywood. In the book *Grierson on Documentary,* Forsyth Hardy has reprinted much of Grierson's writing as a film critic, and his humor, perception, and intellect are combined in a stimulating review of the then-current cinema that is still a joy to read. Grierson loved films, but he despised empty nonsense, trite issues, simplistic solutions, false resolutions, and silly, unreal people. He loved the creation of genuine fantasy, but not the falsification of the real world. He was possessed by a driving desire to bring

The Rink **(1963). (NFB)**

to people an awareness of the social issues of the day in order to make people realize their potential power to change the course of events. He wanted to show them how to rise above the mundane and mediocre, how to be interested in and proud of their own careers, however humble, and how to enjoy their achievements in a world of mass production and stereotyped endeavor. He believed in the strength and the destiny of individuals in a depersonalized age, and he wanted them to be alert, questioning, and informed.

Grierson's mission at the time he came to Canada was to create a flow of information ("propaganda") to the Canadian people about themselves, their fellow men, their country, and its history. He discovered that they had learned little from what had been done in the past. Grierson found himself in a unique position of power, but from a somewhat one-sided standpoint. Documentary film-making was considered, during the early forties, as something of an antidote to the glamorized reality of Hollywood movies. It was the sociological medium to make people aware of the injustice and inequalities of life, as well as the strengths and achievements of the individual. Grierson, how-

Au hasard du temps (Down through the Years) **(1964). (NFB)**

A St-Henri, le 5 septembre (1964). (NFB)

ever, could only make the films required by the various departments of the federal government, and none would be interested, obviously, in portraying social ills that might in themselves be caused by government policies or the lack of them. Even if Grierson invested the films with positive statements and human values, the consideration of cause and effect, or responsibility and blame, would be bound to give rise to controversy. No matter how democratic governments may be, they are sensitive to criticism, are anxious to avoid controversy, and want to remain in power. They are not likely to finance the making of films that might contain the seeds of their later failure at the polls. It has always been extremely difficult to make documentary films that expose social ills, particularly if they are caused by corporations, governments, and people with power, because the production of such films must be financed by a sponsor, and most sponsors are anxious not to offend anyone. If a government is the sponsor, it is even more nervous about offending anyone and is anxious to preserve its own image as a wise and benevolent body.

Freedom of expression for film-makers is possible only for those with sufficient wealth to finance their own work, whether or not they are beginners with a ten-minute documentary or distinguished directors

with years of achievement behind them, making the feature film they have always aspired to create. They should also have financial means great enough to make lack of box-office appeal of no consequence. The high cost of film-making thus rules out almost everyone except the sons of millionaires, who are seldom interested in making revealing films to which audiences might be largely indifferent.

Everyone knows that a painter requires only canvas and oils to create the most controversial pictures; that writers, composer, and playwrights require only paper and pen; the sculptor his chisel and clay. The film-maker, however, requires complicated equipment, raw stock, and elaborate processing methods, which can be enormously expensive, depending on the kind of film being made, and can run from $2,000 to $20,000 a minute. For this reason there always has to be a sponsor, and the man who pays the piper calls the tune, and who expects that tune to bring him back a handsome profit as a result of its public acceptance. However, there are many distinguished film-makers who have successfully managed to please the public, hence the sponsors, too, while still dealing with subject matter that is meaningful to them and has something to say about society and the human condition. The encouraging side to free enterprise is that studios, companies, promoters, or whatever they are called, will finance any film-maker whose work is likely to appeal to the public and make money, whether it is blatant in its mass appeal or a sensitive work of great artistry.

Because sponsors are so necessary, film-makers, whether they make documentaries or feature-length movies, tend to play it safe. They find subjects that interest them, that are not likely to cause controversy, and that will appeal to certain audiences. Within this frame of reference they frequently produce imaginative and appealing films. Documentarians usually end up making pretty films about nature or sponsored films for independent companies and corporations that either advertise what they make or do or act as good public relations films in the form of annual representations of hockey, golf, and football games. Shell Oil of England was one of the few companies to distinguish itself in the production of films of genuine social concern about underdeveloped countries and humanitarian scientific development. Only *This Modern Age,* made by documentarian Sergei Nolbandov for the old J. Arthur Rank Organization in the forties, attempted to tackle urgent social problems and succeeded by simply stating both sides of difficult issues, leaving audiences to make their own judgments. This series ended, somewhat like the bombastic *March of Time* and *Today and Tomorrow,* when the costs of making them became more than their producing organizations could bear. Government film-makers, although not usually thought of in this terminology, have the easier or the most difficult task of all. Their films are not required to make money, they do not have to please audiences, but of course they should please the government. On the other hand, they must convince audiences that their work is not propaganda designed to indoctrinate them with the government's ideology.

John Grierson, although he had sharp encounters and differences of opinion with officials in Ottawa, never really had to face the issue of freedom of expression. With the outbreak of World War II, the entire nation moved into that form of energy and prosperity engendered by the destructive nature of war. Patriotism was the order of the day, and all activities were designed to further and improve the war effort. The films made under Grierson were stirring chronicles of the time. He came to grips with the war, but he was not to depict on film the problems of peace. In 1945 he left the board in the hands of those he had trained so well and returned to England.

5
The National Film Board

At first there were deep fears that the National Film Board would not survive the coming of peace. With the departure of John Grierson, there was indecision and doubts about the future of the role of the film-making agency. The atmosphere in the former saw mill, never the best place to work, reflected gloom and despair as the film-makers attempted to adjust themselves to filming for peaceful purposes, to making films for a doubtful future. Private enterprise, in the form of Famous Players and private production interests, were anxious to see the board disbanded. The government, in spite of all the evidence indicating how essential a Canadian presence was in the cinemas and among the people, was still not convinced that film-making should be one of its major concerns. As usual, a compromise came about that saw the staff and budget reduced, leaving the board to get on with its work— preferably out of sight and out of mind. Ross McLean, who had actually started the board with his famous report eight years earlier, saw Grierson leave with mixed feelings, and for the next five years, with the assistance of Ralph Foster as deputy commissioner, carried out the difficult task of surviving and progressing during the uncertain postwar years.

Under McLean's successor, Arthur Irwin, former editor of *Maclean's Magazine,* the National Film Board moved to Montreal in 1952. The move was opposed by almost everyone, for it was obvious that with the facilities that would be available, the city that housed the NFB would become the center of film-making in Canada. And this proved to be correct. Some argued in favor of Toronto, although there was no reason why one city should be preferred to another. The logical place for the NFB as a government agency was Ottawa, still the neutral ground between Toronto and Montreal. The board in Ottawa was still closer to Montreal than Toronto. But the die was cast, and it is a tribute to Arthur Irwin that he was able to get the government to spend the more than a million dollars (an enormous sum then for such an undertaking) required to construct the new headquarters. The sprawling, colorless edifice, looking more like a prison than a place of creativity, is given over mostly to offices, but contains editing rooms, an animation department, developing and printing laboratories, projection rooms, a large theater, boardroom, cafeteria, the distribution department (which later moved into a building added to the original and named in honor of Grierson), and the information services. Although there are two sound stages, studios are seldom required by the NFB's film-makers since they shoot almost all their material on actual locations, as befits the nature of documentary.

Whether or not this bleak setting and atmosphere depressed the film-makers is difficult to say, but to judge by their work over the years there has been little to inspire them. Like the building they occupy, most of their work has been cold, functional, and efficient. How much is spent on the achievement of efficiency, however, is never really known. Allowing for the fact that film-makers, as artists, should be free to create where, what, and when they choose, and recognizing that the high cost of film-making requires fairly strict budgets, it would seem that far too many films cost

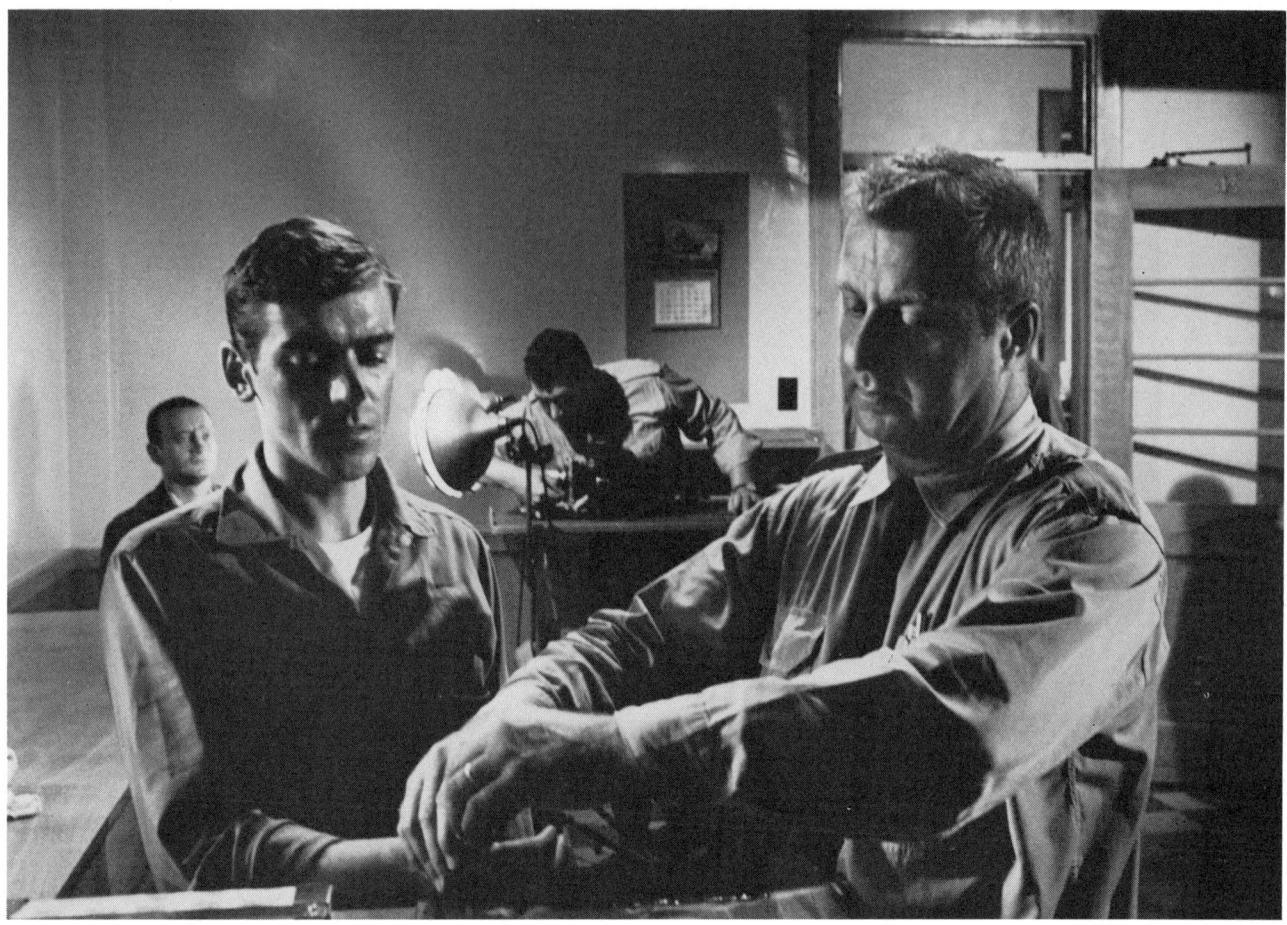

The Correctional Process **(1964). (NFB)**

more than they should have, and too many films were never completed. It is difficult to know at any time what films the board is making and who is making them, and even harder to keep track of completed films and make arrangements to see them.

As an organization producing short films, the board is in a difficult position because the place of the short film in any distribution and exhibition system is uncertain. They are required in cinemas and on television only as "fillers," to round out the main program or to support the feature film, and if the feature runs two hours, which is the length of an average cinema program, they are not required. They are seldom advertized, seldom recognized by the public or the critics, and even at their best, when dealing with matters and subjects that require no more than ten to twenty minutes' running time of the average short film, seldom make an impact on the public or a name for the filmmaker. The only shining exception is the work of Norman McLaren, whose experimental, humorous, and imaginative animations in various techniques have made him and the NFB world-famous. Without the support of the NFB, or in other words, the taxpayer, it might have been difficult, if not impossible, for McLa-

Table 1
Commissioners of the National Film Board
1940–Present

John Grierson	1940–1945
Ross McLean	1945–1950
Arthur Irwin	1950–1955
Albert Trueman	1955–1960
Guy Roberge	1960–1965
Hugo McPherson	1965–1970
Sydney Newman	1970–1975
Andre Lamy	1975–1978
James de B. Domville	1978–1983
François Macerola	1984–

ren to have found the time he required on his experiments.

In producing mainly short films, however, the board has over the years become smothered in its own achievements. It is impossible to remember everything that has been made, and not much stands out in retrospect. That which does, and that has made Canada well known abroad, if not always at home, has mainly been of an abstract nature—experiments in animation and design, in camera and processing effect, in symbolic studies, obscure statements, and the arts and crafts. Very seldom does the board make documentary films that bring home to audiences any sense of social realism relating to the lives of people under stress. It has received praise from sociologists and the like for its *Challenge for Change* series, in which people in cities and the country have participated in the making of films about their lives and the regions they live in, but these films are largely unknown to the general public and are mostly inconclusive examinations of small segments of society.

The board is now more than forty-five years old. Because of its diversity and numbers, assessing what it has produced over the years is extremely difficult. The board has lived for many years on the support of individuals and organizations who have been well aware that without the board, there would have been almost nothing of Canada and its people in the cinemas or television, at home or abroad. Little was ever said of the board's shortcomings and little was known of its truly creative accomplishments. While the CBC is a part of every Canadian's everyday life, and is constantly in the headlines and in people's homes, the NFB has always played a secondary and quieter role in Canada's communications system. It could hardly be otherwise, as the nature of film is different from radio and television. When television was introduced, it was expected that CBC, with its need for filmed programs, would make extensive use of the board and its vast library and enter into production arrangements for continuing series of filmed programs. Although some attempts were made, some series developed and shown, the relationship between the NFB and CBC has been fitful, discouraging, and marked by hostility and acrimony. Too many program directors at CBC are more interested in spending fortunes on mediocre American television series than in trying to achieve a continuing relationship with the NFB. Whatever the failings and drawbacks of the NFB, it has given the taxpayers a far better return than the CBC. Thousands of films made by the NFB are still in distribution, while older ones are safe in their archives and can be seen on request. CBC programs, made at far greater cost, are seen once, frequently destroyed, and seldom available

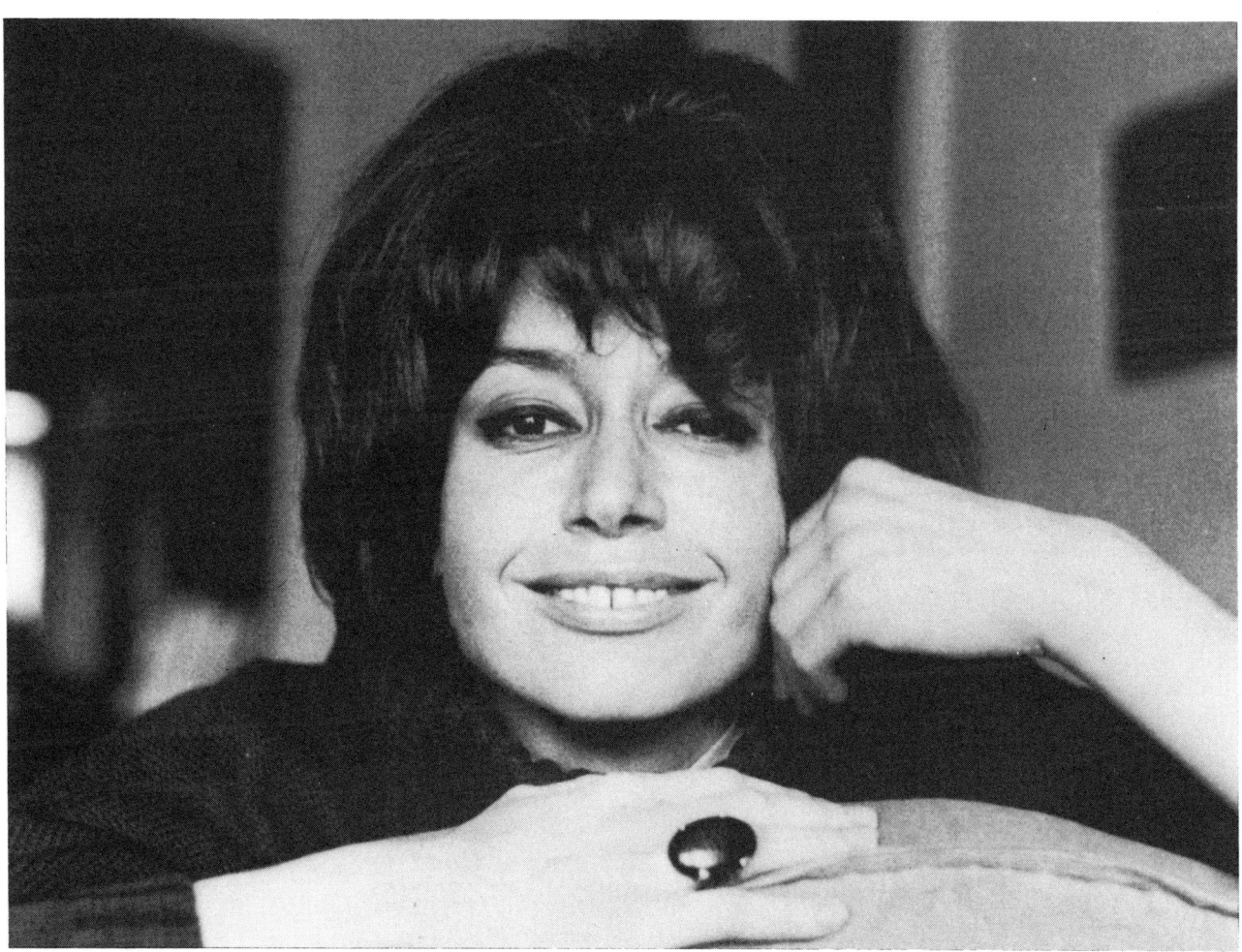

Fabienne sans son Jules (Fabienne) **(1964). (NFB)**

The Hutterites (1964). (NFB)

Mémoire en fête (Walls of Memory (1964). (NFB)

Trail Ride (1964). (NFB)

afterwards for showing under special circumstances to the public or in schools.

Reaching the public has always been far more difficult for the NFB than for the CBC. During pretelevision years, the board, working with a method devised by Grierson, created a unique system of 16mm circuits with traveling projectionists that operated from regional NFB offices across the country. Film councils consisting of interested people from all walks of life were formed in rural and urban centers and regularly held public showings, often followed by discussions of new NFB films, in libraries, schools, city and town halls, federal buildings—anywhere projectors, screens, and chairs could be accommodated. It was here that citizens who were proud of their country first found that encouraging reflection of themselves and their country on the screen. Many programs dealt with specific themes and were arranged for special interest groups. Film councils thrived, although it is doubtful they ever reached the millions of people the NFB claimed in its optimistic press releases of the day. However, they did influence people to talk about what the board was doing, and thus strengthen its place in society. With the coming of television, film councils found their supporters staying home at night to watch the small screen. Films shown in drab halls were no longer appealing. On television, unfortunately, they seldom found NFB films. While both the CBC and private stations do show some NFB films to fulfill Canadian Radio and Television Commission quota re-

quirements, they are usually transmitted at times when audiences are not likely to be watching.

Not all NFB films are suitable for general audiences, either on television or in the cinemas. The board's total output each year is designed to satisfy several masters or special requirements of the government. Government departments require films to inform the public of their programs. These information films are seldom didactic and usually their message is portrayed in an absorbing way, with style and finesse. "Safe" films deal with social behavior, medical problems, science and education, tourism and industrial development. Then there are short films for cinemas that must please Columbia Pictures, their distributor in Canada since Grierson's time. Their subject matter is described as being of "popular interest" and ranges from such topics as a group of students playing violins in a forest to a radio reporter clattering above city traffic in a helicopter. To avoid English and French language difficulties, nearly all cinema shorts are visual and without commentary or dialogue. Half-hour television series deal with people and place, Indian and Eskimo ceremonies and crafts, how supermarkets work, and dozens of other sober subjects. In addition, several feature-length films are included in the NFB's yearly production schedule.

Much of the credit for the board's nervous start in feature films, with *Drylanders* in 1960, goes to Grant McLean, for many years the NFB's director of production, a man dedicated to public service and the Grierson tradition, who overcame opposition from the government, private industry, and American interests, all of whom had no wish to see the NFB widen its activities. The making of dramatized full-length films is now looked upon by almost everyone as normal and desirable; in fact, it has been said by many nationalists that the board should make many more long films and fewer short subjects. About two-thirds of the board's total output each year is in English and one-third in French, and while almost all are rerecorded into other languages for showing abroad, the board stubbornly refuses to make more than a few of its French-speaking films available in English, or vice versa, in spite of the government's insistence on all federal departments making their work available in both languages. At one time, French and English-speaking film-makers worked together, largely because the French-speaking members obligingly spoke English. But in this new age of "cultural sovereignty" for Quebec, the French have shut themselves away in their own division, making their own films, speaking only their own language.

Opinions about the standard of work performed by the board depend entirely on the definition of the term *documentary*. At one time, a film about a city's streets, shops, restaurants, and historic buildings would have

Vaillancourt, sculpteur **(1964). (NFB)**

been termed a tourist or promotion film. A film about slum conditions would clearly be a documentary. Today, the film about the city could qualify as a documentary, partly because it would be more skillfully made. A film about slums would probably not be made until they are demolished and new houses can be shown to have taken their place. This is called a positive statement and no one is offended. The "problem" (slums) was in the past. Today, in Canada at least, standards of film-making at the board and among private producers are high enough that almost all films that are not dramatized subjects qualify as being documentary. The form is sufficient, but what of the content? If, by documentary, visions are conjured up of crusading film-makers taking up the cause of the downtrodden and the oppressed, then the National Film Board is not a documentary film-making organization. If, however, the term means well-made general-interest and technically competent specialized and educational films, then the board has functioned well enough and continues to maintain high standards.

This is not to suggest that the NFB should always be making films about disturbing social situations. There is room for films of positive achievements, of humor

and history, music and successful people. But the board's record shows a considerable amount of the latter and a regrettable absence of inquiry and curiosity into the former. There appears to be little human concern on the part of many of its film-makers, who apparently never read the daily papers to see what is happening around them. There are exceptions, of course, such as *The Things I Cannot Change,* by Tanya Ballantyne.

The board can very easily run afoul of its many masters, the federal government, and the provincial and municipal governments. Some of these agencies still suspect that the board is a federal "snooping" organization come to put them in a bad light, and they are notoriously thin-skinned when it comes to social criticism. Other masters are big and small businesses, self-serving organizations, and the public itself, which consists largely of self-satisfied individuals who have no desire to be informed of other people's misfortunes, or to know how their own selfishness has contributed to a troubled world, or to witness any unpleasant deeds that might be taking place among them. The board remains silent, leaving controversial subjects to the CBC, which can report on them with a sense of immediacy, an excuse the NFB often uses as the reason why it did not film certain matters of the moment.

Over the board's forty years of existence, it has produced around 8,000 films, give or take a thousand. An observer would learn very little about the social and political issues that have affected Canada during this time. It may be true that to venture too far into politics would mean suicide for the NFB or certain dismissal for the commissioner in charge. Many of the board's supporters have long argued in favor of the NFB being given the status of a crown corporation (which Grierson stipulated in his original report), placing it on an equal standing with the CBC and giving it more freedom of expression. Very few persons in power at the NFB seem to want their organization to be anything other than a government department. It does have a great deal of freedom of expression, as presently constituted, but the limits are seldom tested. Reports filter out from time to time that certain films are suppressed, but no one really cares enough to find out what is really happening, and would not likely be told even if they asked. The point that is frequently overlooked, however, is that film-makers can say a great deal about social conditions simply by visual references in humanitarian studies of people. All too often there is no imagination in the way many films are made, and outright social comment is reserved for films made about places outside Canada. Would the NFB make a film such as *Selling Out?* Probably not. It was left to writer Jack Winter and director Tadeusz Jaworski to make this flawed, but compelling and moving film about an old farmer, who on retirement sells his land, which is purchased by a nonresident. It was timely and controversial, it played a large part in the debate on the need for new legislation on the sale of land in Prince Edward Island. No one paid the film-makers to produce this picture. They raised the money themselves because of their interest in the subject. The most pointed political statement the board has made about Canadian politics was in *Propaganda Message,* which being animated, was not real enough to offend anyone in or out of Parliament, and made its tongue-in-cheek statements humorously yet tellingly. Audiences enjoyed it hugely since laughing at their own country's

Waterfowl (1964). (NFB)

La Beauté même (1965). (NFB)

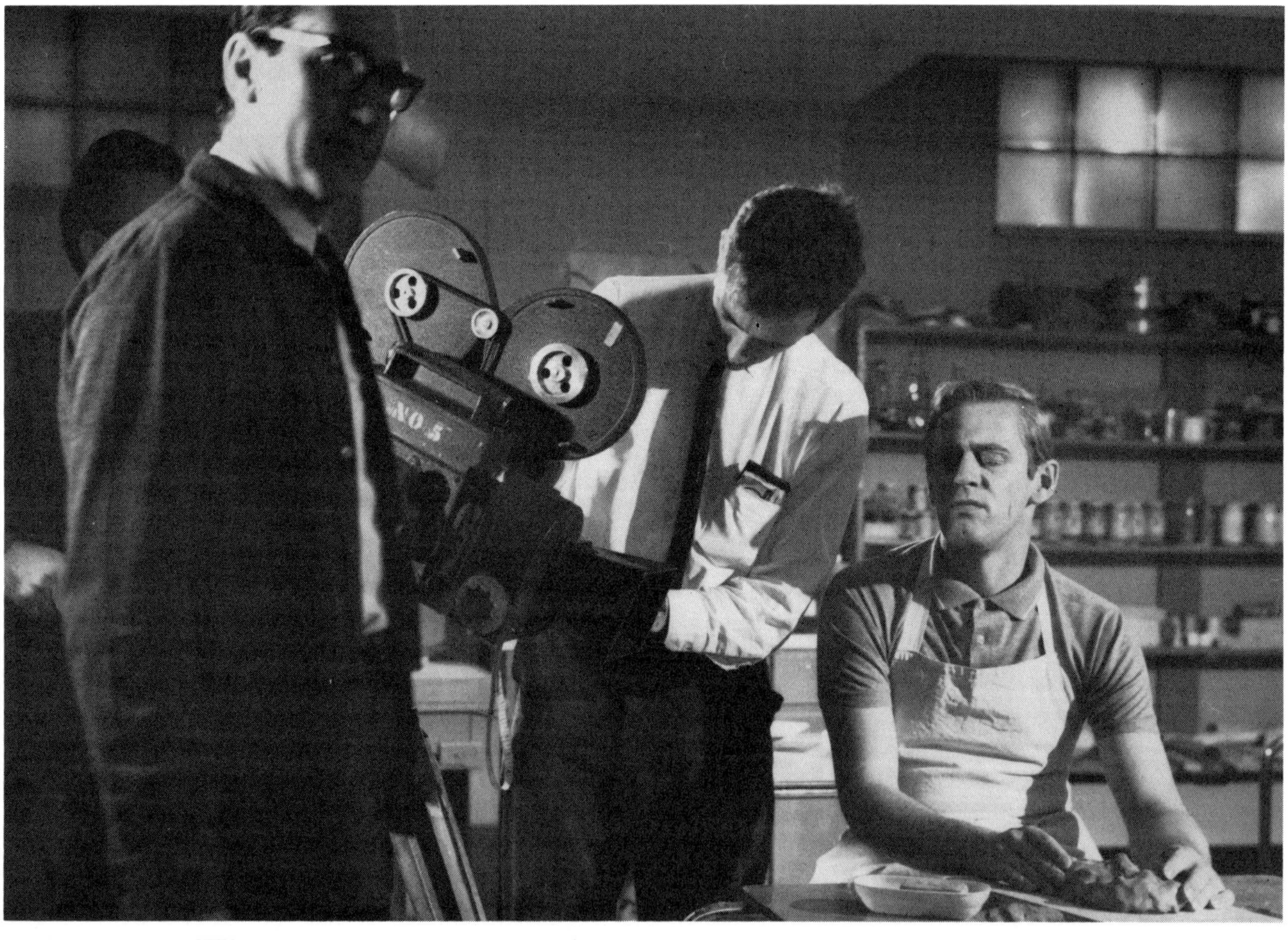

Blindness (1965). (NFB)

Calgary Stampede (1965). (NFB)

political squabbles and mistakes, instead of those of the Americans, is still a novelty in the cinema.

Over the years too much has perhaps been expected of the National Film Board simply because Grierson's great reputation, his outspoken nature, and his humanitarian concerns were expected to bring about controversial results. It is not in the nature of governments to support such an iconoclastic and revolutionary man, and if he had not left, he would soon have trampled over all those exercising authority over him, which would have led to his dismissal. This is not to say that the men who came after him were simpletons. Some were dull, none were film-makers, some used the job as a stepping-stone to other positions (Irwin as high commissioner to Australia, Roberge to Quebec House in London). They became adept at balancing themselves on the fine line between getting results and pleasing superiors. Simply existing was an achievement in itself. It is easy to criticize the National Film Board, but when we remember that first and foremost it is a government department making information films for other government departments, and that this and nothing more is its function, and that it is the only unit of its kind outside the communist countries, then we must recognize it as being an extraordinarily competent organization. The very fact that it secures enough money from the government to make outstanding short subjects for cinemas (which cannot return a profit no matter how successful they are), that it carries out little-heard-of but far-reaching improvements in technical design and manufacture of equipment, and that it has made, since 1954, some twenty-five feature-length films that do contain social observations not permitted in short subjects, then its great value to us is apparent and is a testimony to the men over the years, from Ross McLean to Grant McLean, with their able and concerned producers (Tom Daly, Guy Glover, Colin Low, James Beveridge, et al.), who have proved themselves to be devoted to the principles of public service in motion pictures in the tradition established by Grierson. A counterargument claims, however, that if the board had not existed, something else would have filled the void, that "something" supposedly being private producers, and, further, the fact that the board was in existence, massive and entrenched, under government protection and safe from competition, effectively prevented the development of film-making in all its forms under the banner of free enterprise. Whether this would have been the case or not no one will ever know, but certainly the board, for all its shortcomings, has trained many film-makers and technicians, and it has not prevented several private producers from successfully making advertising and public relations films. The best example of this is F. R. Crawley and Judith Crawley, both of whom worked for Grierson, who left the board to start their own company in Ottawa, and with contracts from the board began a career that has made "Budge" Crawley Canada's best-known private producer. Two of his short subjects, *The Loon's Necklace* and *Newfoundland Scene,* have found a permanent place in Canadian film collections.

Other private producers who survived in a difficult field and gave work and experience to newcomers are Arthur Chetwynd, whose firm became synonymous with sports and nature pictures; Jack Chisholm, whose advertising shorts were internationally recognized; Ralph Ellis, whose Keg Films opened up a new world of nature; Paul Micheau, who made every kind of short subject; and hosts of others working in live action, animation, and television. In some way or other they trace their beginnings and inspirations back to John Grierson. It is said, with some justification, that while several film-makers left the security of the board to succeed or fail in the outside world, too many remained to grow old and tired and unresponsive. Certainly there have been many new young film-makers whose student work has shown great promise and who have been ignored by the board, while European film-makers, whose work and style have little in common with the Canadian experience, were given contracts to work in the country.

Part 2
Success and Struggle
1940–1984

6
The War Years

As far as film-making was concerned, the years 1940–45 belonged entirely to the National Film Board, which produced hundreds of fast-moving, hard-talking, dramatically stated short films about the war years in the series titled *Canada Carries On* and *Eye Witness*. (The board continued making these series until about 1956, when they were discontinued due to the growing reluctance of exhibitors to show any short films with features that frequently ran two or more hours.) There were no dramatized feature-length films made during the war years. The film *Has Anybody Here Seen Canada?* somewhat unfairly criticizes Grierson by saying that he "did nothing to encourage feature films." What would he have encouraged them with? It was all he could do to find enough talented people to keep the NFB working, with so many likely candidates for film-making away serving in the armed forces. It was difficult enough to make documentaries. Had he attempted to use public funds in what would have seemed to be the making of "entertainment films," he might well have wrecked what he created. The politicians believed that there were enough British and American films in the cinemas to keep the public happy. Furthermore, it was only on grounds of "patriotism" that the cinemas were showing NFB shorts. The Hollywood companies would not have tolerated the presence of any Canadian feature films in their territory.

The only feature-length dramatized film shot in Canada during the war years was the 1942 Michael Powell–Emeric Pressburger British production, *49th Parallel* (U.S. title *The Invaders*), a gripping drama about a German U-boat sunk in Hudson's Bay and the survivors' attempts to reach safety in the United States in a difficult trek across Canada. Eric Portman played a thoroughly nasty German, Laurence Olivier a loyal French-Canadian, with other roles taken by Leslie Howard, Anton Walbrook, and the Canadian actor Raymond Massey *(Things To Come, Reap the Wild Wind)*, who was among the early group to find recognition abroad, since there were no opportunities in films at home. Thirty-eight years later, in 1980, Michael Powell came back to Canada to attend a Retrospective program of his films at the Ontario Film Theatre in Toronto. He went to Niagara Falls and stood in exactly the same place where he had taken a shot of the mighty flow of water pouring over the Falls. He remarked that it was probably "the only place in all the locations I had filmed that looks the same!"

On February 6, 1946, only six months after the atom bomb brought the Second World War to its end, the Cold War began in, of all places, the city of Ottawa, Canada's quiet capital. Igor Gouzenko, a cypher clerk in the Russian Embassy, went to the Royal Canadian Mounted Police bearing evidence of a Communist spy ring involving several prominent Canadians, including a member of Parliament and a government scientist. The key agents were attempting to steal the secrets of the atom bomb, and they were duly convicted. But the Russian documents made passing references to other Canadians, and they were summoned before a Royal Commission for questioning. One of them was John Grierson.

The documents had suggested that one of Grierson's

La Forme des choses (Shape of Things) (1965). (NFB)

secretaries was a spy, and that Grierson could be used to help her obtain an important position at the National Research Council. Grierson denied any implication, no charges were ever laid, and he was cleared of any complicity. But the harm was done. In a violently suspicious and anti-Communist society of the day, the continuing progress of John Grierson as a leading figure in the world of cinema had ended. Smeared with "guilt by association," his career in North America was finished. The prime minister, Mackenzie King, to whom Grierson had given loyal service, did not lift a finger to assist his old friend. The incident resulted in Grierson being unable to enter the United States to take up the position offered him as commissioner of the United Nations Film Board. He returned to England instead.

The crisis brought to Canada the first postwar American crew to shoot location scenes for an American movie about the Canadian spy scandal. William Wellman, an accomplished director, filmed _The Iron Curtain_ (also called _Behind the Iron Curtain_), with

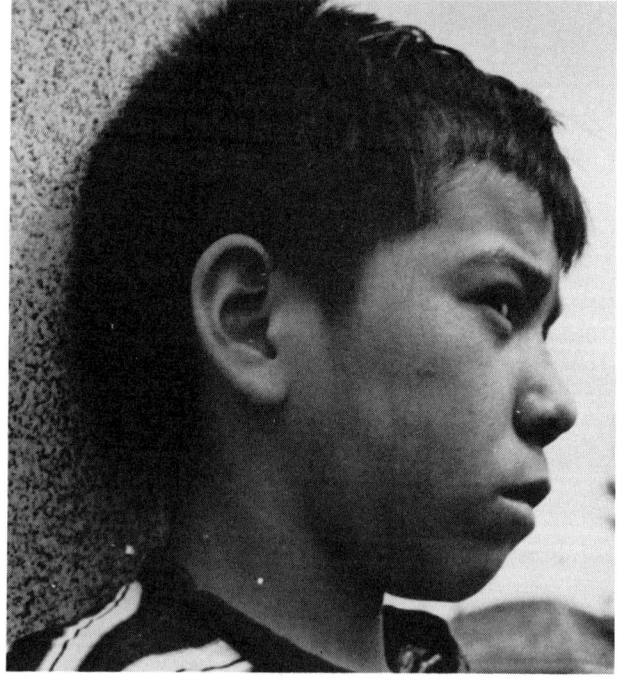

La Monde va nous prendre pour des sauvages (1965). (NFB)

Dana Andrews playing Gouzenko, for Twentieth Century–Fox. However, *The Iron Curtain* was Canadian in only its few murky location shots of dark, snowy streets and a remote Houses of Parliament. Canadians laughed at the film, but it crossed the minds of only a very few that it should have been made by Canadian film-makers, simply because few believed that Canadians could ever make films as well as the Americans.

A man who became important to Canada's film industry and who began his career in the early forties was Hyman Bossin, editor and part-publisher of the former weekly trade paper, *Canadian Film Weekly.* Hye Bossin was an astonishing man in many ways. The son of a poor Jewish immigrant family from Poland, he grew up in Toronto's colorful Spadina district, was largely self-taught, and led an adventurous, often difficult youth, surviving the grim years of the Depression with vigor, determination, and a never-failing sense of humor. He was part of Toronto's early and socialistic group of writers and labor leaders that congregated in the College-Spadina area. He had gone to work for Roddy Brothers Printers as a messenger, advancing to the composing room, where he attained the rank of journeyman compositor. The urge to write kept him up late at night, long after working hours had ceased, and soon he was writing articles and short stories, many of which were published. He left the printing company and went to Hollywood, hoping to become a screenwriter, but circumstances brought him back to Toronto, a city he loved. He was a voracious reader, a gregarious companion, and an untiring conversationalist who loved night life yet never smoked and seldom drank. He loved people, particularly those who worked behind the scenes in the world of entertainment, press and radio-TV, films and publishing. He had a deep and lasting fondness for Toronto and its history. He was also interested in literature and the stage, although he was largely attracted to American enterprise in the popular sense and to the British in the classic sense.

In 1941 he formed a company with N. A. Taylor, exhibitor and producer, to take over the ailing trade paper, *The Exhibitor,* one of Canada's two film trade magazines, the other being *The Canadian Moving Picture Digest,* edited by Miss Ray Lewis. They renamed it *Canadian Film Weekly,* and Hye Bossin remained its editor and publisher until his death in 1964. The *Canadian Film Weekly* afforded him a writing-editing job in which he was his own boss. He proceeded to publish with efficiency and determination, becoming as interested in motion pictures as he was in all other aspects of society. He worked in a constant state of frenzied disorder, with papers, letters, and books piled around him on a desk covered with notes and material. He had no patience with people who made mistakes or who failed to carry out his instructions, and he would fly into rages when things went wrong, were lost, late, or left undone. Yet he was the kindest of men and would never see anyone in want, was deeply troubled by injustice, could tell the difference between genuine people and false friends, and, by keeping in constant touch with everyone connected with the film trade in Canada, mostly in Toronto, produced week after week a highly professional, highly readable paper that faithfully chronicled the daily events of Canadians in the business of films. Working from early in the morning until late at night and on many weekends, Hye Bossin coped with severe financial difficulties, fought constantly for advertising from the American companies who saw no reason why they should support a Canadian trade paper ("let them read *Box Office*"), and edited a far better journal than the country has in these days of Canada Council grants. Now Canadians no longer know who is alive or dead, promoted or retired, and once again, history of a personal kind is slipping away. Hye Bossin made a point of knowing everyone in the trade, seeing, talking, arguing, and fighting with them, telling them what he thought of their actions in forthright and usually humorous terms, unless they

Salut Toronto (Bonjour Toronto) **(1965). (NFB)**

The Sea Got in Your Blood **(1965). (NFB)**

made him so angry that he would then lash out in prolonged fury.

With his outright, honest manner, Hye Bossin survived in a world dominated by men his work depended on; but fighting for his rights and for those of others took a heavy toll of his health and energy. He was a man of integrity and knew what was expected of a trade paper. He never used it to air his views editorially, but he wrote a column called "On the Square," his office originally being at Dundas Square in Toronto, in the Hermant Building, and later in the Twinex Theatres building at 175 Bloor Street East. In this column he wrote of the theater and of books he enjoyed, of writers he admired, and of events and people that interested him. He seldom said an unkind word about anyone, although privately he denounced those who talked loudly of things they knew little about. He would shake his head sorrowfully over Nathan Cohen's often cutting criticism, but admired the man, if not the critic. In the United States he would have passed quite easily as an American, but he had no great love for either the Americans or the British. He loved Canada and always spoke up for this country's

rights and traditions, yet the naive manner of so many Canadians, particularly in matters concerning films, tended to irk him. He was fiercely loyal to the film trade, yet often, like many Canadians, fell into the trap of thinking that any Canadian undertaking was not likely to be successful.

And Bossin was painfully aware that his loyalty was being given to an enterprise that for the most part was not Canadian, did not concern itself with anything Canadian, took millions of dollars out of the country each year, and spent as little as possible in Canada. He was also well aware that the distributors and theater owners could put him out of business overnight if he dared to write a word of criticism about their American ownership. He was also aware that the Canadians who ran these branches were incapable of acting on their own initiative and were unable to take measures not approved by the head offices in New York and, for the most part, saw nothing wrong in this. During the postwar years of the forties and fifties it was actually considered to be un-Canadian to speak up for Canadian films in the face of the American monopoly.

In his paper, filled for the larger part with news

Sire le Roy n'a plus rien dit **(1965). (NFB)**

about American films, Bossin attempted to instill a Canadian flavor by reporting what was happening in the cinemas, from grosses to record runs, openings and closings, new managers, new policies, and visiting personalities. He was a public man and he loved people, and it was in the theaters—not in production (there was none) or in distribution (a mostly office activity)—where he felt very much at home because they involved the public. Here the films were shown, here was excitement, movement, color, and gaiety, and since Bossin was interested in building and architecture it was only natural that his thoughts should turn to the past, to the magic of movies that had sprung from old stores and dilapidated buildings to magnificent and impressive theaters. In the early fifties, knowing well the discouraging background of the subject he was to become deeply involved in, he started to gather together material to write a history of Canadian cinema. He was the first writer to do this, and everything written since then has used his basic research. Much of it was published by him in the *Canadian Film Weekly Yearbooks 1951–70,* but, sadly, like Canadian cinema as a whole, much of the unpublished material seems to have been lost since his death since the manuscript passed to several individuals and the National Film Board, with no one even knowing if it all still exists as a whole.

Thus Canada entered the midforties, the postwar years, with no desire to start making her own films, undisturbed by the fact that the American-owned theaters continued to devote their screens to American productions, that Canadian banks and industry refused to invest in "high-risk" feature films, and that the federal government, ever mindful of objections from Hollywood, was not interested in any form of quotas or levies that might have encouraged the making of Canadian feature films. Only in Quebec was there some hope for aspiring film-makers.

7
Quebec Becomes Active

Over the years very little film-making had taken place in Quebec, a province very unlike the others by reason of its French traditions, language, and religion. In the 1930s, L'Abbé Maurice Proulx, a priest who, like so many of his kind, was fascinated by film and had visited George Eastman's Kodak empire in Rochester, New York to learn how to make films, decided to make a full-length documentary to encourage the colonization of Quebec's northland. Called *Un Pays neuf*, few people saw it, and those who did rejected it on the grounds that it was not an "entertainment."

In 1943, Paul Guevremont, a young actor, appeared in and directed a film for La Société des Missions Etrangères de la Province of Quebec called *A la croisée des chemins,* which was about a man who must decide between his love for a girl and his calling as a missionary. It was said to have been partly produced in China, although how anyone managed to get to China during the war is probably a story in itself. Like *Un Pays neuf* (and anything else that originated in Quebec during this time) it had a religious background to which the devout people of Quebec did not much respond in the movies.

With so little being tried or accomplished in motion pictures in Quebec (not that the rest of Canada was doing any better), it was somewhat unexpected, then, to find that the first postwar feature film to be made in Canada was the French-language *Père Chopin,* a comedy drama with music, directed by Fedor Ozep, who (as is still done) was brought from Hollywood. The production company, Renaissance Films, was formed by Alexandre De Sevre, who ran a dairy and owned several movie theaters. He built a studio on Côtes de Neige Road in Montreal—the same general area of the city where, many years later, the new NFB studios were built. Once again, religion played a large part in this enterprise because the church always kept a steady eye on the cinema and on the prospect of making money. De Sevre, with a sure sense of the power of Catholicism, went into partnership with the church in the form of his spiritual advisor, the L'Abbé Vachet, who promoted the company shares from the pulpit on Sundays and sold them in the sacristy after Mass. But the power of the church was not sufficient to make this venture pay its way. De Sevre made one more picture, *Le gros bill,* and invested money in *Docteur Louise* (*The Story of Doctor Louise,* with Madeleine Robinson, which was Canadian in name only, having been made entirely in France), and *Son Copain,* a France-Canada coproduction with Quebec Productions. This company was formed in 1946 hard on the heels of De Sevre's Renaissance company by Paul L'Anglais and René Germain, who built their own studios in the suburb of Saint Hyacinthe, outside Montreal.

It must be said in fairness to these determined producers that they knew what they wanted to do, they were not "part-time" businessmen in film, and they did not look to the church for permission or support. They considered De Sevre doomed from the start because he wanted to sell Catholic films, and, said L'Anglais, "I don't think you can sell Catholic films any more than you can sell Catholic shoes." However, L'Anglais's start was not too impressive because he aimed

Un Jeu si simple **(1965). (NFB)**

too high in the wrong direction, and his desire to be "international" did not succeed. His first film was *La Forteresse (Whispering City),* made in French and English with three Hollywood actors in the leading roles of the English-speaking version (Helmut Dantine, Paul Lukas, Mary Anderson) and directed by Fedor Ozep (who had earlier directed Renaissance's first film, *Père Chopin).* Mr. Ozep returned to Hollywood after *Whispering City,* where he died on June 20, 1949. L'Anglais learned from his failure, however, and his second film, *Un Homme et son péché (A Man and His Sin),* based on a popular radio serial and thoroughly native to Quebec, was a resounding success. The dialect and the humor was Quebeçois and the audiences knew and loved each character, an obvious fact that producers of English-language films in later years never faced up to when making films for Canadians, preferring instead to think of world audiences that never materialized. So successful was *Un Homme et son péché* that L'Anglais based his third film, *Le Curé de village,* on another radio serial, and this too, was popular in Quebec. Working on the theory that what was popular once would be popular again the second time around, L'Anglais's fourth picture was *Séraphin,* a sequel to *Un Homme et son péché.* This too was a financial success, and all seemed very well indeed with films

Because They are Different **(1966). (NFB)**

The studios of Quebec Productions (ca. 1950).

Producer, Paul L'Anglais.

produced in Quebec. Although L'Anglais had been against religion in films, he had discovered that religion in the makeup of human characters to whom audiences felt a sense of kinship and warmth was certainly acceptable to the people of Quebec. But even this had its limits. In L'Anglais's fifth film, *Le Rossignol et les cloches,* the leading character was a village priest who organized a concert to help pay the cost of new bells for the parish church. The film was a total failure, and to Quebec Productions, lacking financial reserves (as did all producers in Canada) to withstand the failure of a single film, this defeat meant the end of the company.

It was at this time that the minister of trade and commerce, Mr. C. D. Howe (who never went to the movies but did balance the country's books) realized that Canada's alarming postwar imbalance of payments with the United States was draining this country's treasury. Excise taxes were placed on all manner of American goods entering the country. He then noticed that Hollywood was taking out the then-immense sum of twenty million dollars a year in film rentals. It seemed, if only for reasons of hard cash, that the government would at last do something to stop the domination of Canadian cinemas by Hollywood and force the American studios to spend some of that money in Canada. But those who hoped for such a situation to appear did not reckon on the power of the Hollywood companies and the sheer cowardice of Canada's politicians. The commissioner of the NFB, Ross McLean, and his assistant, Ralph Foster, were urging the government to introduce legislation requiring quotas for Canadian films in the theaters. They received a phone call from Francis Harmon, of the Motion Picture Producers of America. He told them quite plainly that if they attempted to go any further

Big Swim (1966). (NFB)

with their plans, he would see to it that they were fired. Eric Johnston, then the head of the MPPAA, came to Ottawa and dazzled Howe with great plans to promote the Canadian tourist trade in Hollywood films if he would desist in any acts to "freeze" Hollywood's profits in Canada. This became known as the (infamous) Canadian Co-operation Project and all hope of a new start for Canadian film-making was lost. Hollywood wined and dined Canadian exhibitors and all politicians, from Prime Minister Lester Pearson down, who all agreed what great fellows the Americans were and how much Canada loved their films! During this time, an anxious Paul L'Anglais tried to reach C. D. Howe. While the Americans found his door always open, L'Anglais could not get a message through. In the film, *Dreamland,* he recalls "I never could get to him. I had no access to him, and the people I trusted to get to him, failed. Howe never tried to help us. On the contrary, he seemed to be the creature of American interests, and in Canada, these were varied and plentiful."

Under the "Canadian Co-operation Project," American producers were to include references to Canada in their screenplays and would film some locations in Canada. The result, however, was that the producers never shot any movies in Canada since they never put into production any picture with Canadian locales. If they did travel to Canada for a few days of filming, it was to use the location to represent someplace else. References to Canada were few and far between and usually uncomplimentary, as the place that thieves and criminals talked of fleeing to when escaping from the FBI. The project was designed primarily to reverse the flow of dollars by encouraging more Americans to travel to Canada for their holidays, and thus improve the tourist trade. The Canadian government was already spending large sums of money doing this. Needless to say, the scheme was an utter flop and petered out in embarrassing silence. Famous Players won the day, and the Canadian government, under St. Laurent (who, when he retired from politics was made a shareholder and a director of Famous Players) made itself look unbelievably foolish.

Quebec had its English-speaking film makers, too. Richard Jarvis had worked with Paul L'Anglais on his first three films, as producer, editor, and director. He decided to make his own films and formed Selkirk Productions with Cecil Maiden. Their first film was *For-*

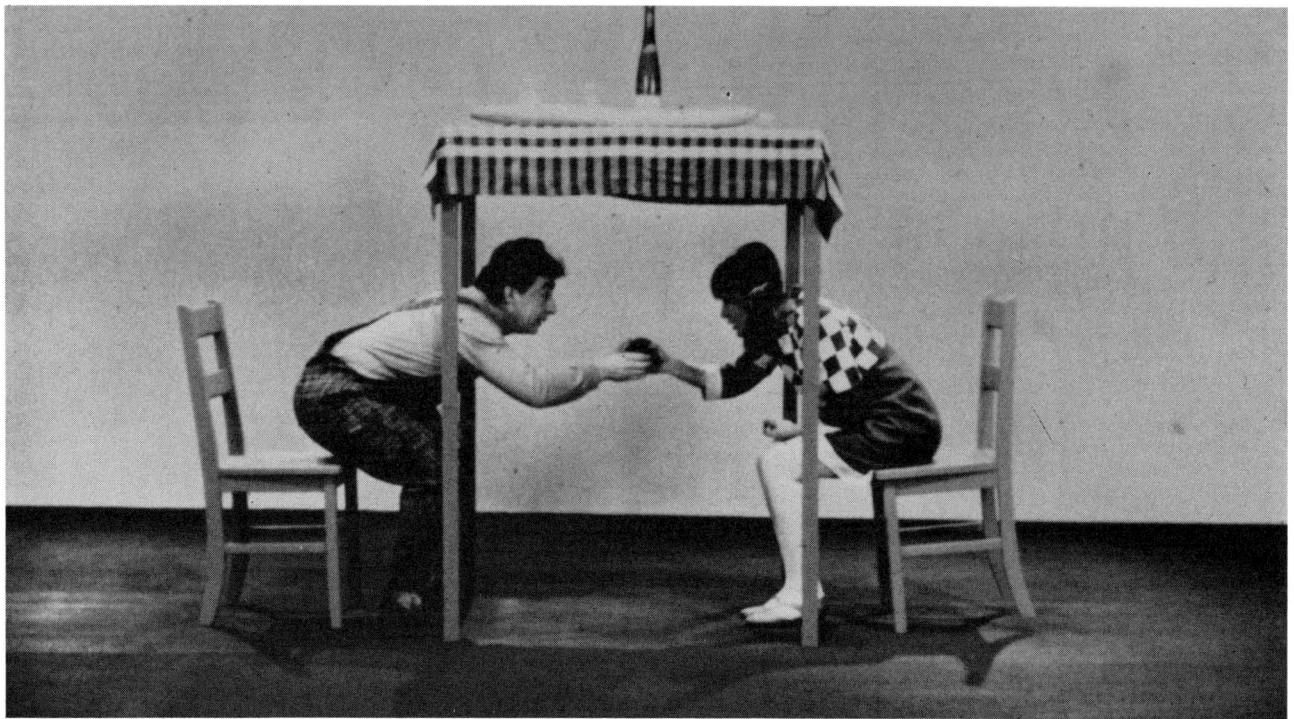

Centennial Fever (1966). (NFB)

Dimension (1966). (NFB)

Feux Follets (Intermede) **(1966). (NFB)**

bidden Journey, with production and direction by Jarvis, and shot at De Sevre's Renaissance Studio. It was their only film, although Jarvis continued to work as a producer on *Coeur de maman* and *L'Esprit du mal* for another short-lived company, Frontier Films. Paul L'Anglais's very real efforts to establish film-making in Quebec may not have succeeded in the way he had hoped—that is, with a firmly established studio similar to a small Hollywood company (Columbia) or an English studio (Ealing). Apart from his films, he did inspire others to try production. This resulted in more French-speaking films such as Excelsior's *Lumières de ma ville,* the longest film made in Canada up until that time and the first (and probably only) Canadian musical; Carillon Pictures, *Etienne Brulé, gibier de potence;* Alliance Films, *La Petite Aurore, l'enfant martyre.* Many of these films were made in the $50,000 budget range and could earn as much as $500,000 in Quebec alone, should they prove popular at the box-office. With this in mind, a well-known French-Canadian actor and playwright, Gratien Gelinas (in later years the first chairman of the Canadian Film Development Corporation), decided to film his hugely

successful play, *Tit-coq.* He asked Paul L'Anglais to be his producer, and the resulting film proved to be an enormous success both critically and financially. In its English sub-titled version, it was the first French-speaking Canadian film to receive successful showings and critical responses throughout the other provinces.

Quebec now led the rest of Canada in feature-film production. Ironically though, at the moment of its greatest success, the movement died and the studios fell silent. The reason was a smaller screen in the homes of millions, television. Audiences stayed away in droves from the cinemas, as they did in the rest of Canada, in Britain, the United States—everywhere. There was competition, and it was in the homes of the people who should have been at the movies. Not until twenty years and more had passed was feature-film-making to come to life again in Quebec.

But throughout these creative years, one cinema in Montreal passed into history. This was the Saint Denis Cinema, where every French-language film received its first showing. It became a mecca for the artists of Quebec, a province that, unlike the others, embraced its stars and celebrated their own background without self-consciousness or embarrassment. The search-lights pierced the dark skies above the Saint Denis with its many "World Premieres," and even if "the world" was confined to an area between Hull and Rimouski, Quebec's actors and writers did actually make a living. And when it ended, it was possible to look back on a program of films that, however naive or intelligent, at least revealed a great deal about the character and collective consciousness of Quebec society, the influence of priests and politicians, and of the restless sense of inferiority brought about by the domination of church and state. With this came the beginnings of the striving for freedom of conscience and strength of will that was to emerge and find further reflection in the cinema of the seventies.

Naturally enough, this constant activity in Quebec did not go unnoticed in Ontario and British Columbia, where films had been made prior to the outbreak of World War II. Not without envy did young men in Toronto and Vancouver, eager to make films, watch the progress of their colleagues in Quebec. The showing of *Père Chopin* in 1945 did not escape the notice of Stirling Campbell, a young man who had been in Hollywood as a second-unit technical director (*Wings,* and so on) during the thirties. He felt the need to make Canadian films, and with actor Austin Willis, and businessman Larry Cromien formed Dominion Produc-

King of Blades (1966). (NFB)

tions to make a Canadian film for double-bill performances. The outcome of their joint efforts was *Bush Pilot.* To make sure of its box-office "acceptability," they used an American writer, Scott Darling, and American actors in the leads, Jack La Rue and Rochelle Hudson. Canadian actors, led by Austin Willis, played some of the supporting roles. Stirling Campbell did not become involved in any additional films, even though the modestly budgeted *Bush Pilot* recovered its costs. His partner, Larry Cromien, did, however, make a second film for another company, called *Sins of the Fathers,* shot at the studios of Quebec Productions. This was in 1947 at a time when sex was never mentioned in the cinema in any kind of forthright manner. This film dared to talk about syphillis and to show medical films of the ravages of venereal disease. Provincial censors and the Legion of Decency permitted the film to be shown on alternate days to segregated audiences of men (one day) and women (the next day). On some occasions, the film was introduced by a "doctor" from the stage! Cromien brought Phil Rosen from Hollywood to direct. When he fell ill, Richard Jarvis took over. The film was not very successful and legal difficulties brought its showings to an end. It was yet another example of a Canadian film made solely because its producers felt that only by using sensational subject matter could a Canadian film hope to succeed. Although proved wrong, they never seemed to learn from the experience.

Apart from the film of the young Stratford (Ontario) Shakespearean Festival's stage presentation of Sophocles' *Oedipus Rex,* directed by Tyrone Guthrie, and an amateur film, *The Little Canadian,* nothing else was filmed in English until ten years after *Bush Pilot*—which had now passed into the realm of running jokes about Toronto's film-making abilities. In 1957, an intense young twenty-four-year-old writer with the CBC, Sidney Furie, expressed his determination to make feature films. Overcoming all obstacles he filmed, in four weeks, *A Dangerous Age,* the story of two young college students (played by American actors) who run away to get married. It received its first showing not in Canada but at London's famous Academy Cinema. It was well received by the critics, and Furie was inspired to make a second film, *A Cool Sound from Hell.* Like *A Dangerous Age,* it was welcomed by critics, shown in England, but not in Canada. Furie, disgusted and dismayed by the lack of trade response to his work, left Canada and went to live and work in London, where he became famous for *The Ipcress File* and other films, before going on to Hollywood.

In the meantime, William Davidson and Norman Klenman (who had produced and written several short films) got together and made a feature, *Now That April's Here,* based on short stories by Morley Cal-

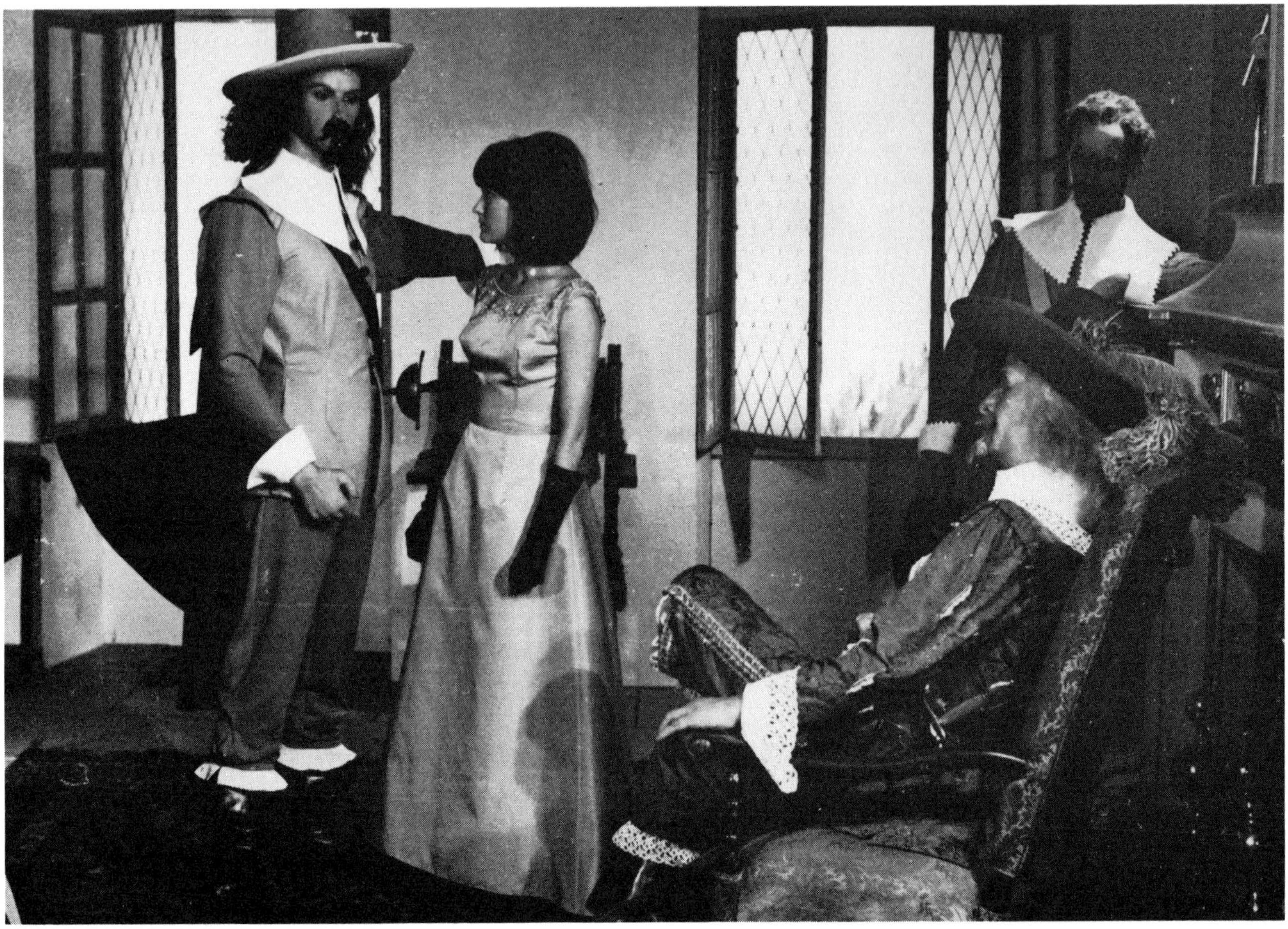

Les Montréalistes **(1966). (NFB)**

Question of Identity **(1966). (NFB)**

laghan. This film did receive a noteworthy première in Toronto at the new Towne Cinema, but unfortunately the occasion was overdone and the public was led to expect a far more ambitious film than the one they saw. Undaunted, Klenman and Davidson, who had planned a sustained program of films (which had never been attempted previously by any producer other than Shipman and L'Anglais), started their second film, *The Ivy League Killers,* deliberately designed as an "action thriller" for the double-bills. It was never shown until five years after its completion, which ended the hopes of Klenman and Davidson to establish a regular production of films in Toronto.

Their efforts, however, inspired Julian Roffman and Ralph Foster (who had previously worked at the NFB) to start their company, Meridian Films (in association with N. A. Taylor, the exhibitor and distributor), and make a second-feature program picture, *The Bloody Brood.* In the familiar desperate attempt to make sure that American distribution would be secured, the three leading roles were played by Americans. Roffman's next picture was *The Mask,* Canada's first 3-D film,

which used Depth Dimension, a process devised by the United Kingdom National Research Council. The technique was better than the content. From these four films emerged *Hired Gun (The Devil's Spawn)* directed by Lindsay Shonteff (who had worked on *Ivy League Killers*). It was shot in eight days, hardly shown, and Shonteff left for England, where he is still working.

With the exception of "semi-feature" films made in Montreal by the NFB in French for showing on the "new medium" of television and the production of American-inspired and American location films in Ontario, there was very little activity between 1958 and 1963. Out in Vancouver, a comparatively unknown British writer, James Clavell, wrote, produced, and directed *The Sweet and the Bitter* (1962) for Commonwealth Productions. It went into legal and financial difficulties and was never shown in Canada. It did get a showing in London five years later. In the same year in Montreal a simple film, *Seul ou avec d'autres (Alone or with Others),* made by students at the University of Montreal as a portrait of student life, received considerable praise and was accepted for showing in the

Summer Pageantry (1966). (NFB)

Critics' Week at Cannes, 1963. It heralded the "new wave" and was totally different in style, form, and technique from any previous Quebec films, being one of the first statements about Quebec's changing society and moral outlook. The young unknown film-makers responsible for this important "signpost" on the way to renewed activity in Quebec have since become distinguished film-makers: Denis Heroux, Michel Brault, and Gilles Groulx.

Not long after this another young film-maker, Claude Jutra, who had become known in Montreal's small but growing film community found wide recognition at Montreal's Film Festival in 1963 with *A tout prendre*. He had won the Best Amateur Award in the first Canadian Film Awards of 1949 for a short work, *Movement Perpetual*. He then went to the NFB where he made short films and the television feature *Les Mains nette. A tout prendre (The Way It Goes* or *Take It All)* was his first independent film, made over a period of two years, according to how much money was available from his parents and friends at any given

time. This was defined as a "personal film" because he told with a considerable amount of frankness and self-indulgence (for those days) of his love affair with a model called Johanne. The fact that she was black and that Jutra depicted some intimate love scenes gave the film a startling quality. It was well received and has become a minor classic. It certainly launched Jutra into a distinguished career, his most outstanding film still being *My Uncle Antoine*. While he received a good deal of attention for this, several of his contemporaries, Bernard Devlin, Leonard Forest, Louis Portugais, Guy Glover, Jacques Bobet, and Victor Jobin, were working quietly at the NFB making small but important trail blazing tele-features such as *Dubois et fils, Les Brûlés, Il était une Guerre, Les Mains nette,* and *Les 90 jours,* which made possible the more ambitious films to come from the NFB in later years.

Ottawa, where apart from the fact that the NFB began there, has its place in film history due to the efforts of one man, F. R. Crawley, a cinematographer, who opened a studio in a former church on Fairmont Avenue in 1946 to make documentary, educational, and business films for sponsors. The studio is still there, functioning much as it always did and is remembered fondly for *The Loon's Necklace* and *Newfoundland Scene,* but Crawley also had his sights set on feature film-making. He achieved his ambition in 1963 with *Amanita Pestilens (Mushrooms),* an advanced (for its time) black comedy about a family man's search for perfection in material things, which led to his ruin. It was directed by a Frenchman, René Bonniere, who had come to Canada to live, and who has since had a distinguished career in television work, together with Norman Campbell, Terence Macartney-Filgate, Harry Rasky, and Ronald Weyman. It was also the first film of a young Montreal actress, Genevieve Bujold, who in later years did become an international star, although in American movies. The fate of *Amanita Pestilens* was that of nearly all English-speaking Canadian films: it was never shown in theaters. But Crawley did not despair and a year later he was to achieve a considerable critical triumph with *The Luck of Ginger Coffey.* Based on Brian Moore's short story of a likable but hapless Irish immigrant and his wife (played by Robert Shaw and Mary Ure) who come to Canada to find a better life, only to find conditions just as difficult as those back at home, it was directed by Irvin Kershner (brought from Hollywood) from Moore's own screenplay, with a mostly British and American crew, but with several good Canadian actors in supporting roles. More important, it emerged looking and feeling Canadian in the way that Canada would seem to appear to new arrivals trying to settle down to a way of life quite different from what they had known before. While *Ginger Coffey* received limited showings, it was widely recognized as a likable

The White Ship (1966). (NFB)

Panorama Studios, Vancouver (1961).

and honest film, one that is just as affecting when shown today as when it was first made. It also opened in New York for a commercial showing.

In Vancouver, the fate of *The Sweet and the Bitter* did not deter a young student from South Africa, Larry Kent, to embark on the hazardous business of making a feature film at the University of British Columbia. Entitled *Bitter Ash,* it dared to deal with shiftless people in a sex-hungry mileau. So restrictive were the provincial censor boards at that time that the theme of the film and a seminude sex scene resulted in the film being banned and seized everywhere Kent attempted to show it. But he knew what he was doing, and on the basis of student screenings alone at a dollar admission he soon recovered his initial $5,000 budget. The film was crude, but it had a cinematic power and enough imagination to make it a compelling film to watch. With a determination and drive seldom seen in young film-makers he went on to make two more quite extraordinary low-budget films, *Sweet Substitute* and *When Tomorrow Dies.*

Perceptive and bleakly romantic, *Sweet Substitute* is about a young man involved with two different kinds of women and is a raw, ragged, and technically impressive film reflecting Kent's inbred vitality and drive, poetic imagination, and compassion for characters torn apart by sexual turmoil.

Larry Kent then went to Montreal, a move which did not seem to serve him well, and the four films he made there, while being technically more competent, lost the vivid and sensitive quality of his Vancouver work. He has since given up the cinema and now works for a Montreal newspaper.

Only three other Vancouver film makers since Kent have shown his imagination: Philip Keatley, Zale Dalen, and Philip Borsos.

Meanwhile, at the National Film Board, dissatisfaction was being expressed by English-language film-makers over the board's continuing production of French-language feature films and documentaries for Quebec, while none were being made in English. The commissioner of the board (Guy Roberge) was decidedly nervous about embarking on the production of full-length English-track features. The board, after all, was a government agency whose mandate had always been interpreted as permission to make short films and only that. While the board knew it could do anything in French and get away with it, the commissioner was fearful that a full-length film with actors would bring the wrath of the Hollywood studios down upon the board. The MPPAA had an open door to the government in Ottawa and anything Hollywood wanted, Ottawa was pleased to give. The sure way of getting at the NFB was to hypocritically remind the public that "the NFB was spending the taxpayers' money" and that to spend it on "entertainment" films was the greatest sin imaginable. There was never any shortage of editorials in the daily papers or letters to the editor that

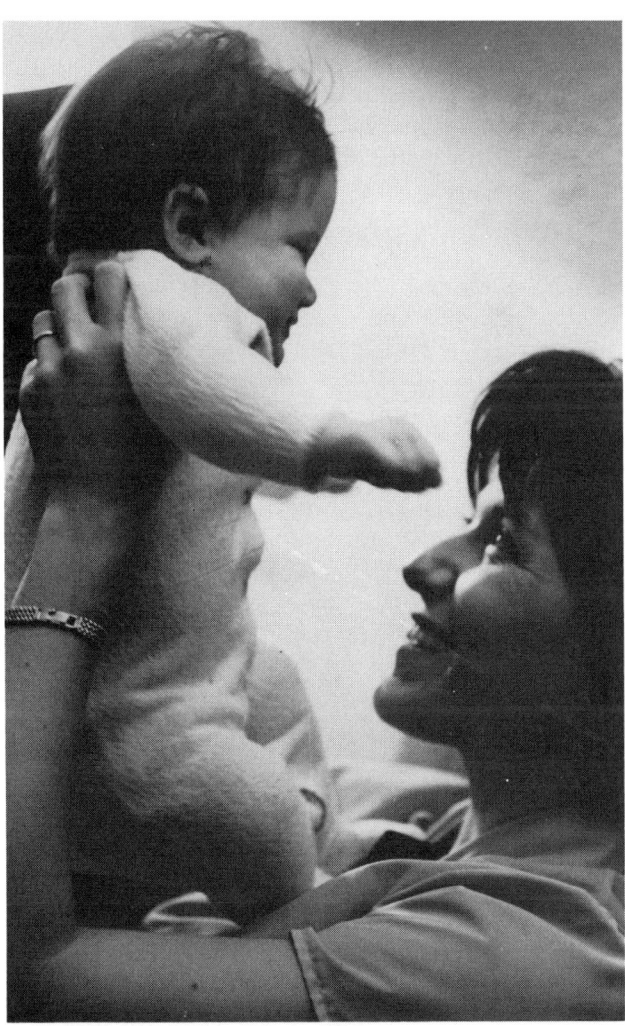

Les Départs nécessaires **(1967). (NFB)**

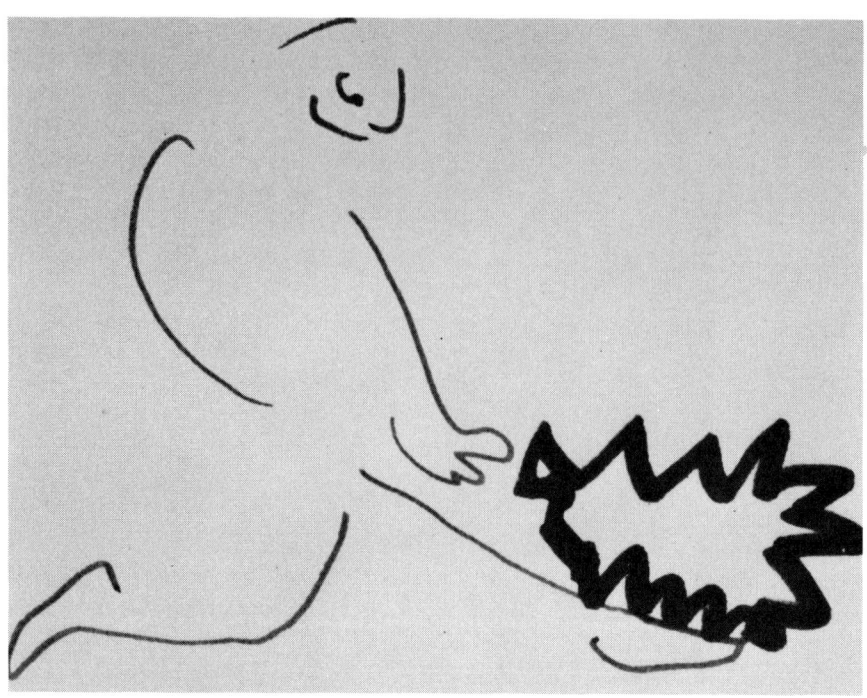

In a Box (1967). (NFB)

did not support the industry's view. For this reason, the NFB was forced to tread softly, and as a result, its first English-language feature, *Drylanders,* took two years to come to the screen (1961–63) and it opened heavily disguised in the publicity as a documentary. It is true that like all of the NFB's feature films, its roots were in the best tradition of Grierson documentary. While the first response of critics and the public was a feeling of disappointment that *Drylanders*—a family saga of survival during the dust bowl depression years in Saskatchewan—was not another *Grapes of Wrath,* it proved to be in subsequent showings a very honest, dignified, and affecting story of a pioneer family's difficulties in settling on the prairies. Thoughtfully directed by Don Haldane, whose earlier work had been in documentary shorts, with a cast that included Frances Hyland (a distinguished actress in later years) and William Fruet (who later became a writer and director), *Drylanders* has passed into history as a most agreeable and memorable film that can be seen many times over with quiet satisfaction. It has the distinction of being the first all-Canadian English-language feature film of the postwar period, and it lives on through the years as a testament to what can be done when film-makers have faith in themselves and in their country. Needless to say, at the time of its release it played in very few cinemas. It was not in the interests of Famous Players to show Canadian films, but Odeon Theatres did give it limited showings because the board had an agreement with Columbia Pictures to distribute its films, and as all Columbia releases went to the Odeon circuit, then Odeon contractually re-

ceived what few features and shorts were made for theatrical exhibition by the NFB.

While *Drylanders* was traditional in its approach and technique, at the time of its production several French-speaking film-makers at the board were making another feature semidocumentary in the "new" *cinema vérité* method. *Pour la suite du monde* was the day-by-day life of the people of the Ile-aux-Coudres and of their attempts to revive the ancient methods used to trap the Beluga whale. In the Grierson-Flaherty mold, it was a remarkable achievement and brought recognition to Michel Brault, Fernand Dansereau, and Pierre Perault, the latter becoming widely known for subsequent work in the *cinema vérité* method. This film was followed by another development in Montreal. Although cooperative film-making was not new (the practice of individuals, usually nonprofessionals, working together without a financial remuneration and hoping for some return from profits—which usually did not materialize), two newcomers to the film scene, Pierre Patry and Jean-Claude Lord, formed Cooperatio Productions and made a thoroughly professional film with a professional cast and crew called *Trouble-Fête.* No one was paid since everyone believed in the film's ultimate financial success, which would thus bring them their fees. Apparently it worked. Once again, this was a film about young people in revolt against authority; it was not sensational, but a responsible work reflecting the changes in society as younger people refused to accept certain patterns of behavior that their families and authorities imposed upon them. Jean-Claude Lord has remained

De mere en fille (1967). (NFB)

active in films as a director (*Bingo* and others) but Patry, after two more cooperative films, went into other business.

In 1963 also came *Lydia,* a feature film made in Toronto under great difficulties by two European filmmakers who had come to live in Canada from Europe, Julius Rascheff and Dedrick D'Allie. A romantic mystery, it is notable for the fact that it was the first appearance of Gordon Pinsent in a feature film. Then just making a name for himself, Pinsent has since become Canada's leading writer and actor in films and television, one of his major accomplishments being *The Rowdyman* (see page 202). Rascheff made a film in London, a mystery called *The Lift.* He then went to the University of Illinois to teach film-making, where he since remains.

The National Film Board made 1964 a memorable year with two documentarylike features, *Le Chat dans le sac* in French by Gilles Groulx (it won the main prize at the Montreal Film Festival) and *Nobody Waved Goodbye* in English, the first feature directed by Don Owen. *Le Chat dans le sac* is about two young Montrealers searching for meaning in their lives. The young man is politically intense but his Jewish girlfriend is quite the opposite, alive, eager, and full of enthusiasm. Like Jutra, Groulx made a personal film in which much of himself was projected in the performance of Claude Godbout. *Nobody Waved Goodbye* is not at all political and uses a semiimprovised style and technique to tell yet another story about a student and his girlfriend, who run away from seemingly uncaring parents. Don Owen, who had achieved recognition for *The Runner* (a short film about Bruce Kidd in 1964), declared at that time his determination to make feature films. The following year he seized his opportunity when the board asked him to make a thirty-minute documentary about why students leave school before completing their studies. Owen devised a film that would obviously run far longer than half an hour. Having to give a reason for the amount of extra stock he was using, Owen showed his exposed film to Grant McLean, head of production, who, impressed with the integrity and moral intent of the story, agreed to let Owen make an hour-long film.

Another major achievement by the NFB was Donald Brittain's *Bethune.* A biographical film, it ranks for sheer power of detail and narrative control with the work of Erwin Leiser or Paul Rotha.

Paralleles et grand soleil (1967). (NFB)

Moreover, its subject, the surgeon Norman Bethune, is not a world-famous figure, despite his early championship of socialized medicine and his work in designing surgical instruments. Out of the assortment of diary extracts, archive material, and recollections by friends and colleagues emerges a dynamic portrait of a personality as complex as Orson Welles's Kane. Aristocratic, authoritarian yet impatient of authority, sybaritic, idealistic, and possessed of immense energy and even artistic talent, Bethune found his destiny in Spain and China. We see him pioneering blood transfusion in a heavily bombed Madrid in 1937 and then performing 115 operations in three days without pause in the Sino-Japanese War. For Bethune, human strife was of constant concern to him, and although politically motivated by communism as a result of the poverty he witnessed in Montreal, he fortunately never lived to see its darker days of Stalinism. His beliefs made him unpopular in his own country for many years.

This film started Brittain on a major career as a documentary film-maker. His collaborator, John Kemeny, did further significant work at the NFB and then made his first independent feature film, *The Apprenticeship of Duddy Kravitz,* directed by Ted Kotch-

eff, a Canadian who had found success in Hollywood (*Who Is Killing the Great Chefs of Europe, Outback*). It was hoped that the success of this film would prompt Kemeny to start a regular production of films in Canada, and that he would establish himself as no one else had done as a producer to whom film-makers could turn with their projects. Instead, he preferred to go to Los Angeles.

The life of Norman Bethune was the subject of two books, one by Roderick Stewart, the other by Ted Allan and Sydney Gordon. Otto Preminger for several years tried to bring Stewart's book to the screen without success, while Kemeny and Kotcheff worked on a multimillion-dollar American production to be filmed in China, starring Donald Sutherland. Nothing came of this. Eric Till directed a television film for CBC with Sutherland (1980) as Bethune and Kate Nelligan playing his wife. The Chinese, to whom Bethune is a hero of epic proportions, made their own film about Bethune in 1964 (*Dr. Norman Bethune [Baiqiuen Dafu]*) with an American actor, Gerry Tannenbaum, as the politically aware and humanitarian doctor.

The Canadian section of the Montreal Film Festivals of 1965 and 1966 was notable for the number of new film-makers it introduced: Gilles Carle with his deft comedy, *The Merry World of Leopold Z* (NFB), which contains all the elements of his style and outlook on life and people that were found in his later work; Fernand Dansereau's grim, dark *Le Festin des morts (Feast of the Dead)* about the Jesuit martyrs, Fathers Lallemand and Brebeuf, who were tortured and burned to death by their disease-wracked converts, the Huron Indians. It was a film so unlike the Western concept of missionaries, cowboys, and Indians that it was strangely disturbing in its vivid portrayal of the clash of wills between two very opposite forms of civilization.

Another name that became known in years to come, Jean-Pierre Lefebvre, first came to attention with *La Révolutionnaire,* a university-made film that dared to express some interestng thoughts about political unrest in Quebec. More a comedy of errors than a political tract, it was either overrated by critics or underestimated by moviegoers, but it set Lefebvre on the road to a succession of strongly personal, independently minded, often difficult films, all of which brought well-deserved recognition to a dedicated film-maker who has always remained true to his beliefs.

Denis Heroux, following *Seul ou avec d'autres,* came up with *Pas de vacances pour les idoles* and *Jusqu'au cou,* both refreshing and free expressions of life in Quebec. Pierre Patry made his two remaining Co-operatio films, both dramas, *La Corde au cou* and *Cain;* Jacques Godbout made a tentative romance-drama, *Yul 871;* Claude Jutra's next film was *Comment savoir,* an interesting statement on the effect of tech-

Flight in White **(1968). (NFB)**

nology on teaching methods, while from Toronto came *Winter Kept Us Warm,* made by David Secter, a student at the University of Toronto. A pleasant story of friendship between two students that may, or may not, have been touched by homosexual undertones, it was one of the first such indications in a Canadian film of a forbidden subject.

Thus was the position of film-making in Canada at the end of 1966, as the nation waited the great celebration of Centennial Year in 1967. It was a promising situation. The province of Quebec had once more taken the lead. Although young film-makers throughout the country were trying to find the ways and means of expressing themselves in the cinema, and while their work received praise at film festivals, the screens of Canada's cinemas were denied to them. They received no financial or moral support from either the provincial or the federal governments, and no one could hope for anything more than the possibility of making one film at a time without knowing what the chances were of getting sufficient money to make a following film. As always they lived in hope, but as in the days of *Dreamland,* most gave up and turned to other occupations. The Quebec film-makers, while often immature, confused, and misguided in their political statements and social observations, were nevertheless forming a body of work that found a

Un Enfant . . . Un Pays **(1968). (NFB)**

sympathetic response from a closed society with its own language and that supported them in a family way. Young film-makers outside Quebec worked on their own, without the sympathy or support of their society, which saw itself as part of the North A'merican English-speaking world that had no particular need for Canadian films which might have spoken for them. It really did not think there was anything worth saying!

The Railrodder (1965). (NFB)

Buster Keaton Rides Again (1965). (NFB)

8
A Turning Point

In 1967 Canada celebrated one hundred years of confederation. To mark this great occasion, the country went on an artistic orgy and a cultural binge the like of which had never been seen before. Fortunately the cinema was not forgotten, although it is a pity that the cinema's seventy years of growth was not a part of Canada's first one hundred years. While the work of the state-financed National Film Board (then twenty-seven years old) had given Canada a secure reputation in the world of documentary, this country, at the most important political and social time of its development, still remained unknown to mass audiences of feature-length films.

Although Canada arrived at the Centennial with her theaters still controlled by American (Paramount–Famous Players) and British (Odeon) interests, with her major distributors American, with most foreign-language films bought for Canada by the Americans, and with no quotas or taxes to aid production, the situation was brighter and more promising than at any other time. With the flowering of artistic achievement in Quebec and a growing number of enthusiastic young film-makers pushing ahead in English-speaking Canada, the government at last recognized the importance of feature film-making as a prime artistic, industrial, and sociological factor in the life of the nation. It came in the form of a government Film Finance Corporation that was empowered to lend up to ten million dollars for the making of feature films. This legislation was the work of the then-unofficial minister of culture, Secretary of State Judy LaMarsh, whose personality, persistence, and deep interest in the arts piloted this controversial bill through Parliament with only one voice raised in dissent.

When one realizes that after the war the government was only too willing to abolish the National Film Board to placate commercial producers and the all-powerful distributors; that the government believed it was not "the government's business to be in film-making," and that it was prevailed upon to retain the board (although drastically reduced in size and staff) only after pressure from responsible citizens and educational groups, it was a heartening, if belated sign of changing attitudes to see the government give its enthusiastic blessing to the loan corporation. It was a happy beginning to the centennial year. With the National Film Board stronger than ever and working to capacity, filled with confidence and making films of great skill and artistry, and with money for features in the offing, one could only hope that Canada's film-makers would make good use of the opportunity, that exhibitors and distributors would support them, and that faith in Canada's ability to be a film-making nation was justified.

It was no doubt inevitable that following the jubilation and achievements of Centennial Year there would be a slowdown during 1968. Part of this was due to a curb on spending by both government and private industry, which spent liberally during 1967. However, as 1968 drew to a close, there was every reason to remain optimistic about future developments in production. The Canadian Film Development Corporation was finally at work and considering the many scripts and proposals submitted to it. The corporation made it

Best Damn Fiddler from Calabogie to Kaladar (1968). (NFB)

Charlie Squash Goes to Town (1969). (NFB)

Evasion des carrousels **(1969). (NFB)**

clear that it would only put money into what appeared to be good commercial subjects, and it interpreted the act under which it administered loan funds in the widest possible sense to encourage the production of movies in Canada by American, British, and other interests. John Terry, managing director of Britain's NFFC (National Film Finance Corporation), visited Canada in an advisory position to the corporation and said that coproductions would be healthy for both sides during this initial period of development.

From Montreal came the sad news of the demise of the International and Canadian film festivals. The festival was closed mainly as a result of protests from film-makers in Quebec who felt that any money that the federal and provincial governments gave to the festival would be better spent on financing production. In view of the large amount of international publicity the festival brought to Montreal and to its determined film-makers, this was a narrow view to take. Vancouver's international film festival, which had struggled through almost ten years of mismanagement yet had always provided good programs, also was not held in 1968.

On the positive side, the annual Canadian Film Awards, which had seen nineteen years of somewhat ineffective celebrating (ineffective in that the award-winning films remained largely unknown to the public) was completely reorganized and taken over by the film-makers' guilds. It planned to have an international jury under the chairmanship of this writer and would show programs of winning films across the country. An indication of the continuing strength and vitality of short film-making and of the growing number of feature-length films then being made could be seen in the number of entries submitted to the awards committee: 12 features and over 170 shorts ranging from fifteen minutes to an hour in length.

On the international scene it was Canada's year at Berlin, where the festival opened with Don Owen's *The Ernie Game* and included Eric Till's Montreal-made, American-financed first feature, *A Great Big Thing,* both films relating the wanderings of lost youths. Also shown was Christopher Chapman's multiple-image 70mm short subject made by the Ontario government for its Expo Pavilion called *A Place to Stand,* which achieved an enormous international success and has been widely shown in theaters throughout North America. Also at Berlin, the Week of Young Cinema was devoted to Quebec-made movies: Michel Brault's *Entre la mer et l'eau douce,* Jean-Pierre

Lefebvre's *La Révolutionnaire* and *Il ne faut pas mourir pour ça,* Arthur Lamothe's *Poussière sur la ville,* Gilles Groulx's *Le chat dans le sac,* Gilles Carle's *Le viol d'une fille douce,* and Larry Kent's *High.* All except *High* are in French.

The National Film Board was widely criticized, along with the CBC, for its features *The Ernie Game* and *Waiting for Caroline,* which went so far over budget without becoming masterpieces that the board probably never wanted to hear the term *feature film* mentioned again. Not daunted, however, it put two more into production, which was the only way to establish a basis for regular production. In the meantime, *Waiting for Caroline,* which cost over $600,000, was sold to United Artists world-wide for $100,000. The board received no praise at all for an excellent one-hour dramatized story of an aging trade union official called *Do Not Fold, Staple, Spindle or Mutilate* with Ed Begley, written by Millard Lampell and directed by John Howe. And undoubtedly, one of its major achievements was Norman McLaren's beautiful *Pas de deux,* a remarkable experiment in which two dancers from Les Grand Ballets Canadiens are seen first as single forms, then are followed by endless reflections of themselves.

The Canadian Film Development Corporation finally appointed an executive secretary in Michael Spencer, formerly of the National Film Board. The corporation was by now fully active but movie-makers who anticipated a small tide of film production assisted by the corporation were rapidly disillusioned and accepted the fact that getting money from the CFDC would be as difficult as obtaining financing from private sources. While the CFDC was not expected to give out loans to every applicant, it was severely criticized for insisting that producers asking for loans should first have distribution contracts backed by money from a distributor. If a film-maker got this far, he could usually raise money elsewhere. Two films went into production with loans from the CFDC, but both would probably have been made without it: *Act of the Heart,* in Montreal, directed by Paul Almond with Geneviève Bujold (Universal), was the outcome of Almond's success with *Isabel* in 1968, and was probably connected with Miss Bujold's appearance in *Anne of a Thousand Days* for Universal, filmed in England with Richard Burton. The second film was *The Blast,* filmed in Vancouver by an American-Canadian company, a story of U.S. "draft dodgers" in Canada, directed by Jules Bricken—and what we now see as the beginning of the Americanization of Canadian feature films.

Some directors were rewarded for their past efforts with awards for "quality film-making" from the CFDC. Allan King and Jean-Pierre Lefebvre each received $14,450 for *Warrendale* and *Il ne faut pas mourir pour*

ca; Gilles Carle, received $13,700 for *Le viol d'une fille douce;* a second award of $13,000 went to Lefebvre for *Patricia et Jean-Baptiste;* $12,300 to Almond for *Isabel;* $10,900 to Michel Brault for *Entre la mer et l'eau douce;* $9,600 to Larry Kent for *High;* to Arthur Lamothe $7,500 for *Poussière sur la ville;* and Camil Adam, $4,100 for *Manette.* These awards were based vaguely on the Swedish system and the British "box-office" fund from which successful films received the highest rewards. Many film-makers felt this money should have been used to make loans more easily available. Consequently the CFDC then announced a system of grants for promising low-budget films.

There was more activity than usual by film-makers from abroad in 1969: Robert Radnitz's Anglo-American production of *My Side of the Mountain* (d. James B. Clark) was shot largely in Quebec; *That Cold Day in the Park* (d. Robert Altman) and *The Mad Room* (d. Bernard Girard) in Vancouver. *The First Time* (d. James Nielson) and *Change of Mind* were filmed in Toronto. All five films were low-budget American productions. Films made by Canadian independents, largely on shoestring budgets, ranged from the University of Manitoba film *And No Birds Sing* (d. Victor Cowie), a charming and perceptive forty-five minute story about a student who falls in love with

Le Quebec vu par Cartier-Bresson (1969). (NFB)

Big Horn Sheep (1970). (NFB)

a girl and then finds out there is nothing between them, to the University of Toronto movie *Stereo,* a beautifully photographed but baffling collection of silent images that have something to do with communication by telepathy. This was the first film of David Cronenberg, who was later to make his reputation with horror movies. In between were the "regulars" who continued to raise money to work: Larry Kent with *Façade* and Fernand Dansereau with *Opération pourquoi.* Allan King completed *A Married Couple* in cinema vérité.

Vancouver staged its International Film Festival again in 1969 but added so many competitive categories for Canadian films that it almost became another Canadial Film Awards ceremony. This latter event, reorganized in 1968, was a tremendous success, with *The Ernie Game* winning the Best Film and Best Director (Don Owen) Award; Genevieve Bujold, Best Actress for *Isabel,* and Gerard Parkes, Best Actor for *Isabel.* The first International Jury consisted of composer David Raksin; director Brian Desmond Hurst; *cineaste* and Professor of French Michel Sanouillet; film-maker Anne-Claire Poirier (NFB), and Toronto critic Joan Fox. The greatest discovery among the almost 200 entries was a marvelous thirty-minute CBC Vancouver TV film by Len Lauk called *The Club Man,* an affecting story of an elderly man near death and his anguish at the changing world around him.

Montreal's festival did not return in 1969. Both the Ontario and federal governments sponsored ambitious multi-screen films for Expo 70 at Osaka. Christopher Chapman *(A Place to Stand)* made the Ontario film, and Roman Kroitor *(Labyrinth)* worked on the official Canadian film with Kon Ichikawa. The screens got larger each time. Meanwhile, the "sensational" technique developed by the Czechs for Expo 67, and which it donated to the Stratford Festival, sat unused in a warehouse. It was too complicated and too expensive to be put to practical use. In Ottawa, Crawley Films, Canada's oldest and largest producer of sponsored and industrial films, celebrated its thirtieth anniversary.

All short films shown in theaters are usually made by the National Film Board. Nineteen sixty-nine saw four productions by independents, an unusual development in view of the high cost of making shorts and the low rentals collected. Actor Albert Waxman directed *Tviggy,* a poetic study of an elfin Jewish girl who dreams of being a model and living in luxury. Don Owen (who returned to this field after *The Ernie Game*) made a beautiful and imaginative study of Buffalo's Knox-Albright Gallery called *Gallery: A View of Time,* quite the best of films in this *genre;* Julius Kohanyi, another determined independent *(Teddy, Little Monday, Henry Moore)* filmed the paintings of Saul Field's Sholom Aleichem Suite under the title *Tevye,* and Robert Applebee made *A Dime's Worth,* a day in the life of a little girl in the city. Also shown in theaters was *Hearts* (heart transplants in Montreal) made by Claude Fournier for L'Office du Film du Quebec. All of these films were visual, without commentary.

Producer John Kemeny, in charge of the NFB's wide-ranging program of films on social problems called *Challenge for Change* (poverty, education, prejudice, ill health, Indian and Eskimo living conditions), announced that so far thirty-seven films had been completed with thirty-six more in production. They were seen mainly on television.

NFB features were *Christopher's Movie Matinee* (Mort Ransen, 90 minutes), an improvised film about students making a film about themselves; *Le Dossier Nelligan* (Claude Fournier, 80 minutes); *Le grand rock* (Raymond Garceau, 90 minutes); *Jusqu'au coeur* (Jean-Pierre Lefebvre, 90 minutes); *Etes-vous donc?* (Gilles Groulx, 90 minutes); *Les Voitures d'eau* (Pierre Perrault, 120 minutes); *Flowers on a One-Way Street* (Robin Spry), a one-hour dramatized documentary on the flower children who became known as "hippies."

Although the Canadian Radio and Television Commission (CRTC) is not primarily concerned with film-making, it did, as a result of its mandate to supervise and watch over the activities of broadcasters, bring about (especially in television) more opportunities for film-makers by establishing a sixty percent Canadian quota for radio and television. As almost everything

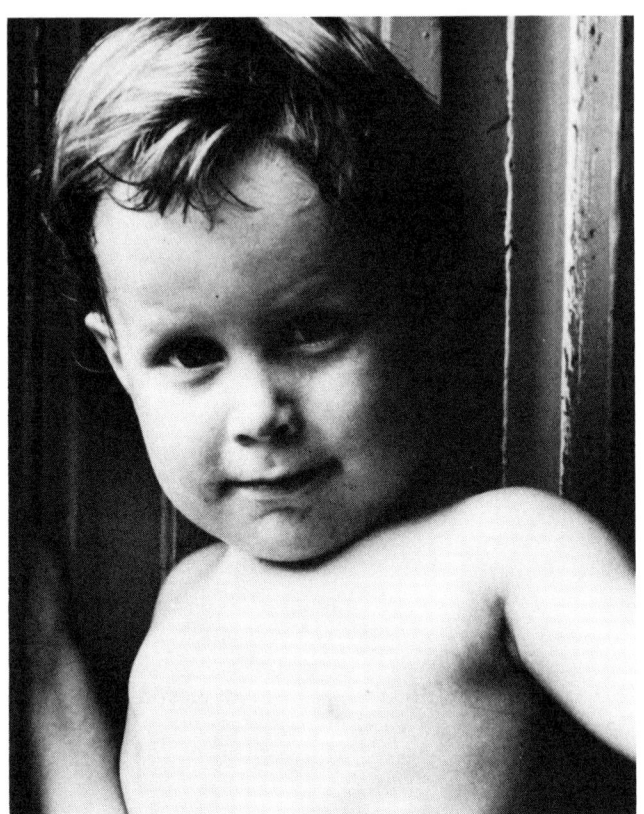

A File for Max (1970). (NFB)

on television these days is filmed material, this meant more work. The actions of the CRTC to force both the CBC and private stations to initiate more Canadian programs and to use less American material was the most encouraging development of 1970.

Under the determined chairmanship of Pierre Juneau, once an administrator at the NFB, the CRTC heartened those individuals who had begun to give up hope of damming the great tide of mediocre American programs. The private broadcasters bitterly opposed the CRTC and lost. The CBC, which went meekly in any direction under weak leadership and started selling the corporation to the advertisers, agreed that it was doing a poor job for Canadian performers and film-makers and. promised to abide by the content regulations.

The other event of the year was the "crisis" at the NFB—actually one of a long, continuing series of problems. Like the CBC, the NFB lacked firm or imaginative leaders, and when the government ordered financial cuts as a result of "austerity regulations," it began to dismiss film-makers. There were immediate protests, and the day was saved by the film-makers themselves, who came together and fought for their very existence. Although some staff members were dismissed, the board remained almost intact—

Here's to Harry's Grandfather (1970). (NFB)

L'Homme et le froid (Below Zero) (1970). (NFB)

but at a great price paid in loss of spirit, morale, and a sense of purpose.

The second annual reorganized Canadian Film Awards competition was again very successful in that it drew 110 entries and brought nationwide recognition to a beautiful, sensitively made NFB fifty-minute dramatized documentary that had earlier been pushed aside and ignored by CBC-TV. Called *The Best Damn Fiddler from Calabogie to Kaladar* (two small communities in the Ottawa Valley), directed by Peter Pearson from a script by Joan Finnegan, it depicts a country family's struggle with poverty and the husband's refusal of welfare assistance. Yet it is not a dismal picture and is infused with a love of life, of children, and of freedom within society no matter how unfavorable its terms may be. The leading actor, Chris Wiggins, won the Best Actor award. Altogether, *Fiddler* won seven major awards from the international jury (Peter Watkins, United Kingdom, Elmer Bernstein and Delmer Daves, United States, and Joan Fox and Marc Gervais, Canada), which unanimously described it as "the best damn film" from anywhere. Kate Reid played the mother and Margot Kidder made her first

screen appearance in this film. This was Peter Pearson's first film, and until the awards were announced, he had been unable to find further work. The film was used as a brilliant example of what Canadians could do if they had the opportunities, and of the kind of material best suited to take the place of the run-of-the-mill American films that dominate Canadian theaters and television—the kind of inexpensive creativity that private broadcasters continue to say they "cannot afford."

The second feature film to be financed in part by the still slow and overly cautious Canadian Film Development Corporation (CFDC) was *Flick,* directed by Gil Taylor and produced by Bill Marshall, who in later years was to become a negative force, unfortunately, in the expanded program of films in the late seventies. An avowed "second feature" from the start by its makers, *Flick* is a competent, straightforward, amusingly horrific attempt to put the young nephew of Frankenstein (Robin Ward) on a Canadian campus and set him to work at the old tricks. Neither funny nor horrific enough, it fails because its makers had no belief in their work other than as a means to make money

The Manhattan Odyssey (1970). (NFB)

Cry of the Wild (1971). (NFB)

quickly in order "to do better next time." Such an enterprise rarely succeeds.

Montreal remained the most important center for feature film-making, with French-speaking directors continuing to raise money and produce on small budgets the most lively and distinctively Canadian films. The ferment for more Canadian programs on television and in theaters was having good, if slow results. Even Famous Players, the American-owned theater circuit, was becoming aware of the need to show an interest in production. Celebrating its fiftieth anniversary, it actually invested money in *Red,* by Gilles Carle, and as a result, the film was guaranteed playing time across the country in FP theaters.

At the National Film Board, Robin Spry, an intelligent and committed film-maker, made *Prologue* (87 minutes), a sympathetic and thoughtful first feature in the documentary style concerning the flower children, the pacifists, and the Chicago riots. Tedious at times, the film was well liked at the London and Venice festivals.

At the CBC, films included Donald Shebib's *Good Times, Bad Times* (40 minutes), a moving and skillful documentary on old soldiers and warfare; *The Style Is the Man Himself* (d. Graham Cameron, 120 minutes), a masterly newsreel depiction of Pierre Trudeau at election time and how he became prime minister; *Dulcima* (d. Rudi Dorn, 90 minutes), a thoughtful adaptation of H. E. Bates's novel, moved to an Ontario town, about a forlorn young girl and a drunkard, well-played by Jackie Burroughs and John Colicos.

Independent production included *Pinter People* (d. Gerald Potterton, 60 minutes), an unusual interview with Pinter and a presentation of his work; *Façade* (d. Larry Kent, 90 minutes), a disappointing feature concerning freakish youth; *Fountains of the Sun* (d. John Feeny, 90 minutes), a beautiful full-length documentary of the Nile, its beginning and end; *Crimes of the Future* (d. David Cronenberg, 60 minutes), another imaginative picture-puzzle from the new avant-garde; and *A Married Couple* (d. Allan King, 96 minutes), in which King takes his *Warrendale* technique into the home to watch a couple battle out their difficulties and save their marriage. Overpraised by devotees of cinema vérité, its realism is doubtful, its honesty suspect, its point and purpose uncertain. The film completely negates the art of film-making and fails to substitute anything of value in its place. One U.S. film was shot on location in Toronto: *Homer* (d. John Trent, 90 minutes), about a boy coming of age and finding his independence from his overbearing, rural father. The cast included Tisa Farrow and Alex Nicol.

The *New York Times* published an article about the rapid development of Canadian feature-film production during 1971 and gave it the somewhat startling headline; "Canadian Films Rival Imports," a situation much to be desired but not likely to be achieved for many years to come. Nevertheless, the situation continued to improve. Where once there were never any Canadian films in Canadian theaters (apart from the few NFB short subjects and those very few features that were buried on double bills in suspect cinemas), in Toronto and Montreal the Canadian film was beginning to appear more often and as a normal part of programming.

The best illustration of this was the gratifying public success of the two major films of 1971; Don Shebib's *Goin' Down the Road* and Gilles Carle's *Red*. In Toronto, *Road* ran for more than two months in a small specialized cinema to great public interest and support. (It later repeated this success in other Canadian towns and in major U.S. cities); *Red* ran for six weeks in a 2,000-seat theater in Montreal to mass approval from everyone. Outside Quebec, *Red* failed to find the same popularity, perhaps due to indifferent showings and a wretched English-dubbing job that destroyed the authentic native values, turning it into a gangster melodrama. Conversely, *Goin' Down the Road* fared better in Montreal. In Alberta, *Red* was not shown as a result of the director's refusal to allow the censor board to make cuts.

Almost immediately following these showings came three more films, *Madeleine Is, The Reincarnate,* and *The Crowd Inside,* the latter two playing side-by-side in a five-auditorium theater. The first, by Sylvia Spring, was a disappointing picture about teenagers in

Aviators of Hudson Strait (1973). (NFB)

105

King of the Hill **(1974). (NFB)**

Vancouver, and one girl in particular who has come under the spell of a sadistic idler. It came and went very quickly. *The Reincarnate* (d. Don Haldane) was well acted and professionally made, but it was only highly colored nonsense about reincarnation. As the subject seemed to have a cult status at the time it was shown, it drew packed houses for weeks on end, which only goes to show that Canadian movies have really arrived when certain bad films can find as large an audience as certain bad films from other countries.

The Crowd Inside was eagerly anticipated, the first film of former actor Albert Waxman (who proved himself with his short, *Tviggy,* in 1968). Starring Geneviève Deloir *(Red),* the story and theme, similar to *Madeleine Is,* concern a young girl surrounded by unhealthy elements and trying to discover herself. While being much superior to Miss Spring's film, it is actually the greater failure because it attempts more in depth and characterization.

Several Quebec film-makers, tempted by the thought of easy money from "skin flicks," concentrated on this type of picture, to the dismay of critics and artists concerned about Quebec life and culture. Two such pictures, *Après-Ski* (d. Roger Cardinal) and

Pile ou face (d. Roger Fournier), although passed by the provincial censor board, ran into opposition in small towns from local priests, who denounced them as "immoral." Considering the hold parish priests once held over the cinema in the days of the Duplessis regime, it was remarkable that so many home made sex films were shown in Quebec without interference from the church.

The economic crisis that affected the NFB in 1970 due to the government's antiinflationary measures brought about the resignation of Commissioner Hugo McPherson. He was succeeded by Sydney Newman, who began his career with the board, moved to CBC-TV, went to the BBC and ITV in London, and returned to take up this appointment. He took over the NFB with almost unanimous acclaim, and at a time when the future of the board was seriously in doubt. With so many feature-length films then being made, the functions of the board were debatable. It appeared to be making fewer short subjects for theaters, and the distribution and exhibition of its films went from bad to worse. Also it was sadly out-of-touch with social issues. In an effort to bridge the chasm of indifference that had existed between the NFB and the CBC, Newman agreed to allow the CBC to use NFB programs with commercial interruptions, a concession not approved by the film-makers. Many people were of the opinion that the NFB should be turned into Canada's national film school.

The coup de théatre came when the CFDC, the Association of Motion Picture Producers and Laboratories of Canada (AMPPLC), and the Department of Trade and Commerce mounted a Canadian week at the Cannes Festival, rented the Vox Cinema, and showed thirty features, with most of the film-makers being flown over to attend. Where only a few short years ago there was never a Canadian feature at Cannes, all of a sudden they seemed to be everywhere. Many of them of course were ordinary, as some first films are bound to be. But the CFDC reasoned that since many other countries put such films on display and made themselves known (if nothing more), Canada was justified in doing the same. And, as is well known, they frequently make money at the box office.

The CFDC under Michael Spencer moved quickly during 1971 and made possible this veritable deluge. Hammered on all sides for having financed pictures described as "sick," "sexy," "immoral," "arty," "obscure," "insignificant," and "American," the corporation carried on doing what it thought was best without losing its small capital of ten million dollars all at once. It used its money on unknowns like Peter Rowe with *The Neon Palace* to professionals like Eric Till and *A Fan's Notes*. It made film production a reality for film-makers who previously would have left the country.

One very obvious fact emerged from the flood of films: too many of the new, young directors wanted to play the *auteur,* in the fullest sense of the world. They wanted to write, produce, and direct. None of them knew how to write for the screen, and few of them had the slightest idea of what constituted a good story. Aimless narratives about aimless youth became a bore. Professionally, most of these features were well made. There was nothing wrong with the often-superb actors, cinematographers, technicians, and laboratories. As directors, most of the film-makers were competent. But the idea that films should not be written, that scripts and stories were old-fashioned, was a drawback that adversely affected the development of Canadian feature films.

Nevertheless in 1972 on every side one heard talk about Canada's "new young film-makers" and of their

Au bout de mon age **(1975). (NFB)**

often heroic efforts to get feature-length films made and, hopefully, shown in cinemas. This was extremely encouraging to supporters of Canadian cinema who, for the past twenty-five years or more, had fought for the recognition of film production as an essential part of Canada's artistic activity and cultural life. Over the span of a little more than three years, Canadian films grew from almost nothing to a great many—although there was not yet anything great among the many. The signs were there: with less self-indulgence and with more attention to screenplays, a recognition of broader social and human issues, and of Canada as a whole, instead of just Montreal and Toronto, Canadian films could become the mirror of the country just as surely as American films have brought the world the American way of life for the past eighty years.

At the Cannes Film Festival in 1971 and 1972 other nations familiar with Canada's quiet and steady production of documentary films were surprised at the seemingly sudden appearance of almost thirty features in French and English, shown mainly to the trade in order to secure foreign sales. The distributors reported excellent results. To most observers, the "skin-flick" phenomenon presented Canada in an entirely new light.

At the same time the public responded and recognized the need to support Canadian movies. In Montreal, it was almost a nationalistic drive that compelled audiences to support any kind of French-language film made in the province. In Toronto, Vancouver, Winnipeg, and elsewhere, audiences felt no compulsion to support Canada's movies unless they were about subjects that appealed to them. This, in the end, was genuine acceptance.

The NFB found its greatest success in 1972 with a feature-length film that no one expected would ever find an audience. Claude Jutra's *Mon Oncle Antoine* (rejected by the Cannes selection committee in 1971) languished in darkness until September, when it was discovered at the Stratford International Film Festival by Canadian critics, and a few weeks later by the international jury of the Canadian Film Awards, which gave it eight Etrogs, the official Awards statue. The tremendous publicity created by these two events brought the film to the attention of exhibitors and the public, and it opened in Toronto's Cinecity Cinema and played for twenty weeks to enthusiastic audiences. This success was repeated in Montreal, Vancouver, and other cities. Keeping in mind that several films made in Montreal were successful financially in Quebec but not elsewhere, one can say that *Mon Oncle Antoine* joined Allan King's *Warrendale* and Donald Shebib's *Goin' Down the Road* to make a trio of successful movies. For the National Film Board it was a victory after many years of feature-length film production that did not find sufficiently large enough

Sand Castles (1977). (NFB)

audiences to cover production costs. Otherwise it was a quiet but steady year for the board under its new commissioner, Sydney Newman, with the number of NFB short films shown in theaters reaching the highest level in the board's existence. The many French-language films made by the NFB, however, remained unknown outside Quebec since the board still refused to make English-language versions available of all but a very few.

The year 1973 revealed clearly that film production in Canada centered predominantly in Montreal, with Toronto and Vancouver lagging behind. There was a vitality, a sense of purpose, and a characteristic lively air of freedom about Quebec films in French that seemed to elude the directors of Canadian films in English. While talk in Toronto frequently concerned the definition of what constituted a Canadian film, the *réalisateurs* of Montreal went ahead and made films about their province and society, giving little thought to whether they would be "international" enough to get back production costs. As a result, many of their films, particularly those of Gilles Carle, did find international audiences, while others on small budgets appealed to local audiences and covered their costs in Canada, even if they did not travel far beyond Quebec.

Film-makers elsewhere tended to be dominated by a concern for other markets and by an anxious desire to lose what Canadian identity their subject material may

Special Delivery (1978). (NFB)

have had in order to attract mass audiences. This rationale led to movies like *The Neptune Factor*, which satisfied no one and reflected little credit on Canadian production. Some film-makers in provinces other than Quebec were often inhibited by the desire to make "something worthwhile," which led to long delays while they pondered the nature of what they wanted to do next. Directors in Montreal, however, took simple subjects and quickly turned them into inexpensive and light-hearted trifles, which resulted in an impressive number of movies that made Quebec the best-known part of Canada to the rest of the world.

At one time a feature-length film was a clearly defined part of cinema language. Today works that might have been once called documentary, amateur, unprofessional, educational, television, and more, find their way into cinemas and make it somewhat difficult to distinguish their origin when all are totaled for the year. However, it would be safe to say that Canadian production for 1973 was around the thirty-odd mark. The annual report of the Canadian Film Development Corporation stated that since 1971 the number of films it had invested money in was around one hundred. The president, Gratien Gelinas, noted with satisfaction that the federal government had renewed the CFDC's mandate with a further $10 million. He added that "as attendance at theatres is constantly decreasing and it is

evident that the cinema is no longer the popular attraction it once was, film producers should now turn to other means to develop a new flexibility in bringing their work before the public." The report then recommended that film-makers, "to ensure a prosperous future, should pay particular attention to television. Moreover, it seems to us that provincial governments with jurisdiction over theatres, could contribute to the growth of our cinema by investing in production either wholly or partially, the taxes collected at the box office."

The one province that was increasingly moving to support film-making was, of course, Quebec. According to the Throne Speech from the National Assembly, the government intended to establish a Cinematographic Centre with the status of an independent corporation "in order to develop within a Quebec context the powerful cultural means of expression that the cinema represents, and thus fulfill the expectations of the profession." The center would incorporate all present government film agencies with an annual budget of $3 million. The Ontario government also considered similar legislation based on a report from a committee. As it turned out, the Quebec center was established as the Quebec Film Institute in 1979. The Ontario government shelved its report, which was prepared by John Bassett.

109

In feature production, the French-language unit of the National Film Board made more films than the English-language division, with Clement Perron's *Taureau* and Francis Mankiewicz's *Le Temps d'une chasse* preeminent. *Cold Journey,* a story about a young Indian boy's struggle with a white man's school and life on the reservation, was started as a feature film, but was eventually shown on television. Gilles Groulx's *Vingt-Quatre heures ou plus* was reported to have displeased Commissioner Sydney Newman, who found that it advocated "the rejection of Canada's political and economical system." Charges of censorship were raised, but the different points of view were reconciled.

Canada's third official year at Cannes was the most successful to date from both a commercial and artistic point of view. At Cannes two aims are pursued by participating nations: one is to present the best work under the auspices of a distinguished festival, a showplace where the world may see what film-makers are capable of doing; and the second is to put on the marketplace all manner of films that, the producers hope, will find buyers and audiences.

In the first category Canada was strongly represented by four films: Gilles Carle's *La Mort d'un bucheron* (Death of a Lumberjack), Claude Jutra's *Kamouraska,* William Fruet's *Wedding in White,* and Denys Arcand's *Rejeanne Padovani.* The market showings included the first projections of Harvey Hart's *The Pyx* with Christopher Plummer and Donald Pilon, Don Shebib's *Between Friends,* the NFB's *OK la liberté,* Larry Kent's comedy *Keep it in the Family,* and about fifteen other movies produced during the year, mostly in French in Montreal. Two of the most popular, *Quelques arpents de neige* (The Rebels) and *Les Colombes* (The Doves), appeared for the first time in dubbed-in English versions. Judging from the results, little was learned from the poor job done a few years ago on Gilles Carle's *Red.*

All films in French shown in the competition, whether they were from France, Belgium, Switzerland, or Canada, carried English subtitles, a convenience readily appreciated by non-French-speaking distributors, critics, and festival directors. On the market, the percentage of films with English subtitles continued to grow, but most French-speaking Canadian films carried no subtitles (with the exception of those distributed by Rock Demers's Faroun Films), which led distributors and critics to complain that even if they understood French, they could not understand

Solzenitsyn's Children Are Making a Lot of Noise in Paris (NFB)

Bravery in the Field (1979). (NFB)

the Canadian-accented French; and therefore, how could the producers expect to sell their films under this handicap or get them reviewed in the international journals?

Whether this was a handicap to sales or not remains a debatable question, as do all aspects of the chancey business of selling films. But most Canadian producers and distributors at Cannes expressed satisfaction with the enterprise, and there is no doubt that the world was becoming aware of the fact that in five short years Canada had become a film-producing nation with an impressive and considerable output.

The greatest achievement of 1973's organizing committee, made up of officials and staff from the secretary of state's office, CFDC, the National Film Board, trade groups, and the Ministry of Trade and Commerce of the federal government (which paid most of the costs), was to present a unified Canadian effort, not a predominately Quebec-oriented enterprise at the expense of the national government. They managed this feat, in spite of the fact that the majority of Canadian films were spoken in French.

The suggestion made in 1973 by the CFDC and followed up by many organizations campaigning for more Canadian films on cinema and TV screens—that both public and private TV stations and networks show more Canadian films—brought positive results in 1974.

The Sweater (1980). (NFB)

111

Steady as She Goes (1981). (NFB)

Both the CBC and CTV networks bought almost every well-known Canadian feature made during the past five years for showing during the 1974 winter season. Helpful though this was for the Canadian presence on television, the money paid was small in comparison to original production costs. Since no quotas were established for cinemas, however, the additional television showings were possibly the only way Canadians not living in urban centers could see these films, a fact that strengthened the CFDC position that cinemas were becoming obsolete and television would become the most important means of transmission in the very near future. If the CFDC believed this, producers argued, then it should be prepared to provide full financing for features, and not just one-third as it presently does in most cases. This in turn has led to proposals that CBC-CTV-CFDC should jointly finance movies for television and leave out the troublesome issue of trying to get them widely shown in cinemas. At that time only large cities saw Canadian films, and not for long.

The first English-language film to set box-office records comparable to many French-language productions was *The Apprenticeship of Duddy Kravitz,* ironically enough filmed not in Toronto, but in Montreal, where the story of a young Jewish boy on the make for fame and fortune takes place in the late forties. Written by Mordecai Richler and directed by returning expatriate Ted Kotcheff, it is an efficient if cramped and untidy picture, and one that takes the "sell-out" mentality of so many English-speaking producers and directors to the limit since five of the main roles were played by American actors and the cameraman and composer were British. It was argued that since Canadians have so little confidence in themselves, the reason for the film's success was due to the American actors.

9
Saving the Industry?

In Toronto, Montreal, Winnipeg, and to a lesser degree, Vancouver, 1975 was marked by great conferences and confrontations between trade and professional organizations, unions, guilds, and societies, and any number of major and minor government officials, during which the participants put forward their views on what should be done to "save the industry." The secretary of state's film department appeared to remain quite unmoved by the storm, but the provincial governments of Ontario and Quebec did respond, although not quite in the manner anticipated. Ontario, which had formed a ministry of culture, promised legislation to bring about quotas and levies by midsummer. However, when the ministry was asked how the box-office levy would be administered, an official thought it would be a "good idea" to let the Americans have it to make films in Ontario. The government of Quebec, pressed for years by the trade to bring in a film act to protect Canadian (Quebec?) films, did just that, but with such stringent government control that it amounted, according to the organizations that asked for it, to legislation akin to totalitarian rule. The trade, both English-speaking and French-speaking, did achieve one impressive result: unanimity. Governments defended their lack of action on the grounds that the many organizations representing the various parts of production did not know what they wanted and all spoke with different voices, contradicting each other. They changed this by presenting a united front. The federal government did heed the call to restore previously disallowed tax concessions, but on a more sensible basis. Producers could write off 100% of capital costs providing the motion picture represents "significant Canadian participation." This stipulation was added to prevent promoters from writing off films with American stars, directors, and writers.

There were many film-makers, members of the public, and officials connected with the trade, however, who felt that quotas, levies, and other schemes would be too late. With theaters then charging $3.50 admission prices, only "big" pictures that promised audiences some immediate satisfaction were drawing good attendances. The smaller film, no matter how excellent was ignored because the public knew that shortly it would be showing on television. Discussions took place that dealt with the possibility of Canadian features being made primarily for CBC-TV, without commercial interruptions and financed jointly by the CBC and the CFDC. This had been the pattern in Germany for the past few years.

During 1968–75, the CFDC had invested $17.2 million in production, which represented 160 motion pictures. It had prompted private investors and producers to make available another $52 million. Of its $17 million-odd, the CFDC has earned back $2.7 million on its investments, a fifteen percent return. The fact that so little has been recovered is not really important when one considers the work and experience that the money provided, and that it made possible a Canadian presence on the world's screens and in a home market traditionally swamped with American movies. The CFDC completed its 1974/75 fiscal year by investing $3.5 million in twenty-four movies. Of these, eleven were low-budget productions suitable for television

113

Not a Love Story (1981). (NFB)

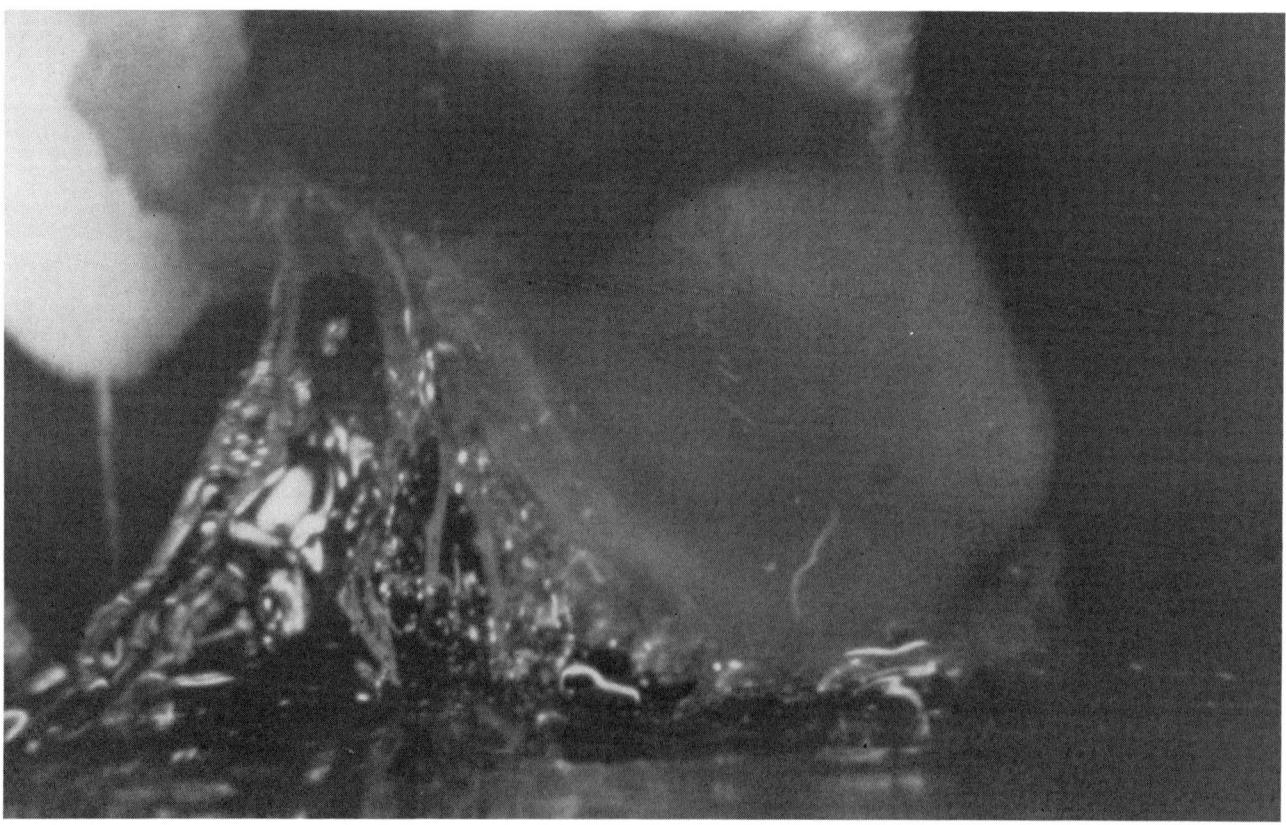

Zea (1982). (NFB)

and, in effect, providing opportunities to first film-makers (the first of these projects to be successful was Brian Damude's remarkable *Sudden Fury*); four were major English-track films from Toronto, and nine were major French-track films from Montreal. During this period the CFDC earned back a record $830,000, a $50,000 increase over the previous year. Of the total, between $100,000 and $200,000 came from sales to television networks and a large part of the remainder came from the success of *Duddy Kravitz* and two commercial U.S.-Canadian potboilers, *Black Christmas and Sunday in the Country*. The CFDC's executive director, Michael Spencer, who had long advocated a quota system, also declared that a five percent levy against box-office grosses would make a great deal of difference in the amount of money available for production. The huge sum of $180 million was taken in at cinema box offices in 1974, most of which left the country. As Spencer said, in an interview at Cannes for the CBC, "Five per cent of that is $9 million and this sum, with the CFDC's money would help to make 25 features per year, or one per million of our population. It works this way in other countries, why not here?"

However, all the expectations aroused by the spate of meetings with government officials in 1975 came to nothing. Quietly, sadly, the film-makers and their supporters came to realize that there never would be any quotas and levies, and that distributors and exhibitors, for the most part, would continue in the same old way—which is the American system with predominantly American films. The secretary of state, the Hon. Hugh Faulkner, announced an agreement with Famous Players and Odeon on "voluntary quotas," but no one expected anything from it. The only "Canadian" films the circuits will show willingly are those with American actors and directors, Canadian backgrounds that pass for U.S. locations *(The Little Girl Who Lived Down the Lane, Shoot, Echoes of Summer, The Breaking Point)*, and distribution that is mainly American.

As a result of this disheartening situation, many Canadian film-makers (to judge by their mediocre work on view at Cannes) turned in frustration to shoddy treatments of sensational subjects to appeal to the lowest tastes *(East End Hustle, Point of No Return, L'Eau chaude, l'eau frette, Death Weekend)* in a desperate attempt to get their films into theaters. But

Every Child (1981). (NFB)

Ted Baryluk's Grocery (1982). (NFB)

while exhibitors were prepared to show junk from other countries, they had no faith in the box-office appeal of the Canadian equivalent! To be fair, the secretary of state cannot seek legislation through the Dominion Government to obtain quotas and levies on theaters because the provinces claim that under the BNA (British North America Act) they alone have jurisdiction over cinemas and the censoring of the films shown in them. Mr. Faulkner met with provincial ministers and encouraged them to act in concert and enact the necessary legislation. They did absolutely nothing, which is why no legislation was introduced to Parliament. The Quebec government, which is more interested in film as an expression of its cultural identity than are the other provinces, was too involved with the costly Olympic Games to pay attention to motion pictures. The fact is that before 1976 no one had legally challenged the assumption of the provincial governments that they have jurisdiction over cinemas and motion pictures, a control that had not been envisioned at the time the constitution was written.

In 1976 a journalist, Gerard McNeil, of Halifax, took the government of Nova Scotia to court because the censor board had banned *Last Tango in Paris*. He won the case. The court said that provincial governments had the right to classify films, but not to interfere with the right of freedom of expression by cutting and banning them. Obscenity is a matter fully provided for by the nation's Criminal Code. Nova Scotia appealed this decision to the Supreme Court of Canada, but unfortunately the decision was not upheld.

Another legal action was taken by a group of filmmakers and artists who, at the annual Winnipeg Symposium, filed an application with the combines investigation branch of the department of consumer and corporate affairs for an inquiry into the market practices of the foreign-controlled theatrical film distribution and exhibition system in Canada. The film companies always seem to wriggle out of these inquiries, and in this case they did again. However, there were some encouraging signs. The minister of communications, the Hon. Jeanne Sauve, announced that a pay-TV cable service would be licensed by the government with funds intended for programs. However, it was not until 1982 that pay-TV licenses were finally issued.

The National Film Board was given a new commissioner, André Lamy, who had many years of experience in both the private and public sectors. He followed Sydney Newman, whose term expired in 1975. Mr. Lamy had a difficult task ahead of him in attempting to revive the board from the stupor that had overtaken it and made it an almost-forgotten institution. He did not succeed.

The Saskatchewan government, alone among the provinces, took the welcome step of investing $300,000 in Allan King's film of W. O. Mitchell's well-known story, *Who Has Seen the Wind,* which was filmed in the province.

In October 1976 the Canadian Film Awards Festival and competition returned, after a year's absence, at the Shaw Festival, Niagara-on-the-Lake. A successful event with over 250 films of all kinds, the winning feature was Michel Brault's *Les Ordres.* The Best Actor award went to Stuart Gillard *(Why Rock the Boat)* and Best Actress award to Margot Kidder *(A Quiet Day in Belfast* and *Black Christmas).* Both artists then went to work in the United States.

Also in 1976 occurred the sad demise, then in its twentieth year, of the Stratford International Film Festival, the first of its kind in North America when it started in 1956. The new artistic director, Robin Phillips, abolished it as being "out-of-place" in a small town.

Across the Pacific, Australian film-makers continued to move ahead with faith and confidence in their country and in their ability to make successful films about Australian subjects with their own talented performers and technicians. Unfortunately, the same cannot be said of Canada, where schemes for a new beginning took root in Centennial Year with the formation of the CFDC, which inspired the Australians to do likewise. Instead, their Canadian counterparts continue to slip backwards in a confused state of desperation and uncertainty.

A new secretary of state, John Roberts, was appointed in 1977 (his department is responsible for policy and funding). His first move was to announce a proposed levy on the box-office, something that the former secretary of state said could not be done by the federal government since cinemas were a provincial responsibility. And nothing was done.

Taking over the feature-film market were the financiers, the tax-consultants, the investors, the "fast buck" operators, and the "package" promoters. For the promoters, *coproduction* has been the magic word and deed. Needless to say, this hybrid form of film-making, which only the French and Italians seem to have made workable without undue loss of native values, has worked to the total disadvantage of Canada. *Angela, Alien Encounter, Breaking Point, Disappearance, Echoes of Summer, Equus, Full Circle, Goldenrod, King Solomon's Treasure, Leopard in the Snow, The Little Girl Who Lives Down the Lane, Le Malefice, Ragtime Summer (Age of Innocence), Shadows in an Empty Room, Shadow of the Hawk, Shoot, The Uncanny, Welcome to Blood City,* are but a

few titles on the ever-lengthening list, some official coproductions, others American-dominated. Of eleven major coproductions with France, England, and Italy, only three were directed by Canadians, only two written by Canadians, and no resident Canadian actors were employed in major roles.

Yet when Canadians who wanted to make genuinely Canadian films protested this sell-out, the backers of these mostly dubious enterprises dismissed them as being "provincial" and talked about this being the way to create the "Canadian motion picture industry." Some technic..ns obtain work, it is true, but they are the last to be chosen for the major jobs. Backgrounds sometimes emerge, such as the streets of Montreal and the countryside of Ontario, but for the most part these are "foreign" films that, when shown at home or abroad, have little or nothing Canadian in them.

This fact is of no importance to their promoters. What emerged quite clearly during the seventies was the knowledge that politicians and producers alike, along with a large part of audiences, had been reared so extensively over the years on American films and

Miller Britten (1982). (NFB)

"E" (1982). (NFB)

television that they only recognized Canadian work as being praiseworthy when it looked American and was made by Americans. No matter what concerned nationalists say, the businessmen carry on (helped, regrettably, by taxpayers' money from the CFDC), using non-Canadian performers in inferior films that take advantage of complicated tax benefits.

The use of non-Canadian performers by producers and CBC television become so widespread that finally, in exasperation, ACTRA (the actors' and writers' union) "blacked" certain CBC productions that used non-Canadians (mostly Americans) and denied many work permits. Immediately ACTRA was shot down in flames by editorial writers and members of the public who deplored the ACTRA move as "narrow" and "parochial" and uttered dire predictions about Canadians being denied the great talents of the world, and how they would soon be living in a "Canadian ghetto." The sad truth is that when it comes to arts and entertainment, music and literature, the majority of Canadians live on American material and creations and would not want it any other way.

The situation in Quebec was no less depressing. Only the causes were different. For the most part, various syndicates and unions involved in production,

distribution, and exhibition seemed to have been at each other's throats or at odds with producers, which resulted in strikes and lengthy disputes that curtailed production. Also, although the province was then intent on separation from Canada proper, the public, although seemingly caught up in the frenzy, had not responded to French-language Canadian films as greatly as before, which meant financial difficulties for filmmakers, whose costs kept rising in an already small market. The decline in cinema attendance might have been due in part to the increase in admission prices; moreover, there was less need for the people of Quebec to see themselves on the screen since CBC's French-language Radio-Canada concerns itself greatly with the lives of the people in the province. Yet the film artists in Quebec, some dedicated to separatism, continued to reflect their society and develop a popular audience. In short, their films had a sense of character and place. The long-awaited Quebec Film Institute became a reality, although not yet in 1977 a force in production. The intent of the institute was to bring all film production in the province under government control or supervision in exchange for financial benefits.

In its annual report, the CFDC gave the number of

films produced in 1976 as eleven English-track (ten in Ontario, one in British Columbia) and seven French-track from Montreal. Five of the English-track and one of the French-track films were made under the "special investments programme" for low-budget first features.

Canada's best directors were working precariously in television in 1977: Claude Jutra *(Dreamspeaker, Ada)*, Peter Pearson *(Kathy Karuks Is a Grizzly Bear)*, Don Shebib *(The Canary)*, Eric Till *(Bethune)*, Michel Brault *(Le Son des Français)*, Denys Arcand *(Duplessis)*, and Francis Mankiewicz *(A People Problem)*. Gilles Carle was trying to get *Exit*, a musical drama, into production, and filled in time with *L'Ange et la femme*, with Carole Laure and Lewis Furey, and *A Thousand Moons* for television. Allan King was editing *Who Has Seen the Wind* (from the book by W. O. Mitchell), a film he finally put into production in Saskatchewan after years of effort. Ted Kotcheff was still trying to raise money to film Mordecai Richler's *St. Urbain's Horseman*. It is obvious that the stories that imitated Hollywood and were supposedly commercial found production funds while the projects Canada's best directors wanted to film went begging for money—and the CFDC stood by and did almost nothing. No one seemed to think of the stimulating effect a few valuable, respectable, honest Canadian films, would have had on flagging pride and morale.

The National Film Board continued its program of bland documentaries for television, while severely curtailing its important schedule for short subjects for cinemas. Its technical experiments, particularly in 3-D and holography, were impressive, yet, in spite of criticism it still stubbornly refused to make many of its French-language feature and documentary films, which were frequently outstanding, available to the rest of Canada with English sub-titles *(Famille et variations, La Fleur aux dents*, to name only two). The NFB, as a government agency, appears to have decided long ago that Canada is two countries and so far as French and English-language films are concerned, they shall remain separate. In addition to its operations in Montreal, the NFB opened regional production centers in Halifax, Toronto, Winnipeg, Moncton, and Vancouver. Film-makers in these cities were given the opportunity to tell stories that had not been possible when all films had originated from Montreal.

On the surface, 1978 seemed a better year than most; four films *Outrageous, Why Shoot the Teacher, Who Has Seen the Wind*, and *J. A. Martin, Photographer*, made an impact on the public's awareness of

The Tender Tale of Cinderella Penguin (1982). (NFB)

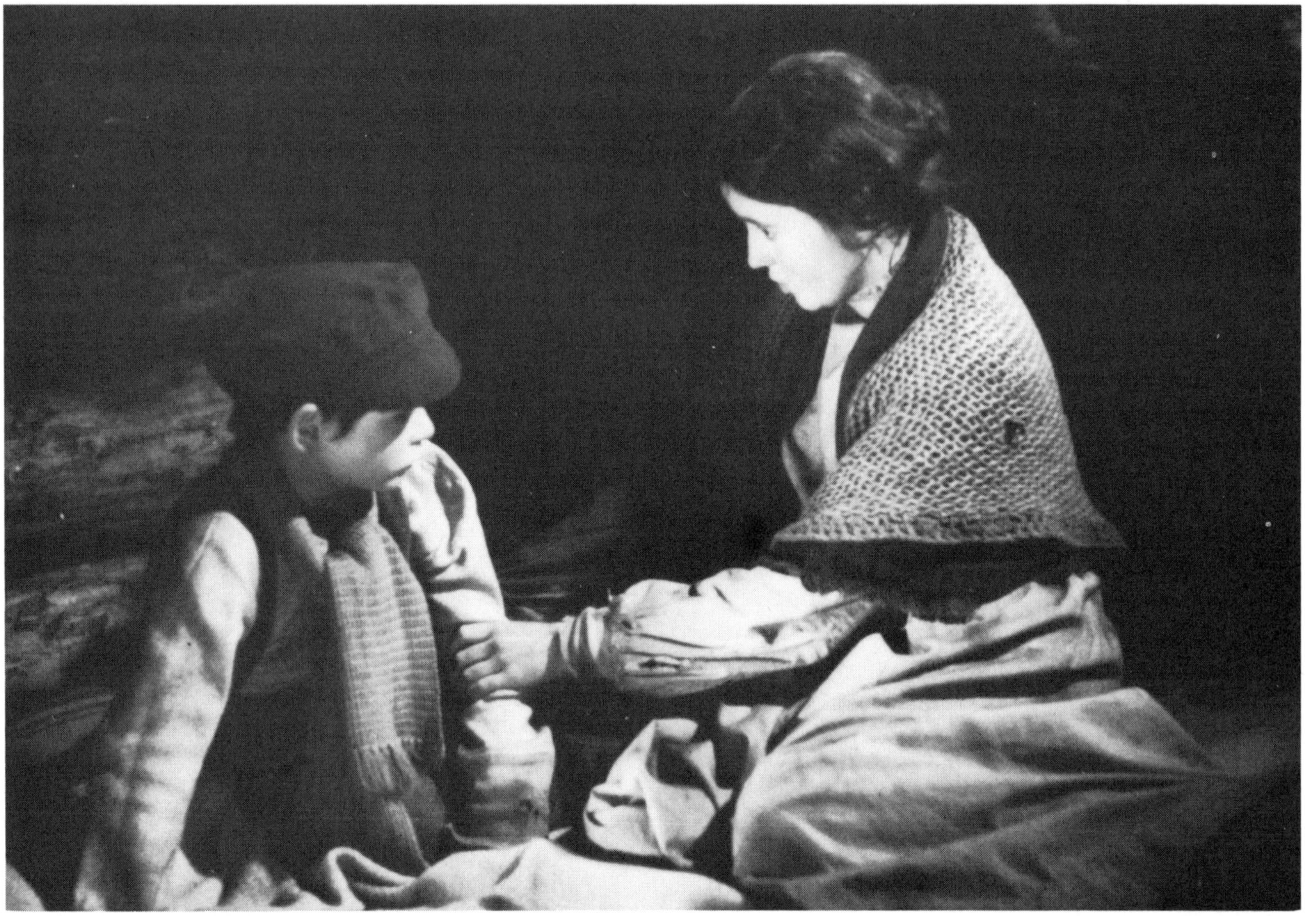

The First Winter (1982). (NFB)

Gala (1982). (NFB)

Canadian films as few had previously ever done. Undoubtedly, *Outrageous* (directed by Richard Benner), shot quickly but professionally on 16mm and a very low budget, was the most popular. An amusing yet sad story of a homosexual female impersonator (Craig Russell) who befriends a somewhat quirky young woman (Hollis McLaren) and gives her the opportunity to be herself, the film seized the public's attention, caught fire at the box office, and went on to successful showings in New York and at the Berlin Film Festival. *Why Shoot the Teacher,* vigorously advertised by its distributor, Ambassador Films, also became talked about and was widely shown. Based on a novel of the same name by Max Braithwaite, the movie concerns a young teacher's first year at a school on the prairies during the Depression and is marred only by Bud Cort's performance as the young man—he was clearly quite out of his depth and range of understanding. As with the appearance of José Ferrer in Allan King's *Who Has Seen the Wind,* these non-Canadian actors are required to be a part of these films by investors who think that because of their "names," the movies will easily get American distribution and exhibition. The fact that this seldom happens does not deter other

investors in the slightest. Ironically, the film that was successful in the United States, namely *Outrageous,* did so without any of the actors being American or well known to anyone. The picture was Canadian, and the film-makers were not afraid to set it in Toronto and to name places and people even if they were unknown to audiences outside the country.

Who Has Seen the Wind, from the book by W. O. Mitchell, set in Saskatchewan, is the old story of a boy growing up and becoming aware of life's realities and his family's frailties. Little fault can be found with the acting and direction, but the film, although beautifully photographed, tends to fall into a series of episodes that never made a convincing whole. The storm scene and the teacher's encounter with the trustees contain a vigor not present throughout the remainder of the film. The fourth film, Jean Beaudin's *J. A. Martin, Photographer,* was more a success with the critics than with the public. It did no business in the provinces outside Quebec and was not greatly successful even there. At times the movie tends to be as lifeless as Mr. Martin's photography, and the use of constant fadeouts, as though to render the whole into an impression of still pictures similar to the work of the photographer,

The Kid Who Couldn't Miss **(1982). (NFB)**

War Story (1982). (NFB)

makes the film somewhat tedious. Monique Mercure's understanding performance as the wife, however, is beautifully etched and deservedly won her the acting prize at Cannes and the CFA Award. Marcel Sabourin, who seems to appear in almost every other film made in Quebec, gives further strength to the portrait of the quiet and methodical photographer.

Two more films, *One Man,* written and directed by Robin Spry (NFB) and Zale Dalen's *Skip Tracer,* a remarkable first feature shot in Vancouver, were widely talked about but hardly seen in cinemas. In the first, a factory owner played by Barry Morse is polluting a neighborhood, children are dying, and a crusading TV reporter (Len Cariou) must decide whether to remain silent about it or lose his family (Jayne Eastwood) and his job. In the second film, a debt collector (David Petersen) finally comes to hate himself for what he is doing to people who have fallen on bad times. The failure of the exhibitors to give these films the showings they deserved made the promises of the trade to the naive politicians responsible for encouraging film-making sound even emptier than usual.

It might be argued that with four films being quite widely released, the trade was getting behind Canadian movies at long last, but this was not really the case. It simply happened that they came along at a time of intense pressure applied by the film-makers' own organizations and related groups and individuals. The theaters were forced to do something, but keeping up the pressure was extremely difficult. It became even harder when there were no productions to back it up, as was the case in the latter part of 1978.

The Cinema Canada showings at the Cannes Festival every May are an indication of whether it will be a good or bad year for Canadian movies: judging by what was shown in 1978, the result was dismal. Although fourteen new films were raked up from somewhere (none in French, which reflected the severe drop in production in Quebec, due to economic and political conditions), there was not very much national awareness at all. The titles and the stars of the films tell us why: *Deadly Harvest* (Clint Walker), *Two Solitudes* (Stacy Keach, Jean-Pierre Aumont), *Power Play* (Peter O'Toole, David Hemmings), *Blood and Guts* (William Smith), *Blackout* (Jim Mitchum, Robert Carradine), *Tomorrow Never Comes* (Oliver Reed, Stephen McHattie), and *High Ballin'* (Peter Fonda). Donald Sutherland appears in two coproductions, *Blood Relatives* (Chabrol) and *The Disappearance* (Stuart Cooper). Although *I Miss You, Hugs and Kisses* is set in Toronto and is based on an actual murder case, the star is Elke Sommer. *The Third Walker,* set in Cape Breton, stars Tony and David Meyer from the Royal Shakespeare Company. Only three films made use of casts comprising all-Canadian actors: *I, Maureen, The Fighting Men,* and *Panique.* No wonder Canadian actors continued to lead the ranks of unemployed!

The political stage in 1978 continued to be a nonstop comic opera. Its "singer" was Secretary of State John Roberts, who emerged as a weak and timid figure. He did take a plan to Cabinet to tax money earned by U.S. distributors, but it was thrown out, partly because the Cabinet was frightened of retaliation by the Americans and because the politicians as a whole have never understood the powerful, persuasive effect of motion pictures.

The National Film Board won two Academy Awards: *I'll Find a Way,* the story of a nine-year old handicapped girl, directed by Beverly Shaffer, won the Best Live Action Short award, and *Sand Castle,* directed by Coe Hoedeman, was Best Animated Film. Two other NFB films were also nominated: *High Grass Circus,* by Tony Ianzelo and Torben Schioler (traveling circuses), in the documentary category, and *The Bead Game,* by Ishu Patel, in the animated short category. The NFB previously won Academy Awards in 1949 for *Churchill's Island* and in 1952 with Norman McLaren's *Neighbours.* Since the board came into ex-

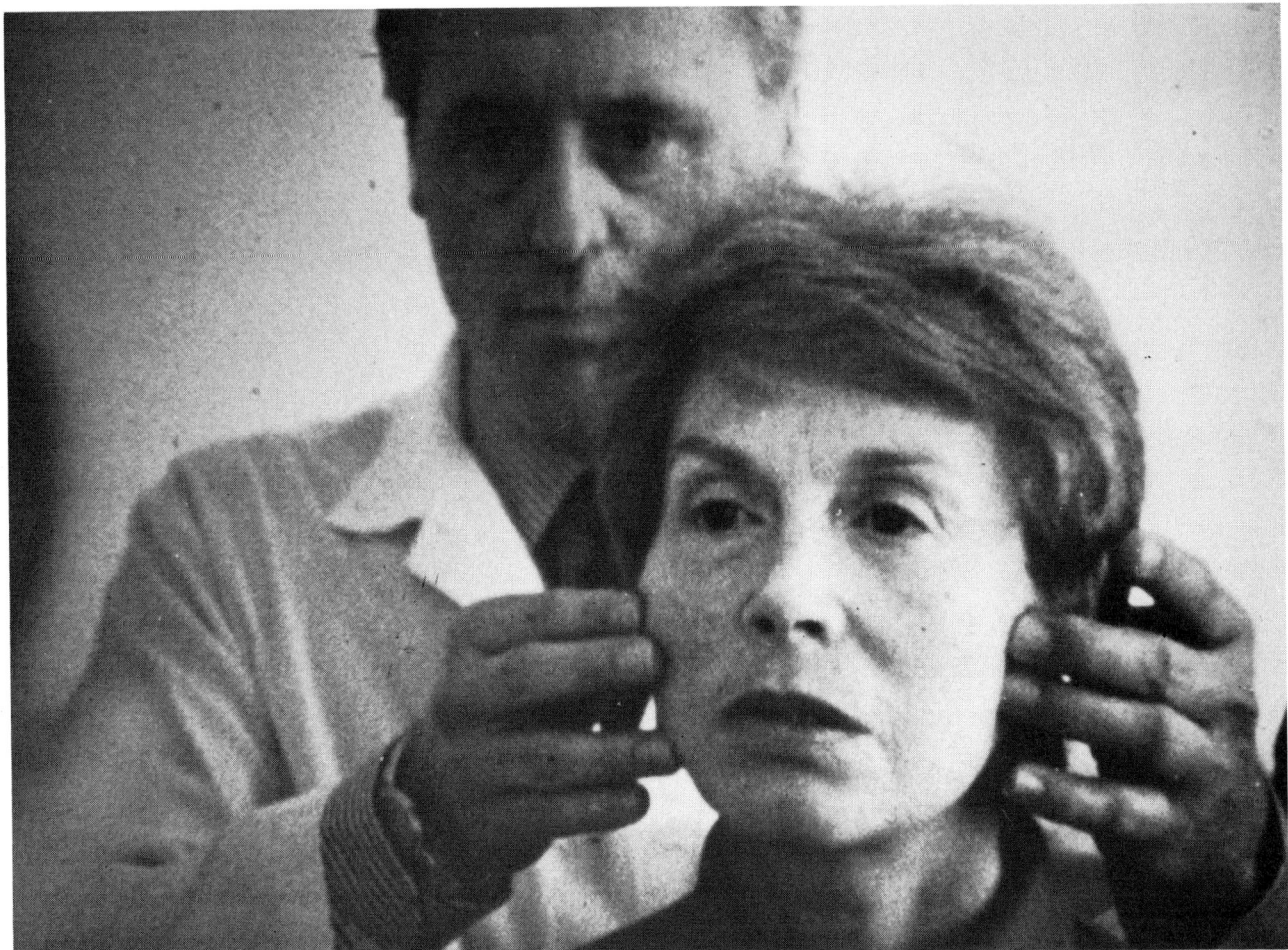

Daisy: The Story of a Facelift (1982). (NFB)

istence in 1940, a total of forty-nine of its films had been nominated for Academy Awards, up until 1984.

The only film in competition at Cannes in 1978 was the NFB's short subject *L'Affaire Bronswik,* a humorous comment on social behavior that revolves around a certain make of television set that induces people to buy things they do not want or need (d. Robert Awad and André Leduc).

10
"International Films"

In the space of one year, from 1978 to 1979, Canada achieved the dubious distinction of being the only nation in the world to turn its film production over to "international films" and in doing so sold itself into oblivion. The cash returns for this sellout were said to be considerable, and the returns in terms of national identity and the recognition of Canadian life and characters were almost nil.

A combination of factors made this event possible. First, the director of the CFDC (Canadian Film Development Corporation), Michael Spencer, although due to retire was hastened from his position to make way for the new director, Michael McCabe. While Mr. Spencer rarely approved the investment of CFDC funds in films that were not Canadian with Canadian performers, Mr. McCabe and the new chairman, Michael Vennant (who replaced Gratien Gelinas), had no such scruples. In fact, McCabe's ambition seemed to be to stamp out native Canadian films on the grounds that they lose money and are of no value to anyone. Instead, the less truly Canadian films seemed, the more willing he appeared to invest in them. Second, the Dominion Government's tax shelter concessions, introduced to encourage investors to put money into genuinely Canadian films, was subverted to permit private investors to claim tax concessions for financing these international productions. If these producers and investors had their way, no films would probably even be made in Canada. They are getting around this by investing in coproductions made in countries with which the CFDC has signed treaties. Needless to say, the advantages are all with the other countries and not with Canada.

What were the 1979 results from this boom in the Canadian "film industry"? *Murder by Decree* (d. Bob Clark), shot entirely in London, and whose strengths are that it appears to be British and that James Mason and Christopher Plummer are very good; *A Man Called Intrepid* (d. Peter Carter) with David Niven, Michael York, Barbara Hershey, and Gayle Hunnicut—a commonplace wartime spy melodrama; *A nous deux* (d. Claude Lelouche) with Catherine Deneuve and Jacques Dutronc—a French film in which the two criminal adventurers finally arrive in Canada, only to leave it immediately (in thirty degrees below Farenheit temperatures) for New York; *Agency* (d. George Kaczender) with Robert Mitchum, Lee Majors, and Valerie Perrine, in which Montreal plays New York in an advertising agency where CIA agents plant subliminal messages—much to the pain of honest admen; *Bear Island* (d. Don Sharp) with Donald Sutherland, Vanessa Redgrave, Richard Widmark, and Christopher Lee, based on Alistair Maclean's novel of the search for missing German gold; *City on Fire* (d. Alvin Rakoff) in which Montreal is again passed off as a corrupt American city burning from an oil refinery explosion, with Barry Newman, Ava Gardner, Henry Fonda, and Shelley Winters; *The Shape of Things to Come* (d. George McCowan) a truly awful followup of the H. G. Wells classic with Jack Palance, John Ireland, and, suffering terribly, Barry Morse; *Fast Company* (d. David Cronenberg), a silly racing car melodrama with William Smith, John Saxon, and strong U.S.-oriented backgrounds; *Meatballs* (d. Ivan

The Pedlar **(1982). (NFB)**

Reitman) with Bill Murray, Harvey Atkin, and Kate Lynch—a juvenile jamboree of summer camp misdemeanors; *Running* (d. Steven Stern) in which Toronto stands in for New York City and Boston for athlete Michael Douglas's attempt at an Olympic comeback, with Susan Anspach; *Wild Horse Hank* (d. Eric Till), with Linda Blair trying to save a herd of wild horses in Alberta, which is supposed to be the United States. This last film was made by the producer of the successful film *Outrageous,* which obviously gave him no incentive to create a second truly Canadian film.

Following these were Don Shebib's *Fish Hawk,* with Will Sampson; *Stone Cold Dead,* with Richard Crenna and Paul Williams; *It Rained All Night the Day I Left,* with Tony Curtis and Sally Kellerman; *The Changeling,* with George C. Scott; *Double Negative,* with Anthony Perkins; *Title Shot,* with Tony Curtis; *Yesterday,* with Vince Van Patten, Eddie Albert, and Cloris Leachman. Finally, add Dino Risi's Italian film *Caro Papa,* which, like *A Special Day,* we were solemnly assured, is one of the CFDC's great Canadian co-productions. Hardly a day passed without more announcements of million-dollar productions with American actors and stories. Others who also entered

Something Hidden: A Portrait of Wilder Penfield **(1982). (NFB)**

the tax-concession arena were Garth Drabinsky, William Marshall, Henk Van der Kolk, Robert Lantos, Stephen Roth, Sandy Howard, Robert Cooper, and Ronald Cohen, most of whom were involved in some way with monied interests in Los Angeles. Most regrettably, their association, the Canadian Association of Motion Picture Producers (CAMPP), was also instrumental in bringing to an end that honorable thirty-year-old institution, the Canadian Film Awards. This came about because the CFA would never recognize these "international" films as being worthy of awards. (It was replaced by the Academy of Canadian Cinema, whose members are "in the industry." The academy held its first awards, the "Genies," in an Oscar-imitation ceremony in February 1980.) The justification most frequently put forward by the promoters of these "international" films was that they gave work to technicians and laboratories. The fact that this relegated Canadians to their familiar role of drawers of water and hewers of wood for mostly outside interests seemed not to worry the public and certainly not the politicians at all. At Cannes in 1979, McCabe and his brigade blew the loudest among the trumpet-blowers about "Canada Can and Does." But no one knew what Canada did

that was *Canadian* in the way that they knew for example, what made Australia truly Australian. The official 1979 entry at Cannes was Gilles Carle's *Fantastica.*

While many of these hybrid, pseudo-American co-productions were made in Montreal, Canada's French-language film-makers in Quebec looked upon them with utter disdain and, recovering from 1978's slump, made several interesting films (including seven features) about Quebec's changing society. While, to be fair to the CFDC, some of the films received money from the corporation, others were made with financial assistance from the new Quebec Film Institute, under the direction of Rock Demers, formerly of Faroun Films (though Demers was forced to resign in June 1979). The CFDC's participation may have been prompted in part by charges made against McCabe by the French-speaking film-makers' association to the effect that he was misusing public funds in financing so many non-Canadian films. Among the new Quebec productions are Jean-Claude Lord's *Eclair au chocolat,* a sensitive study of a mother-and-son relationship; Jean-Pierre Lefebvre's *Avoir seize ans (To Be Sixteen),* a likable discussion of student fears and anx-

Getting Started (1983). (NFB)

127

Nose and Tina (1983). (NFB)

language film-makers do not find this satisfaction and since their work does not portray their country and its people, their films will very quickly be forgotten.

In 1979 the NFB celebrated its fortieth anniversary with, among other things, a new commissioner. James de B. Domville replaced André Lamy, who left before his full term and moved to the CBC. The fifty-five-year-old Domville, who was the deputy film commissioner, previously held executive positions with the National Theatre School, Expo '67, and the Theatre du Nouveau Monde. He took over a film board that had had its budget cut by some seven million dollars, that was no longer making feature films, that no longer had any short subjects in the cinemas, and that many observers thought had "been trapped by its own age." While the NFB had made several interesting films that had been seen on television, the CBC steadfastly refused to make use of the board's talents and facilities by granting it a regular place in its programming. And while libraries and schools were still firm supporters of the NFB, making good use of its films, Canadian educational authorities still used seventy percent American material in its audio-visual requirements.

The board won another Academy Award in 1979 for

ieties; *L'Arrache-Coeur,* Mireille Dansereau's drama of a young married woman trying to break away from the domination of her mother; Francis Mankiewicz's *Les Bons Debarras,* a study of a mother-and-daughter relationship; Jean-Claude Labrecque's *L'Affaire Coffin;* Jean Beaudin's *Cordelia* (NFB); and André Blanchard's *L'Hiver blue,* which won the Association of Quebec Film Critics Award. Family passions are aroused in *Contre Jour* by Jean-Guy Noel, and teenagers get a going-over once again in Paul Tana's *Le Danseur.* Among the documentaries are *Les Enfants du Quebec,* Michel Moreau's examination of the different social climates of Quebec's children; Arthur Lamothe's *Innu Asi,* a study of the people of Labrador; Diane Letourneau's *Les Servantes du bon Dieu,* in which an order of domestic nuns talk about their lives, and finally, *Les Voyages de Tortillard,* Peter Sanders's full-length animation of a young boy's travels through time. The writers, directors, technicians, and actors have made interesting low-budget films about themselves and their province (which is, to them, their country), films that will endure, to be used not just as entertainment but for the study of sociology. English-

After the Axe (1983). (NFB)

the animated short *Special Delivery,* by Eunice Macauley and John Weldon. Two full-length documentaries from the board were *Has Anybody Here Seen Canada?* and *Mourir à tue-tête.* The first (d. John Kramer) is the second part of *Dreamland,* a history of the Canadian cinema, and brings the chronicle up to 1952. To look at it is to wonder why Canada cared so little about its film-making and to understand why we have the films that are being made today. The second, by Anne-Claire Poirier, is a dramatized account, intense, powerful, and frequently moving, of the effects of rape and its consequences. Norman McLaren was reported to be making a new film about ballet called *Narcissus.* Finally, *Going The Distance* (d. Paul Cowan) is an imaginative portrayal of the 1978 Edmonton Commonwealth Games.

Continuing their triumphant return in 1979, Quebec film-makers had ten more films finished or ready for showing: André Forcier's *Au claire de la lune;* Louise Carré's *Ça peut pas être l'hiver on n'a même pas eu d'Eté;* François Labonte's *Château de Cartes;* Paul Tana's *Les Grands Enfants;* Michel Moreau's *Une Naissance apprivoisée;* Raphael Levy's *Le Noel de Madame Beauchamp;* Vincent Davy's *Les Tresor de nouvelle France;* Paule Baillargeon and Frederique Collin's *La Cuisine rouge;* and two from André Melançon, *L'Espace d'une été* and *Planquez-vous, les Lacasse arrivent.*

Also filmed in Montreal, in English, were Claude Fournier's low comedy, *The Clean-Up Squad;* George Mihalka's *Pinball Summer* (the latter prompted no doubt by the success of 1979's de-countrified *Meatballs*); and Larry Kent's *Yesterday* (retitled *Scoring*), which suffers from a poor script and dull characters.

After enormous publicity, many of the shoddy pictures made in Canada but supposedly taking place in the States, came and went within a week or two. *The Changeling* (d. Peter Medak) a creaking, old-house melodrama with George C. Scott, was one exception. Coming along just in time to catch the end of the psychic horror cycle, it probably had the longest run of its kind. But it still had a long way to go to earn back its enormously inflated production cost, reported to have been around $10 million. *Jack London's Klondike Fever* (d. Peter Carter) with Rod Steiger and Jeff East played for two weeks, never to be seen again. This practice began with *Welcome to Blood City* and *Leopard in the Snow,* which after all the ballyhoo, were never shown. Quebec films, on the other hand, are so much a part of the province, its history, and its life and traditions that they live on, teaching new generations a sense of identity. The last English-speaking film to fall into this category was *Skip Tracer* (1977).

How the English-track producers went on claiming they were making films for the masses when the masses were obviously not much interested in their

Earle Birney: Portrait of a Poet (1983). (NFB)

paltry efforts was just one more factor belying their outrageous claims to be putting Canada "on to world screens." The CFDC's advertising at Cannes in 1980 would have had the world believe that "in two short years Canada has risen to the front rank of the world film industry. This is good news for us and great news for you. Because Canada's got great pictures for sale this year—with fast action, high passion and terrific entertainment. What makes our pictures great pictures?" The CFDC might have well asked the question. Neither this ad-agency boasting nor its practitioners could answer, because greatness was nowhere apparent. And the American company, Carolco, candidly admitted in print at Cannes that "we have a number of Canadian films, because it seemed to us that after we had invested in *Silent Partner,* there was a lot of tax money in Canada, which interested us. We became famous in Canada for the work we had done so it seemed logical for us to continue there, especially since the films are not particularly Canadian. We use American stars which help to sell the pictures."

Canadian directors who work on these films pay a high price in terms of their reputations.

Thanks for the Ride (1983). (NFB)

When Ross Dimsey, the director of the Victoria Film Corporation, introduced the series of new Australian films at the Ontario Film Theatre in 1981, he explained in detail the workings of Australia's new tax allowance scheme and the regulations that would prevent its misuse in the way the similar plan, introduced in Canada, had destroyed the national character of English-speaking Canadian films. Just as the awareness of Australia's films had become world-wide, with the films themselves in the mainstream of exhibition, distribution, and review, so the dismal nature of Canada's pseudo-American films made under the tax allowance scheme has also become known within international film circles—and greatly to the detriment of the country's reputation in the cinema.

Thankfully, however, 1981 was not as bad as the two preceding years and the number of Canada's "Stars and Stripes" films seemed to have dropped (or more of them just simpy disappeared). With the resignation of Michael McCabe, from the CFDC (he was replaced by André Lamy) there was a much greater awareness in government circles and among the public of the sheer idiocy of Canada's English-track production. Francis Fox, the new secretary of state and minister of Communications, was said to be opposed to Canadian films trying to be American, and having Canadian cities disguised as U.S. cities and employing non-Canadian ac-

tors in leading roles. The regulations under which films could claim tax exemptions were to be tightened to prevent these abuses. They were not.

The three main films shown at Cannes in 1981 were Donald Shebib's *Heartaches,* Gilles Carle's *Les Plouffe,* and Ralph Thomas's *Ticket to Heaven. Heartaches* tells a simple story about two young women of differing personalities who work in a mattress factory, and are delightfully played by Margot Kidder and Annie Potts, with Winston Rekert in the unusual (for him) role of a romantic Italian. The obligatory American actor is Robert Carradine in the role of a boyfriend, a part that any ten unemployed Canadian actors could have taken with ease. While Toronto is not disguised as an American city and its impressive skyline is frequently shown, great care is taken by the producers never to identify the city in any natural way as the cities in the films of other countries would be. Posters on walls announce the election of "Councilman," when the term used in Canada is "Alderman." A story going round Cannes told of Shebib's difficulties with the producers in keeping American flags out of the film. To do this, he had to agree not to show any Canadian flags!

Shebib's attitude about the noncharacter of his past three films, *Second Wind, Fish Hawk,* and *Heartaches,* seemed ambivalent. It is worth noting that the

Norman McLaren's Narcissus **(1983). (NFB)**

feature film he made for CBC television, _The Fighting Men_ (1977), concerning the Canadian army, shows his work in a different light simply because he knew _where he was_ in the events being depicted and _who his characters were_ in playing out the events in their lives and _where they lived._ But Shebib never quite recovered the wonderfully free and natural spirit of _Goin' Down the Road, Rip-Off,_ and _Between Friends,_ which characterized his early period.

Ticket to Heaven with Nick Mancuso and Saul Rubinek does not hide its Canadian origin, even though much of it takes place in San Francisco where a Toronto youth, downhearted at the ending of a love affair, becomes indoctrinated by a religious cult. It was the first feature film by Ralph Thomas, who had made several important films for CBC-TV. The weakness of _Ticket to Heaven,_ shot in the documentary style of television, is in its failures to convince us that the young man could be so easily "taken in" by the cult, and to make us care very much for him when he is "taken over." Otherwise it is a capable and timely statement.

Riopelle (1983). **(NFB)**

131

Gilles Carle's *Les Plouffe* was a surprise in many ways: with his *Fantastica* disliked by many critics and not finding much success in the cinemas, it might well have been some time before he worked again. But one of the strengths of film-making in Quebec is that talent which misses out at times is never buried for long, and Carle found great success with his new film, an affectionate "scrapbook" of scenes of life of the old Quebec, before and during the last war, of the old generation, quaint and humorous in their outlook and their ways, scolded by church and state and defiant of *les anglais*. Based on an extremely popular radio series written by Roger Lemelin during the time in which it is set, the film depicts a past lifestyle that charms audiences as a wonderfully warm and nostalgic memory. There are three versions of *Les Plouffe*—the original four-hour version that opened in Quebec City, which was followed by a shorter version for general release, and a two-hour version subtitled for English-speaking audiences. A six-hour version was shown on television in the autumn in French and English.

Faced with the confidence, determination, and commonsense attitude of the Australian and New Zealand film-makers, who were at Cannes in force, Canadian producers stood revealed in all their incompetence and greed. Instead of bragging, in 1981 they complained to the daily press that their films were not screened in the competition. However, if they had looked at the films that were shown and studied the names of their directors and learned about Cannes and the world of film-making, they might have realized why their basically simple films were seldom accepted in competition. Some twenty-odd other countries already had been making much better films for a very long time and were seldom, if ever, in competition. They never complained about it, though, and continued to go to Cannes regularly and show their films in other programs.

The failure of the Canadian system that was designed to help film-makers was shown by the absence at Cannes of Zale Dalen's first film since *Skip Tracer*. Called *The Hounds of Notre Dame* (which makes it sound, unfortunately, like one of the never-ending stream of horror films), it is rather a likable, very human, well-directed "day in the life" of Father Athol Murray, who founded Notre Dame College in Regina, Saskatchewan, in 1940. He was a controversial figure, in trouble with the church and the authorities, and is

Massabielle (1983). (NFB)

Les Adeptes (The Followers) **(1983). (NFB)**

marvelously well played by Thomas Peacocke, who captures the personality of the original to the life, according to those who remember the fighting priest. The film recalls the old Hollywood films of sentimental, fighting priests, but avoids all such comparisons since it is again similar to a documentary but with all the humanity and drama of a modestly made yet intelligently thoughtout recreation of a past life. The "Hounds" in the title, by the way, refers to the school's hockey team.

Robin Spry's much-anticipated *Suzanne* received its first showing at the 1981 Toronto Film Festival, and although it disappointed many critics it was the first English-speaking film to be genuinely Canadian since *Skip Tracer* in 1977. Like *Les Plouffe* and *Hounds of Notre Dame,* it was an attempt at social history in terms of the individual and took place during what is now known as the "nostalgia era" for the movies, the early fifties, complete with naughty moments in the back seats of cars and school belles in convent uniforms. Suzanne is a French-Canadian girl of a Scottish-Canadian father who is victimized by men and torn between English and French cultures. The acting is superlative, from Jennifer Dale as Suzanne, Gabriel

Arcand as her gentle lover, and Winston Rekert as a "rebel without cause" and her true passion in life, who brings to the film a genuine sense of tragedy. The film, however, lacks a depth and conviction that should make us care more deeply about the characters and the situations.

The great disappointment of 1981, however, was the work of Claude Jutra. Once Canada's finest director, he became something of a hack for producer Beryl Fox. Their first film, *Surfacing,* which at least had good intentions, was a complete failure; their second film, *By Design,* was worthless. A coy and unpleasant comedy-drama about a lesbian couple who want to adopt a child, it bounces erratically from pillow to post, managing to be offensive about everyone and everything it touches.

Perversely, Quebec, the province that gives Canada the most difficulties over political and cultural matters, gave Canada its one distinguished film in 1982. The once-exasperating (with his obscure work) Jean-Pierre Lefebvre, who turned the corner in his discovery of the human psyche in *Les Dernières Fiançailles (The Last Betrothal),* was back again with *Les Fleurs sauvages (The Wild Flowers)* and was invited to participate

Kate and Anna McGarrigle (1983). (NFB)

in "The Directors' Fortnight" at Cannes where his film won the International Critics' Award for its "poetry, warmth and human tenderness."

The National Film Board struggled through another year coping with budget cuts and criticism of its role in the trade, its spending, the nature and quality of its work, and its very necessity to cultural life. The board much to its surprise found itself in the glare of publicity over a documentary on pornography called *Not A Love Story: A Film about Pornography,* which, typically is not so much about pornography in Canada but in New York City. Because it was made by women film-makers, Bonnie Sherr Klein and Anne Henderson, and reflects the feminine point of view, it received well-deserved support. However, male critics who found the film lacking were severely castigated by women's groups and individuals for not being sympathetic to the way women feel and for exhibiting feelings of male superiority. The film was banned from commercial exhibition in Ontario.

One of the best documentaries made by the NFB for many years was *A War Story,* directed by Anne Wheeler. In it she tells the story of her father, Dr. Benjamin Wheeler, and his years in a Japanese prisoner-of-war camp in Formosa. Dr. Wheeler was a doctor with the British-Indian army sent to Singapore at the time of the Japanese invasion. After the surrender, he and hundreds of British soldiers suffered dreadfully at the hands of the Japanese, and many more would have died had it not been for the care and devotion of Dr. Wheeler. The film is a clever amalgamation of archive footage with reenacted scenes, and Donald Sutherland reads excerpts from the doctor's diaries written to his wife and sons. *A War Story* is a very moving and authentic film that reminds us of a subject little dealt with since *The Bridge on the River Kwai.* Barry Greenwald, who received critical acclaim for his first student film, *Metamorphoses* (1979), made a one-hour documentary for the NFB entitled *Taxi,* which is a look at the taxi business in Toronto and the lives of the drivers. It is funny, concerned, and revealing.

The most unexpected development to take place in the normally untroubled exhibition scene in Canada was the introduction in 1983 of the familiar practice (to U.S. exhibitors) of the previously unknown (to Canadian exhibitors) system of going to distributors and bidding for their films.

A historical note puts the matter into perspective: since about 1919 when Paramount began to acquire, in Canada, its powerful chain of cinemas known as Famous Players, the Canadian film business in all its aspects (save that of the government funded National Film Board) has been totally controlled and dominated by the major Hollywood studios and their distributing companies. This is why there has never been any sustained indigenous film production in this country, other than that which takes place in French-speaking Quebec.

This control would not have been entirely possible were it not for the fact that the public was satisfied with American films and expressed no great desire to see Canada on the screen in the same way as it watched the depiction of all aspects of American life in Hollywood films.

But getting what few Canadian films were made onto the screens was almost impossible because they were controlled by Famous Players, which, in the old days, followed an aggressive policy of making sure that only U.S. films were exhibited. Being owned by Paramount, Famous Players naturally gave this company the "most favored studio" treatment, and all others followed. In the United States at this time, of course, the studios owned not only their own distributing companies, but their own circuits of cinemas.

When, between 1949 and 1951, the U.S. Department of Justice ordered the studios to sell their cinemas under the antitrust laws, no such law existed in Canada, and Paramount was not required to sell its holdings here. The only alternative distribution system came about in the late 1940s when J. Arthur Rank (later Lord Rank) created the Odeon circuit in Canada when he found it impossible to get his films shown on Famous screens. A "gentleman's agreement" was then reached between Odeon, Famous and the major distributors as to who would show what films from which companies in various cities, and this very convenient arrangement held sway in the distribution-exhibition system up until early in 1983, when the unexpected happened.

The Cineplex company, the first new major exhibitor in Canada since Odeon, built twenty-one mini-16mm-cinemas in the futuristic Eaton shopping center in Toronto, with the intention of showing foreign films to "ethnic audiences." The policy was soon abandoned in favor of showing American films in 16mm once they had finished their runs with Famous and Odeon.

Then it became dissatisfied with this move, changed its projectors to 35mm, and tried to obtain first-run films. The distributors, not wanting to jeopardise their position with Famous and Odeon, refused to let Cineplex have first-runs on the grounds that it did not have

A Time to Rise (1983). (NFB)

135

In Search of Farley Mowat (1983). (NFB)

enough screens to return bigger grosses than the other circuits.

Cineplex then filed a restraint of trade complaint against the distributors with the anticombines department of the national government, and much to everyone's surprise, quick action followed which led to the distributors meeting with government representatives and agreeing to introduce a bidding system. Now there are no more predetermined "splits" and "gentlemen's agreements" between Odeon and Famous. Whoever puts up the most money gets the films.

Over the years, several failed attempts were made to break the monopoly held by Famous Players over securing first-run films, and later, the Famous Players–Odeon arrangement with distributors. The most recent was in 1978 when the Rocca Theatre chain, a small independent group in the Maritimes, sued Warner Brothers as a test case claiming that it never had the opportunity to bid for first-run films. As the case pro-

ceeded under the provincial Nova Scotia Theatres Act instead of under the laws of the federal anticombines act, Rocca lost his action and everything continued as before—until recently, when, faced with federal law, the distributors agreed, through the Canadian Moton Picture Distributors Association, to introduce the bidding procedure.

Needless to say, Famous with its more than four hundred screens across Canada in the important first-runs will still get the most profitable films, the "big pictures"; but at least, the practice could be said to fit the principles of free enterprise. The result so far has meant unprecedented paperwork for the circuits' head offices, which they previously were not required to contend with, and even more money for the distributors. If anything, the dollar drain in rentals, remitted to the United States and running around $100 million annually, will now be greater. Cineplex is now getting first-runs with a limited number of pictures, but is paying heavily for them, with returns at the box office depending on the popularity of each film shown.

Surprisingly, with Famous Players actually strengthening its position under the bidding system, the news was made public later in the year that Gulf and Western (which owns Paramount, hence Famous Players too) has put the cinema circuit up for sale. The cinemas themselves are mostly leased, leaving only seats, screens, and sound systems as actual assets to be sold. Gulf and Western, apparently sold all the real-estate assets of Famous to a former company executive in 1982. G & W said it was selling Famous Players because it "decided it did not want to be in the exhibition business in the long term." Showing movies is expected to become a "slow or no-growth" business because viewers are getting an increasing amount of entertainment on their home television screens. In the past Famous Players had always been profitable. Its profit went from about $11 million in 1979 to an estimated $13 million in 1980, then down to $4 million in 1981. It seems unbelievable that after sixty-five years of dominating the Canadian cinema scene, the once mighty Famous Players has become a property that no one really seems to want, and, in spite of the tremendous grosses for some films, must make its profits mainly on popcorn and Pepsi! But within the year, the bidding system drove Odeon into bankruptcy. The company was bought by Cineplex and merged with it, creating a new monopoly, and the old situation once more of two major circuits. "Bidding" also forced the closing down of scores of independent cinema owners.

In Quebec, the provincial government finally put into effect its long-announced plans to curb the power of Hollywood by passing laws that call for all films not distributed worldwide by American companies to be distributed in Quebec province by Canadian (i.e. Quebec) companies, with a ten percent tax on the

Devil at Your Heels **(1983). (NFB)**

American companies to be used for production in the province; these statutes also require the subtitling or dubbing into French of all films following their first runs in their original versions. Jack Valenti, head of the MPAA, on a visit to the Montreal International Film Festival, expressed his anger at the thought that a previously docile domain of Hollywood was attempting to break free from its control. While in the past, the national government always caved in to pressure from Hollywood to abandon any legislation that would improve conditions for Canadian film-makers, the Quebec government remained unmoved.

And Pay-TV came to Canada in 1983. It was generally forgotten that Canada was the first country in the world to have Pay-TV in 1958 when Famous Players, of all likely candidates, started a system called Trans-Canada Telemeter in a suburb of Toronto named Etobicoke. It lasted one year. Television, because of its newness, was still an attraction. Not enough people subscribed to commercial-free TV to make it profitable, and Famous Players gave it up. History now repeats itself. After a year of intense campaigning and lobbying for licenses from the CRTC, the Commission approved three national companies: First Choice Canadian (which then promptly dropped Canadian from its title), Super Channel, and C-Channel. The winners (and the other applicants to operate this potentially lucrative service) fell over themselves promising Canadian films and programs, with millions of dollars of work for "the industry." The CRTC regulations were supposed to make sure they lived up to their promises; no one expected that they would; no one expected the CRTC to compel them to do so. Existing television stations are past masters at evading content rules. The Pay-TV companies were not to be involved in production themselves, but would commission producers to provide them with programs and motion pictures. The individuals who lined up at Ottawa's doors were those who had ruined the film business, and when they received licences they promptly brought up the films they had made (and which had never been shown), and paid American producers to film their U.S. programs in local studios to qualify for Canadian content. The public, however, was not impressed, and the networks found it much harder than they anticipated to obtain the number of subscribers necessary to make their operations pay. C-Channel was the first to go bankrupt. Directed to audiences who, it was thought, would want to see filmed opera, ballet, theater, and the better films, it did not last six months. Possibly this minority audience preferred seeing theater live on stage, or, what it did require on television it found on the CBC, TVOntario, and PBS, the latter coming in from U.S. border stations and on regular cable service. The two remaining Pay-TV companies found themselves in financial straits. First Choice was saved at the eleventh hour by Astral Films, a long-established Canadian company itself experiencing financial difficulties until it produced the two mindless *Porky*'s films. With the profits from them, Astral invested $2.5 million in First Choice to buy a nine percent share in the company. To obtain permission from the CRTC to carry out this transaction, Astral agreed to stop making films in order not to provide unfair competition to other producers selling films to the network. Astral also started negotiations to purchase Famous Players cinemas, but nothing came of it.

Distressing as this period has been with its resultant frustration for those who have for so long worked to create an indigenous body of film-making, the year was not without its cheerful aspects in the form of four praiseworthy films: two English-track, *The Terry Fox Story* and *The Grey Fox;* two French-track, *Rien qu'un jeu* and *La Quarantaine;* and a further body of work

For the Love of Dance (1983). (NFB)

Prisoners of Debt: Inside the Global Banking Crisis (1983). (NFB)

from Quebec supported by the Quebec Film Institute. The *Terry Fox Story* would be hard to believe were it not for the fact that everything about it is true. Terry Fox, a young Vancouver athlete who lost a leg to cancer, overcame his despair and vowed to run across Canada (almost three thousand miles) from Newfoundland to British Columbia to raise money for cancer research. It was a mostly discouraging act for him at first, with few people thinking very deeply about the heroic task he had undertaken. By the time the public at large realized what courage and determination he was showing in face of great pain and adversity and the worsening of his health, it was too late to cheer him to the finish line in his own town. He was forced to abandon his run, after reaching the halfway mark, to return to the hospital, where he later died. By now, the public was so affected by his perseverance that an enormous TV telethon took place which raised the unheard of sum of $10 million for cancer in the name of Terry Fox.

The film manages to relate much of this with commendable restraint and insight. It is not entirely successful, looking at times like a stodgy television documentary-drama. It is made completely believable, however, by the extraordinary performance of Eric Fryer as Terry Fox. He himself also lost a leg as a result of cancer, and he knows the feelings and emotions that possessed Terry Fox. Knowing them and portraying them, however, are two entirely different matters, yet this young nonprofessional player conveyed the fear, the pain, the despair, and the moments

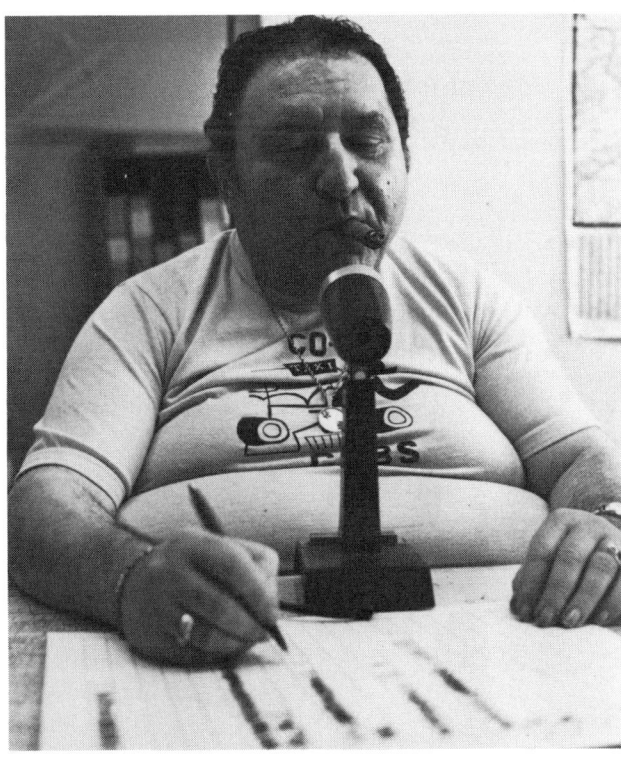

Taxi (1983). (NFB)

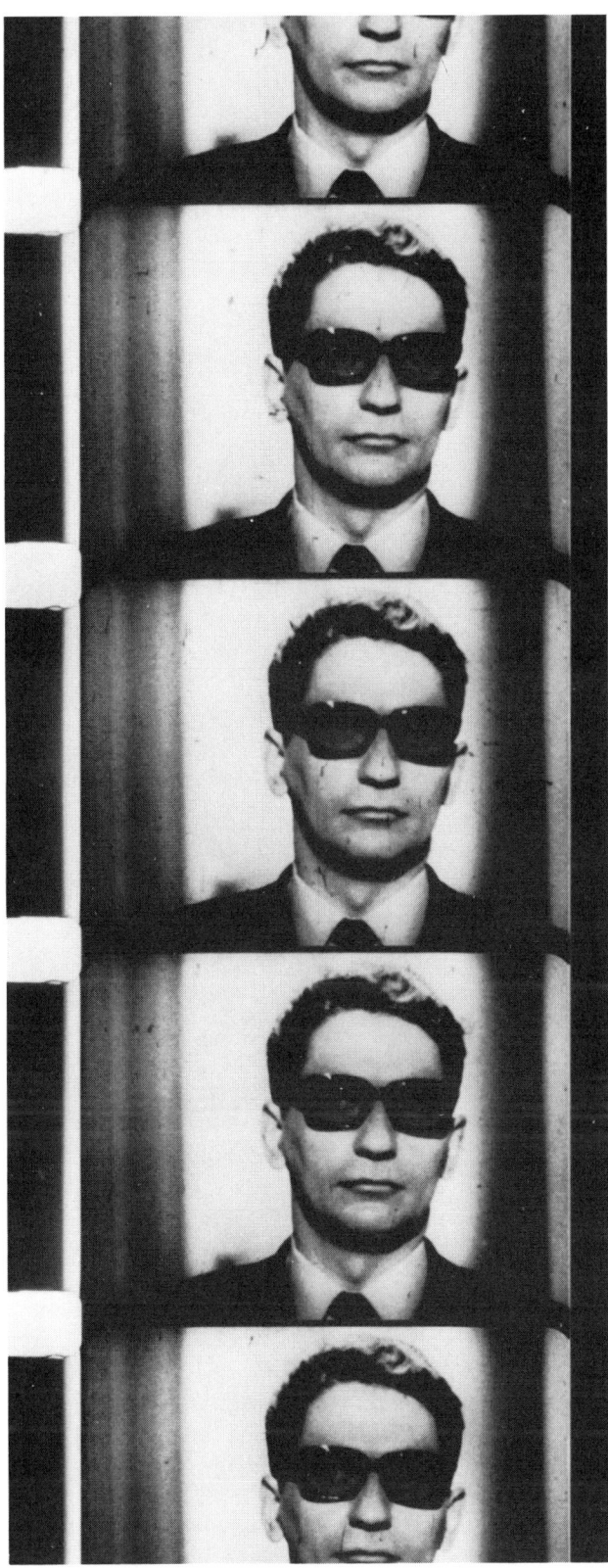

Deux épisodes dans la vie d'Hubert Aquin (1983). (NFB)

F. R. Scott: Rhyme and Reason (1983). (NFB)

of pleasure that were felt by Fox in a consistently believable way. Considering that the image of the real Terry Fox had but recently faded from the television screens, it is remarkable how easy it is to accept Eric Fryer as being Fox. The film does not make a saint out of its subject. He was in real life difficult—rude and impossible at times, with good reason—and Fryer, working from a superficial screenplay by American writer Edward Hume, shows this forcefully yet naturally, as well as cleverly imitating the up-and-down, hop-and-skip walk of Fox, with his arms held across his chest, which so many millions of TV viewers came to know so well. Some of the most poignant moments are those that take place in the Maritimes when Fox, cresting a hill, sees the long, lonely, and empty road stretching miles ahead of him over hill after hill. These beautifully visual scenes (Richard Ciupka) brought home to audiences the sheer physical courage and endurance required by Terry Fox to cover the distance he did.

Capably directed by Ralph L. Thomas (whose first film was *Ticket to Heaven*) and with a fine supporting cast, *The Terry Fox Story* was produced by Robert Cooper, one of the leading exponents of pseudo-American Canadian films. This being so, no one would have been surprised to find that Terry Fox was running between Chicago and Los Angeles. Fortunately, this was not the case, and the film becomes one of the very few made in this country that shows the vast and changing landscapes of this enormous and beautiful land—and a glimpse of cities as well. At the Venice Film Festival in 1982, an American student taking part in a discussion on Canadian cinema remarked that she had heard a lot about Toronto being an attractive city, but she had never seen it on the screen. It appears as itself this time. The obligatory American presence is required as a result of money from Home Box Office, and this is provided by Robert Duvall, in the small role of the Cancer Society representative who accompanies Fox on the later part of his run. At least, Duvall is a decent actor, but in the naturalistic style of this picture, his presence is out of key. The banal score is by Hollywood composer, Tom Conti, and it is to the film's credit that it survives in spite of it. To some, the whole idea of a man's physical handicap being turned into a press and public relations carnival ("You must be in Barrie by six o'clock to meet the delegation") and being heartlessly exploited, even for a charitable cause, is utterly distasteful. One of the virtues of this film is that it maintains an air of objectivity about this heroic if somewhat misguided event, which speaks for itself.

The Grey Fox, dare it be said, for fear of striking a carping note, cannot rid us either of the American influence, dealing as it does with an American train robber in Canada at the turn of the century. This, like *Terry Fox,* is a true story, but not as true as *Terry Fox;* its deviations from what Bill Miner might have done and whom he met become acceptable as being part of western mythology because they are presented with artistry, deep feeling, and imagination. The writer and director have used the character and his deeds to relate history with meaning and significance within a social context. Were it not for the fact that Bill Miner was a somewhat unsuccessful train robber, that he was neither brutal nor a killer, it would be hard to sympathize with him or to accept this film even in spite of

its poetic vision and beautifully told story. This film, five years in preparation, with three years elapsing between the start of production and its first showing at Taormina (where it received two prizes), has brought to its director all the pain, frustration, and financial headaches that so many film-makers experience in getting their first feature made.

Phillip Borsos, born in Australia, moved to Canada at the age of five, and grew up in British Columbia. His first short film, *Cooperage* (1976) startled the International Jury (bored by dozens of dull documentaries) at the Canadian Film Awards that year with its original and striking portrayal of the art of barrel making. The next year he did the same with *Spartree* (1977) a short film about lumberjacks. Two years later, in 1979, he made another remarkable short documentary showing the manufacture of *Nails,* for which he was nominated for an Academy Award. He then started working on *The Grey Fox* with the energetic young Vancouver

Hugh MacLellan: Portrait of a Writer **(1983). (NFB)**

producer, Peter O'Brian. It is entirely in keeping with Borsos's work that he should be concerned with past and present, although there is not such a gap between the old and new in *The Grey Fox* as there is in his short films. With a pleasing sense of consistency he interpolated black-and-white archive footage into *Cooperage, Spartree,* and *Nails* to show how the work depicted was done at the turn of the century. In *The Grey Fox,* Bill Miner comes out of San Quentin after serving thirty-three years for robbing stage coaches, and goes to one of the new movie halls. There he sees Edwin S. Porter's *The Great Train Robbery,* which we, the audience, watch with him. Whether Miner actually was inspired in his new career as a result of seeing this film, no one really knows, but it is a delightful motivating force and is entirely in keeping with the style of Borsos's short films.

After botching his first train robbery in the States, Miner crosses into British Columbia and tries his luck on the Canadian Pacific Railway. He also meets an outspoken middle-aged woman, a photographer by profession, who finds it hard going in a man's world, delightfully played by Jackie Burroughs. A charming romance develops between them; later he goes away to hold up another train, is caught by the North West Mounted Police and goes back to prison. We are asked to believe that he escapes, joins his lover, and that they live happily ever after—which is what we would like to believe. The facts are that he went back to the States, continued to rob trains, and died in prison in Georgia in 1913.

Beautifully and dramatically photographed by Frank Tidy, *The Grey Fox* takes the life of a man who was not widely known or written about and embellishes his petty crime and brief encounters with a fine sense of drama and social history. Miner is played as a dignified, cultured, and kindly man by Richard Farnsworth. In this instance, it is entirely proper that an American actor should play the role, and it is doubtful that a better choice could have been made. Farnsworth had been a stuntman since the early days of film, from the age of seventeen, and worked on many of John Ford's films. His first acting role was as Jane Fonda's father in Alan Pakula's *Comes a Horseman.* With his sad eyes, gentle manner, and gentlemanly bearing, it is hard to understand why he is a bandit. The film is not too explicit in this regard, yet Farnsworth conveys with few words, together with Borsos's marvelous visual sense, the restlessness within him, the search for adventure, the need to be independent, carrying out his hold-ups quietly and without physical violence.

The director has been faulted for being slow in his pacing and muted in his excitement; but this is not a western, and it was not intended to be; rather, it is a movingly-told story of a man who, by his own choice, lives on the wrong side of the law. It is also a very clear statement that Canadian pioneer days were very different from those of the United States—if the hundreds of westerns we have seen over the years are to be believed! One of the many refreshing scenes shows the North West Mounted Police rounding up the Grey Fox and his men—without a chase, without a shot being fired, in a most civilized manner. Further mention should be made of Jackie Burroughs as Kate. A distinguished stage actress who has had few film opportunities, she brings a lively splash of color and flamboyancy into the picture, providing a welcome, yet never false contrast to Farnsworth's courtliness—one vociferous rebel attracted to an enigmatic one!

The Grey Fox is a remarkable entry in the limited Canadian film field. As a quietly-told romantic drama, its intimate character details and visual splendors (particularly the train photography) introduce a director of style, thoughtfulness, and imagination. We can only hope the system will not fail as it has failed Shebib, Zalen, Spry, and so many fine directors, to give him further opportunities to enhance our limited world of feature film-making.

The NFB. A national government study on the state of the arts (The Applebaum-Hebert Report) recommended the disbandment of the NFB as a production and distribution agency, turning it instead into a train-

Cries from the Deep (1983). (NFB)

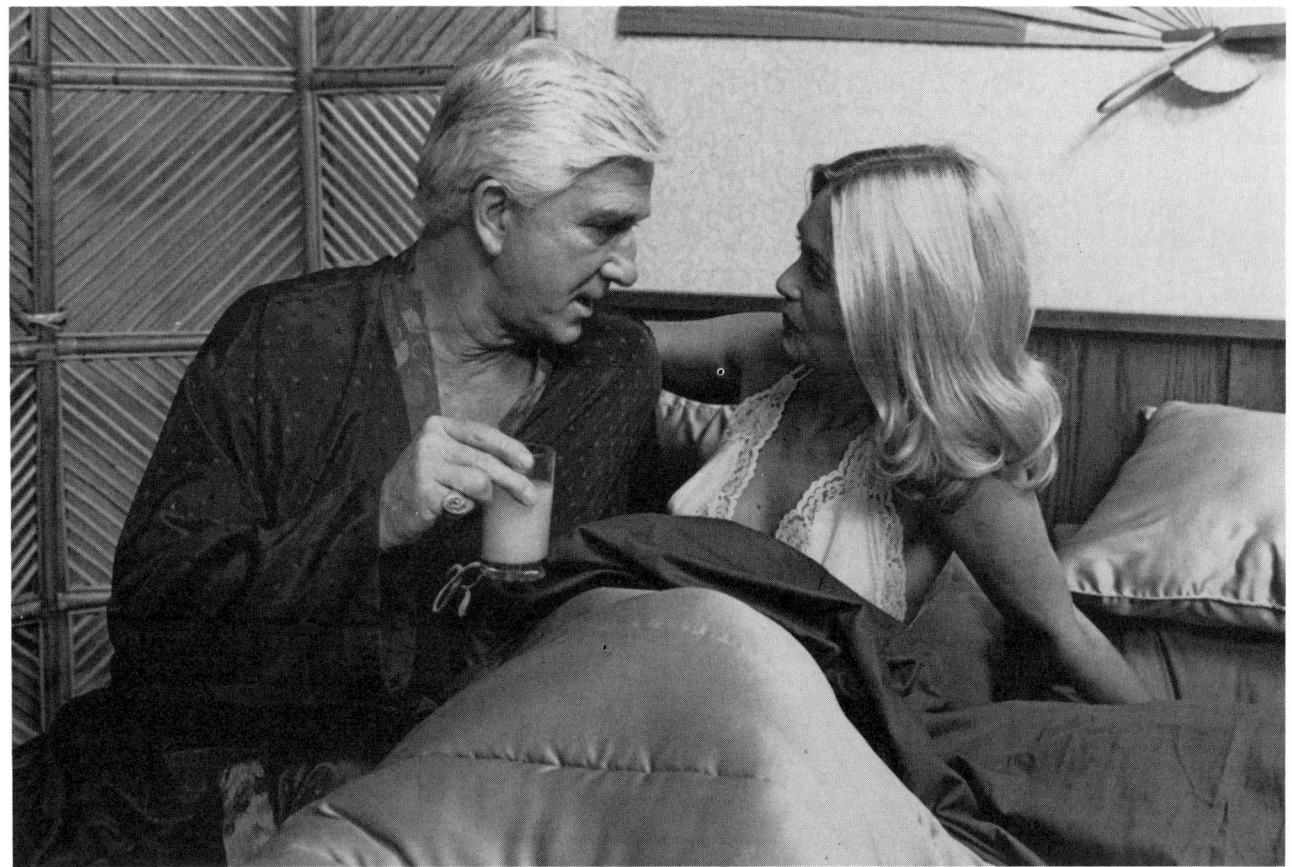

Choice of Two **(1983). (NFB)**

ing school. The board fought back, supported by hundreds of organizations and individuals, and so far the government has ignored the report's advice. Just as the board found itself in the limelight in 1982 for *Not a Love Story,* this year it was startled to receive unimaginable publicity in the United States (and subsequently in Canada) when the U.S. Department of Justice designated three NFB documentaries, *If You Love This Planet, Acid from Heaven,* and *Acid Rain: Requiem of Recovery,* as being "foreign propaganda" under a wartime ruling that gave the government the power to control films reflecting "a foreign government's point-of-view." The three films were suspect because of their direct or implied criticism of the way in which the United States is handling the issue of nuclear war, and because its industries are responsible for much of the acid rain falling in Canada and ruining the lakes and forests. Under this order, distributors were required to list the names of persons attending projections of the films. Concerned Americans who were outraged over governmental restraint of freedom of expression, countered this order in the courts with the result that a judge in California declared the Department of Justice ruling to be "unconstitutional." (His decision was later appealed to a higher court and overturned.) The films themselves are simple yet ef-

fective, with *If You Love This Planet* being no more than an illustrated lecture by Dr. Helen Caldicott on the need for nuclear disarmament.

Some five years and five hundred films later at a cost estimate between $800 and $900 million (probably more), the great Canadian English-language "film boom" collapsed. This would be a sad occasion if the films that had been made were distinguished in any way and contributed to the artistic well-being of the country. But such was not the case. The collapse is actually a cause for relief because it brings to an end Canada's ignominious role as the world's leading imitator of American films and makes possible yet again a chance for another beginning to a new and better period. Of this huge sum of money, only about $50 million is said to have been recovered by investors, and the state lost more money, in taxes, than it would have done had it directly subsidized indigenous Canadian films through a properly constituted CFDC. Few individuals other than anticinema elements in government and business would complain unduly about this loss if we could point with satisfaction to several hundred titles of genuine Canadian films which, like the majority of other nations' films, were about this country and its people. It is difficult, however, to find ten such movies among the tide of imitation-American films that our speculators, promoters, brokers, and investors, who by manipulating the liberal points system set up by the Capital Costs Allowance plan (which supposedly guarantees the Canadian nature of enterprises submitted for approval), managed to put into production on inflated budgets with great profit to themselves. Hundreds of technicians did find work, but not many actors, directors and writers benefited from this "Hollywood North" activity because the subjects were not Canadian and the so-called creativity came from outside the country—usually cast-off material and talents from Los Angeles. Now the bragging is over, and the sickness has all but passed as production comes to a standstill and everyone is out of work again and cast aside, having been used for dubious means. If this recession had come about after a genuine renaissance of Canadian films, the film-makers could at least have consoled themselves that they had worked on material they were proud of and which would become an important part of our film history. But this unfortunate period yielded nothing of worth; because they worked in material that was not permitted to be national, but was deliberately contrived to be "international" in ap-

peal, not a single actor, director, cameraman, or writer was established in domestic or international cinema. As a result, this work found its only successes to be a few releases in the United States, with the rest consigned to the lower depths of the European and South American markets.

Yet few individuals in government film departments, in the trade, and in the media want to recognize this. "The films turned out not to be very good," "We did too much too soon," "We were inexperienced," are comments uttered with a lack of understanding so typical of the entire situation. No one will admit that (with few exceptions) all everybody in government and business wanted were imitation American movies. Even after this failure, those involved in finding a way out still think American rather than Canadian when talking of film production. The provinces (except Quebec) spend thousands of dollars attempting to attract American producers to film in their "marvelous mountains and lovely lakes and bustling cities," but their film departments (unlike the Australian states) never seem to think how important it is to make money available to local film-makers with ideas. Alberta announced plans to build a $20 million film studio com-

Something to Celebrate (1983; director Donald Brittain is shown). (NFB)

144

Home Feeling: Struggle for a Community (1983). (NFB)

hope, the latest rage, the next rainbow to chase; and the Canadian Film Development Corporation, which is not in a position to develop anything these days, cheerfully talks about "coproductions" as though they are the answer to our difficulties in presenting ourselves to the world. What coproductions we have made so far have all been to the benefit of the other country and not to Canada and its film community.

Of the 500-odd English-language films made during this period all but twenty-five have employed non-Canadian actors in the leading roles, predominantly of course, Americans. This fact is devastating in what it tells us about the mentality of Canadian producers and their lack of faith in Canadian actors, and leads us to reflect on what might have happened to the careers of Canadian actors, writers, directors, technicians, had they been given the opportunities handed out so willingly to non-Canadians.

We are forever being told we are "a young and inexperienced country" and that we are finding our way. This has become a banal and tiresome statement, and should be discarded. Canada was born long before the movies were invented. They are the one art we could have made our own, as the Americans have done. There is nothing wrong with our film-makers and artists, only with our producers who, as Alexander Walker wrote when deploring the internationalists, "are part of a clique in search of the Holy Grail of Hollywood." They will never find it, but they will ruin us in the search.

The Americans have finally come to realize what has been happening: a reviewer for *Variety,* writing about *Screwballs,* a Toronto-made youth sex-comedy, ends by saying "one wonders why all these vulgar studies of randy young Americans come from north of the border." The way in which these Canadian films have portrayed Americans as silly and unpleasant people is sheer effrontery, and if Hollywood films were to portray Canadians in the same light the uproar would be heard across the land.

An interested observer visiting this country and looking at the film scene would find, however, that few individuals in or out of the profession show any concern over what has happened. The period of "the boom" will be excused on the grounds that it gave work to technicians, "pumped" millions of dollars into hotels and restaurants and related businesses, and served as "a training ground." But this could have been just as easily accomplished by making indigenous films which, even if they had been unsuccessful at the box office, could not possibly have lost more money than did the pseudo-American productions. Aided and abetted by all branches of the media, which hailed every new undertaking as a further example of our great "Hollywood North" activity (little realising that this is actually what English-track film-making in

plex, which is not required, on the doubtful basis that because *Superman* used locations there, the next *Superman* would be filmed in its entirety in the province instead of at Pinewood studios. Nothing is said about making funds available to Alberta's film-makers, who can hardly be called such as no money is forthcoming to provide them with the means to make films. Toronto and Montreal are well equipped with studios and laboratories to carry out regular work and are seldom pressed for business. So desperate is the trade, the government, and certain parts of the media to claim successes in production that we witness the absurd spectacle of proponents of non-Canadian motion pictures becoming highly excited over the reported financial successes of *Quest for Fire* and *Atlantic City,* on the grounds that because Canadian money was invested in them, they are true Canadian film achievements. Some rocky location work was done in Canada for *Quest for Fire,* and what few Montreal- and Toronto-based actors are in them are, of course, gnawing on bones as usual. But coproductions are the white

Canada became—an outpost of Hollywood) and praised it indiscriminately, those close to the workings of the business still believe there was nothing wrong about the "boom" years. They deluded themselves into believing that "our films made a global impact" and talked endlessly about "the international recognition" accorded to us abroad. What they do not want to recognize is that our international reputation for English-track films is disclaimed for the absurdity of failing to find its roots in its own country.

This period of the American-Canadian film is actually the largest and most expensive manifestation of Canada's infatuation with everything American. It runs through all the arts and entertainment, the social services, sports, music, education, medicine, the press, business big and small, reaching into all levels of government. Should an expert be wanted in any field of counseling, consulting and conference making, an American will be chosen. The fact that a Canadian might be just as good or better is ignored. Private television stations devote themselves almost exclusively to American programs, with news broadcasts heavy with reports on international events from the American networks. Commentators asked to speak about the latest crisis in world affairs will probably be American. It seems that turning to Washington is far more exciting than turning to Ottawa.

Hand-in-hand with this infatuation with U.S. life goes the widely-held belief in "the free-market" principle, the proponents of which believe that no support, subsidy or safeguards should be extended by governments to any form of endeavour, and in particular, to the arts and entertainment. These unbelievably short-sighted individuals, many in high-places, claim that if something Canadian is good enough it will find its own way in the market-place and make a profit. If it does not, it is because the American product must be better. It is almost impossible to get the proponents of this belief to understand that if opportunities are denied to artists and businessmen to get to the market because it is controlled from outside the country, or is part of a system that emanates from outside the country (as the film business is in Canada), or is run by Canadians who are addicted to American products and programs, then the artist or businessman cannot be expected to bring his work before the public and compete. Ask a filmmaker what the "free-market" is when he tries to sell his film to a television station that is only interested in showing cheaply-priced American programs.

Partly because of this situation, the bulk of moviegoers, usually between the ages of sixteen and twenty-five, are quite satisfied with a steady diet of Hollywood films. Having grown up with them on television, they feel they belong to the life the films portray, and Canadian subject matter can be an alien intrusion, like a French or an Italian movie. This

La Bête lumineuse (The Shimmering Beast) (1982). (NFB)

Americanization of the film world extends to such events as the Toronto Festival of Festivals—which reflects its immaturity by claiming to be "the world's largest publicly attended festival," as if Moscow and Bombay, to name only two, did not exist. Every year the Festival brings in American critics to program certain sections when there are many young Canadian film enthusiasts who are capable of doing this, but are never given the opportunity. The Festival is American-oriented in names and appearance. To the Festival's credit, however, after taking note of the criticism made of its activities, it did mount in 1984 a fairly comprehensive and expensive retrospective devoted to Canadian films, features, and documentaries, going back to the silent period. This was done in association with the National Film Archive in Ottawa. The Academy of Canadian Cinema, a small copy of its big relation in Hollywood, celebrates each year its recognition of Canada's American "B" pictures with an American-styled awards ceremony called "The Genies," thus making the real issue of what Canadian

Magic in the Sky **(1983). (NFB)**

production should be into a tiresome, foolish, flag-waving imitation of what the Americans do so much better.

This is all related to the activities of the government agencies which are supposed to support Canadian films and television, and thus, directly, the actors, writers, technicians, and directors. These agencies are the Canadian Film Development Corporation (CFDC) and the Canadian Radio and Television Commission (CRTC) and the Capital Cost Allowance (CCA). These organizations, which began with high hopes and great promises, have not in performance lived up to these high expectations. The CFDC gives so little encouragement to film-makers it has become a travesty of what it set out to be; the CRTC allows the television and Pay-TV companies to do almost exactly as they like; and the CCA permits the points system, which determines how "Canadian" a feature film is, to be juggled around at will, resulting in films that have nothing to do with Canada being passed as eligible for certification. Their actions (or lack of them) are a cause for despair, and they are presided over by politicians and bureaucrats who make themselves look foolish by issuing provocative statements about how they will call the Americans to task for dominating the market, and then back down. Hardly a month goes by

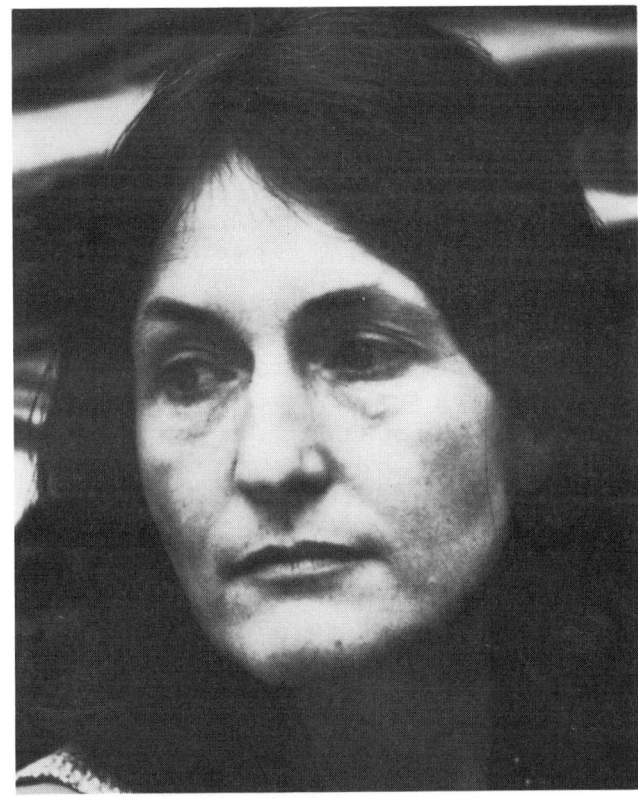

If You Love This Planet **(Dr. Helen Caldicott, 1983). (NFB)**

147

Standing Alone (1983). (NFB)

Among the five thousand or so feature films made in Canada during the past eighty years, successes have been few and far between, failures have been many and often, and few among the latter could be called noble. For this, and many other reasons relating to Canada's social and economic situation, Canadians have come to believe that when some among them decide to enter film and television there is little expectation that they will succeed. Success in this instance will be measured not by how good a film or television program may be as a Canadian work in the definitive sense, but by how good they are at being American. The public is not surprised when Norman Jewison, Arthur Hiller, Ted Kotcheff, Daniel Petrie, Sidney Furie, and others go to Hollywood and become successful directors (together with writers and actors) because they know so much about American life as a result of growing up in Canada that it is second nature for them to become American in their film work—although there is something about their approach to American films which is, while difficult to describe, a Canadian sensibility. Those who remain at home to struggle against the system to create a Canadian vision on the screen are often thought not to be good enough. If they were, they would be in Hollywood.

A Canadian screen character is not thought of as being a virtue by the public at large, and as a result of eighty years of this kind of conditioning few people ever expect Canadian films to be successful, either commercially or artistically. When successful films do appear, such as *Les Plouffe, The Grey Fox, The Terry Fox Story,* they are welcomed as exceptions to the rule—a fluke perhaps not likely to be repeated, and considerably diminished in their success should they fail to receive critical approval in New York. The favorable verdict of critics abroad on any Canadian artistic endeavor that travels outside the country is desperately sought by an immature press and public alike. Few seem to think that to please ourselves is enough. "Is it good enough to be international?" is the most tiresome aspect of creativity in Canada today. If praise abroad is not forthcoming, gloom follows, previous success at home is minimized, and everyone returns to the comfort and security of being American at the movies and in television. After all, it is reasoned, we are not responsible for the failures of the Americans. We can laugh at them, criticize them for not being good enough; we took none of the risks, and we can triumph vicariously in their successes because we enjoy them too. Such are the ambivalent, subjective feelings and thoughts of the average movie-going and television-watching Canadian.

There is no greater disappointment to those who do care than the indigenous films that fail. They provide continuous ammunition to those who say, in private, at conferences, in "letters to the editor," that Canadians

without a new "policy" being announced, a new committee being formed, which comes to nothing, much to the derision of the free-market supporters, and much to the despair of those who support a greater Canadian presence in films and television and deplore the way in which incompetent officials make government support of the arts seem so silly and ineffective when, properly managed, it is a force for good. The latest policy is a $380 million production fund for television films raised through an eight percent tax on Cable-TV, worked out by the CFDC. Any stipulation that the film should be set in Canada is unlikely. The Minister of Communications is also preparing a new "policy" on distribution and exhibition. Naturally, the sum total of all this is to make the entire issue of Canadian production seem tiresome, foolish, and parochial, and the involvement of government in film as being clumsy and harmful. The wrong people are given positions which, in the hands of the right people, might make a radical change in the situation.

cannot make films, that we should not try to compete with the Americans, but should bury ourselves in the safety of coproductions with other countries.

The final months of 1983 saw one major failure, *The Wars;* one minor failure, *Dead Wrong;* and two, *The Tin Flute* and *Maria Chapdelaine,* which, in spite of many admirable qualities, were not the satisfying works that had been expected. *The Wars* is the film version of Timothy Findley's highly acclaimed novel about the son of a wealthy, but neurotic, Toronto family who joins the army to fight for Canada during World War I. Apart from *Carry On Sergeant* (1928) there have been no feature films made showing the part played by the Canadian Armed Forces during the world wars, and so naturally enough, with memories of *Journey's End* and *The Big Parade* strongly in mind, *The Wars* was greatly anticipated as a major work that would fill this void in film history. But even before it opened, after a delay of two years, stories were rife about the difficulties that plagued the production, of the wars between those working on the picture, and of the rapidly rising production costs. In one respect, history repeats itself. *Carry On Sergeant* was directed by the cartoonist, Bruce Bairnsfather, an Englishman, without previous film experience. Fifty years later, our second war film was directed by the stage director, Robin Phillips, an Englishman without previous film experience who had established his reputation as the petulant and temperamental director of the Shakespeare Festival at Stratford, Ontario. Regrettably, in spite of an excellent cast including Brent Carver and Martha Henry, and some magnificent photography, the screenplay by the author is awkward and stilted, the characters are dull and uninteresting, the direction heavy-handed rendering the whole into an unconvincing and contrived portrait of a family at war mostly within itself. There is no life to what we see, no humor, no genuine sense of tragedy; we are left with an overblown, pretentious statement of little value and of nothing memorable. The minor film, *Dead Wrong,* concerns a decent fellow, played by the remarkable actor, Winston Rekart, who goes to Colombia to sail a

Singing: A Joy in Any Language **(1983). (NFB)**

Flamenco at 5:15 (1983). (NFB)

yacht back to Vancouver with a consignment of drugs. The Mounties on the case (of whom Britt Ekland is one) together with the Canadian army, are portrayed as silly asses; the whole is tedious, confused, and unconvincing. Everything about this misguided effort is dead wrong! Popular melodrama, so much a staple of American films, has its place in Canadian cinema too, but when it is shown in such juvenile terms, it is not surprising that the public feels embarrassed over such an enterprise and finds its beliefs in the weaknesses of Canadian films justified by efforts such as *Dead Wrong.*

In the case of *Maria Chapdelaine,* this is a film by Canada's leading director, the distinguished Gille Carle, which simply does not live up to expectations. Granting the fact that Louis Hemon's once-popular story of pioneer life in Quebec is now considered old, tired, and quaint, Carle, in spite of several clever directorial devices, fails to bring the events to life, or indeed, to give any life to the whole or to create any emotional depth to the characters, especially the young lovers played by Carole Laure and Nick Mancuso, who look too old for their parts. The settings are not convincing, the period feels wrong. It seems that Carle, afraid of being called "old-fashioned" for taking

War (1983). (NFB)

150

an "old-fashioned" book to the screen, has no fashion at all, resulting in a film without style or spirit.

The Tin Flute (Bonheur d'occasion) on the other hand, directed and photographed by Claude Fournier, conveys a deep sense of feeling and commitment by the film-maker in bringing to the screen the darkness and despair, the moments of laughter and hope, in the life of an ordinary family in Montreal during the thirties. Entirely true to Gabrielle Roy's fine novel, it comes to us, unfortunately, in fits and starts and episodic sequences, having been edited down to its two-hour length from a five-hour miniseries for television. Among the actors, Marilyn Lightstone (who played the mother so beautifully in *Lies My Father Told Me*) is again extremely effective as the long-suffering, but entirely believable mother. Although it has similarities to *Les Plouffe,* it brings back memories not so much of this film but of Gratien Gelinas's *Tit-Coq* (1954). Speaking of *Les Plouffe,* we now have another episode in the life of this family, entitled *Le Crime d'Ovide Plouffe (The Crime of Ovide Plouffe),* in which Ovide (Gabriel Arcand) becomes involved in a melodramatic plot which sees his wife killed in an airplane blown up by his sexually frustrated employee. That the story seems disconcerting in time, place, and plot is explained by the fact that once again cinema audiences are suffering for the sake of television. This version is two hours of a six-hour miniseries, the cinema part being directed by Denys Arcand, the TV part by Gilles Carle, who directed the first *Les Plouffe.* These are enormously expensive and complicated undertakings with huge casts and period locations, involving private companies, the CBC, and the NFB, and which, in spite of shortcomings, are a tribute to the film-making capacities of Quebec province. Another French-speaking film of merit is Bruno Carrière's *Lucien Brouillard,* a flawed, sometimes awkward, but well-meaning study of a young man, convincingly played by Pierre Curzi, one of Quebec's leading actors, who is so concerned about the welfare of others, particularly the poor and the unemployed, that he becomes a social activist. His zeal, however, gets out of bounds; he becomes caught up in politics, goes too far, and finds himself in prison. His friends

The Children's Crusade (1984). (NFB)

and family desert him, and his growing madness leads him to attempt an assassination of the premier of Quebec (in the manner of *The Manchurian Candidate*) in a political subplot that is far-fetched and unconvincing—true though some of its implications about political double-crossing may be.

Among the remaining films of 1983 is an oddity that marks a turning point as the imitation-American period fades out. This is *Strange Brew*, a comedy quite unlike any other, introducing to the cinema two clever comedians, Dave Thomas and Rick Moranis, playing Bob and Doug McKenzie—the McKenzie Brothers of the brilliant Canadian television comedy program "SCTV," probably the only Canadian comedy apart from CBC radio's "Royal Canadian Air Farce," to find wide popularity with American audiences satirizing, as it does, so many well-known situation shows, quizzes, and soap operas. The McKenzie Brothers always appeared at the end of the show as beer-swilling "hosers," a new term to describe amiable working-class individuals, who here live up in "The Great White North" (as Canada is always conceived to be by many Americans), and who appear to subsist on Canadian bacon and beer. Their comments were entirely improvised and heavily laden with such phrases as "take off," and full of sentences or remarks ending with "eh," a pattern of speech for many Canadians in ordinary conversation. The satire was everywhere apparent; sometimes it worked and sometimes it did not, but it was always good fun—never long enough to become tiresome whether they were successful or not. No Canadian producers saw fit to bring them to the screen, but MGM did, and the studio did not insist that the comedians change their Great White North routine to somewhere in the United States, giving the lie to those Canadian producers who excused their imitation-American films on the grounds that Hollywood refused to recognize Canadian places. (Of course, changing the locale of the McKenzie Brothers would have ruined their act, because almost overnight they established a recognized Canadian characteristic, one which many think is low-class and best not talked about, and to attempt to Americanize it simply would not work.) So their film, *Strange Brew*, is strange indeed. Needless to say, it is set in a brewery where the brothers indulge their thirst for the product. Weird and bizarre events take place, and while there are several flat spots as in most comedies, it nevertheless contains many uproarious moments and well-devised comic sequences, and is as completely and naturally Canadian as the *Carry On* comedies are British. Among the many comments on current affairs is the portrait of the Queen hanging in a mock courtroom and next to it, a portrait of Prime Minister Pierre Trudeau. Popular television personalities seldom take the public into the cinema with them when they turn to films, but *Strange*

Brew was an exception, taking in over $2 million in cinemas in Canada—an impressive sum for such a film. As comedy has never been a high point in Canadian films, plays, and literature, it was perhaps difficult for the public to accept the fact that not only was this a Canadian film, but also a frequently very funny one.

Just as Winston Rekart, Brent Carver, and Nick Mancuso were misued, respectively in, *Dead Wrong, The Wars,* and *Maria Chapdelaine,* so Alan Scarfe, in spite of a very convincing performance, is wasted in a peculiar film from Vancouver called *The Deserters,* directed by Jack Darcus. Again, obsessed with the American fact, this improbable film concerns an aggressive sergeant in the U.S. Army who crosses into Canada to bring back two young American soldiers who have fled the Vietnam war. In many respects this is a filmed play that propounds some good ideas about morality and duty, and the way certain individuals think and feel about war and their relationship with each other. But it is underdeveloped and, in the end, all rather false and pointless.

Also made in Vancouver was Paul Almond's *Ups and Downs,* which, seemingly an antidote for *Porky's* and *Meatballs,* tries to portray life in a private school with humor, respect, and a sense of decency. But any film-maker dealing with these "out of fashion" values in today's youth films needs a script strong in story and characterization. This film limps along from one incident to another, episodic in nature, peopled by students who are likable, but little else. While filmed on actual locations using students, it oddly enough takes care to iron out any Canadian references. None of these intelligent, upper-class students seems to refer to where he or she comes from, reads a paper, listens to the radio, or watches television, which would let us know that the location is Vancouver. This school could be in England or New England until the interested moviegoer reads the small print in the final credits, which list the names of the schools used for locations.

At the other end of the creative scale is another Vancouver film called *The Big Meat Eater.* This is a "no budget" semistudent effort by a group of young enthusiasts that good humoredly piles horror on horror in a lunatic version of all the known aberations ever depicted in this kind of film. From Winnipeg comes the self-consciously artistic *Latitude 55,* directed by John Juliani, in which a woman lost in her car in a heavy snowstorm, appears to be rescued by a kind of primitive man, a snow-covered Robinson Crusoe, who takes her to his log cabin and shows her how to survive on what seems to be an endless diet of potatoes. Another play on film, it attempts to illustrate the values of a simple life compared to the woman's presumably artificial existence as an official in the provincial ministry of culture, yet there appears to be no point to their boring relationship; the whole is tedious and tired, and when it is all over the woman is found dead in her car! *20th-Century Chocolate Cake* is a self-indulgent little personal film by Lois Siegal of Montreal consisting of a collage of bits and pieces of old and new film, animation and cut-outs, about nothing in particular. In Halifax, Nova Scotia, a province that contains a number of hopeful young film-makers, Paul Donovan, directed his second feature film, *Siege,* based on the police strike that took place in Halifax in 1982. Regrettably it sacrifices the true drama and social implications of the event for B-picture sensationalism.

For the tenth year, Jean-Pierre Lefebvre was invited to Cannes, this time to show *Le Jour "S . . ." ("S" as In . . . A Sentimental Tale)* made with his new collaborator, Barbara Easto, and shown in the program, *A Certain Regard.* Here, with gentleness and wry humor, Lefebvre depicts the events in the day of a young man who is looking forward to meeting his girlfriend later that evening. As the day proceeds, he finds himself taking a sentimental journey into the past remembering romantic occasions as he observes different women—and then unexpectedly meets his former wife. This is a delicate and fragile series of happenings and characterizations, which only Lefebvre could spin in such a pleasing way. All the women are played by the charming Marie Tifo, while Pierre Curzi, the tense social agitator in *Lucien Brouillard,* here gives a contrasting performance as the likable young man. Lefebvre's contemporary, Jean-Claude Labrecque, was also invited to show *Les Années de rêves (Years of Dreams and Revolt)* in the Directors' Fortnight. This is a fast-moving, yet sadly superficial look at the sixties in Quebec seen through the eyes of a young couple, newly married, with a child on the way. The film explores how they survive various events including de Gaulle's arrogant visit, the kidnapping of James Cross, the coming of Expo, and all the talk and underground activity relating to Quebec's surge for independence. The radicals and the militants are depicted as some kind of heroes, but the narrative, written by Robert Gurik and Marie Laberge, is one-sided and slipshod. Labrecque, however, has directed it with a fast pace and brings out some good performances from a mostly believable cast.

On the market showings, it was a pleasure to find Don Owen's anticipated follow-up of his classic 1964 film, *Nobody Waved Goodbye.* Titled *Unfinished Business,* we find that twenty years later, Peter and Julie are divorced and their nineteen-year-old daughter is living with her mother, who works in a radio station, with little time to spare for family matters. Isabelle (nicely played by Isabelle Mejias) is lost and bewildered by life and its contradictions; in particular, she becomes aware of the horror of nuclear warfare and joins a protest group, becoming involved with an unorthodox young man (Peter Spence). In an ending that parallels the closing events of the former film, she decides that running away to Montreal will not solve anything and remains to work out her dilemmas. Her boyfriend joins her, which is a victory on her part, but for what purpose? A lively cast of players brings a great deal of honesty and feeling to the script by Owen, who has directed with insight and concern. The use of rock music to express the feelings of today's youth tends to minimize the drama for older audiences, but the youth market may respond more positively. The CFDC (Canadian Film Development Corporation), which has reduced its standing to further depths by changing its name to Telefilm (it sounds like a small-time 16mm distributor instead of what it should be, a government organization with stature and dignity), refused to help finance the Lefebvre and Labrecque films, but did assist *Unfinished Business,* which leaves more money, presumably, for the CFDC to go chasing around the world trying to draw up useless coproduction agreements.

It is encouraging to note that as this period ended, a Canadian film about a genuine American subject, *Running Brave,* came to the screen and atoned somewhat for the worthless material of the past five years. Financed by the wealthy Ermineskin Band of Cree Indians from Calgary, it tells the story of the American Indian athlete, Billy Mills, who ran the 10,000-meter race and won the Olympic medal for the United States in Tokyo in 1964. Obviously influenced by *Chariots of Fire,* it is a long way down the scale compared with it, but on its own level it is a decent, honest film, with Robbie Benson giving a convincing performance as Mills and Pat Hingle playing his trainer with sympathy and understanding. Many Indians were deeply disappointed that an Indian actor did not play Mills, but it was reported that Mills himself insisted on Benson playing the role. *Running Brave* was directed with the customary skill and sensitivity we have come to expect from Donald Shebib, but unfortunately, he had his name removed from the film after a dispute with the producer over the final editing. While the finished version may not be the work Shebib wanted it to be, he has nothing to feel ashamed about.

In June 1984, the Minister of Communications announced his long-awaited, two-years in preparation film policy. It was news for one day and then—silence. This unexpected response occurred because the report said almost nothing, and as a result there is hardly anything to say about it; furthermore it is so badly written that it is hard to know what it is saying and what it stands for. The words "focuses" and "culture" are repeated *ad infinitum,* and the whole looks and sounds like a report from an advertising agency trying to sell a doubtful deal to a gullible client. In this case, however, it is a report from an incompetent government department to an indifferent public, a public that has come to expect nothing from an agency whose task it is to foster indigenous Canadian film-making and has repeatedly failed to do so because, like so many of the producers it supports and who are bent on selling out Canada to Hollywood, it lacks vision and resolve and appears not to believe in the cause it should espouse.

Mr. Fox shook his fist at the Americans again, from a safe distance, but as always, for the wrong reasons. He spoke about the cinemas' refusing to show Canadian films, but overlooked the fact that there are hardly any movies made in this country, which might honestly be called Canadian, for them to show. If he is shedding tears over the hundreds of pseudo-American films made here by our shabby producers over the past five years under the Capital Costs Allowance plan, then he cries alone, as the majority of them are a disgrace to this country and best left unshown. The genuine films, among them *The Grey Fox, Strange Brew, Ticket to Heaven, Suzanne, Maria Chapdelaine, Les Plouffe, The Tin Flute, The Wars, Bay Boy,* have been seen with varying degrees of success depending on the cinemas in which they were shown, their publicity, the reviews, the competition from other films, and the time of the year they opened—all factors that affect the outcome of any film, no matter where it is from, within the complex business of exhibition.

The policy does not significantly address the far more important subject of film distribution. In almost every other country, American films and others are distributed by local companies, but in Canada, all the American studios control their own distribution and maintain a tight grip on the showings of their films from head offices in New York and Los Angeles. This is an intolerable situation, which severely limits the possibilities of Canadian films getting into theaters. Independent Canadian distributors are rapidly going out of business since they cannot buy rights because of Hollywood's monopoly; and there are not enough Canadian films made to keep them in business. So they fail, and control by Hollywood grows stronger.

Although the report drones on about the need for Canadian identity, the most notable production activity (mainly in Toronto) since it was announced is an even greater number of American films and Canadian-American films with Hollywood players than were previously made, all heavily American in cast and content. The great betrayal, of course, coming almost immediately after the report, was the announcement by the producers of Mordecai Richler's *Joshua Then and Now* that the two most important roles in the book—Joshua, the central part, and his father—are played by two American actors, James Woods and Alan Arkin. The excuse, as always, is that as this is a $10 million production, and that box-office names must be used in order to secure showings of the film in the United States. Since when did the names of James Woods and Alan Arkin sell $10 million films? Once again, the many splendid Canadian actors who could have played these parts with a Canadian sensitivity are overlooked or forced to take the supporting roles. Woods is no more likely to project the complex and very Canadian character of Joshua than Richard Dreyfuss did as Duddy Kravitz. And now we are told that Nicolas Cage is the only suitable actor to play Ned Hanlan, in *The Boy in Blue,* a film about the world-champion sculler. Are Canadians on the screen forever to be represented by Americans?

No other country is so beholden to the American film industry as Canada. Our producers have consistently used American actors to play Canadians, who, quite naturally through the force of their personalities, turned their characters into Americans. The policy report should be asking why we are making $10 million productions of *Joshua* and *Louisiana,* which cannot earn their costs back in Canada (and sometimes not even abroad) instead of ten $1 million films, similar to the many British and Australian movies that would show this country to the world as they do theirs.

But the policy report, and the various regulations of the CFDC, the CCA, and the CRTC, do not rectify this. They do not ask why we cannot make films for ourselves instead of losing our characters in the greedy chase for the American market. Films about ourselves with our own actors would be far more appealing to audiences abroad. The CFDC, rather than encouraging and working with directors such as Don Shebib, Robin Spry, Zale Dalen, Micheline Lanctôt, and the many others who struggle to realize their projects, prefers instead to travel the world signing useless coproductions, the limited benefits from which are always in favor of the other countries, not Canada. It finally came up against the truth when the Australians refused to have anything to do with our shoddy practices; it learned what it had previously refused to recognize: that the world is contemptuous of our mostly "international," non-Canadian films.

Then there is the NFB—praised over the table while being kicked down into the cellar. The government's plans for the board would seem to spell an end to its valuable work. At times, the board leaves a lot to be desired, but it cannot always turn out masterpieces, and in the light of the failure of our cinema and TV films over the years, it has kept the fabric of our motion pictures Canadian in such a deep and lasting manner that the NFB is as much a part of people's lives as the CBC—without the CBC's appalling commercialism. To say—as the Applebaum-Hebert Report did—that the board has become irrelevant to our lives is absurd. The commissioners obviously did not go into the hundreds of small towns and cities whose public libraries and museums keep up regular showings of its films. There are many subjects that private producers cannot film because no one will pay them to make them. Without the NFB, what little there is of Canada on the TV, cinema, and library screens today would diminish into a few fleeting images.

The policy report's only positive aspect is in its description of the huge broadcast-film fund, variously mentioned as being worth $130 million to finance film programs for television. It would be interesting to hear from the media TV reviewers, many of whom seem to reside permanently in Hollywood, what genuine Canadian films are in production from the CBC and independent producers as a result of the infusion of funds from this scheme. We live in hope of interesting work to come reflecting the many phases of life in this country, but the statements being made by producers create unease: they are the tired excuses about the existence of Canadian films depending on working with American networks, studios, actors, and writers instead of our own, which previously resulted in the finished films being more about the United States than this country. Why is that producers seem to have the power to decide the noncharacter of Canadian films, with artists having no part to play and nothing to say?

Conclusions

In 1982 the National Film Theatre in London held a retrospective program of the films of the Quebec film-maker Jean-Pierre Lefebvre. The writer of the notes accompanying the announcement of this event pointedly remarked that "in recent years the Canadian industry's bad imitations of American potboilers have won few admirers abroad. But there is another Canadian cinema coming primarily out of Quebec." One could add to this that even if the potboilers were good imitations, it is doubtful that they would find admirers; but strange as it may seem, those pseudo-American films, good or bad, do have admirers in Canada, particularly in the popular press.

One hears a great deal about how Canadians are indoctrinated into the American way of life by the number of American films in their cinemas, by the amount of American programing on Canadian radio and TV stations, and by the flood of American books and magazines available in every variety and drugstore, bookshop and library. What no one can properly assess is the effect this has on Canadians, particularly the younger generation, in turning them into Americans. One hopes that the very act of living and being educated in Canada would help to offset this influence, but the fact is very obvious that there is so much that is American-influenced and inspired in every aspect of daily life, particularly on television and in the cinema, that Canadian character and identity are all but swamped. It is not funny when lawyers relate that people arrested by the police expect their arraignment and subsequent trial to proceed according to what they see on American television, or that children going to school expect to find the Stars and Stripes flag in their classroom.

Is it because so many Canadians live an American lifestyle through film and television that they are neither surprised nor disturbed on finding that Canadian films are really American? The way in which people show little concern about it would seem to bear out this contention. Furthermore, they react with hostility to those who question the Americanization of Canadian films, as though the expression of these doubts is an indication of anti-American feeling. The response is usually a defensive "What's wrong with being American?" or "What's wrong with admiring American films?" (the implication being that they are always better than Canadian programing), and "We should be grateful to have the Americans as our neighbors."

It goes without saying that no sensible person denies or disputes these feelings, not would anyone want to see the imposition of controls (which would be unworkable, anyway) on the amount of American material available in this country. But why does this admiration and acceptance of American films and television always seem to preclude the acceptance of and to deny the reality of anything Canadian? One of the penalties Canadians pay for acceptance of all things American is the loss of knowing what it really means to be Canadian. How far we have lost this is shown in our ready acceptance of the true-blue and honest portrayals of American society and settings in American films to the extent that, having so submerged our thoughts and feelings about anything Canadian, our country no longer exists in the form of subject, place, or presence to be considered worthwhile depicting in the cinema or on television.

To ask or expect, then, producers to make Canadian films that are set in and identify Canada (as all American films identify their place of action and backgrounds of their characters) with Canadian actors portraying Canadians, is to make oneself seem rather quaint and ridiculous. Who needs Canada on the screen? The academics of the cinema courses, the columnists and reporters in the media, and the politicians in the provincial and federal governments all seem to think it is beneath their dignity and out of the range of their concerns to even ask for such a reasonable state of affairs. Even worse, just to discuss the matter would make them seem petty and less international in outlook. Being a Canadian means being broad-minded enough to accept everything the world has to offer, while showing no concern whatsoever over the fact that little from one's own country is in evidence. No one objects to producers making decent profits from decent pictures, since this is the only way they can stay in business. But there are very real grounds on which to object when they make personal profits (as most have done) while making films at the taxpayers' expense that have nothing to do with Canada and all too often lose the money invested in them by others. The producers (who are more akin to hustlers than the serious producers one finds in Los Angeles and Europe) claim they give work to Canadian technicians, laboratories, and film-makers. However, they certainly are not giving work to Canadian actors, who must stand aside for Americans who, in most cases, are no more "box-office magic" than many of Canada's lesser known, but far more talented actors who remain unknown because their producers do not provide them with opportunities. But what does it profit creative people to be working on horror films and similar inanities that have no relevance to their lives or their society? This is precisely where Quebec film-makers have the advantage over their counterparts in the rest of Canada. They know who they are, what they are saying, and the lives they are depicting. As a result, Quebec has established its separate identity through the cinema.

All film-making is creative, and all film-makers take pride in their work. Most of them would like this work to reveal something about who they are and their backgrounds. This seldom happens in Canadian films. The producers deny them the opportunities that Quebec film-makers have, claiming that since Canadians are first cousins to the Americans and speak the same language, then their films should be like Americans' films. This is nonsense. Canada has much to portray that would be appealing to English-speaking audiences everywhere, just as the Australians have shown us fascinating glimpses of their life and history. Can any producer prove that *Meatballs* would have been any less successful in the United States had it contained a few matter-of-fact Canadian references? I doubt it. Did *Middle Age Crazy* have to be set in Houston? Are there no husbands in Canadian cities who get that middle-age feeling? Did *The Changeling* (filmed in Vancouver) have to pretend the setting was Seattle? Would Americans have recoiled in alarm and stayed away on hearing that the locale was Vancouver? Did *Threshold* have to be set in Washington? Do we not have extremely clever heart surgeons at work here? One could go on and on with the number of Canadian films that prefer to speak of Americans than of Canadians, made by producers with a sell-out mentality.

Audiences accept the fact that American films will be naturally American, that if a film is French, then it will be about France, and so on with German, Russian, British, Italian, and Swedish films; but when one expects that Canadian films should be about Toronto, Hamilton, London, Calgary, Edmonton, and places between and beyond, with references to the police force, newspapers, schools, shops, politics, streets and buses, and more, such statements are met with a stare that suggests that such activities in a Canadian setting would have no interest to anyone and would not be worthy enough to be put on film. Such is the subjugation of the Canadian identity in the mind of the general public. Yet when good Canadian films do appear and are given the opportunities to reach audiences, such as *Goin' down the Road, Outrageous,* and *The Grey Fox,* the public will respond, as if awakened from a trance, to the fact that there is a Canadian reality that makes interesting screen material. Unfortunately, there are so very few genuine Canadian films in English that the spark of interest is quickly extinguished. This has been an important factor over the years contributing to the public's indifference.

To add to one's confusion over what is and is not Canadian on the screens these days, Canada now has, in addition to films made in Canadian cities that are supposed to represent those in the States, "Canadian films" that were not made here and have nothing to do with the country and its people. Columnists and television reporters proudly referred to the "Canadian films" *Atlantic City* (formerly *Atlantic City USA*), which was nominated for an Academy Award, and *Quest for Fire,* an expensive oddity about prehistoric man that came to Canada as a France-Canada coproduction. There is very little about these films (and there are others) that is Canadian other than the money invested in them. Does the fact that they were paid for entirely or in part by Canadian banks and investment houses make them Canadian? The producers think so, of course, because they deal only in terms of commerce. But films are much more than this. They are a reflection of a country and its society, and values such as this cannot be found in films that are little more than international financial transactions. Where there is no creativity and no subject matter that is clearly Canadian, then by no stretch of the imagination can we say the result is Canadian. The supporters of these commercial transactions claim that Hollywood companies invest money in films made abroad that are not American. Sometimes they do, but Americans always have the interests of America at heart, and such films are never without creative participation by Americans or without reference to American influence. Furthermore, most countries with a steady production of indigenous motion pictures can afford, in the cultural as well as financial sense, to make some films that are not about themselves so to speak, because they are but a few among the many which are authentic. Canada has no indigenous films outside those made in Quebec, so how are we to find any satisfaction at all in such movies as *Atlantic City* and *Quest for Fire?* Are we supposed to feel pride because we made it possible for two French directors to make non-Canadian films? Most of us do not. The cynics will reply that what is important is that the films were made; but this is a glib, pseudointellectual reply. At this level we could go on forever making films that have nothing to do with the country that paid for them.

Motion pictures mean much more than this, and money is not always the deciding factor in determining the nationality of a film. An American company might, shall we say, finance entirely the making of a film of Mordecai Richler's *St. Urbain's Horseman* (a much-bandied-about possibility) in Montreal, written and directed by a Canadian with Canadian actors and technicians. This, quite simply, would be a Canadian film. But why should an American company do this? Yet they are more likely to do so because Canadians lack the desire and determination to do this themselves. Unfortunately, the moneymen in Canada's film activity have no faith in their country, no vision, and no imagination, and the CFDC does nothing to change this dismal state of affairs.

Producers are quick to excuse their non-Canadian films on the grounds that Canada has no writers and no stories to tell. However, the journal *Books in Canada* and the book-review sections of the daily newspapers are filled, month after month, with reviews of Canadian novels and works of nonfiction, most of which, even if not great literature, would make splendid films revealing the life and history of the country, quite apart from providing some extra money for the authors. Together with many fascinating Canadians plays that lend themselves to adaptation to the screen, we could be seeing a steady flow of small, intimate, inexpensive (by the $12 million standard), important films that would identify Canada, would please audiences in cinemas and on television, and would provide a visual record of times past and present. (Students in film courses at universities study American life in American classic films almost exclusively, and together with what they see in the cinemas and on television come to think this is their life too. There are no Canadian films to provide them with a counterbalance.) But time after time, film-makers, as well as producers, drawn hypnotically toward the United States, announce their interest in American books, subjects, and screenplays. There is nothing, it seems, of value in Canada. Just as discouraging is the fact that on those rare occasions when Canadian books of merit are filmed, such as Margaret Atwood's *Surfacing* and Hugh MacLennan's *Two Solitudes,* the producers fail them and distort them by using non-Canadian actors. The one worthwhile aspect about *Surfacing* is that it proves that what is said about Canadians being American, with no difference between them, is simply not true: the use of Joseph Bottoms and Kathleen Beller in *Surfacing* caused considerable damage to the essential Canadian quality of the story. They were out of place and out of their depths.

The use of film as historical evidence has tended to provoke argument about the value of newsreels and documentaries, but seldom about the value of the feature film. Yet it is the feature film that more accurately reflects the assumptions of the society that both produces it and flocks to see it. Whether we like it or not, the popular films of their time will tell future historians more about their societies than studies and surveys in documentary.

Understandably, contemporary historians and politicians have found an assertion such as this difficult to accept. It is partly a puritanical snobbery that still regards the cinema as lowbrow and vulgar, and partly a conservatism that accepts fiction, drama, and painting as historical evidence, but not motion pictures. Film becomes the medium through which an understanding of changing social attitudes becomes possible—but this is not the case in Canada. We have never made enough feature films about the various aspects of life to provide historians, researchers, sociologists, even audiences, with the evidence that can plainly be found in the films of other countries.

Will this situation ever change? It has yet to change in over eighty years of motion picture history.

One would need to be an incurable optimist to believe there is a promising future after so many disheartening setbacks. At one time, these could have been attributed to lack of money and opportunity and to absence of interest and support by governments. The failure of the tax-shelter (CCA) era, however, and the latter period of the CFDC, is tragic when considering the amount of money that was made available by the state, so little of which resulted in memorable films. Countless opportunities have been missed; there are very few chances left to put matters right. This state of affairs will not change until men of vision, courage, and belief in Canada are given the opportunity to run the CFDC, the NFB, and the CBC—and when private enterprise comes to understand that it cannot go on living high from paying low prices for American programing.

If there is a future, it lies predominantly with the CBC, which when stripped of its bureaucratic vice-presidents and commercials and its unwarranted infatuation with ratings, should associate itself with the NFB and independent film-makers, and, with the films of Britain's Channel Four and the BBC in mind, set about creating a continuous, living portrayal of Canadian life in all its many varied, dramatic, and colorful aspects. There will be no change, however, until all those concerned with making films for cinemas and television learn to put the interests of Canada first.

Part 3
The Credits
Canadian Films 1945–1984

The films listed in this section include the premiere or release date opposite the title, the production or releasing company, credits, place of premiere, running time, distributor (when applicable), cast, and brief description. Abbreviations used are: *prod.* (producer), *rel.* (release), *dir.* (director), *scen.* (writer), *cam.* (cinematography), *ed.* (editor), *prem.* (premiere), and *dist.* (distribution).

This filmography does not claim to list every film made in Canada. It primarily concerns those films made for showings in cinemas. However, when others such as documentary, television, or experimental films move into the theatrical distribution system, many are included. Canada's American films and some co-productions are noted, but American films shot on location in Canada or in studios for Pay-TV are not included.

For information other than that given here, the reader is referred to the detailed indexes, *Canadian Feature Films, Part 2: 1941–1963,* edited by Peter Morris (CFI: Ottawa, 1965); *Canadian Feature Films, Part 3: 1964–1969,* edited by Piers Handling (CFI: Ottawa, 1976); and to *New Canadian Films* and *Copie Zero* (1968 to 1984), published by the Cinémathèque Québecoise, Montreal.

PERE CHOPIN   April 1945

Prod. co. Renaissance Films; *dir.* Fedor Ozep; *scen.* Jean Desprez; *cam.* (b&w) Don Malkames; *ed.* Georges Freedand; *music* Rudolph Goehr. *Prem.* St. Denis Theatre, Montreal; 108 min.

Roles	*Cast*
Paul Dupont	Marcel Chabrier
Madeleine	Madeleine Ozeray
Le Prêtre	François Rozet
Pierre Dupont	Pierre Durand
Roger	Guy Moufette
Ginette	Ginette Letondal
Pierrot	Louis Rolland

Le Père Chopin **(1945).**

Comedy drama with music about two brothers from France who live in Quebec. One plays the organ and is very poor, the other is a financier and very rich.

BUSH PILOT   Nov. 1946

Rel. Dominion Productions Limited; *prod.* Larry Cromien; *dir.* Sterling Campbell; *scen.* Scott Darling; *cam.* (b&w) Edward Hyland; *sound* Edward Fenton; *ed.* Jack Ogilvie; *music* Morris C. Davis. 63 min.

Roles	*Cast*
Paul	Jack La Rue
Red	Austin Willis
Hilary	Rochelle Hudson

also: Frank Perry, Joe Carr, Florence Kennedy, Robert Christie, Gordon Burwash, Nancy Graham.

Romantic melodrama concerning the rivalry of two airmen brothers for the same girl.

La Forteresse **(1947).**

LA FORTERESSE (Whispering City)   Sept. 1947

Rel. Eagle Lion—J. Arthur Rank Film Distributors (Canada) Limited; *prod. co.* Quebec Production Corporation; *prod.* Paul L'Anglais; *dir.* Fedor Ozep; *scen.* Rian Jones and Leonard Lee, from an original story by George Zuckerman and Michael Lennox; *cam.* (b&w) Guy Roe; *music* Morris C. Davis; "Quebec Concerto" by André Mathieu; *Prem.* St. Denis Theatre, Montreal. 98 min. In French and English. The English version, *Whispering City,* starred Helmut Dantine, Paul Lukas, and Mary Anderson.

Roles	*Cast*
Michel Lacoste	Paul Dupuis
Marie Roberts	Nicole Germain
Albert Fredericks	Jacques Auger
Renée Brancourt	Mimi d'Estee
Edward Dupont	John Pratt
Nun	Lucie Poitras
Blanche Lacoste	Joy LaFleur
Police Inspector	George Alexander
Asst. Police Inspector	Henri Poitras

Pathological and romantic crime melodrama concerning the homicidal machinations of a seemingly immaculate patron of classical music.

SINS OF THE FATHERS   July 1948

Rel. Canadian Productions; *prod. co.* Larry Cromien Productions; *prod.* Cyril Strange; *dir.* Phil Rosen and Richard Jarvis; *scen.* Gordon Burwash; *cam.* (b&w) William Steiner; *music* Morris C. Davis; *ed.* Richard Jarvis. *Prem.* Royal Alexandra Theatre, Toronto, 93 min.

Roles	*Cast*
Dr. Ben Edwards	Austin Willis
Patsy Curran	Joy LaFleur
Marty Williams	John Pratt
Daphne	Phyllis Carter
Leona	Suzanne Avon
Charlie Mitchell	Frank Heron
Ellen Carter	Mary Barclay
Higgins	Gerald Rowan
Shorty	Norman Traviss

Anti-venereal disease melodrama set in a small Canadian town.

THE BUTLER'S NIGHT OFF   1948

Prod. co. Mount Royal Films; *dir.* Roger Racine; *scen.* Anton Van der Water, based on a story by Silvio Narizzano; *dial.* Stanley Mann; *cam.* (b&w) José Mena; *music* Neil Chotem. No release. 57 min. *Cast:* Paul Colbert, Peter Sturges, Eric Workman, Mary Lou Hennessy, Charles Rittenhouse, William Shatner, Maurice Gauvin, Robin Pratt, Michael Oliver, Leroy Fallana, Ken Ito.

Thought to be a comedy-drama about a butler who becomes romantically involved during his off-duty hours. William Shatner later found fame as a Shakespearean actor and as Captain Kirk in the long-running television series, *Star Trek*. He also played the Captain in Robert Wise's film version and in two subsequent versions.

LE CURE DE VILLAGE   Nov. 1949

Prod. co. Quebec Productions Corporation; *prod.* Paul L'Anglais; *dir.* Richard Jarvis; *scen.* Robert Choquette, based on his radio play; *cam.* (b&w) Roger Racine; *music* Morris C. Davis; *mus. dir.* Jean Deslauriers. *Prem.* St. Denis Theatre, Montreal, 85 mins. *Distr.* France-Film.

Roles	Cast
Le Curé	Ovila Legare
Juliette Martel	Lise Roy
Lionel Theberge	Denis Droulin
Marten	Paul Guevremont
Le Notaire	Camille Ducharme
Le Bedeau	Eugene Daignault

Le Curé de village (1949).

Le Gros Bill (1949).

La Veuvre Sirois	Jeanne Quintal
Honorine	Blanche Gautier
Mlle Jolicoeur	Juliette Huot

A tale of a Quebec village priest who is the religious head, counselor, and final authority in the town.

LE GROS BILL   Oct. 1949

Prod. co. Renaissance Films; *dir.* René Delacroix; *scen.* Jean Palardy; *cam.* (b&w) Jean Bochelet; *music* Maurice Blackburn. *Prem.* St. Denis Theatre, Montreal. 85 min. *Dist.* France-Film.

Roles	Cast
Clarina	Ginette Letondal
Bill	Yves Henry
Tante Mina	Juliette Beliveau
Alphonse	Maurice Gauvin
M Chouinard	Paul Guevremont
Mme Chouinard	Amanda Alarie
Arthur	Paul Berval
Le Notaire	Fred Ratte
Le Curé	Claude Lapointe

A Texan comes to Quebec to claim a farm he has inherited from his father. Unable to speak French, he runs into difficulties with the townspeople.

UN HOMME ET SON PECHE   Feb. 1949

Rel. Quebec Productions. *Prod.* Paul L'Anglais; *dir.* Paul Gury; *scen.* Claude Henri Grignon, from his radio play; *cam.* (b&w) Drummond Drury; *music* Hector Gratton. *Prem.* St. Denis Theatre, Montreal. 80 min. *Distr.* France-Film.

Roles	Cast

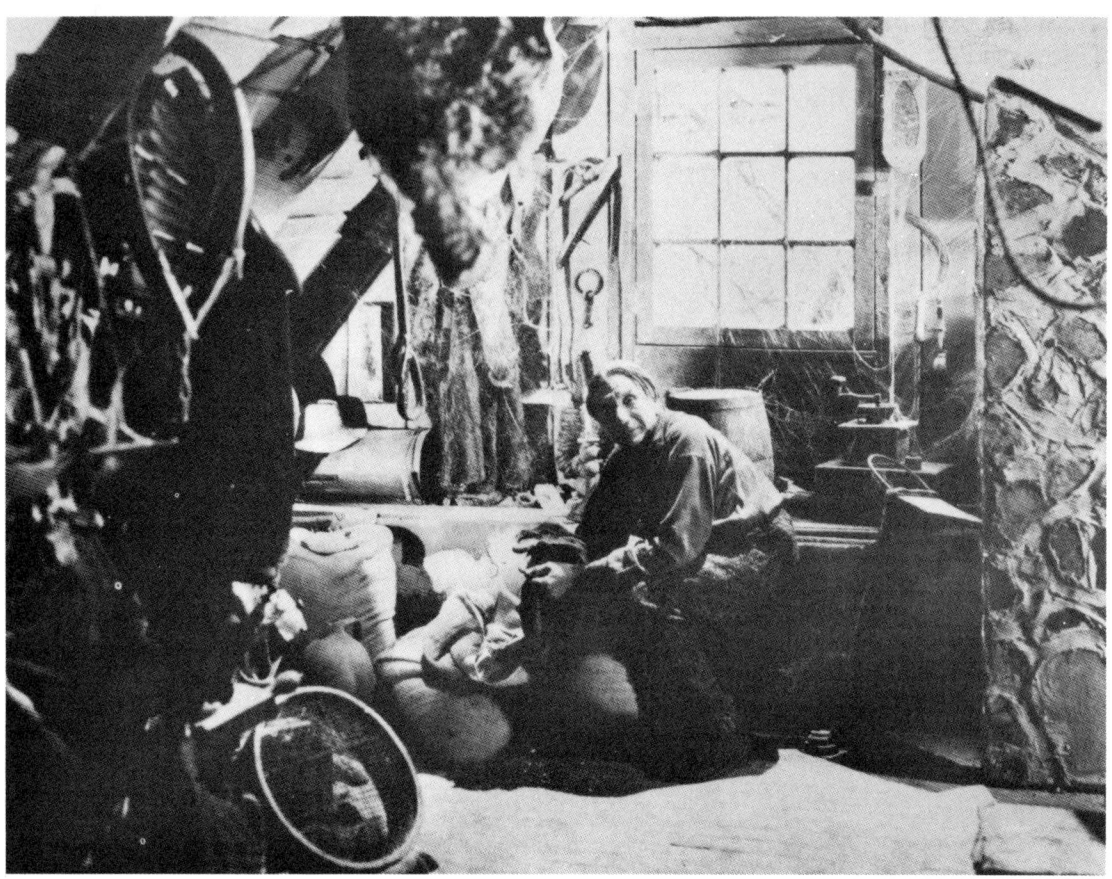

Un Homme et son péché **(1948).**

Séraphin **(1949).**

Seraphin	Hector Charland
Donalda	Nicole Germain
Alexis	Guy Provost
James de Bois	Henri Poitras
Artemise	Suzanne Avon
Wabo	George Alexander

Incidents in the life of the miser Seraphin and his pretty wife, Donalda.

SERAPHIN   Feb. 1950

Rel. Quebec Productions. *Prod.* Paul L'Anglais; *dir.* Jean Boisvert; *scen.* Claude-Henri Grignon; *cam.* (b&w) Drummond Drury; *music* Arthur Morrow. *Prem.* St. Denis Theatre, Montreal. 105 min. *Distr.* France-Film.

Roles	*Cast*
Seraphin	Hector Charland
Donalda	Nicole Germain
Alexis	Guy Provost
Artemise	Suzanne Avon
James de Bois	Henri Poitras
Waho	Arthur Lefebvre
Le Curé Labelle	Eddy Tremblay
Le Bébé	Alain Boisvert
Le Dr. Cyprien	Marcel Sylvain
Delima	Jeannette Teasdale
Mlle Angelique	Antoinette Grioux_

The further adventures of Seraphin the miser. A follow-up to *Un Homme et son péché*.

FOBIDDEN JOURNEY   Sept. 1950

Rel. United Artists; *prod. co.* Selkirk; *prod./dir./scen.* Richard Jarvis and Cecil Maiden; *cam.* (b&w) Roger Racine; *music* Oscar Morowetz. *Prem.* Princess Theatre, Montreal. 95 min.

Roles	*Cast*
Jan Bartik	Jan Rubes
Mary Sherritt	Susan Douglas
Professor Bartik	Gerry Rowan
Joe	Richard Kronold
Stub	Max Shoub
Shipping Agent	Rupert Caplan
Mme Duval	Blanche Gautier
Student	John Colicos
Aunt Sherritt	Eleanor Stuart
Dancer	Elizabeth Leese

Political melodrama about a fugitive from behind the Iron Curtain who gains illegal entry into Canada in order to spread anti-Communist propaganda.

LUMIERES DE MA VILLE   Oct. 1950
(Lights of My City)

Prod. co. Excelsior Film; *dir.* Jean-Yves Bigras; *scen.*

Les Lumières de ma ville (1950).

Jean Marie Poirier; *cam.* (b&w) Roger Racine; *music* Allen McIver. *Prem.* St. Denis Theatre, Montreal. 125 min. *Distr.* France-Film.

Roles	*Cast*
Roger Martin	Guy Maufette
Hélène Clement	Huguette Oligny
Marcel	Pierre Berval
Monique Fontaine	Monique Leyrac
The Editor	Albert Duquesne
The Captain	Paul Guevremont
Impresario	Maurice Gauvin
Denise	Denyse Proulx

Romance dealing with the affairs of a nightclub singer, a composer, and an author.

SON COPAIN   Dec. 1950
(The Unknown from Montreal)

Son Copain (1950).

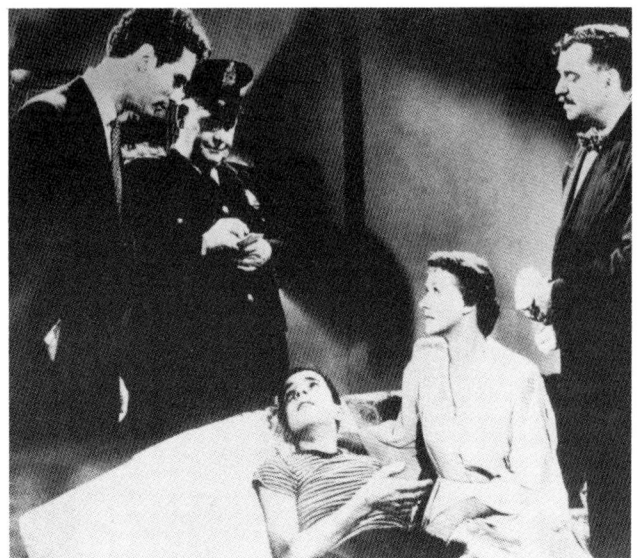

Le Rossignol et les clôches **(1951).**

Prod. co. Quebec Productions Corporation and Eclectiques Film of Paris; *prod.* Paul L'Anglais; *dir.* Jean Devaivre; *scen.* Charles Exbrayat, Jean Devaivre and Ted Allan; *cam.* (b&w) Philippe Agostini; *music* Joseph Kosma. *Prem.* St. Denis Theatre, Montreal. 110 min. *Distr.* France-Film.

Roles	Cast
Pierre	René Dory
Hélène	Patricia Roc
Paul	Paul Dupuis

Anton	Albert Miller
Lawyer	Guy Maufette
RCMP Agent	Armand Leguet
Anton's friend	Jacques Langevin

A chase-melodrama set in Paris and Quebec about a Royal Canadian Mounted policeman whose friend is an acquaintance of a supposed murderer whom the RCMP seek to arrest. In two versions, English and French, with the same cast.

ROYAL JOURNEY   Dec. 1951

Documentary. *Rel.* United Artists (USA), Columbia (Canada), and GFD (UK); *prod. co.* National Film Board; *prod.* Tom Daly; *dir.* David Bairstow; *cam.* (Eastman Ektacolor) Osmond Borrodaille, Ron Alexander, Dennis Gillson, Bob Humble, Wally Sutton, Grant McLean, and Lorne Batchelor; *ballet sequence dir.* Gudrun Parker; *ed.* Victor Jobin and Ronald Dick; *tech. super.* Gerald Graham; *music* Louis Applebaum; *commentary* Leslie McFarlane. *Prem.* Nelson Theatre, Ottawa. 52 min.

A fascinating record of the Canadian tour of Princess Elizabeth and Prince Philip during Autumn 1951. *Royal Journey* was the first film to use the new Eastman Ektacolor process.

LE ROSSIGNOL ET LES CLOCHES   March 1952

Prod. co. Quebec Productions Syndicat du Film

Etienne Brûlé, gibier de potence **(1952).**

La Petite Aurore l'enfant martyre (1952).

Gerard Barbeau; *prod.* Richard Jarvis; *dir.* René Delacroix; *scen.* Joseph Schull; *cam.* (b&w) Roger Racine; *music* Allen McIver; *musical dir.* Jean Deslauriers. *Prem.* St. Denis Theatre, Montreal. 92 min. *Distr.* France-Film.

Roles	Cast
Guy	Gerard Barbeau
Nicole Payette	Nicole Germain
René	Jean Coutu
Le Curé	Clement Latour
L'Evêque	Hector Charland
Madame Boyer	Juliette Beliveau
Jeanne	Juliette Huot
Antonio	Ovila Legare

Musical comedy about the efforts of a village curé to raise money to buy new bells for the church.

LA PETITE AURORE,   April 1952
L'ENFANT MARTYRE

Prod. co. Alliance Cinematographique Canadienne Inc.; *dir.* Jean-Yves Bigras; *scen.* Emile Asselin; *cam.* (b&w) Roger Racine; *music* Germaine Janelle. *Prem.* St. Denis Theatre, Montreal. 104 min. *Distr.* France-Film.

Roles	Cast

Aurore	Yvonne Laflame
Marie-Louise	Lucie Mitchell
Théodore	Paul Desmarteau
Le Curé	Marc Forrez
Delphine	Therese McKinnon
Catherine	Jeannette Bertrand
Abraham	Jean Lajeunesse
Le Docteur	Roland D'Amour
Maurice	Roch Poulin
Tante Malvina	Nana de Varenne

Psychological study of a woman's hatred of her stepchild, based on an actual case in which the child was cruelly murdered.

ETIENNE BRULE,   Sept. 1952
GIBIER DE POTENCE
(The Immortal Scoundrel)

Prod. co. Carillon Pictures; *prod./dir.* Melburn Turner; *scen.* Jeannette Downing, adapted from the book *The Immortal Scoundrel* by J. H. Cranston; *cam.* (Anscolor) Melburn Turner, Georges Delanae, and Claude Rondeau; *sound* Stanley Clemson and Tom Derbyshire. *Prem.* St. Denis Theatre, Montreal. 100 min. *Distr.* France-Film.

Roles	Cast
Etienne Brulé	Paul Dupuis

Tit-Coq (1953).

Samuel de Champlain	Jacques Auger
Agonsa, Huron Princess	Ginette Letondal
Gayonena, Huron Princess	Paulette Deguise
Janendo, Huron Warrior	Gabriel Gascon
Serge Pelletier	Guy Hoffman
Père Jean de Brebeuf	Lionel Villeneuve
Sagida, Huron Doctor	Louis Thomas
Ojekwa, Iroquois Chief	Pierre Dulos
Odoneo, Huron Chief	Aimé Maior
Nika, Huron Warrior	Thomas Taylor
Admiral Kirk	Donald McGill
Aide-de-Camp de l'Admiral	Peter Jennings
Un Chief Indien	Tom Grand Louis
Mousquetaires	Pierre Rondeau and Réal Lemieux

Early French-Canadian history of the adventures among the Indians of Etienne Brulé, an early explorer and protégé of Champlain. The first full-length Canadian film in color.

TIT-COQ   Feb. 1953

Prod. co. Gratien Gelinas Productions; *prod.* Gratien Gelinas; *assoc. prod.* Paul L'Anglais; *dir.* René Delacroix; *codir.* Gratien Gelinas; *scen.* Gratien Gelinas, from his play of the same name; *prod. mgr.* Roger Garand; *photog. dir.* Akas Farkas; *cam.* (b&w) José Mena; *ed.* Anton Van der Water and Roger Garand; *sets* Michel Ambrogi; *music* Morris C. Davis and Maurice Blackburn. *Prem.* St. Denis Theatre, Montreal. 104 min. *Distr.* France-Film.

Roles	*Cast*
Tit-Coq	Gratien Gelinas
Marie-Ange	Monique Miller
Father Desilets	Fred Barry
Padre	Paul Dupuis
Germaine	Denise Pelletier
Jean-Paul Desilets	Clement Latour
Aunt Clara	Juliette Beliveau
Mother Desilets	Amanda Alarie
Camp Commander	George Alexander
Leopold Vermette	Jean Duceppe
Rosie	Corinne Conley
Uncle Alcide	Henri Poitras

Tit-Coq, a shy, unhappy little man, without friends and self-conscious of his illegitimate birth, finds unexpected happiness in his love for Marie-Ange. But while he is away during the war, her parents persuade her to marry another man. On his return, Tit-Coq again finds himself alone in the world.

COEUR DE MAMAN   Sept. 1953

Prod. co. Frontier Productions Ltd.; *prod.* Richard Jarvis; *dir.* René Delacroix; *scen.* René Delacroix, from a play by Henri Deyglun; *photog. dir.* Drummond Drury; *cam.* (b&w) José Mena; *ed.* Anton Van der Water; *sound* Marc Audet; *music* Germaine Janelle. *Prem.* St. Denis Theatre, Montreal. 108 mins. *Distr.* France-Film.

Roles	*Cast*
Marie Paradis	Jeanne Demons
Celeste	Rosanna Seaborn
Suzy	Denyse St-Pierre
Jacques	Jean-Paul Dugas
Francois	Paul Guevremont
Doctor	Paul Desmarteaux
Joseph	Jean-Paul Kingsley
Pauline	Yvonne Laflamme
Msgr. Payot	Henri Norbert

The trials of a mother, following the death of her husband, when her son, who is her only means of support, is sent to prison after being falsely accused of a crime his father had committed.

L'ESPRIT DU MAL   Feb. 1954

Prod. co. Frontier Films Ltd.; *prod.* Richard Jarvis; *dir.* Jean-Yves Bigras; *scen.* Louis Pelland, from an original story by Henri Deyglun; *photog. dir.* Osmond Borradaile; *cam.* (b&w) M. Jackson Samuels; *ed.* A. Van der Water; *sound* Marc Audet and André de Tonnancour; *musical dir.* Jean Deslauriers. *Prem.* St. Denis Theatre, Montreal. 90 min. *Distr.* France-Film.

Roles	*Cast*
Virginia Trudeau	Rosanna Seaborn
Ginette Trudeau	Denyse St. Pierre
Brassilov	Roger Garceau
Johnny Macdonald	Robert Rivard
Mr. Trudeau	Camille Ducharme
Pierre	Pierre Valcour

Coeur de maman (1953).

Mrs. Macdonald	Marthe Thiery
Mr. Macdonald	Edouard Wooley
Maid Justine	Christianne Ranger

also: Jean Marc Morissette, Paul Blouin, Pierrette Lachance, Josee Vincent. This was the last Quebec feature-fiction film for ten years.

A conniving stepmother attempts to marry her daughter to the mentally retarded son of a wealthy family.

THE LITTLE CANADIAN   June 1955

Prod. co. St. Lawrence Pictures Corp. Ltd.; *prod.* Melburn Turner; *dir./scen./ed.* Melburn Turner; *cam.* (Ansco color) Joe Robb; *sound* William Foster; *sets* Ethel Beedell. *Prem.* Odeon, Kingston. 75 min.

Roles	*Cast*
The Deacon	Wallace Havelock Robb
Bruce Lawrence	Robert Agar
Joan Todd	Diane MacMillan

also: Edythe Millman, Ronald Grant, Gary Shortcliffe, Margaret Shortcliffe, George Grant, Airlie Robb, Allan Anderson, William Angus, Kerrie Meek, Kevin Robert Turner, David William Robb, and Duke, the Wonder Dog.

Rustic comedy about an eccentric writer living in the country and a youth who marries his daughter.

Shot in 16mm and enlarged to 35mm.

LA SACRIFIEE   Sept. 1955

Prod. co. Centre sociale de cinématographie de Montreal; *prod.* Benjamin Belisle; *dir./cam.* (b&w) Benjamin Belisle; *scen.* Paul Gauthier; *ed.* Benjamin Belisle and Madame Belisle; *music* Madeleine Tremb-

lay; *post-synchronized sound* Fernande Beaulieu. *Prem.* L'Islet. 94 mins.

Cast: Pierrette Gosselin, Denise Bourque, Thérèse Bourque, Renée Gamache, and Jean Morin.

A young woman is secretly in love with a young doctor, who has similar undeclared feelings for her. However, her sister is jealous of this relationship and wants to destroy it, so she declares her love for the doctor. The other sister leaves for a convent.

(Shot on location in 16mm in Chicoutimi, Jonquiere, L'Islet, Montmagny, and in the main centers of Lac St.-Jean and Abitibi in the autumn and winter of 1955, this was very much a cooperative venture, although Belisle financed the whole production. It was both his and Gauthier's first feature, designed more as a learning project than a film that would be released. It was shot when those involved could take the time away from their regular jobs and consequently was quite difficult to make. Belisle has made only one other feature, *L'amour du couple* (1973). There is virtually no written material on *La Sacrifiee.*)

LE VILLAGE ENCHANTE   March 1956

Prod./dir. Marcel Racicot and Réal Racicot; *scen.* Réal Racicot; *music* Emilien Allard; *nar.* Pierre Dagenais. *Prem.* St. Denis Theatre, Montreal. 62 mins. *Distr.* France-Film.

A chapel bell with magical qualities affects the lives of a group of Canadian pioneers clearing land in the wilderness. When the bell rings, the dry land yields a bountiful harvest, enemies are reconciled, and a child brightens a lonely home.

The first Canadian feature-length animated film. The authors devoted all their spare time for six years in order to produce it, but it was not a success. Critics

L'Esprit du mal (1954).

found the script and dramatic construction weak and the animation a pale imitation of Disney.

OEDIPUS REX   Aug. 1956

Prod. co. Oedipus Rex Productions Ltd.; *prod.* Leonard Kipnis; *assoc.* Samuel E. Friedman; *dir.* Tyrone Guthrie; *cam.* (color) Roger Barlow; *ed.* Irving Lerner; *music* Louis Applebaum; *costumes, sets, masks* Tanya Moiseiwitsch. *Prem.* Edinburgh Film Festival 1956. 75 min. *Distr.* (USA) Motion Pictures Distributors, Inc., N.Y. Photographed in Eastmancolor at Canadian Film Industries Ltd., Toronto.

Roles	*Cast*
Oedipus	Douglas Campbell
Jocasta	Eleanor Stuart
Creon	Robert Goodier
Tiresias	Donald Davis
Priest and Herdsman	Eric House
Shepherd	Tony van Bridge
Messenger	Douglas Rain
Chorus Leader	William Hutt
Daughters	Nomi Cameron and Barbara Franklin
Nurse	Gertrude Tyas
Members of the chorus	Robert Christie, Roland Bull, Edward Follows, Bruno Gerussi, David Gardner, Edward Holmes, Richard Howard, Roland Hewgill, James Manser, Louis Negin, Grant Reddick, William Shatner, Bruce Swerdfager, and Neil Vipond.

Based on the tragedy by Sophocles. The son of a king kills his father in error and marries his mother. On becoming king, he discovers the truth of his situation, puts out his eyes, and ends his life wandering in exile.

A film of the play as staged by the Stratford Shakespearean Festival of Stratford, Ontario, 1955.

A DANGEROUS AGE   May 1958

Prod./dir./scen. Sidney J. Furie; *cam.* (b&w) Herbert S. Alpert; *ed.* David Nicholson; *art dir.* Harry Maxfield; *music* Phil Nimmons. *Prem.* Academy Cinema, London. 70 min. *Distr.* (UK), Films de France. Filmed in Toronto at Meridian Studios and on location in 1957.

Cast: Ben Piazza, Anne Pearson, Aileen Seaton, Kate Reid, Shane Rimmer, John Sullivan, Austin Willis, Barbara Hamilton, Lloyd Jones, and Claude Rae.

Unpretentious romantic melodrama describing a young couple's unsuccessful attempts to wed without their parents' consent.

NOW THAT APRIL'S HERE   June 1958

Prod. co. Klenman-Davidson; *prod.* Norman Klenman and William Davidson; *dir.* William Davidson; *scen.* Norman Klenman, from four short stories by Morley Callaghan; *photog. dir.,* William H. Gimmi CSC; *cam.* (b&w) M. Jackson Samuels; *sound* James Willis; *ed.* Klenman-Davidson; *costumes* Thelma Timmins; *music* John Bath. *Prem.* Towne Cinema, Toronto. 90 min. *Distr.* (Canada) IFD. Filmed on location in Toronto. Introduced by Raymond Massey.

Silk Stockings: Don Borisenko, Judy Welch, Beth Amos, Michael Mann, Sheila Billings, and Pam D'Orsay. *Rocking Chair:* John Drainie, Katherine Blake, Alan Hood, and Art Jenoff. *The Rejected One:* Tony Gray, Nancy Lou Gill, Fred Diehl, Paisley Maxwell, and Josephine Barrington. *A Sick Call:* Walter Massey, Georges Toupin, Kathy McNeil, Anna Collings, and Ralph Carston.

Silk Stockings is about a shy young boy attracted to his landlady's daughter. He buys her a pair of stockings for her birthday, but when she wears them to go out with her boyfriend he attempts to stop her. *Rocking Chair* tells of a widower and his lonely life now that his wife is dead. His wife's close friend, an unmarried woman, tries to befriend him and make him forget the past. *The Rejected One* is about a young man from a reserved family who falls in love with a simple shopgirl, and of her first meeting with his family. *A Sick Call,* the final story, is concerned with a husband who opposes the visit of a priest to his sick wife, fearing that the church will come between them.

This film was the first feature by the partnership of Bill Davidson and Norman Klenman, though they had earlier made several documentaries and worked as a writer/director team on CBC's *Graphic*. They purchased the film rights to Callaghan's four stories (published in the collection *Now That April's Here* in 1936) in July 1957, began casting in November 1957 and shooting on February 1, 1958. During the four-week shooting schedule they filmed entirely on location with interiors shot in a variety of homes and buildings. The production cost $75,000. An adaptation of the screenplay for the four episodes was published in *Liberty,* July, August, September, and October 1958.

Exterior scenes for the following British and Hollywood films were shot in Canada during 1957 and 1958:

Hollywood productions

WOLF DOG	Fox-Regal Films
FLAMING FRONTIER	Fox-Regal Films
	(Both filmed in Ontario)

The Abbey of Monte Cassino (1959).

British productions

HIGH TIDE AT NOON   Jaro
(Filmed in Nova Scotia)

INTENT TO KILL   Zonic
(Filmed in Montreal)

THE BLOODY BROOD   Oct. 1959

Prod. co. Kay Film Productions, Meridian Studios, Toronto; *prod./dir.* Julian Roffman; *assoc. prod.* Yvonne Taylor and Ralph Foster; *orig. script* Anne Howard Bailey; *scen.* Elwood Ullman and Ben Kerner; *photog. dir.* (b&w) Eugen Shuftan; *sound* Jack Locke; *ed.* Robert Johnson; *art dir.* David Ballou; *sets* Robert Byrnes; *costumes* Marie Day; *music* Harry Freedman. 70 min.

Cast: Jack Betts, Barbara Lord, Peter Falk, Robert Christie, Ronald Hartman, William Brydon, Ronald Taylor, Michael Zenon, Sammy Sales, Kenneth Wickes, George Sperdakos, Billy Kowalchuk, Carol Starkman, Rolf Carston, and Ann Collins.

A tale of love, murder, and pursuit among young people of the Beat Generation.

A COOL SOUND FROM HELL   Nov. 1959
(The Young and the Beat)

Prod./scen./dir. Sidney J. Furie; *ed.* David Nicholson; *cam.* (b&w) Herbert S. Alpert; *art dir.* Jack McCullough; *music* Phil Nimmons. 70 min. Distribution: International Film Distributors. Filmed at Toronto International Film Studios and on location.

Cast: Anthony Ray, Kim Smith, Ronald Taylor, Madeleine Kronby, Alan Crowfoot, Murray Westgate,

Tom Harvey, Walter Massey.

A young man becomes disillusioned with the activities of the Beat Generation.

IVY LEAGUE KILLERS   1959

Prod. co. Ivy League Films Ltd.; *prod.* Norman Klenman and William Davidson; *dir./ed.* William Davidson; *scen.* Norman Klenman; *photog. dir.* (b&w) William Gimmi; *cam.* M. Jackson Samuels; *sound* James Willis; *score* John Bath; *song (words and music)* Igors Gavon; *costumes* Thelma Timmins; *art dir.* Leif B. Pederson. 70 min. (Released in 1964 under the title *The Fast Ones.*) Distribution: Astral Films. Filmed on location in Toronto.

Cast: Don Borisenko, Don Francks, Barbara Bricker, Barry Lavender, Patrick Desmond, Jean Templeton, Martin Lager, Jon Ringham, John Paris, Igors Gavon, George Carron, Boyd Jackson and the Black Diamond Riders, Rolf Carston and Art Jenoff.

A group of rich, idle youths think up "the perfect crime" to demonstrate their superiority over a rival motorcycle gang. They underrate the initiative of their victim and find themselves involved with the police.

THIS MOST GALLANT AFFAIR   Nov. 1959

Documentary. *Prod./dir.* Arthur J. Kelly; *scen.* Agnes M. Anderson; *tech. sup.* Curtis Harrison. 70 min. *Distr.* (Canada) Rank Film Distributors Ltd. *Narration* John Fisher.

A color film shot in 16mm and printed in 35mm about the Dieppe Raid using actual newsreel photography of Canadian forces engaged in the event.

THE ABBEY OF MONTE CASSINO   1959–60

Semi-documentary. *Prod. co.* Arthur J. Kelly Productions (Brantford, Ontario); *prod.* Arthur J. Kelly; *asst. prod.* Curtis Harrison; *scen.* Agnes M. Anderson; *tech. work* Crawley Film Ltd., Ottawa. 60 min. *Narration* Hugh Bender. From actual wartime footage of the Italian battle. In both color and b&w.

The film deals with Canadian and U.S. soldiers in the Battle of Monte Cassino and the reluctance of the Allies to bomb the famous Monte Cassino Abbey occupied by German troops.

HIRED GUN (The Devil's Spawn)   1959

Prod. co. Dairy Production; *prod./dir.* Lindsay Shonteff; *asst. prod.* James Beggs; *scen.* Lindsay Shonteff; *photog. dir.* (b&w) Herb Alpert CSC; *sound* Les Hadley; *ed.* Lindsay Shonteff; *continuity* Christine Murray; *sets* Edgar Keenan; *costumes* Malabar Ltd.; *optical effects* Film Opticals Ltd.; *theme song* "Hired

Gun," Lesley Pouliot; *music* Fred Tudor. 60 min. Distribution: Astral Films. Filmed on location and at Meridian Studio, Toronto.

Cast: Don Borisenko, Tess Tory, Jan Shannon, Art Jenoff, Ken James, Gordon Clark, James Beggs, Michael Zenon, Buddy Fernes, Jim Peddie, Ed Holmes, Bill Williams, James Barron, Mike Conway, Spud Abbot, Al Waxman, Bert Hilkman, and Garrick Hagon.

A gunfighter, hired by farmers to stop the molestation of their women by cowboys from a large ranch in the district, is killed by a farmer with whose wife he becomes involved.

WINGS OF CHANCE   March 1961

Prod. co. Tiger Productions; *exec. prod.* Lorne H. Reed; *prod.* Larry Matanski; *prod. mgr.* Jack L. Copeland; *dir.* Edward Dew; *scen.* Patrick Whyte, based on the John Patrick Gullese novel *Kirby's Gander; cam.* (color) Leonard Claremont; *ed.* Walter Hannemann; *music* Michael Anderson. 76 min. Distribution: Universal Films. Filmed in Calgary and on location in Alberta.

Cast: Jim Brown, Frances Rafferty, Richard Trotter, and Patrick Whyte.

The hazards and experiences of a bush pilot in Northwestern Canada.

THE MASK (The Eyes of Hell)   1961

Prod. co. Taylor-Roffman with Beaver-Champion Productions; *dir.* Julian Roffman; *assoc. prod.* Yvonne Taylor, Frank Taubes, Sandy Haver, and Jean Lenaur; *ed.* Stephen T. Mar; *scen.* Frank Taubes and Harry Olive; *photog.* (b&w), Herbert Alpert; *special process photog.* (using StereoVision camera developed by the UK National Research Council) James B. Gordon; *special effects* Herman G. Townsley; *stereoscopic control* Charles W. Smith; *sound* Willard B. Goodman; *score* Louis Applebaum. 95 min. *Distr.* Warner Bros. In 3-D.

Cast: Paul Stevens, Claudette Nevins, Bill Walker, Anne Collings, Leo Leyden, Martin Lavut, Norman Ettinger, Eleanor Beecroft, Bill Bryden, and Ray Lawler.

A psychiatrist is visited by a man who claims to have committed a murder while under the influence of an Indian ritual mask unearthed in South America. Though the psychiatrist is sceptical, he himself experiences fearful hallucinations and a compulsion to strangle his receptionist. When a colleague demands tests of the mask under his supervision and his fiancée threatens to tell the police, the psychiatrist goes berserk. The police eventually overcome him as he

tries to strangle his fiancée and the mask is returned to the museum.

IT HAPPENED IN CANADA   1961

Prod./dir./scen./photog./ed. Luigi Petrucci; *music* Carmine Rizzo. 96 min. (b&w). Italian dialogue.

Cast: Nello Zordan, Gisela Zdunke, Dedena Morella, and Pino Ubaldo.

Produced independently in Toronto in 1960–61. Premiere (with English subtitles) at the Christie Theatre, Toronto, February 27, 1962. No general release in Canada. Released in Italy by Italo-American Films.

Rita, a young Italian teacher, comes to Canada to meet Andrea, the man her parents have arranged for her to marry. Andrea is a 45-year-old widower and Rita finds she cannot love him but her desire to return to Italy subsides when she falls in love with Carlo, Andrea's handsome nephew. Carlo is a wastrel who has fathered an illegitimate child by his earlier love, Carmela, but he soon turns into a hard-working laborer under Rita's influence. Carlo is killed in an accident. Rita determines to return to Italy but is again prevented by the death of Carmela. She decides instead to care for the now-orphaned child.

A production by enthusiastic nonprofessionals. Petrucci had studied at the Rome Film School but worked for eight years in Canada as a salesman to save enough money to make this film. The actresses were all local amateurs. It was photographed entirely in Toronto; only the music and sound track were prepared in Italy. Production, on a low budget, took almost two years.

1 + 1 (The Kinsey Report;   Aug. 1961
Exploring the Kinsey Report)

Prod. co. Flourite Ltd.; *prod./scen./dir.* Arch Oboler, and based on his play *Mrs. Kingsley's Report; photog. dir.* (b&w) George Jacobson; *music* John Bath; *ed.* Charles W. Schaeffer; 114 min. *Prem:* Stratford Film Festival. Film is in six parts with Leo G. Carroll as the star. Leading players in the stories: *Honeymoon:* Hilda Brauner and William Taylor. *Homecoming:* Kate Reid, Ernest Graves, and Richard Janaver. *The Divorce:* June Duprez, Austin Willis, Douglas Rain. *Average Man:* Jane Rose and Truman Smith. *Baby:* Rita Gardner and Jack Betts.

Professor Logan addresses a symposium on the Kinsey Reports. As he discusses the various statistics, individual members of the audience reflect on their personal experiences. *Honeymoon*—a newly married couple wonder if they were right to have had premarital sexual relations. They decide they were because the world might have ended before they married. *Homecoming*—a lonely wife feels she is growing old and passionless through the continued absence of

Les Brûlés (The Promised Land) **(1958).**

her husband on business. When he returns home after a long trip she confesses that, although she loves him deeply, her loneliness has led to her infidelity with another man. *The Divorcee*—a divorcee is taken advantage of by a distinguished middle-aged playboy. *Average Man*—a fat businessman regrets that he is not represented in the statistics in the Kinsey Report and sets out to taste the "forbidden fruit." He meets a former girlfriend, tries to seduce her, but she has to baby-sit for her grandchildren. *Baby*—a young wife dares not tell her husband she is pregnant and tries to secure an illegal abortion. The sordidness prevents her from going through with it and she confesses to her husband, who in fact is overjoyed. The film ends with *Lecture Hall,* a general discussion by members of the symposium. This was an unusually frank subject for its time, but foolish in treatment.

Hollywood Productions, 1960–61

The Canadians (Fox) and *Nikki, Wild Dog of the North* (Disney) were filmed entirely in Canada during 1960–61.

TEN GIRLS AGO   1962

Prod. co. Am-Can; *prod.* Ed Gollin; *dir.* Harold Daniels; *scen.* Peter Farrow; *photog. dir.* Lee Garmes; *cam.* (Eastmancolor) Jackson Samuels; *ed.* Dave

Nicholson; *sound* Russ Heisey; *makeup* Valerie Shand; *music and songs* Joe Hartnell and Sammy Fine. 95 min. Distribution: IFD (Canada) and U-I (USA) (not released). Produced in Eastmancolor and Panavision.

Cast: Buster Keaton, Bert Lahr, Eddie Foy, Jr., Dion, Risella Bain, Jan Miner, Diane Scaville, Beth Jones, Marguerite Gray, Austin Willis, and Eric Clavering.

A musical-comedy satire on the television industry.

LES BRULES (The Promised Land)   June 1962

Prod./dist. National Film Board of Canada; *prod.* Léonard Forest, Guy Glover; *dir.* Bernard Devlin; *scen.* Devlin, based on the novel *Nuages sur les brûlés (Clouds over the Clearing)* by Hervé Biron; *cam.* (b&w), Georges Dufaux; *ed.* David Mayerovitch. French and English versions. Released in four parts on CBC-TV and as a film running 97 min. (Produced in 1958.)

Cast: Félix Leclerc, Jean Lajeunesse, J. Leo Gagnon.

An interesting re-creation in dramatized form of the story of the settlement of the Abitibi region of Quebec during the Depression years of the thirties. The new community must suffer fires, storms, and social difficulties before an established order is created with the building of homes, the church, and the school.

Pour la suite du monde (1963).

Hollywood Productions, 1961–62

Exteriors for *Big Red* were filmed in Quebec during the summer of 1961 and *The Incredible Journey* was shot in Toronto in the fall of 1962. Both were Walt Disney productions released through Empire.Universal Films Ltd. in Canada.

POUR LA SUITE DU MONDE   May 1963
(So That the World Goes On)

Documentary. *Prod. and Dist.* National Film Board of Canada; *prod.* Fernand Dansereau; *dir.* Pierre Perrault and Michel Brault; *cam.* (b&w), Michel Brault and Bernard Gosselin; *ed.* Werner Nold; *sound* Marcel Carriere; *music* Jean Cousineau, guitar, and Jean Meunier, flute. French language with English subtitles. First shown at the Cannes Film Festival 1963 as the official Canadian entry. 105 min.

Cast: Leopold Tremblay, Alexis Tremblay, Abel Harvey, Louis Harvey, and Joachim Harvey.

This film in the Flaherty tradition tells of the people of the Ile-aux-Coudres (an island in the St. Lawrence, 70 miles downstream from the city of Quebec) and of their attempts to revive the hunting of the Beluga whale. Among the customs revived with this endeavor are the Lenten festivities, the auction sales for the benefit of souls in purgatory, and the jigs and customs dating back to the discovery of Canada.

SEUL OU AVEC D'AUTRES   May 1963
(Alone or with Others)

Prod. co./rel. Association Générale des Etudiants de l'Université de Montréal; *prod.* Denis Heroux; *dir.* Michel Brault and Gilles Groulx; *scen.* Denys Arcand and Stephane Venne; *cam.* (b&w) Michel Brault; *music* Stephane Venne. Shown in the Critics' Section out-of-competition at the Cannes Film Festival 1963. 65 min. In French.

Cast: Nicole Braun, Pierre Letourneau, Marie-José Raymond, Michelle Boulizon, Carl Mailhot, and Marcel Saint-Germain.

This film combines the styles and techniques of the "new wave" and "cinéma vérité" movements to reveal the lives of several students, who talk into the camera about their thoughts and problems.

THE SWEET AND THE BITTER   1963

A tout prendre (1963).

Drylanders (1963).

Prod. co. Commonwealth; *prod./scen./dir.* James Clavell; *cam.* (b&w) Monk Askins; *score* Paul Dunlop; *ed.* Douglas Robinson. 91 min. *Distr.* (UK) British Lion. (The film was made in 1963. There was no North American release due to legal difficulties.) (James Clavell later found fame as the author of *Shogun* and other novels.)

Cast: Yoko Tani, Paul Richards, Torin Thatcher, Jane Mallett, Ishimoto, and Verle Cooter.

A love story about a Japanese girl and a Canadian boy set in Vancouver.

A TOUT PRENDRE   Aug. 1963
(Take It All) (The Way It Goes)

Prod. co. Les Films Cassiopée–Orion Films; *dir./scen./ed.* Claude Jutra; *cam.* (b&w) Michel Brault and Jean-Claude Labrecque; *music* Jean Cousineau and Maurice Blackburn. *Prem.* Montreal Film Festival 1963. 90 min. *Distr.* Columbia Pictures. In French with English, with subtitles and narration.

Cast: Claude Jutra, Johanne, and Victor Desy.

Claude Jutra portrays his failed love affair with Johanne in a personal film of a real-life experience.

DRYLANDERS   Sept. 1963

Prod. co. National Film Board of Canada; *rel.* Columbia Pictures; *prod.* Peter Jones; *dir.* Donald Haldane; *scen./story* M. Charles Cohen; *narr. scen.* William Weintraub; *cam.* (superscope b&w) Reginald Morris; *ed.* John Kemeny and Kirk Jones; *music* Eldon Rathburn. *Prem.* Cinema Theatre, Swift Current, Sask. 70 min.

Cast: Frances Hyland, James Douglas, Lester Nixon, Mary Savage, William Fruet, Don Francks, and Irene Mayeska.

Family life on the prairies during the years of the great drought and depression.

AMANITA PESTILENS   Aug. 1963

Prod. co. Crawley Films (Ottawa); *prod.* F. R. Crawley;. *dir./ed.* René Bonnière; *scen.* David Walker; *cam.* (color) Frank Stokes; *music* Lawrence Crosley. 90 min. In French and English versions. *Prem.* Stratford Film Festival.

Cast: Jacques Labrecque, Huguette Oligny, Geneviève Bujold, Benoit Girard, Roger Garçeau, Blake James, Jacques Normand, Julien Lippe, Jean Louis

Amanita pestilens (1963).

Barbara Ulrich in *Le Chat dans le sac (The Cat in the Bag)* (d. Gilles Groulx, 1964).

Millette, Gabriel Vigneault, Georges Cortez, Pierre Baron, Denise Bombardier, Ronald France, J. Leo Gagnon, Giselle, Juliette Huot, Françoise Lemieux, and Yvon Leroux.

A comedy-satire showing how a suburban family in Montreal destroys itself in the attempt to achieve materialistic perfection in life. (Originally titled *Ville Jolie*). This was Geneviève Bujold's first film.

BITTER ASH   Oct. 1963

Prod./dir./scen. Larry Kent; *photog.* (b&w) Richard Bellamy; *ed.* Richard Bellamy and Larry Kent; *music* Jack Dale. 79 mins.

Cast: Alan Scarfe, Lynne Stewart, Phillip Brown, Douglas Reid, Jocelyn Thomas.

A drama about a shiftless, talentless playwright who lives off the money his pregnant wife earns as a waitress. After a party, a sex-hungry woman friend pays him to go to bed with her. As a result his wife goes to bed with a young printer after a chance meeting. The wife ends up hating both the husband and the printer.

LE CHAT DANS LE SAC   Aug. 1964
(The Cat in the Bag)

Documentary. *Prod. co.* National Film Board of Canada; *exec. prod.* Jacques Bobet; *dir./ed.* Gilles Groulx; *cam.* (b&w) Jean-Claude Labrecque; *music* Coltrane, Vivaldi, Couperin. *Prem.* Montreal Film Festival 1964. 74 min. In French with English subtitles.

Roles	*Cast*
Barbara	Barbara Ulrich
Claude	Claude Godbout
Manon	Manon Blain

Peter Kastner and Julie Biggs in *Nobody Waved Goodbye* (d. Don Owen, 1964).

Jean-Paul   Jean-Paul Bernier
Véronique   Véronique Vilbert
Toulouse   André Leblanc

also: Paul-Marie Lapointe, Jean-V. Dufresne, and Pierre Maheau.

An improvised documentary set in the world of theater and journalism in Montreal in the early sixties, concerning a young real-life couple (the girl is Anglo-Canadian and Jewish, the man is Quebecois, seeking for his identity) who are on the verge of separating. Generally considered to be the first film to mark Quebec's new beginning in the cinema.

THE LUCK OF GINGER COFFEY   Nov. 1964

Prod. co. Crawley Films (Ottawa), and Roth-Kershner Productions (Hollywood); *prod.* Leon Roth; *dir.* Irvin Kershner; *scen.* Brian Moore, from his novel of the same name; *cam.* (b&w), Manny Wynn; *prod. designer* Harry Horner; *ed.* Tony Gibbs; *music* Bernardo Segall. 100 min. *Distr.* Continental Distributing Co. *Prem.* Place Ville Marie, Montreal.

Cast: Robert Shaw, Mary Ure, Liam Redmond, Tom Harvey, Libby McClintock, Leo Leyden, Powys Thomas, Tom Kneebone, Les Yeo, Vern Chapman, Paul Guevremont, Barry Stewart, Arch McDonnell,

Bob Howay and Carol Pastinsky in *Sweet Substitute* (d. Larry Kent, 1964).

Ivola Legare, Jacques Godin, Maurice Beaupre, Sydney Brown, Juliette Huot, and Paul Hebert.

How a likable Irish immigrant attempts to find a job in Montreal and a new understanding with his wife.

LYDIA   Aug. 1964

Prod. co. Libra Films; *prod.* Julius Rascheff; *dir.* Diederick d'Ailly; *scen.* Diederick d'Ailly, Burton Krancer, and Julius Rascheff; *cam.* (color) Julius Rascheff; *ed.* Julius Rascheff; *music* André Hajdu. *Prem.* Montreal Film Festival 1964. 83 min.

Cast: Gordon Pinsent, Anna Hagan, Benentino Costa, and Malena Anusaki.

A love story filmed on location in Greece. Pinsent (in his first film) plays an American with an incurable illness who visits a Greek island to find peace and come to terms with himself. He also finds love, which is related to a local legend, but gives up the girl because he has no future.

NOBODY WAVED GOODBYE   Aug. 1964

Prod. co. and Dist. National Film Board of Canada; *prod.* Roman Kroiter; *scen./dir.* Don Owen; *cam.* (b&w) John Spotton; *ed.* Donald Ginsberg and John Spotton; *music* Eldon Rathburn. *Prem.* Montreal Film Festival 1964. 80 min.

Roles	Cast
Peter	Peter Kastner
Julie	Julie Biggs
Father	Claude Rae
Mother	Charmion King
Sister	Toby Tarnow
Friend	Ron Taylor
Agent	Robert Hill
Sergeant	Jack Beer
Probation Officer	John Sullivan
Julie's Mother	Lynne Gorman
Personnel Manager	Ivor Barry
Landlord	Norman Ettlinger
Car Park Attendant	John Vernon

A funny and sad depiction of Peter, charming and impulsive, who leaves home to escape his nagging middle-class parents with their materialistic values, only to discover that the world outside can be just as harsh and intolerant. (Owen made a sequel, *Unfinished Business,* in 1984.)

SWEET SUBSTITUTE (Caressed)   Nov. 1964

Prod./scen./dir. Larry Kent; *cam.* (b&w) Richard Bellamy; *ed.* Sheila Reljac; *music* Jack Dale. *Prem.* University of British Columbia. 90 min.

Cast: Robert Howay, Carol Pastinsky, Angela Gann, Lanny Beckman, Robert Silverman, Bill Hartley, Mitzi Hurd, and Virginia Dunsaith.

A lively, active teenage boy can't concentrate on his studies because he is obsessed with sex. A pleasant, plain girl satisfies his demands and sees him through his scholarship, but becomes pregnant as a result. He then abandons her and becomes engaged to a socially acceptable, but less-accessible woman.

TROUBLE-FETE (Trouble Makers)   March 1964

Prod. co. Cooperatio; *prod.* Jean-Claude Lord; *dir.* Pierre Patry; *scen.* Jean-Claude Lord and Pierre Patry; *cam.* (b&w) Jean Roy; *ed.* Lucien Marleau; *music* Claude Leveille. *Prem.* St. Denis, Montreal. 95 min. *Distr.* France-Film.

Cast: Percy Rodriguez, Henri Tremblay, Yves Corbeil, Jean-Louis Paris, Jean-Paul Brodeu, Jean-Pierre Souriol, Gabriel Vigneault, José Léon, Yves Lapointe, Rita Imbault, André Lafrance, Claude Palmieri, Yvon Deschamps, Mirielle Lachance, Robert Desroches, Rejeanne Desrameaux, Lucie Mitchell, Monique Aubry, Ernest Guimond, and Alain Michel.

The life of a college student in Montreal who revolts against the authorities, his family, and his friends in his struggle to find a meaning to his existence.

WHEN TOMORROW DIES   Jan. 1965

Prod./dir. Larry Kent; *scen.* Robert Harlow and Larry Kent; *cam.* (b&w) Douglas McKay; *ed.* Hajo Hadeler; *music* Jack Dale. *Prem.* Lyric Theatre, Vancouver. 91 min.

Cast: Patricia Gage, Douglas Campbell, Neil Dainard, Lanny Beckman, Nikki Cole, Diane Filer, Francesca Long, Rex Owen, Louise Payne, and Patricia Wilson.

A young housewife and mother finds that her daily existence has become dull and empty as both her husband and children are too taken up with their own affairs to bother about her. Feeling alone and rejected, she goes back to studying in an attempt to brighten her life. She meets a professor and finds him attractive, but after a brief liaison she knows that life with him would be no different than with her husband. For her tomorrow will be just like today.

CAIN   April 1965

Prod. co. Cooperatio; *prod.* Pierre Patry and Jean Roy; *dir.* Pierre Patry; *scen.* Jacques Proulx, from the novel *Les Marcheurs de la Nuit* by Réal Giguere; *ed.* Lucien Marleau; *cam.* (b&w) Jean Roy; *music* Jean Cousineau; *songs* "La Ballade des Pendus" sung by Francois Villon, "Les Chansons d'Antan" sung by Marie Senecal. *Prem.* St. Denis Theatre, Montreal. 90 min.

Ginette Letondal and Réal Giguère in *Cain* (d. Pierre Patry, 1965).

Roles	*Cast*
Luc	Yves Létourneau
Jean	Réal Giguere
Marie	Ginette Letondal
Olga	Ginette Letondal
Nicole	Gabbi Sylvain
Maurice	Yvon Dufour
Landru	Ronald France
Laura	Gaetane Letourneau
Mme Toupin	Rose Rey Duzil

A group of people in Montreal, friends and enemies, lovers and lost souls, are caught up in unexpected murder and violence, which most do not comprehend nor wish to become involved with.

BETHUNE   Jan. 1965

Documentary. *Prod. co.* National Film Board of Canada; *exec. prod.* Guy Glover; *scen./prod.* Donald Brittain and John Kemeny; *narr. scen.* Lister Sinclair; *cam.* (b&w) Robert Humble, François Seguillon, and Murray Fallen; *res./ed.* John Kemeny; *comm.* Donald Brittain. 59 min.

Norman Bethune was a doctor, thinker, and philosopher. Compiled from films, photographs, and stories contributed by people who knew him, this film pieces together an impressive biography of a remarkable man. His legend, strengthened by his premature death, lives on in China, where they call him "the White-One-Sent."

COMMENT SAVOIR   April 1965

Documentary. *Prod. co.* National Film Board of Canada; *prod.* Marcel Martin; *dir.* Claude Jutra; *res./comm.* Jean Lemoyne; *cam.* (b&w) Bernard Gosselin; *ed.* Werner Nold; *anim.* Pierre Hebert. 90 min.

An attempt to explain the increasing use and effectiveness of technology in the classroom.

LE FESTIN DES MORTS   May 1965
(Mission of Fear)

Documentary-dramatization. *Prod. co.* National Film Board of Canada; *prod.* André Belleau; *dir./ed.* Fernand Dansereau; *scen.* Alex Pelletier; *cam.* (b&w) Georges Dufaux; *music* Maurice Blackburn. 80 min. *Prem.* Cinema Place, Ville-Marie, Montreal.

Cast: Alain Cuny, Jean-Guy Sabourin, Jacques Godin, Jean-Louis Millette, Albert Millaire, Yves Létourneau, Monique Mercure, Maurice Tremblay, Jacques Kasma, François Guillier, Ginette Letondal, Janine Sutto, Jean Perraud.

A stark, unadorned, and philosophical film about the martyrdom of Jesuit missionaries among the Huron Indians, 1611 to 1760. Some murky observations about courage, death, and religion.

LA NEIGE A FONDU SUR   Aug. 1965
LA MANICOUAGAN
(The Snow Has Melted on the Manicouagan)

Prod. co. National Film Board of Canada; *prod.* Marcel Martin; *scen./dir./ed.* Arthur Lamothe; *cam.* (b&w) Gilles Gascon; *music* Maurice Blackburn. 95 mins.

Cast: Monique Miller, Gilles Vigneault, Margot Campbell, Jean Doyen.

An atmospheric mood piece photographed in the winter at the giant dam that Quebec Hydro built in the northern wilds of the province. The slight story concerns the wife of a worker who is bored with her dreary existence in this wilderness of construction, who walks around in the snow recalling how she met her husband, and goes to the landing field to catch a departing plane. But she remains when her husband tells her how much his work means to him.

A scene from *Le Festin des morts (Mission of Fear)* **(d. Fernand Dansereau, 1964).**

Guy L'Ecuyer and Paul Hébert in *La Vie heureuse de Leopold Z (The Merry World of Leopold Z)* (d. Gilles Carle, 1965).

LA REVOLUTIONNAIRE   Aug. 1965
(The Revolutionaries)

Prod. co. Les Films Jean-Pierre Lefebvre; *scen./dir.* Jean-Pierre Lefebvre; *cam.* (b&w) Michel Regnier; *ed.* Marguerite Duparc; *music* Folklore played on the fiddle by Lionel Renaud; *anim.* Pierre Hebert. Shown outside the Montreal Film Festival 1965. 70 min.

Cast: Louis St-Pierre, Louise Rasselet, Alain Chartrand, Robert Daudelin, Michel Gauthier, René Goulet, Pierre Hébert, Camil Houle, Richard Lacroix, Jacques Monette, Michel Patenaude.

This first film by Jean-Pierre Lefebvre, shot in a few weeks on 16mm with hardly enough cash to buy raw stock, should be considered only as a determined initial effort at learning how to make a film by going out with a camera and putting desire into practice. As such it comes off fairly well and is frequently commendable, but it falls victim to obvious shortcomings such as not enough cross-cutting, shots held for too long, a complete lack of characterization, awkwardness, and uncertainty. The slight story is intended to be a comic look at a group of ineffectual youths who call themselves revolutionaries for a free Quebec and go into the cold, snowbound countryside to an old house for training purposes. This kind of activity soon palls and

they end by accidentally eliminating each other. The treatment wavers between satire and seriousness and results in considerable monotony and some foolishness. However, a sequence depicting a brief history of Canada filled in with scratchy animation effects is ingeniously done.

LA VIE HEUREUSE DE LEOPOLD Z   Aug. 1965
(The Merry World of Leopold Z)

Prod. co. National Film Board of Canada; *prod.* Jacques Bobet; *scen./dir.* Gilles Carle; *cam.* (b&w) Jean-Claude Labrecque; *ed.* Werner Nold; *music* Paul de Margerie. *Prem.* Montreal Film Festival 1965. 70 min. *Distr.* Columbia Pictures, French, dubbed into English.

Roles	*Cast*
Leopold	Guy L'Ecuyer
Théophile	Paul Hébert
Josita	Suzanne Valery
Mme Tremblay	Monique Joly
The Son	Jacques Poulin

Leopold, a plump, amiable, happily married man, drives a snowplow for the city of Montreal. It is Christmas Eve and the snow is falling heavily. Between cleaning streets he takes out a loan, buys his wife a fur coat, and takes care of his cousin, a night-club singer. Throughout his long and tiring day he is watched by his foreman, who suspects he is up to other things. This is a lively, spirited, deftly handled comedy with serious undertones, an auspicious beginning for Gilles Carle, who, if nothing else, has made winter and its snow seem entirely natural and frequently funny.

WINTER KEPT US WARM   Sept. 1965

Prod. co. Varsity Films; *prod./dir.* David Secter; *scen.* John Porter; *cam.* (b&w) Robert Fresco and Ernest Meersholk; *ed.* Michael Foytenyi; *music* Paul Hoffert. *Prem.* Cardiff Commonwealth Film Festival 1965. 81 min.

John Labow and Joy Tepperman in *Winter Kept Us Warm* (d. David Secter, 1965).

Roles	Cast
Douglas	John Labow
Peter	Henry Tarvainen
Beverly	Joy Tepperman
Janet	Janet Amos
Arthur	Iain Ewing
Nick	Jack Messinger
Larry	Larry Greenspan
Hall Porter	Sol Mendelson
House Don	George Appelby

A University of Toronto and Ryerson College student film, *Winter* convincingly expresses the feeling of postadolescent torment of a secret love. It is a psychological study of two boys, one a sensitive new student from the country, the other the confident man on campus. Contrary to convention, it is the womanizing older boy who falls in love with the younger one, making the point that it is often the quiet misfit who is more secure than the brash and friendly fellow.

LA CORDE AU COU   June 1966

Prod. co. Cooperatio; *prod./dir.* Pierre Patry; *scen.* Claude Jasmin, from his novel; *cam.* (b&w) Jean Roy; *ed.* Lucien Marleau; *music* François Cousineau. *Prem.* St. Denis Theatre, Montreal. 93 min.

Roles	Cast
L'acteur	Jacques Auger
Aline	Andrée Boucher
Le chauffeur	Gilbert Chenier
Achille	Roland D'Amour
Père de Léo	Henri Deyglun
Ubald	Jean Duceppe
Bedeau	Camille Ducharme
La religieuse	Tania Fedor
Gaugsteins Jr.	Ronald France
Léo	Guy Godin
Xavier	Ernest Guimond
J-P. Brazeau	Gaetan Labreche
Suzanne	Andrée Lachapelle
Bozo	Guy L'Ecuyer
L'étudiant Faucheur	Richard Martin
Amédée	Jean-Louis Millette
Mère de Léo	Lucie Mitchell
Frère d'Amédée	Gilles Normand
Driftman	Henri Norbert
Rémy	Jean-Louis Paris
Lucienne	Denise Pelletier
Micheline	Monique Sirois
Annette	Gabbi Sylvain

One night at a party, Léo murders the girl he loves. He runs away, and thus begins his long and tragic flight from justice.

YUL 871 (Montreal Flight 871)   Aug. 1966

Prod. co. National Film Board of Canada; *prod.* André Belleau; *dir./scen.* Jacques Godbout; *cam.* (b&w)

Georges Dufaux; *ed.* Victor Jobin; *music* François Dompierre and Stephane Venne. *Prem.* Montreal Film Festival 1966. 70 min. Dist: Columbia Pictures.

Roles	Cast
Jean	Charles Denner
Marguerite	Andrée Lachapelle
Girl	Francine Landry
Antonio	Paul Buissonneau

also: Jean Duceppe, Jacques Desrosiers, Jacques Normand, Louise Marleau, Claude Prefontaine, Les Jerolas, Victor Desy, Bouda Bradon, Violette Bussy, Connie Kilbourn.

The tale of a Frenchman on a two-day business trip to Montreal who brings with him memories of his childhood. He searches for relatives living in the city and meets a woman with whom he has a love interlude before flying back to Paris.

THE OFFERING   Nov. 1966

Prod. co. Secter Films; *prod.* Samuel Roy; *dir.* David Secter; *scen.* David Secter, Martin Lager, Iain Ewing, Jan Steen, and Gillian Lennox; *cam.* (b&w) Stanley Lipinski; *ed.* Tony Lower; *music* Paul Hoffert. *Prem.* Odeon Danforth Cinema, Toronto. 80 min.

Roles	Cast
Mei-lin	Kee Faun
Gordon	Ratch Wallace
Jung-ling	Ellen Yamasaki
Jack	Marvin Goldhar
Tien	Gene Mark

David Secter, 23-year-old director of *Winter Kept Us Warm,* the University of Toronto film that brought him a measure of fame, raised some $50,000 to make this, his second film, and while a brave effort it fails due to a poor script and lack of knowledge of his subject. The weak story concerns a romance between a Chinese dancer, a member of the visiting Peking Opera Company, and a stage hand at the theater where she appears. The film's saving grace is some bright black-and-white photography of Toronto.

WARRENDALE   Jan. 1967

Prod. co. Canadian Broadcasting Corporation; *prod.* Patrick Watson; *dir.* Allan King; *cam.* (b&w) William Brayne; *ed.* Peter Moseley. 105 min. Dist: Columbia Pictures. Although commissioned by the CBC, the Corporation refused to show the film because the children in it used then-forbidden four-letter words. It was shown in specialized cinemas instead.

This "cinema direct" study of disturbed children, at a home in Toronto called Warrendale, shows the special treatment devised for them by the director, Doctor Brown. No attempt is made to impose a dramatic story on the events of the day. Quite by chance, as the filmmakers were at work, the home's cook, much-liked by the children, died suddenly, adding a drama not envisioned by the director. There is no commentary, and the picture has a disturbing effect on audiences, leading them to wonder perhaps what parents are doing to their children in this age of psychotics and psychiatrists. *Warrendale* was shown in the Critics' Section at the Cannes Film Festival 1967 and was selected as the first feature to be presented by the New Cinema Club in London.

LE REGNE DU JOUR   April 1967
(Duration of the Day)

Prod./rel. National Film Board of Canada; Jacques Bobet and Guy L. Cote; *dir.* Pierre Perrault; *cam.* (b&w) Bernard Gosselin; *ed.* Yves Leduc; *music* Jean-Marie Cloutier. *Prem.* at the Critics' Week at Cannes Film Festival, 118 min.

Cast: Alexis Tremblay, Leopold Tremblay, Raphael Clement, Louis Brosse, Robert Martin, Louis Lemarchand, Marie Tremblay, Marie-Paule Tremblay, Fran-

Charles Denner and Andrée Lachapelle in *Yul 871* (d. Jacques Godbout, 1966).

A scene from *Warrendale* (d. Allan King, 1966).

çoise Montagne and Christiane Greillon.

Filmed in the "cinema direct" method. Less a motion picture and more a filmed conversation, the film follows Alexis Tremblay and his wife as they go to New York's aquarium to see the whale they caught in the previous film, *Pour la suite du monde* (1963). From there they go to visit relatives in France for the first time. Refreshing, often warmly funny, it's a "look in" on family life. It raises once again the question of the validity of the *cinema-vérité* technique as the last word in realism once it becomes apparent that the people being photographed are aware of the camera and modulate their behavior accordingly, or start to act for the cameras.

THE ERNIE GAME   Nov. 1967

Prod. co. National Film Board of Canada and Canadian Broadcasting Corporation (NFB-CBC); *exec-.prod.* Robert Allen; *prod.* Gordon Burwash; *scen./dir.*
Don Owen; *cam.* (Technicolor) Jean-Claude Labrecque; *ed.* Roy Ayton; *music* Kensington Market. *Prem.* CBC-TV, November 8, 1967, 86 min. *Distr.* Columbia Pictures.

Roles	*Cast*
Ernie	Alexis Kanner
Donna	Judith Gault
Gail	Jackie Burroughs
Ernie's accomplice	Derek May
Social worker	Anna Cameron
Singer	Leonard Cohen
Ernie's friend	Louis Negin
Landlady	Corinne Copnick
Neighbor	Roland D'Amour

A dull fellow playing a dull game. A fragmentary nonstory film about a shiftless young man in Montreal precariously close to insanity and unable to face life. He survives by imposing on two girls, by using people, by talking of the things he plans to do but is incapable

Alexis Kanner in *The Ernie Game* **(d. Don Owen, 1967).**

William Needles and Alexandra Stewart in *Waiting For Caroline* **(d. Ron Kelly, 1968).**

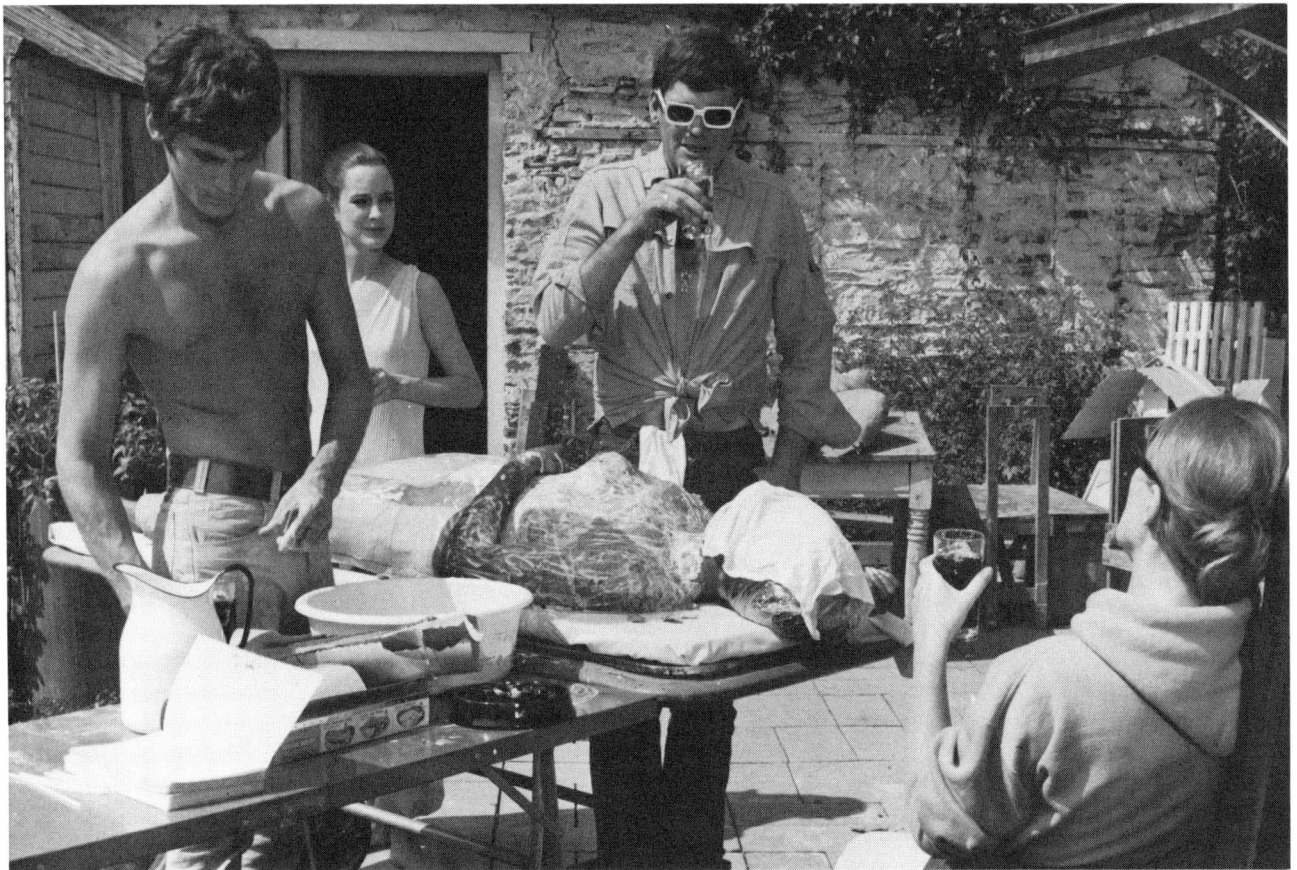

Robin Ward, Marc Strange, and Marigold Charlesworth in
The Paper People **(d. David Gardner, 1967).**

of carrying out. But we never really know him, particularly from Kanner's self-indulgent performance. The two girls are the Donna and Gail of Owen's earlier short film, *Notes for a Film About Donna and Gail.* Seen in retrospect, *The Ernie Game* did at least presage an entire generation of American and European films dealing with gloomy, uncertain, and boring individuals. Compared with most of them, it holds up rather well.

WAITING FOR CAROLINE   Nov. 1967

Prod. co. National Film Board of Canada and Canadian Broadcasting Corporation; *exec. prod.* Robert Allen; *prod.* Walford Hewitson; *dir.* Ron Kelly; *scen.* George C. Robertson and Ron Kelly; *cam.* (Technicolor) Denis Gillson; *ed.* Barrie Howells; *music* Eldon Rathburn. *Prem.* CBC-TV, November 29, 1967. 86 min. *Distr.* Columbia Pictures (Canada), United Artists (USA).

Roles	Cast
Caroline	Alexandra Stewart
Peter	Robert Howay
Marc	François Tasse
Emily	Sharon Acker
Stephen	William Needles
Lally	Aileen Seaton
M. Simard	Paul Guevremont
Jean-Pierre	Daniel Gadouas
Mme Simard	Lucie Poitras
Yvette	Monique Mercure
Hagan	Reg McReynolds
Louis	Paul Buissoneau

Ron Kelly, who established his reputation with his interesting work for CBC and NFB in documentary and television, entered feature film-making with this beautifully made, expensively mounted piece of romantic melodrama concerning a woman and her love for two men, one from Quebec and one from British Columbia. Between the snows of one province and the rugged mountains of the other, it is a somewhat boring business waiting for Caroline to make up her mind and decide between the two.

THE PAPER PEOPLE   Dec. 1967

Prod. co. Canadian Broadcasting Corporation; *exec. prod.* Robert Allen; *prod.* Ted Zarpas; *dir.* David Gardner; *scen.* Timothy Findley; *cam.* (Eastmancolor) Ernest Kirkpatrick; *ed.* M. C. Manne; *music* John Coulson. First shown on CBC's "Festival," December 13, 1967. 90 min. (This was the CBC's first feature film

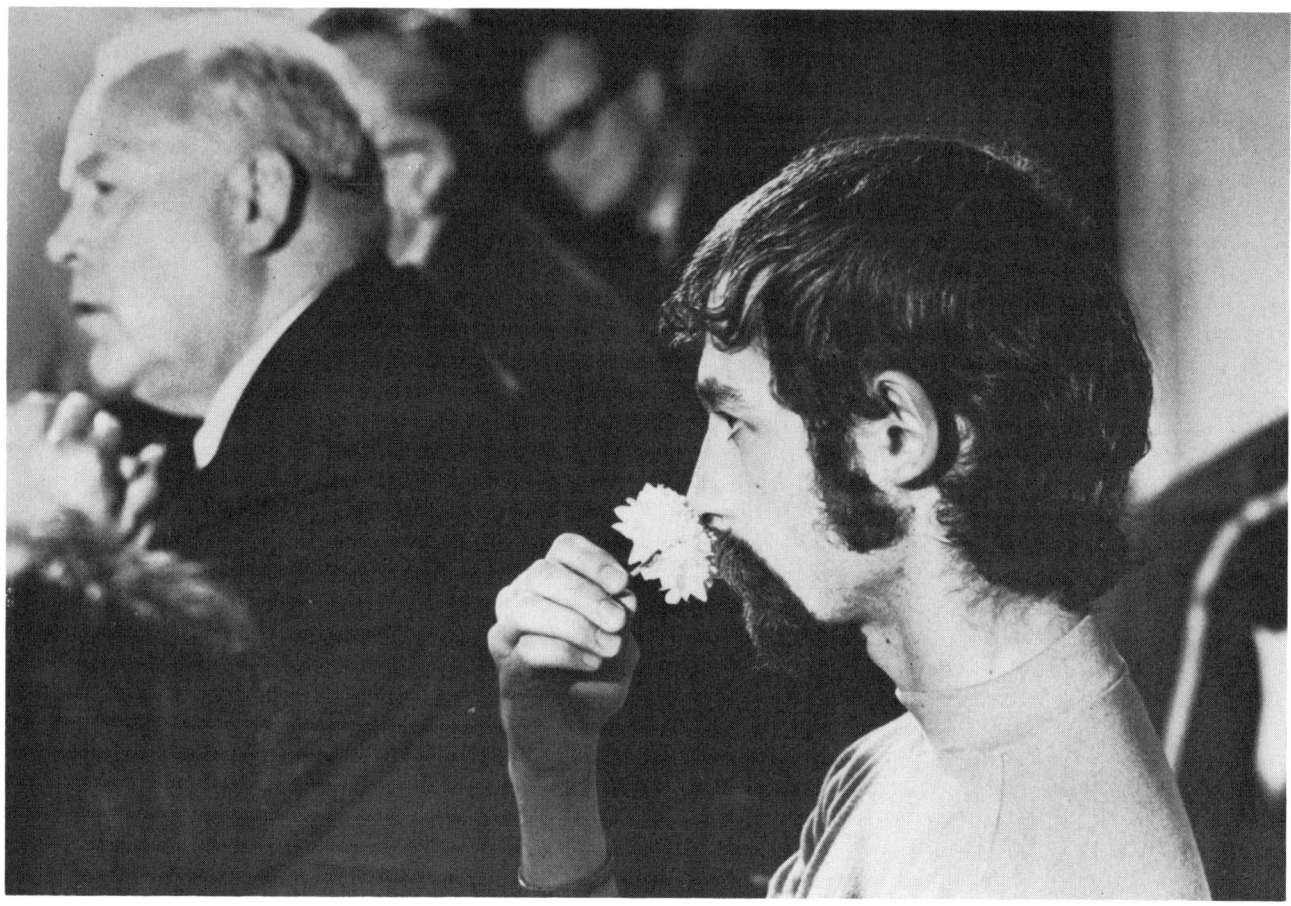

A scene from *Flowers on a One-Way Street* (d. Robin Spry, 1968).

production under its own auspices.)

Roles	Cast
Jamie Taylor	Marc Strange
Janet Webb	Marigold Charlesworth
Carrie	Lucy Warner
Michael	Robin Ward
Rosamund Davis	Kate Reid
Mrs. Taylor	Hilary Vernon
Maxine	Brett Somers
Elizabeth	Sabina Maydelle
Daniel	Clifford Trevor
Tonya	Stevie Wise
Patrick	Ed McGibbon
Bernice	Claudette Houchen
Anastasia	Liz Creighton
Marco	Adam Ludwig
Harold	Don McGill
Wilfrid	Graham McCannell

also: Elizabeth Ward, Sheila Haney, Audrey Kniveton, Michael Payeur, and D'Arcy Guthrie.

This frequently silly, pretentious, and ambiguous film on the familiar theme of an eccentric, wilful, and selfish artist who makes paper sculptures of people he doesn't like and then burns them, draws great strength from the remarkable acting performances by the entire cast, notably Marc Strange (the moody young man later seen in *Isabel*), and from the vivid and imaginative direction of David Gardner, who makes much of Timothy Findley's erratic script. Findley, who also wrote *Don't Let The Angels Fall,* was at this time one of Canada's most promising and skillful young writers and found recognition in later years for his novels and the film of one of them, *The Wars* (1982).

FLOWERS ON A ONE-WAY STREET July 1968

Documentary. *Prod. co./rel.* National Film Board of Canada; *prod.* Joseph Koenig; *scen./dir.* Robin Spry; *cam.* (color) Martin Duckworth and Jacques Fogel; *ed.* Christopher Cordeaux; *music* The Beatles and Ravi Shankar. *Prem.* CBC-TV, July 7, 1968. 60 min.

Somewhat like a first cousin to *Christopher's Movie Matinee,* shown the following year, this film was also shot in Toronto's Yorkville district, then the home of the "hippie" movement, and concerns itself mainly with the confrontation that took place between the representatives of the Canadian Youth Council and those of City Hall, who opposed the council's request for closed streets and freedom from police "harassment." An interesting social document on a time that has quickly passed.

ISABEL
July 1968

Prod. co. Quest Films; *prod./scen./dir.* Paul Almond; *cam.* (Technicolor) Georges Dufaux; *ed.* George Appleby; *music* Harry Freedman. 108 min. *Distr.* Paramount.

Roles	Cast
Isabel	Geneviève Bujold
Jason	Marc Strange
Uncle Matthew	Gerard Parkes
Eb	Elton Hayes
Viola	Ede Kerr
Herb	Albert Waxman
His friends	Ratch Wallace, Lynden Bechervaise
Postmaster	Eric Clavering
Fisherman	Rob Hayes
Storekeeper	J. Donald Dow

A young girl returns to her home in the lonely Gaspé region of Quebec and becomes aware of strange influences at work around her. Beautifully photographed, sensitively acted and directed, splendidly brooding and atmospheric, this first feature by former CBC-TV director Paul Almond tells a fascinating tale of suppressed sex, subjective fears, and psychotic fancies.

ENTRE LA MER ET L'EAU DOUCE
July 1968
(Between Sweet and Salt Water)
(Drifting Downstream)

Rel. Glendon Films; *prod. co.* Cooperatio; *prod./dir.* Michel Brault; *scen.* Michel Brault, Denys Arcand, Marcel Dube, Gerald Godin, and Claude Jutra; *cam.* (b&w) Bernard Gosselin, Jean-Claude Labrecque, and Michel Brault; *ed.* Werner Nold; *music* Claude Gauthier. 90 min. In French. Shown at the Berlin International Film Festival, Young Films of Canada Week, July 1968.

Cast: Geneviève Bujold, Claude Gauthier, Louise Latraverse, Paul Gauthier, Robert Charlebois.

Michel Brault, an exponent of "cinema-direct" films for the National Film Board, made his first feature in

Geneviève Bujold in *Isabel* (d. Paul Almond, 1968).

fictional and dramatized form, with strong factual, political, and documentary overtones throughout.

It is a somewhat depressing story filmed against drab locations of a young man (Claude Gauthier) who leaves his home and work on Quebec's North Shore to try his luck in nearby Montreal. Here he gets a succession of jobs and meets and falls in love with a pretty waitress (Geneviève Bujold) working in a run-down cafe. Unexpectedly, he finds a career as a chansonnier and is attracted to another woman. Although he achieves success in the so-called world of wealth and glitter he has lost the girl, the only person who meant something to him, and he remains as lonely and unfulfilled as in his previous life.

A GREAT BIG THING   July 1968

Prod. co. Argofilm (Canada) Limited; *prod.* Martin Rosen; *dir.* Eric Till; *scen./story* Terence Heffernan; *cam.* (Eastmancolor) Jean-Claude Labrecque; *ed.* Ralph Rosenblum; *music* Robert Prince. 83 min. Shown at the Berlin International Film Festival, Young Films of Canada Week, July 1968.

Roles	Cast
Vinny	Reni Santoni
Michelle	Louise Latraverse
Morrie	Paul Sand
Lauriea	Marcy Plotnick
Appie	Gerard Parkes
Holly	François Yves Carpentier
Eve	Roberta Maxwell
Ray	Leon Pownall
Bill	Heath Lamberts

Similar in many ways to *The Ernie Game,* and also filmed in Montreal, this U.S.–Canadian picture, financed by American producer Martin Rosen, was yet another in the growing line of plotless, unresolved pictures about disoriented youth. In this instance, it is a 23-year-old, who while not entirely unlikable or even criminal, is irresponsible, unreliable, annoyed with the world, and unable to know himself or to come to terms with life. This was Eric Till's first feature film.

HIGH   July 1968

Prod./scen./dir. (Montreal) Larry Kent; *rel.* Joseph Brenner Associates; *ed.* Pierre Savard; *cam.* (b&w and color) Paul Van der Linden; *prod. asst.* Robert Linnell; *music and songs* The Sidetrack. 85 min. *Prem.* Presidium Theatre, San Francisco.

Roles	Cast
Vicki	Astri Thorvik
Tom	Lanny Beckman

also: Peter Matthews, Joyce Cay, Denis Payne, Carol Epstein, Doris Cowan, Mortie Golub, Al Mayoff, Melinda McCracken, Janet Amos, Gary Eisencraft, Paul Kirby, Jack Epstein, Peter Pyper, Daphne, Sue, and Kirsten.

At the Montreal Film Festival held in September in association with Expo 67, this picture by Larry Kent was scheduled to be shown as part of the series devoted to Canadian films, but at the last moment a license was refused by the Quebec Board of Censors.

Largely improvised, with standard fragmentary narrative, *High* concerns a group of young people whose lives are without purpose and who indulge in a dreary round of pot, dormitory sex, and petty crime.

IL NE FAUT PAS MOURIR POUR ÇA   July 1968
(Don't Let It Kill You)

Rel. Film Canada Presentation; *prod. co.* Les Films Jean-Pierre Lefebvre; *dir.* Jean-Pierre Lefebvre; *scen.* Jean-Pierre Lefebvre and Marcel Sabourin; *cam.* (b&w) Jacques Leduc; *ed.* Marguerite Duparc; *music* Andrée Paul. 90 min. In French. Shown at the Berlin International Film Festival, Young Films of Canada Week, July 1968.

Cast: Marcel Sabourin, Monique Champagne, Suzanne Grossman, Claudine Monfette, Lucille Belanger, André Page, Denise Morelle, Gabbi Sylvain, Gaetan Labreche, Zivart Cankul, Lusarif Atamoglu, Fleur-Ange Laplante.

Another story of a strange young man in Montreal, this one an amiable, innocent eccentric who, to use the director's description, wants to change many things but finds that they change him. The narrative shows little evidence of these intentions, and for the most part what little action there is remains perplexing. The pace is ponderously slow, the conversations long and without camera movement or much change of viewpoint. Undoubtedly the character, casually played by Marcel Sabourin, who wrote the script with Lefebvre, is an interesting one and the ideas put forward are valuable and worthy of consideration. But their expression ultimately becomes tiresome. The occasional moments of wit, warmth, and charm are all too rare.

POUSSIERE SUR LA VILLE   July 1968
(Dust from Underground)

Prod. co. Cooperatio film; *prod.* Pierre Patry and Jean Roy; *dir./ed.* Arthur Lamothe; *scen.* André Langevin, from his novel; *cam.* (b&w) Guy-Laval Fortier; *music* Gilles Vigneault. 90 min. In French. Shown at the Berlin International Film Festival, Young Films of Canada Week July 1968.

Cast: Guy Sanche, Michele Rossignol, Henri Norbert, Nicole Filion, Gilles Pelletier, Nicolas Doclin, Roland Chenail, Victor Desy, Paul Guevremont, Pierre Dupuis, Rose Rey Duzil, Rejane Desameaux, Louisette Dussault.

Ineffective story of a smalltown doctor living in the frozen countryside with a bored and unfaithful wife.

LE VIOL D'UNE JEUNE FILLE DOUCE July 1968
(The Rape of a Sweet Young Girl)

Rel. Film Canada; *prod. co.* Onyx Films; *prod./scen./dir./ed.* Gilles Carle; *cam.* (Eastmancolor) Bernard Chentrier; *music* Pierre Brault. Shown at the Berlin International Film Festival, Young Films of Canada Week, July 1968. Opened at Cinecity, Toronto, September 17. 83 min.

Cast: Julie Lachapelle, Jacques Cohen, Daniel Pilon, Katerine Mousseau, Donald Pilon, André Gagnon, Jacques Chenail, Suzanne Kay, Claude Jutra, Larry Kent, Guy Marcenay, Arnie Gelbert, Francine Monette, Frank LeFlagis, René Bail, Michel le Bourhis.

This film is Gilles Carle's second feature, but it fails to reach the modest level of achievement he attained in his cheerful, likable first film, *La Vie Heureuse de Leopold Z*, made for the NFB. *Rape* (which closed the week of Canadian films at Berlin and opened one soon afterwards in Toronto) is an independent production made by Carle's own company, Onyx Films of Montreal. It is supposed to be a comedy, but black or white, there's nothing funny about its sketchy story. Apart from some occasionally humorous and apt statements in the dialogue, which would seem to indicate that Carle is attempting to make references to the way life and other people continually "rape" each other in the metaphysical sense, there is little point, purpose, or enlightenment to be found here.

CHRISTOPHER'S MOVIE MATINEE   April 1969

Prod. co./rel. National Film Board of Canada; *prod.* Joseph Koenig; *dir./ed.* Mort Ransen; *cam.* (Eastmancolor) Martin Duckworth. *Prem.* National Film Theatre, Ottawa. 90 min.

Cast: The Students: Graham Bourns, Jan Cassen, Malcolm Dean, Roger Dowker, Tom Evans, Doreen Foster, Lari Frolick, Cindy Glickman, Peter Keefe, Joyce Moore, Cathy Masmith, Harold Shore, Chris Whiteley, Ken Whiteley. The Band: Darius Brubeck, Alexander Crawley, Amos Garrett, William Hawkins.

This film about students, made primarily for them, normally would not be considered as coming within the orbit of public cinema were it not for the fact that the growth of student participation in film-making and appreciation had become so enormous as to be considered "commercial" in its own sphere, with "campus" exhibition yielding profitable returns for low-budget productions such as this one.

There is no writing credit since no script was used. In *cinema vérité* fashion, the content consists of moments of life among a group of students in Toronto. The director, 25-year-old Mort Ransen, whose work with the board concerned the "problems of youth" (notably *No Reason to Say,* a dramatized documentary on pupils who drop out of school), intended to make a study of student behavior, attitudes, and beliefs. The students, however, wanted to make the film themselves, and so Ransen and his crew let them have their way, providing token instructions on points of technique.

Throughout, the young people try to express their thoughts and feelings about themselves and society, to understand the adults and the causes of conflicts between them and the forces of authority. Nothing is resolved, confusion remains, and life seems to have no direction.

DON'T LET THE ANGELS FALL   May 1969

Rel. Columbia Pictures; *prod. co.* National Film Board of Canada; *prod.* John Kemeny; *dir.* George Kaczender; *story* Timothy Findley; *scen.* Timothy Findley and George Kaczender; *cam.* (b&w) Paul Leach; *ed.* Michael McKennirey; *music* The Collectors. At the Cannes Film Festival 1969. 97 min. The first Canadian dramatized feature film to be shown in competition at the Cannes Film Festival.

Roles	Cast
Robert	Arthur Hill
Barbara	Sharon Acker
Myrna	Charmion King
Guy	Jonathan Michaelson
Mrs. Pelletier	Monique Mercure
Diane	Michele Magny
Prostitute	Andrée Lachapelle
Michael	John Kastner
TV Host	Peter Desbarats
Mr. Ferguson	Ian Ireland
Miss Agnew	Madeleine Rozon
Teacher	Gwyn MacKenzie
Gladys	Eileen Clifford
The Boss	Len Watt
Police Sergeant	Walter Massey
Elderly Woman	Violet Bussey
Old Man	Walter Wakefield
Other Man	Don MacIntyre
Young Man	Jonathan Booth
Well-dressed Woman	Valda Dalton
Script Assistant	Astrid Thorvik
Girl in School	Janly Levene
12-year-old Girl	Erica Gold
Office Boy	Bill Glazer
Policeman #1	Gordon Reid
Policeman #2	Brian Weber

A well-made and acted film in which the theme of alienation is cleverly expressed in symbolic terms; the film begins with the death of a dog on the street and a closeup of the wife's hearing device, which cuts her off from life and her husband. There is a mother living up on the third floor whose demanding voice is heard, but who is never seen. The narrative is framed by a television program, which eventually proves to the husband how uninvolved he has become in society. His office is a prison of plate glass and steel, created for official business methods that dehumanize the people and make even his secretary an unknown quality.

LE GRAND ROCK   May 1969

Prod. co. National Film Board of Canada; *rel.* Columbia Pictures; *prod.* Guy L. Cote; *dir./scen./ed.* Raymond Garceau; *cam.* (Eastmancolor) François Seguillon; *music* Eldon Rathburn. Shown at Cannes Film Festival (non-competing) 1969. 73 min. In French.

Roles	*Cast*
Le Grand Rock	Guy Thauvette
Regine	Francine Racette
Freddie	Jacques Bilodeau
Johnny	Ian Ireland
Charlie	Pat Gagnon
Paulus	Ernest Guimond
The Dancer	Naomi Carter

Here is a film of a genre ignored by most Canadian movie-makers in favor of the "personal statement": the action melodrama of the individual in a rugged environment who wants to remain free. The plot concerns Rock Duchesneau, a "big" young man who works when he wants to at whatever he likes and who lives as he pleases. But marriage to the town's pret- tiest girl begins his downfall. Set against the once largely unfamiliar rural background of Quebec it contains some observant views of local customs and behavior, particularly in the beer parlor—the community meeting place.

JUSQU'AU COEUR   May 1969
(Straight to the Heart)

Prod. co. National Film Board of Canada; *rel.* Columbia Pictures; *prod.* Clement Perron; *dir./scen.* Jean--Pierre Lefebvre; *cam.* (Eastmancolor) Thomas Vamos; *ed.* Marguerite Duparc; *transp.* Denis Gillson; *anim.* Pierre Hebert; *spec. eff.* André Roy; *music* Robert Charlebois. At Cannes Film Festival (non-competing) 1969. 92 min.

Cast: Robert Charlebois, Claudine Monfette, Claudette Robitaille, Paul Berval, Denis Drouin, Pierre Dufresne, Luc Granger, Gaetan Labreche.

A young man's message is that no matter what society does to destroy the individual, to murder his soul, to operate on his brain, it cannot conquer his heart. Our life, says writer-director Lefebvre, is science-fiction; we live in an oppressive world. There is much talk of destiny of parallel lives, the mystery of existence, the matter of choice, of the effect of advertising on individuals, of love and death, the bomb and aborted children. Much of this apparently is directed to Quebec

**Charmion King and Arthur Hill in *Don't Let The Angels Fall*
(d. George Kaczender, 1969).**

A scene from *Les Voitures d'eau* (d. Pierre Perrault, 1970).

society.

VALERIE   May 1969

Prod. co. Julien Parnelle; *rel.* Cinepix; *dir.* Denis Heroux; *scen.* Louis Gauthier; *cam.* (b&w) René Verzier; *ed.* Jean Lafleur; *music* Joe Gracy and Michel Paje. Shown on the market at the Cannes Film Festival, 1969. 95 min.

Cast: Danielle Ouimet, Guy Godin, Michel Paje, Yvon Ducharme, Claude Prefontaine, Andrée Flamand, Kim Wilcox, Pierre Paquette, Hugo Gelinas, Henri Norbert, Clemence Desrochers.

With *Valerie* Denis Heroux joined the sex film game with financially rewarding results. Heroux, who made films for the National Film Board and Canadian Broadcasting Corporation for several years, independently slapped together a film so simple and naive that its chances of success seemed nonexistent in view of the extremes to which sex films had gone. But it was this very simplicity (and a low production budget) that was responsible in part for its success.

Valerie, a simple, physically well-endowed T-shirt type, flees a convent, finds the boys slow, becomes a topless dancer, takes to the money-making world of high-class call girls, and actually ends by finding "true love" with an artist (the father of a small son), who is madly in love with her and prepared to forget her follies.

LES VOITURES D'EAU (Water Cars)   May 1970

Documentary. *Prod. co.* National Film Board of Canada; *prod.* Jacques Bobet and Guy L. Cote; *dir./ story* Pierre Perrault; *cam.* (b&w) Bernard Gosselin; *ed.* Monique Fortier. Shown in the Critics' Section at the Cannes Film Festival, 1970. 110 min.

Cast: Laurent Tremblay and his sons Aurele and Yvan, Eloi Perron, Neree Harvey, Joachim Harvey, Leopold Tremblay, Alexis Tremblay, Grand Louis Harvey.

This is the third of Perrault's *cinema vérité* studies of the Tremblay family, who live on an island off the mainland and speak an ancient form of French. This time, the family and its friends are involved in building a magnificent wooden boat, in the way in which their ancestors would have done. Gentle, amusing, tender, and kind, this is a poetic film about rugged and independent people, beautifully observed and a social document for all time.

Daniel Pilon in *Red* (d. Gilles Carle, 1970).

RED   May 1970

Prod. co. Onyx Films; *rel.* Cinepix; *prod.* Pierre Lamy; *scen./dir.* Gilles Carle, with Ennio Flaiano; *cam.* (color) Bernard Chentrier; *ed.* Yves Langlois; *music* Pierre F. Brault. Shown at the Marché du Film, Cannes Film Festival, 1970. 101 min.

Roles	*Cast*
Red	Daniel Pilon
Georgette	Genevieve Deloir
Frederic	Gratien Gelinas
Elizabeth	Fernande Giroux
Amedee	Paul Gauthier
Jerome	Claude Michaud
Bill Sullivan	Donald Pilon
Detective Brunelle	Yvon Dufour
Catherine	Sylvie Heppel
Joachim	Raymond Cloutier
Domino	Katerine Mousseau
Georges	Aurele Dion
Jack	Michel Leblond
The Sargent Senecal	Jean-Pierre Cartier
The Sargent Brown	Beaudoin Rousseau
Land Surveyor	Serge Deyglun

A strange collaboration between Gilles Carle and the Italian writer Flaiano has resulted in a film that sounds French, looks Italian, and follows the violent traditions of American cinema. The story of a homeless, restless, rootless young man who is part Indian, part Quebecois, concerns his violent encounters with women and the establishment until his heavily symbolic death. Well shot and acted, it takes Carle further into professionalism, but away from a true reflection of the French-Canadian society. (This was the first film in which Famous Players, the leading Canadian cinema circuit owned by Paramount, invested money.)

LA CHAMBRE BLANCHE   May 1970
(The House of Light)

Prod. co. Jean-Pierre Lefebvre (Cinak); rel. Faroun Films; scen./ed./dir. Jean-Pierre Lefebvre; cam. (b&w Panavision) Thomas Vamos; music Walter Boudreau. Shown at Quinzaine des Réalisateurs, Cannes Film Festival, 1970. 80 min.

Cast: Marcel Sabourin and Michele Magny

Another film from productive and highly individualistic Jean-Pierre Lefebvre. This is a stylistic, ritualistic, beautifully staged, composed, and photographed black-and-white study of a man and his wife, set against mainly snowy landscapes seen through their window. Told with ambiguity and lack of narrative concern, typical of Lefebvre, it is described as (and often is) a poem to love, beauty, honor, and to the conscience and contradictions of human nature.

ENTRE TU ET VOUS   May 1970

Prod. co./rel. National Film Board of Canada; prod. Jean-Pierre Lefebvre; scen./dir. Gilles Groulx; cam. (b&w) Michel Brault; ed. Jacques Kasma. Shown at Quinzaine des Réalisateurs, Cannes Film Festival, 1970. 65 min.

Cast: Pierre Harel, Paule Baillargeon, Dolores Monfette, Manon D'Amour, Denise Lafleur, Susan Kay.

This Jean-Pierre Lefebvre picture, this time with Gilles Groulx, is better seen after reading the director's intentions and meaning of the seduction of a woman by a man and of the individual by society, a story told in seven sequences and separated by the then-familiar scenes of student protest (shown in "negative" process).

Q-BEC-MY-LOVE   May 1970
(A Commercial Success)

Prod. co. Jean-Pierre Lefebvre (Cinak); rel. Faroun Films; scen./ed./dir. Jean-Pierre Lefebvre; cam. (b&w) Thomas Vamos; music Andrée Paul. Shown at Quinzaine des Réalisateurs, Cannes Film Festival, 1970. 80 min.

Cast: Anne Lauriault, Jean-Pierre Cartier, Larry Kent, Denis Payne, André Caron, Judith Pare, Raoul Duguay.

Among Quebec's many vigorous and determined movie-makers, none had achieved a reputation quite so quickly and as widespread as Jean-Pierre Lefebvre. It's only fair to point out, however, that he did so mainly by making baffling and convoluted films that his many supporters in Montreal and festival-goers could not help but talk about. He was not likely to find a mass and responsive audience. This film is rather like a scrapbook of bits and pieces of unrelated scenes in a nonmusical revue. Satirical and contemporary, all are paraded in a hit-or-miss fashion, some very funny,

others tedious, dull, and childlike, accompanied by a jumble of sounds and words, tricks, and tomfoolery. Scenes appear to be added at random until feature-length time is achieved. The whole abounds in bare breasts, bottoms, pubic hair, and copulation, about which there is no misunderstanding. While the uninitiated tried to puzzle it out, Lefebvre, one suspects, was laughing quietly up his sleeve. Shown at Osaka, it was also Canada's new invited entry at Berlin in 1970.

GOIN' DOWN THE ROAD   July 1970

Prod. co. Evenden; rel. Phoenix Films; prod./ed./dir. Donald Shebib; story Donald Shebib and William Fruet; scen. William Fruet; cam. (color) Richard Leiterman; music Bruce Cockburn. Prem. New Yorker Cinema, Toronto, July 3, 1970. 90 min.

Roles	Cast
Peter	Doug McGrath
Joey	Paul Bradley
Betty	Jayne Eastwood

and: Nicole Morin, Pierre LaRoche, Gayle Chernin, Ted Sugar, Don Steinhouse, Ron Martin

With few exceptions, the film-makers of any country late in establishing itself with its own feature-length fare must of necessity go through a long and vexing period during which their films fail to find a public large enough to make them financially successful. This was the situation in Canada during 1965 to 1970 as film after film came and went, frequently receiving praise abroad but finding little praise or rentals at home. Experienced observers knew that nothing would change until a certain film comes along that, for a number of reasons, will "catch fire" on its opening, intrigue the public, and suddenly make Canadian films a professional reality and a fact of life.

This long-awaited moment finally arrived with Don Shebib's Goin' Down the Road, which opened to impressive grosses in Toronto and without the supposed benefits of a New York premiere or as an entry in a European festival. Ironically, this success was achieved with a simple drama about class life. Brought in for around $78,000 by 32-year-old Shebib, who was trained in the documentary school of the University of California, CBC, and the National Film Board of Canada, and who found recognition in 1969 for his 45-minute study of old soldiers called Good Times, Bad Times, this first feature is a pleasure to watch and refreshingly free of all the fashions and fads and familiar hangups that infest youth-oriented cinema.

Written by Shebib and William Fruet, the story concerns two simple maritimer provincials who leave their poverty-stricken region and take to the road leading them to Toronto, where, in the big city, they feel sure they will find work, money, and a better life. Without education or skills of any kind, they find they are doomed to a useless existence even worse than what they have left behind.

There are minor technical failures but they never

Paul Bradley and Doug McGrath in *Goin' Down the Road* **(d. Don Shebib, 1970).**

mar this very human and compassionate film, made under great difficulties by a determined young film-maker, who, with his first feature film, found a well-deserved success and made the road easier for others.

ACT OF THE HEART   Sept. 1970

Prod. co. Quest Films; *rel.* Universal; *prod./scen./dir.* Paul Almond; *prod.* Peter Carter; *cam.* (Technicolor) Jean Boffety; *ed.* James Mitchell; *music* Harry Freedman and Gilles Vigneault. 103 min.

Roles	Cast
Martha Hayes	Geneviève Bujold
Father Michael Ferrier	Donald Sutherland
Johane Foss	Monique Leyrac
Russell Foss	Bill Mitchell
Housekeeper	Suzanne Langlois
Adele (at Radio-Canada)	Sharon Acker
Diedrich	Ratch Wallace
Parks Commissioner	Jean Duceppe
Coach Ti-Joe	Gilles Vigneault
Choirmaster	Eric House
Party Guests	Jean Dalmain, Claude

	Jutra, François Tasse
The Northern Stars	Members of Les Hurricans de Ville-Emard
The Church Choir	Members of St. Philips Church

Paul Almond must be recognized as one of Canada's few individualistic film-makers with the courage to express himself without regard for any standard forms or fashions. Following *Isabel,* a tortured tale of a young girl's projections of a terrible past into an awkward present, Almond takes up the matter of religious fervor, which literally burns up his heroine: a young girl who wants to touch God, and falls in love with a priest, who leaves the church. Neither finds happiness. Beautifully made and acted, it is not always convincing and remains emotionally unaffecting.

Other Films in 1970

Deux Femmes En Or (Two Women of Gold) (d. Claude Fournier), a funny sex film whose financial success helped Quebec films back into steady production; a modern version of wives who pay the tradesmen with favors instead of money: with Monique Mercure, Louise Turcot, Marcel Sabourin, Donald Pilon, Donald Lautrec, Jean Lapointe, Olivier Guimond.

A Matter of Fat (d. William Weintraub), a study of a man who shed half his body weight under special treatment.

Neon Palace (d. Peter Rowe), a lively study of the pop art and youthful practices of the fifties and sixties.

L'Initiation (d. Denis Heroux), another comedy about sex and near-sin with Chantal Renaud and Danielle Ouimet.

Love In a Four-Letter World (d. John Sone), more sex, this time in English.

Megantic Outlaw (d. Ron Kelly), a striking drama for CBC-TV based on the true story of a young outlaw in the Quebec Eastern Townships of the early 1880s, with Gary McKeehan, Carol Lazare, Jane Mallet, Ratch Wallace, Lloyd Bochner, Harry Finlay.

Wow (d. Claude Jutra), a film Jutra perhaps should not have made, particularly for the NFB, since it deals in a supposedly comic way with would-be anarchists.

Geneviève Bujold in *Act of the Heart* (d. Paul Almond, 1970).

Great Coups of History (d. Jack Darcus), a charming romance-drama about a young boy who learns of love from an older woman, with Delphine Harvey, Ellis Pryce-Jones, set in Vancouver.

Zero the Fool (d. Morley Markson), a black comedy in an experimental vein with Gerald Cogan and Penelope and Daniel Greff.

Canadian Film Awards 1970

The 22d annual competition attracted 125 entries, 14 of them features, the rest documentaries, television, and public relations films running from five to fifty minutes. The jury consisted of John Grierson, Jan Kadar, Miklos Rozsa, and Canadian critics Louise Bresky and Marc Gervais. In the main categories the winner of the best feature award was *Goin' Down the Road;* best direction: Paul Almond (*Act of the Heart*); best actress: Geneviève Bujold (*Act of the Heart*); best actors: Paul Bradley and Douglas McGrath (*Goin' Down the Road*); best documentary under thirty minutes: *KW-Plus* (Aimé Danis–Quebec Hydro); best documentary over thirty minutes: *Wild Africa* (John Livingston—CBC); best public affairs TV film: *The Little Fellow from Gambo* (Julian Biggs—NFB). The awards and reception were held in public in Canada's largest theater, the Imperial, in Toronto, instead of being part of a professional dinner. For the first time all the jury screenings were open to the public in the St. Lawrence Theatre in order to make entries better known, and programs of the award-winning films were shown across the country in Vancouver, Edmonton, Regina, Winnipeg, Ottawa, Montreal, Charlottetown, Halifax, Fredericton, and St. John's, Newfoundland.

MON ONCLE ANTOINE   May 1971
(My Uncle Antoine)

Prod. co. National Film Board of Canada; *rel.* Gendon Films; *prod.* Marc Beaudet; *dir.* Claude Jutra; *scen.* Clement Perron; *cam.* (Eastmancolor) Michel Brault; *music* Jean Cousineau. Shown at Week of Canadian Cinema, Cannes Film Festival 1971. 110 min.

Roles	*Cast*
Benoit	Jacques Gagnon
Carmen	Lyne Champagne
Antoine	Jean Duceppe
Alexandrine	Monique Mercure
Joseph Poulin	Lionel Villeneuve
Cecile	Olivette Thibault
Elise	Helen Loiselle
Fernand	Claude Jutra

Claude Jutra, like many film-makers, started his career by trying new techniques and abstractions in form and style, but found that narrative and characterization were more important than manipulations of people and camera for the sake of experiment. As a

Jacques Gagnon and Jean Duceppe in *Mon Oncle Antoine* (d. Claude Jutra, 1971).

result, *My Uncle Antoine* is his best film and one of the finest Canadian films of this period.

The familiar story of a village boy growing into manhood and discovering the world and his family anew is beautifully told and acted. Its eternal truths restated make it a compelling and thought-provoking family drama. Although the story takes place in the '40s, the depicted values, behavior, and morality of a small Quebec town are probably not much different today.

L'ACADIE, L'ACADIE   May 1971

Prod. co./rel. National Film Board of Canada; *prod.* Guy L. Cote and Paul Larose; *dir.* Michel Brault and Pierre Perrault; *cam.* (b&w, 16mm) Michel Brault; *ed.* Monique Fortier; *sound* Serge Beauchemin; *rerecording* Roger Lamoureux. Shown at Week of Canadian Cinema, Cannes Film Festival 1971. 117 min.

A *cinema vérité* documentary of a student protest at the University of Moncton in 1968–69 over French-language rights in the province of New Brunswick and other related grievances: a useful document for the future.

THE APPRENTICE (Fleur Bleue)   May 1971

Prod. co. Potterton Productions; *rel.* Faroun Films; *prod.* Donald Brittain; *dir.* Larry Kent; *scen.* Edward Stewart; *cam.* (Eastmancolor) Jean-Claude Labrecque; *music* Roger Gravel. Shown at Week of Canadian Cinema, Cannes Film Festival 1971. 85 min. In French and English.

Cast: Steve Fiset, Celine Bernier, Susan Sarandon, Jean-Pierre Cartier, Paul Berval, Gerard Parkes, Carole Lord, Nana de Varennes.

The story of a Montreal youth whose apprenticeship in life is "doomed to failure." There are some heavy-handed references to French-English animosities, but what could have been a funny, vital, revealing and ultimately tragic story of Quebec society is rendered superficial and unconvincing.

FAUT ALLER PARMI LE MONDE   May 1971
POUR L'SAVOIR
(It is Necessary to Be among the
Peoples of the World to Know Them)

Prod. co. Media (with various Quebec organizations); *dir./ed.* Fernand Dansereau; *cam.* (Eastmancolor, 16mm) Michel Brault; *music* Michel Garneau. Shown at Directors' Fortnight, Cannes Film Festival 1971. 100 min.

This is a long, *cinema vérité* talk picture, done in TV style in which Fernand Dansereau and Michel Brault, noted for their separatist inclinations, visit several towns and cities in Quebec and talk about the various grievances, both real and imagined, of certain groups in the province. Being "among the peoples of the world" to Brault and Dansereau means being "among the people of Quebec." For them, none other exists. This is made clear in the film. Competently done, it is bound to seem monotonous to all but the fiercest separatists, and they have heard it all before.

LES MALES (The Men)   May 1971

Prod. co. Onyx Film and France Film; *rel.* Faroun Films; *prod.* Pierre Lamy; *dir./ed./scen.* Gilles Carle; *cam.* (Eastmancolor) René Verzier; *music* Stephane Venne. Shown at Week of Canadian Cinema, Cannes Film Festival 1971. 113 min.

Cast: Donald Pilon, René Blouin, Andrée Pelletier, Katerine Mousseau.

Backwoods comedy of two clods in the wilderness who have abandoned civilization, but one day decide to hunt for a woman. With its local jokes and provincial references, *Les Males* was a runaway success in Quebec, but was probably too regional to find large audiences elsewhere.

LE MARTIEN DE NOEL   May 1971
(The Christmas Martian)

Prod. co. Faroun Films and Les Cineastes Associés; *rel.* Faroun Films; *dir.* Bernard Gosselin; *scen.* Roch Carrier; *cam.* (Eastmancolor) Alain Dostie; *spec. sound eff.* Robert Laferriere; *music* Jacques Perron. Shown at Week of Canadian Cinema, Cannes Film Festival 1971. 65 min.

A delightful film for young children about a friendly Martian who lands in Quebec's northern woods at Christmas time. He is discovered, lost and cold, by two children who take care of him, and after a snowmobile chase by the villagers, send him on his way again in his twinkling red space craft. A forerunner to *E.T.*

LES MAUDITS SAUVAGES   May 1971
(Those Damned Savages)

Prod. co. Cinak production; *rel.* Faroun Films; *prod./scen./dir.* Jean-Pierre Lefebvre; *cam.* (Eastmancolor) Jean-Claude Labrecque; *ed.* Marguerite Duparc;

music Vivaldi and others. Shown at Directors' Fortnight, Cannes Film Festival 1971. 107 min.

Cast: Pierre Dufresne, Nicole Filion, Rachel Cailhier, Jacques Thisdale, Denise Morelle, Marcel Sabourin, Roger Garceau, Gaetan Labreche and Denis Andre.

In his first film in color, Lefebvre attempted to "repossess," or make contemporary, certain historical facts and characters and place them in the present to show us that society's attitudes, particularly towards humanity, have not changed. These observations revolve around an Indian maiden and a trapper, with the action, if it can be so described, wandering between 1670 and 1970 settings. The belief that life is an "eternal tragicomedy" is hardly original, but Lefebvre has tried to put it all into a different context in restating it.

STOP   May 1971

Prod. co./rel. National Film Board of Canada; *prod.* Pierre Gauvreau; *dir.* Jean Beaudin; *scen.* Clement Perron; *dial.* Minou Petrowski; *cam.* (Eastmancolor) Georges Dufaux; *ed.* Sidney Pearson; *music* Pierre F. Brault. Shown at Week of Canadian Cinema, Cannes Film Festival 1971. 85 min.

Roles	*Cast*
Charles	Raymond Bouchard
Francoise	Danielle Naud
Diane	Marie Tifo

Another *Stop The World I Want To Get Off,* more likely to evoke the response, "stop the film, I want to get out." Once again, the story of people destroying themselves in the human jungle for materialistic purposes and unable to commit themselves to each other or to communicate, all heavily laced with solemn sex both real and imagined. It should have been stopped before it began.

THE ONLY THING YOU KNOW   Aug. 1971

Rel. New Cinema; *prod./dir./scen./ed.* Clarke Mackey; *cam.* (color) Paul Lang; *music* Paul Craven and Iain Ewing. First shown by Canadian Filmmakers Distribution Centre, Rochdale College, Toronto. 80 min.

Cast: Ann Knox, John Denos, Alan Royal, Iain Ewing, Linda Huffman, Hugh and Eileen McIntyre.

A remarkable first feature about a young girl, dissatisfied at home with her tiresome parents, who falls in love with her schoolteacher but finds that romance and affection are hard to find. While a good deal of improvisation is noticeable, the sensitive depiction of the subject matter and the insights it reveals into the nature of the girl's disposition and outlook on life are honest and affecting.

Prod. co. Agincourt International presentation of a John F. Bassett production; *dir.* George McCowan; *scen.* George Robertson; *cam.* (Eastmancolor) Don Wilder; *ed.* Kirk Jones; *music* Ron Collier; *songs* Frank Moore, sung by Moore and Trudy Young. *Prem.* Odeon–Carlton Theatre, Toronto. 90 min.

Roles	*Cast*
Billy Duke	Art Hindle
Sherri Lee Nelson	Trudy Young
Barney Job	Frank Moore
Joe MacMillan	Steve Pernie
Mrs. Duke	Kay Hawtrey
Max	George Eaton
Bud	Robin White
Gerry	Perry Thompson
Graydon Hunter	Austin Willis
Fred Wares	John Vernon
Greg Walsh	Sean Sullivan
Grace Wares	Vivian Reis
George Armstrong	George Armstrong
Mrs. Hunter	Susan Douglas
Leaf Doctor	Harold Ballard

also Derek Sanderson

Hockey is Canada's leading sport, but few films have ever been made about it. This love story with a hockey background is often trite and overly sentimental, yet it has about it an authentic air of what the sport means to Canadians, and its settings and acting performances cannot be faulted.

Other Features Shown at "Cinema Canada," Cannes Film Festival 1971

The Crowd Inside (d. Al Waxman). First film of actor Waxman, in a creditable attempt to explain young girl's discovery of self in a nightmare of sex and drugs. Geneviève Deloir, Alan Dean.

The Reincarnate (d. Don Haldane). Confused and talkative attempt at reincarnation mixed up with black magic and virgin sacrifice. Jack Creeley, Trudy Young.

L'Amour humain (d. Denis Heroux). Nun and priest leave their orders, get married, and come to accept sex without guilt. Louise Marleau, Jacques Riberolles.

Seven Times a Day (d. Denis Heroux). Sex comedy about an architect who is worried over his capacity for sex. Shot in Israel. Rosanna Schiaffino, Jean Coutu.

Madeleine Is. . . (d. Sylvia Spring). Another young girl mixed up in the hippy world of sex and drugs, trying to find out who she is. Nicola Lipman, John Juliani.

Inside Out (d. Graham Parker). Unusual attempt at Second World War spy story with Canadian soldiers for a change. Carole Laure, John Juliani, Ratch Wallace.

The Last Act of Martin Weston (d. Michael Jacot). Shot in Czechoslovakia, somewhat bizarre tale of an engineer who rigs up his suicide, but we don't really know why. Jon Granik, Milena Dvorska, Albert Waxman, Nuala Fitzgerald.

Golden Apples of the Sun (d. Barry Angus McLean). McLean's first film, of boy and girl in the woods, surrealism, sex, and uncertainty as to what it all means. Percy Harkness, Elizabeth Suzuki, Derek Lamb.

Loving and Laughing (d. John Sone). Sex comedy about young people and the free life. André Lawrence, Celine Lomez.

Pile Ou Face (d. Roger Fournier). Sex comedy among skiers. Nathalie Naubert, Jean Coutu.

Canadian Film Awards 1971

The 23d annual competition attracted 143 entries, 12 of them feature-length: *The Crowd Inside, Tiki Tiki* (an animated children's film from Potterton Productions, Montreal), *Loving and Laughing, Fortune and Men's Eyes* (Harvey Hart's American film [shot in Montreal] of John Herbert's play about men in prison), *I'm Going to Get You Elliott Boy* (filmed in Edmonton), *The Reincarnate, Rip Off, The Apprentice, The Only Thing You Know, Life and Times of Chester Angus Ramsgood* (filmed in Vancouver), *The Proud Rider,* and *Foxy Lady.*

The jury was Edgar Anstey, Louise Bresky, Bosley Crowther, Alex North, Jiri Weiss, and Jean-Pierre Tadros. All films were shown to the public free of charge at the St. Lawrence Centre, Toronto, during four days of screening sessions lasting from 9 A.M. to midnight. Awards were presented by Darryl F. Zanuck at a dinner for film-makers at the Royal York Hotel. It was here that John Grierson made his last public appearance in Canada before his death early in 1972.

The winning films: best documentary under 30 minutes: *The Sea* (NFB); best documentary over 30 minutes: *Les Philharmonistes* (NFB); best education film: *It Starts at the Top* (Chetwynd Films, Toronto); best animation film: *Evolution* (NFB); best TV drama: *The Megantic Outlaw* (CBC); best TV/information and public affairs: *The Human Journal* (CTV); best theatrical short: *Don't Knock the Ox* (NFB); best arts and the artist: *Found Sculpture* (ETV); best nature and wildlife: *Temples of Time* (NFB); best travel and adventure: *Under the Sun* (Chinook Films, Edmonton); best sports and recreation: *Ski de Fond* (NFB); best public relations film: *Shebandewan—a Summer Place* (Westminster Films, Toronto); best sales film: *Containerization* (Canawest Films); best experimental film: *Essai à la Mille* (Jean-Claude Labrecque); best feature film: *Mon Oncle Antoine* (NFB); best director: Claude Jutra

(Mon Oncle Antoine); best screenplay: Clement Perron *(Mon Oncle Antoine);* best cinematography: Michel Brault *(Mon Oncle Antoine);* best editing: Douglas Robertson *(Fortune and Men's Eyes*—Cinemex, Canada); best sound: Roger Lamoureux *(Mon Oncle Antoine);* best musical score: Jean Cousineau *(Mon Oncle Antoine);* best actor: Jean Duceppe *(Mon Oncle Antoine);* best actress: Ann Knox *(The Only Thing You Know*—Clarke Mackey Films); best supporting actor: Danny Freedman *(Fortune and Men's Eyes*—Cinemex, Canada); best supporting actress: Olivette Thibault *(Mon Oncle Antoine);* best art direction: Potterton Productions *(Tiki Tiki).*

Special Jury Awards went to: Multiscreen Corporation for "outstanding technical achievement with respect to the IMAX System" and to Clarke Mackey for "outstanding achievement in making his first feature film, *The Only Thing You Know.*"

A FAN'S NOTES   May 1972

Prod. co. Coquihala; *rel.* Warner Bros; *prod.* Martin Davidson; *dir.* Eric Till; *scen.* William Kinsolving, from the novel by Frederick Earl Exley; *cam.* (color) Harry Makin; *ed.* Michael Manne; *music* Ron Collier. In competition at Cannes Film Festival 1972. 90 min.

Roles	Cast
Fred	Jerry Orbach
Patience	Patricia Collins
Mr. Blue	Burgess Meredith
Moms	Rosemary Murphy
Poppy	Conrad Bain
Bunny Sue	Julia Robinson

Based on Frederick Exley's novel in which the narrative is sustained on a fragile thread of thoughts, fantasies, hopes, and despairs, Eric Till has made an imaginative film on an extremely difficult cinematic subject. Ranging from comedy to sadness, black humor to madness, he tells of the unhappiness of a typical North American man who finds that nothing in life has any value. Wanting to be a leader, a hero, a creator, he must accept the fact that his abilities and intelligence will not permit him to be more than a par-

Marcel Sabourin, J. Leo Gagnon, and Luce Guilbeault in *La Maudite Galette* **(d. Denys Arcand, 1972).**

Gordon Pinsent and Will Geer in *The Rowdyman* **(d. Peter Carter, 1972).**

ticipant and a spectator, in sports and in the arts. That he finally comes to terms with his own nature and recognizes his limitations is his final victory. Jerry Orbach gives a funny and deeply felt performance as the "fan," the supporting cast is excellent, and Eric Till has cleverly combined disparate elements into a thoughtful, symbolic study of today's dissatisfied society.

LA MAUDITE GALETTE   May 1972
(That Darned Loot)

Prod. co./rel. Cinak-Carle-Lamy; *prod.* Pierre Lamy; *dir.* Denys Arcand; *scen.* Jacques Benoit; *cam.* (color) Alain Dostie; *ed.* Marguerite Duparc; *music* Gabriel Arcand. Shown at Critics' Week, Cannes Film Festival 1972. 108 min.

Roles	Cast
Berthe	Luce Guilbeault
Ernest	Marcel Sabourin
Roland	René Caron
Uncle Arthur	J. Leo Gagnon
Ti-Bi	Gabriel Arcand
Rosaire	Jean-Pierre Saulnier

Had it moved a little faster and talked a little less, this would have been a superior crime thriller with a neat, twist ending making it suitable for wide popular exhibition. A wickedly black film about a poor plumber, his wife and children, Ernest, their hired-hand and lodger, and the robbery and murder of a rich old uncle, the story variations make an engrossing drama. Unfortunately, the director is dedicated to long, Godardish sequences that slow the pace, introduce tedium, and blunt the satirical ending. Its observations about human nature, however, are deadly accurate.

THE ROWDYMAN   May 1972

Prod. co. Agincourt; *rel.* Crawley Films; *prod.* Lawrence Dane; *dir.* Peter Carter; *scen.* Gordon Pinsent; *cam.* (color) Edmund Long; *ed.* Michael Manne; *music* Ben McPeek. *Prem.* Odeon-Carlton Theatre, Toronto. 95 mins.

Roles	Cast
Will Cole	Gordon Pinsent
Andrew Scott	Frank Converse
Stan	Will Geer

Ruth Lowe	Linda Goranson
Carol Scott	Sabina Maydelle
Constable Williams	Ted Henley
Mary Cole	Estelle Wall
Constable Bill	Stuart Gillard
Walt	Austin Davis
Woman on train	Dawn Greenhalgh

Gordon Pinsent is one of Canada's best-known actors, and, like many of his fellow artists, he was anxious to get films made to provide more opportunities for them. With his own life and Newfoundland in mind, he wrote this screenplay about a forthright, boisterous, independent, fun-loving rascal who finds himself ultimately alone in society. Made entirely on location, with Peter Carter (from CBC-TV) directing his first feature, and with the veteran producer, F. R. Crawley, making this venture possible, the result is a sharply observed study of the simple life and its island people, honest and engaging, with screenwriter Pinsent, who was born in Newfoundland, leaving it to actor Pinsent to make up for certain dramatic weaknesses in the narrative. There are many marvelous moments, notably the scenes between Pinsent and Will Geer, and the whole has a charm and energy that carries it over less articulated sequences.

LA VRAIE NATURE DE BERNADETTE May 1972
(The True Nature of Bernadette)

Prod. co. Carle-Lamy; *rel.* France-Film; *prod.* Pierre Lamy; *scen./dir.* Gilles Carle; *cam.* (color), René Verzier; *ed.* Gilles Carle; *music* Pierre F. Brault. In competition at Cannes Film Festival 1972. 97 min.

Roles	*Cast*
Bernadette	Micheline Lanctot
Thomas	Donald Pilon
Rock	Reynald Bouchard
Octave	Maurice Beaupre
Moise	Ernest Guimond
August	Julien Lippe

Donald Pilon and Micheline Lanctot in *La Vraie Nature de Bernadette (The True Nature of Bernadette)* **(d. Gilles Carle, 1972).**

Felecien	Robert Rivard
Antoine	Willie Lamothe

Bernadette is a pretty young wife and mother who leaves her city home and family to find freedom and purity in the fresh clean air of country life. Taking over an old farm, she also provides sexual gratification for a variety of men, young and aged, crippled and robust. She persuades a mute, abandoned child to speak and finds a horde of handicapped villagers at her door begging for a miracle cure. Meanwhile, two of her visitors turn on her household with guns, a young boy is shot, and farmers dump their produce on the highway in a revolt that is never really explained. While Gilles Carle's vitality as a film-maker never seems to flag, he doesn't give himself enough time to work out or properly motivate his screenplays, which results in slap-dash ideas and incidents, superficiality, melodrama, and ultimately confusion. Fortunately, he has injected a good deal of comedy into the proceedings, and is helped considerably—by the appealing performance of Micheline Lanctot—in getting away with subject matter that only Bunuel has treated successfully.

Films Shown at "Cinema Canada," Cannes Film Festival 1972

L'Amoureuse (d. Jean-Paul Sassy). A young woman escapes from a psychiatric institution and takes refuge in the home of an architect. Sex and madness ensue in confused measure. Benoit Girard, Anna Gàel.

L'Apparition (d. Roger Cardinal). A parody on religious fanaticism and those who profit by it. Slight and uncertain. Pierre Labelle, Guy L'Ecuyer.

Another Smith for Paradise (d. Thomas Shandel). Dismal tale of big business, unfaithful wife, and other assorted agonies. Henry Ramer, Frances Hyland.

Cannibal Girls (d. Ivan Reitman). Girls who eat men. A horror in every sense. Andrea Martin, Eugene Levy.

C'est bien beau l'amour (d. Marc Daigle). Three months in the life of six young people seem like an eternity. Ann Brackman-Janvier.

La Conquête (d. Jacques Gagnon). A married couple meet and fall in love. Much soul-searching. Michele Rossignol, François Tasse.

Le Diable est parmi nous (d. Jean Beaudin). Romance, magic, and murder in a melodrama of mysterious deaths. Louise Marleau, Daniel Pilon.

Ever After All (shown last year as *Golden Apples of the Sun*).

Le Grand Sabordage (d. Alain Perisson). Canada-France coproduction about two children in the city.

Nathalie Drivet, Luce Guilbeault.

IXE-13 (d. Jacques Godbout). Often funny but somewhat strained version of comicstrip super spy. André Dubois, Carole Laure, Luce Guilbeault.

Out of Touch (d. John Gaisford). Nude therapy group encounter led by obnoxious psychologist.

The Proud Rider (d. Chester Stocki). Motorcycle melodrama. Jeremy Kane, Karen Gregory.

Rip Off (d. Donald Shebib). Four youths try to start a commune. Lively comedy about growing up. Don Scardino, Ralph Endersby.

Les Smattes (Wise Guys) (d. Jean-Claude Labrecque). Two young men in the Gaspé fight for their rights and become outlaws. Fine color photography. Daniel Pilon, Donald Pilon, Louise Lapare, Marcel Sabourin.

Tiens-toi bien après les oreilles a Papa (What the Hell Are They Complaining About) (d. Jean Bissonnette). Very funny but sometimes heavy-handed satire on French-English relations within a Montreal insurance firm. Dominique Michel, Yvon Deschamps, Dave Broadfoot.

JOURNEY   Sept. 1972

Prod. co. Quest; *prod.* Paul Almond; *scen./dir.* Paul Almond; *cam.* (Eastmancolor), Jean Boffety; *ed.* Paul Almond and Honor Griffith; *music* Luke Gibson. *Prem.* Canadian Film Awards, Toronto, 1972. 87 min. *Dist.* Astral Films.

Roles	*Cast*
Saguenay	Geneviève Bujold
Boulder Allin	John Vernon
Vid	George Sperdakos
Piers	Elton Hayes
Luke	Luke Gibson

The story is situated outside the normal frame of space and time. It begins with a girl floating down the deep and mysterious Saguenay River. She is rescued by a man who carries her back to a community in the wilderness called Undersky. Its inhabitants live close to the earth in houses and clothes they have made themselves, living off the land they have cultivated. There the girl, a lonely person who cannot make friends, begins to come back to life, to speak and move. She falls in love with the man. But her presence results in strange dark deeds that mar the happiness of the commune. There is nothing for the girl to do but return to the river, where once again she floats away into another world.

Journey was described by Almond as the last of his trilogy (*Isabel* and *Act of the Heart*), but it is difficult to find any direct relationship between the three films other than that of the painfully obscure. The awe-

Geneviève John
Bujold Vernon

Journey
72-710

John Vernon in _Journey_ (d. Paul Almond, 1972).

somely beautiful, mist-shrouded mountainous region of Tadoussac in Quebec seems at times to be enough to sustain the film, but eventually the metaphorical and unfathomable tale drowns in its incomprehensible screenplay. The considerable acting abilities of both John Vernon and Geneviève Bujold cannot hide their own lack of understanding of what they are supposed to represent in Almond's allegory.

LE TEMPS D'UNE CHASSE   Oct. 1972
(The Time of the Hunt)

Prod. co. National Film Board of Canada; *prod.* Pierre Gauvreau; *scen./dir.* Francis Mankiewicz; *cam.* (color) Michel Brault; *ed.* Werner Nold; *music* Pierre F. Brault. *Prem.* Cinema Parisien, Montreal. 90 min.

Roles	*Cast*
Willie	Guy L'Ecuyer
Richard	Marcel Sabourin
Lionel	Pierre Dufresne
Michel	Olivier L'Ecuyer
Monique	Luce Guilbeault
Waitress	Frederique Collin

Francis Mankiewicz's first film was the first important work of the new Canadian cinema. It has much in common with *Wedding in White,* except for its setting, which is almost entirely outdoors. Three men leave Montreal at dawn to go on a weekend hunting trip, a common practice in Canada. They are three foolish men who must rid themselves of the frustrations of domestic life by proving their virility in a desperately cheerful attempt to find an animal to kill, a woman to sleep with, and friends to get drunk with. They succeed in none of their desires and find only increased despair and emptiness in their lives. Here is one of those rare films that never takes a false step nor contains an unnecessary scene. Achingly real, beautifully written, honest, and perceptive, it never compromises or exploits the weakness and despair of its characters. The cast is superb, the technique imaginative and unobtrusive.

WEDDING IN WHITE   Oct. 1972

Prod. co. Dermet Productions; *prod.* John Vidette; *scen./dir.* William Fruet (based on his play); *cam.* (color) Richard Leiterman; *ed.* Tony Lower; *music* Mi-

Frédérique Collin and Marcel Sabourin in *Le Temps d'une chasse (Once upon a Hunt)* (d. Francis Mankiewicz, 1972).

Ian Kymlicka. *Prem.* Uptown Theatre, Toronto. 106 min. *Dist.* Cinepix Ltd.

Roles	Cast
Jim	Donald Pleasence
Jeannie	Carol Kane
Mary	Doris Petrie
Sandy	Leo Phillips
Jimmy	Paul Bradley
Billy	Douglas McGrath
Sarah	Christine Thomas
Dollie	Bonnie Carol Case

William Fruet's first film is his strong adaptation of his play of the same name about a Scottish Presbyterian family in Toronto during the Second World War. Essentially a study of small-minded people living in small, dingy homes, in which a lost and pathetic daughter is made pregnant by the beer-drinking friend of her brother who is home on leave from the army, the film sensitively and knowingly depicts the bleak outlook, attitudes, and banality of hopeless people un-aware of the possibilities of a better life. It is marvelously well-acted, accurately written and observed, and only occasionally overmagnified. Terrible-tempered Donald Pleasence and a resigned Doris Petrie as the parents are drawn from life itself and the re-creation of the period is claustrophobically depressing.

TAUREAU   Nov. 1972

Prod. co. Dist. National Film Board of Canada; *prod.* Marc Beaudet; *dir./scen.* Clement Perron; *cam.* (color) Georges Dufaux; *ed.* Pierre Lemelin; *music* Jean Cousineau. 90 min.

Roles	Cast
Taureau	André Melancon
La Gilbert	Monique Lepage
Denise	Michele Magny
Gigi	Louise Portal
Serge	Marcel Sabourin

The writer of Jutra's *My Uncle Antoine,* Clement

Perron, turns to writing and directing in this film, which is a somewhat sensational and derivative tale of lust and life in a village of demented souls in a country town in Quebec.

Canadian Film Awards 1972

The awards in 1972 went to the following—best feature film: *Wedding in White;* best direction: Gilles Carle *(La Vraie Nature de Bernadette);* best editing: Danielle Cagne *(La Vie revée);* best cinematography: Michel Brault *(Le Temps d'une chasse);* best screenplay: Gilles Carle *(La Vraie Nature de Bernadette);* best sound recording: Claude Hazanavicius *(Le Temps d'une chasse);* best sound re-recording: Film House *(Face Off);* best musical score: Pierre Brault *(La Vrai Nature de Bernadette);* best sound mixing: Honor Griffith/John Kelly *(Journey);* best actor, Gordon Pinsent *(The Rowdyman);* best actress: Micheline Lanctot *(La Vrai Nature de Bernadette);* best supporting actor: Donald Pilon *(La Vrai Nature de Bernadette);* best supporting actress: Doris Petrie *(Wedding in White);* best art direction: Karen Bromley *(Wedding in White);* The Wendy Michener Award for Outstanding Artistic Achievement: Mireille Dansereau *(La Vie revée);* Special Jury Award: Francis Mankiewicz *(Le Temps d'une chasse);* International Jury Award: Quebec Film Office *(Un Petit Canard pas comme les autres* [short subject]); best documentary: Tadeusz Jaworski *(Selling Out).*

The International Jury consisted of: Maurice Blackburn, Jay Leyda, Dusan Makavejev, Satyajit Ray, Jean-Pierre Tadros, and Leslie Wedman.

LA MORT D'UN BOUCHERON   Jan. 1973
(Death of a Lumberjack)

Prod. co. Carle-Lamy; *prod.* Pierre Lamy; *dir./scen./ ed.* Gilles Carle; *cam.* (color) René Verzier; *music* Willie Lamothe. *Prem.* Princess Theatre, Montreal. 115 min. *Dist.* New World Mutual.

Roles	Cast
Marie	Carole Laure
Robert	Daniel Pilon
Blanche	Denise Filiatrault
Armand	Willie Lamothe
Charlotte	Pauline Julien
Ti-noir	Marcel Sabourin

A humorous, sad, and violent account of a village girl who goes to Montreal to find her long-lost father, and of the encounters in which she finds herself. A typical Carle film—friendly, perceptive, sensually aware, and never dull. Carole Laure is provocative and engaging—and went on to more important roles.

A QUIET DAY IN BELFAST   Feb. 1973

Prod. co. Twinbay Media International; *rel.* Ambassa-dor Films; *prod./dir.* Milad Bessada; *scen.* Jack Gray, based on a play of the same name by Andrew Angus Dalrymple; *cam.* (color) Harry Makin; *ed.* Simon Christopher Dew; *music* Greg Adams and Eric Robertson. *Prem.* International Cinema, Toronto. 91 min.

Roles	Cast
John Slattery	Barry Foster
Bridgit Slattery and Thelma	Margot Kidder
Peter O'Lurgan	Sean McCann
Charlie McLarnon	Leo Leyden
Tim Horgan	Mel Tuck
Mrs. McDuatt	Joyce Campion
Mike Mahoney	Sean Mulcahy

This is an odd story filmed on location in Ireland and concerning its present-day troubles, revolving around a small betting shop and its varied customers. It is not without interest, and Margot Kidder is very good in her dual role.

THE RAINBOW BOYS   March 1973

Prod. co. Potterton Productions; *rel.* Mutual Films; *exec. prod.* Murray Shostak; *prod.* Anthony Robinow; *scen./dir.* Gerald Potterton; *cam.* (color) Robert Saad; *ed.* Marlene Fletcher; *music* Howard Blake. *Prem.* Odeon-Fairlawn, Toronto. 92 min.

Roles	Cast
Logan	Donald Pleasence
Gladys	Kate Reid
Mazella	Don Calfa

also Leonard George, Stanley James, Greg George, Bernard Edwards, Isaac Paul, Frederick Earl, Yvonne Weisner, David Thomas.

Outdoor comedy, filmed against the rugged beauty of British Columbia, concerning a comical goldminer and his attempts, with two looney friends, to find a lost mine. Broad and often boring.

KAMOURASKA   March 1973

Prod. co. Carle-Lamy Parc Films; *prod.* Pierre Lamy and Mag Bodard; *dir.* Claude Jutra; *scen.* Anne Hébert and Claude Jutra based on the novel by Anne Hébert; *cam.* (color) Michel Brault, François Protat, and Jean-Charles Tremblay; *ed.* Renée Lichtig, Françoise London, Madeleine Guerin, and Susan Kay; *music* Maurice Le Roux. *Prem.* St. Denis Theatre, Montreal. 123 min. *Dist.* Cinepix Ltd.

Roles	Cast
Elizabeth	Geneviève Bujold
Dr. George Nelson	Richard Jordan
Antoine	Philippe Leotard
Aurelie	Suzie Baillargeon
Jerome	Marcel Cuvellier

A scene from *A Quiet Day in Belfast* (d. Milad Bessada, 1973).

A romantic and passionate tale of Quebec in 1839 concerning a wife who relives her past while tending her dying husband. Jutra's film is astonishing in its sweep and power, yet the characters are subtlely delineated and its depiction of the past is detailed and vividly expressed. (The original version of 173 min. was shown on Pay-TV in 1984.)

REJEANNE PADOVANI   March 1973

Prod. co. Cinak; *prod.* Jean-Pierre Lefebvre; *dir.* Denys Arcand; *scen.* Denys Arcand and Jacques Benoit; *cam.* (color) Alain Dostie; *ed.* Marguerite Duparc; *music* Gluck and Boudreau. *Prem.* Cinema Vendome, Montreal. 94 min. *Dist.* Cinepix Ltd.

Roles	Cast
Vincent Padovani	Jean Lajeunesse
Rejeanne Padovani	Luce Guilbeault
Jean-Leo	Roger Lebel
Stella	Margo McKinnon
Minister	René Caron
Aline	Therese Cadorette
Jean-Pierre	Jean-Pierre Lefebvre
Hélène	Frédérique Collin
Dominique	Pierre Theriault
Lucky	Gabriel Arcand

Tannenbaum	Henry Ramer

A forthright melodrama about corruption in Quebec in the construction business, with strong political overtones and caustic comments about businessmen and their deals with governments.

KEEP IT IN THE FAMILY   April 1973

Prod. co. Dal Productions; *rel.* Cinepix; *prod.* John Dunning and Andre Link; *dir.* Larry Kent; *scen.* Edward Stewart; *cam.* (color) Roger Moride; *ed.* Larry Kent; *music* Paul Baillargeon. *Prem.* Westmount Square Theatre, Montreal. 91 min.

Roles	Cast
Celia	Patricia Gage
Roy	John Gavin
Karen	Adrienne La Russa
Alex	Allan McRae

Silly domestic sex-comedy in which a young married couple, annoyed by the refusal of their parents to subsidize their extravagant living, plan to seduce the parents in revenge.

U-TURN   April 1973

Prod. co. George Kaczender; *rel.* Cinepix; *dir.* George Kaczender; *scen.* Douglas Bowie; *cam.* (Eastmancolor) Miklos Lente; *ed.* George Kaczender; *music* Neil Chotem. *Prem.* Avenue Theatre, Montreal. 97 min.

Roles	Cast
Scott	David Selby
Paula and Tracy	Maud Adams
Bonnie	Gay Rowan
Prof. Bamberger	William Osler
Holly	Diane Dewey

A young lawyer is so struck by a pretty girl he meets at the ferry that he spends the next two years in a desperate search for her. He finds her but she is married with children, and he leaves her more unhappy than before. Romantic but wearying.

After many short films at the National Film Board and the feature *Don't Let The Angels Fall,* this was Kaczender's first independent film.

SLIPSTREAM   May 1973

Prod. co. Pacific Rim Films; *rel.* Cinepix; *prod.* James Margellos; *dir.* David Acomba; *scen.* William Fruet, from an original story by David Acomba; *cam.* (color) Marc Champion; *ed.* Tony Lower; *music* Brian Ahern,

Kate Reid in *The Rainbow Boys* (d. Gerald Potterton, 1973).

Roger Lebel and Luce Guilbeault in *Rejeanne Padovani* (d. Denys Arcand, 1973).

Van Morrison, and Eric Clapton. *Prem.* Lethbridge, Alberta. 92 min.

Roles	Cast
Mike Mallard	Luke Askew
Kathy	Patti Oatman
Alec	Eli Rill
Terry	Scott Hylands
Hitch	Danny Friedman

A first feature by Acomba about a reclusive discjockey on the prairies who broadcasts hard-rock music and takes a dim view of life and love. Beautifully photographed, but dramatically confused.

MONTREAL MAIN   Sept. 1973

Prod. co. President Film; *rel.* Faroun Films; *prod.* Frank Vitale and Allan Moyle; *dir.* Frank Vitale; *scen.* John Sutherland; *cam.* (b&w) Erich Block; *ed.* Frank Vitale; *music* Beverly Glenn-Copeland. *Prem.* Montreal Film Festival, 88 min. Improvised by a nonprofessional cast.

Roles	Cast
Frank	Frank Vitale
Johnny	John Sutherland

Christopher Plummer in *The Pyx* (d. Harvey Hart, 1973).

also Dave Sutherland, Anne Sutherland, Peter Brawley, Pam Marchant, Allan Moyle, Jackie Holden.

A well-intentioned but depressing story about a relationship between a mature man and an adolescent boy, set in an artists' colony in Montreal in which everyone is thoroughly unhappy about life.

THE PYX   Sept. 1973

Prod. co. Maxine Samuels–Julian Roffman; *rel.* Cinepix (Cinerama in U.S.A.); *dir.* Harvey Hart; *scen.* Robert Schlitt, from a novel by John Buell; *cam.* (color) René Verzier; *ed.* Ron Wisman; *music* Harry Freedman, songs composed and sung by Karen Black. *Prem.* Place de Ville Cinema II, Ottawa. 111 min.

Roles	Cast
Elizabeth Lucy	Karen Black
Jim Henderson	Christopher Plummer
Pierre Pequette	Donald Pilon
Keerson	Jean-Louis Roux
Meg	Yvette Brind'Amour
Superintendent	Jacques Godin
Herbie Lafram	Lee Broker
Jimmy	Terry Haig
Worther	Robin Gammell
Sandra	Louise Rinfret

The strange and troubling tale of a night world, where a beautiful callgirl becomes involved in religious hocus-pocus. A first cousin, far removed, to *Rosemary's Baby*.

Y'A TOUJOURS MOYEN   Sept. 1973
DE MOYENNER
(There's Always a Way to Find a Way)

Prod. co. Cinevideo–Les Films du Nouveau Monde–Cinemas Units–Tele-Capitale; *rel.* Distributions Cine-Capitale; *dir.* Denis Heroux; *scen.* Marcel Lefebvre; *cam.* (color) René Verzier; *ed.* Yves Langlois; *music* Marcel Lefebvre. *Prem.* Palace Theatre, Montreal. 92 min.

Roles	Cast
Yvan	Yvon Ducharme
Sam	Jean-Guy Moreau
Willie Turgeon	Willie Lamothe
Marie	Danielle Ouimet
Mother Superior	Dominique Michel

A tired and predictable slap-dash comedy about a bank teller who finds himself in all kinds of trouble as a result of his brother-in-law, who wants to get rich quick.

Henry Beckman, Charles Shamata, and Hugh Webster in *Between Friends* (d. Don Shebib, 1973).

Nancy Belle Fuller and Donnelly Rhodes in *The Hard Part Begins* (d. Paul Lynch, 1973).

BETWEEN FRIENDS   Oct. 1973

Prod. co. Clearwater Films; *rel.* New Cinema; *prod.* Chalmers Adams; *dir.* Donald Shebib; *scen.* Claude Harz; *cam.* (color) Richard Leiterman; *ed.* Tony Lower; *music* Matthew McCauley. *Prem.* Ontario Film Theatre, Toronto. 91 min.

Roles	*Cast*
Toby	Michael Parks
Ellie	Bonnie Bedelia
Chino	Chuck Shamata
Will	Henry Beckman
Coker	Hugh Webster

After having been good friends in California, two young men meet again in Toronto and decide to steal the payroll of a mining company in Sudbury, northern Ontario. The scheme fails. A story as bleak as the winter snows and as desperate as the characters themselves, this is a poignant, understanding, and extremely honest film that further enhances the reputation of Donald Shebib *(Goin' Down The Road)* as Canada's best film-maker working in English. The moral of the film is clearly stated: there is no easy way out of life's difficulties, whether they are emotional or physical, unless the individual is prepared to face them with confidence and determination.

THE HARD PART BEGINS   Oct. 1973

Prod. co. Odyssey Films Ltd.; *exec. prod.* Ratch Wallace; *prod.* John Clifford Hunter and Derrett Lee; *dir.* Paul Lynch; *scen.* John Clifford Hunter; *cam.* (Kodak color) Robert Saad; *ed.* William Gray; *music* Ian Guenther. *Prem.* Filmexpo, National Arts Centre, Ottawa. 80 min. *Dist.* Cinepix Ltd.

Roles	Cast
King	Donnelly Rhodes
Jenny	Nancy Belle Fuller
Duane	Paul Bradley
Alice	Linda Sorenson
Roxon	Robert Hawkins
Al Dawson	Doug McGrath
Mechanic	Les Carlson

and Neil Vipond, Vinetta Strombergs, Marie Fleming, Cliff Carroll, Hugh Curry, David Daniels.

A film about a down-and-out country-and-western singer traveling around the small towns of Ontario, containing a strong emotional appeal and realistic settings, providing an arresting insight into character and motivation.

PAPERBACK HERO   Oct. 1973

Prod. co. Agincourt International Ltd.; *rel.* New Cinema; *prod.* James Margellos and John F. Bassett; *dir.* Peter Pearson; *scen.* Les Rose and Barry Pearson; *cam.* (color) Don Wilder; *ed.* Kirk Jones; *music* Ron Collier. "If You Could Read My Mind" written and performed by Gordon Lightfoot. *Prem.* Paramount Theatre, Saskatoon. 94 min.

Roles	Cast
Rick	Keir Dullea
Loretta	Elizabeth Ashley
Pov	John Beck
Joanna	Dayle Haddon
Big Ed	Franz Russell
Burdock	George R. Robertson

and Margot Lamarre, Ted Follows, Linda Sorenson, Les Ruby, Jacquie Presly, Chet Robertson, Winnie Rowles.

A far-fetched mini-western about a skirt-chasing hockey hero who shoots up the town whenever he pleases. One of the increasing number of films that was undecided about whether to be Canadian or American.

Franz Russell in *Paperback Hero* (d. Peter Pearson, 1973).

J. Leo Gagnon and Marthe Nadeau in *Les Dernières Fiançailles (The Last Betrothal* (d. Jean-Pierre Lefebvre, 1973).

LES CORPS CELESTES   Nov. 1973
(Heavenly Bodies)

Prod.. co. Mojack Carle-Lamy; *rel.* Cine-Art; *prod.* Pierre Lamy; *dir.* Gilles Carle; *scen.* Gilles Carle and Arthur Lamothe; *cam.* (color) Jean-Claude Labrecque; *ed.* Renée Lichtig; *music* Phillipe Sarde. *Prem.* Cinema Fleur de Lys, Montreal. 104 min.

Roles	*Cast*
Desmond	Donald Pilon
Rose-Marie	Carole Laure
Sweetie	Micheline Lanctot
Betty	Judi McDonald
Helen	Sheila Charlesworth
Katie	Reda Markovits
Brigitte	Claudie Verdant
The Polish	Dominique Charron
Lorenzo	Yvon Barrette
Parish Priest	Jacques Dufilho

A slight but lively comedy with serious undertones about a pimp who arrives in a small mining town with seven prostitutes and plans to open a whorehouse and enjoy himself on the proceeds. The coming of the Second World War changes his plans.

LES DERNIERES FIANCAILLES   Nov. 1973
(The Last Betrothal)

Prod. co. Cinak and Prisma Films; *rel.* Faroun Films; *prod.* Marguerite Duparc and Bernard Lalonde; *dir./scen.* Jean-Pierre Lefebvre; *cam.* (color) Guy Dufaux; *ed.* Marguerite Duparc; *music* André Paul. *Prem.* Cinémathèque Québecois. 91 min.

Roles	*Cast*
Rose Tremblay	Marthé Nadeau
Armand Tremblay	J. Leo Gagnon
The Doctor	Marcel Sabourin

Armand Tremblay, 78, and his wife, 75, have lived together for more than fifty years on a piece of land they cleared themselves. Their solitude is almost total, and their days are filled with the simple acts of working, eating, sleeping. The film closes with their deaths. While it seems only to watch, this is an unexpectedly tender, evocative, and entirely beautiful study that makes an ordinary existence one of happiness and serenity, conveyed by Lefebvre's style of long takes, slow panning shots, and a remarkable observance of real time.

THE HEATWAVE LASTED   Dec. 1973
FOUR DAYS

Prod. co./rel. National Film Board; *prod./scen./dir.* Douglas Jackson; *cam.* (color) Douglas Kiefer; *ed.* Eddy Le Lorrain; *music* Ben Low. *Prem.* National Film Board Theatre, Montreal. 84 min.

Roles	Cast
Cliff	Gordon Pinsent
Barbara	Alexandra Stewart
Cuozzo	Lawrence Dane
Gabriella	Domini Blythe
Harry	Albert Waxman
Inspector	Ron Hartman
Jennifer	Judy Ann Davies
Sterzi	Jon Granik
Wife	Joan Blackman
Bob	Jean-Roger Periard

A Montreal television cameraman accidentally witnesses a heroin deal and finds himself involved with the underworld. A taut and tightly told contemporary

Donald Sutherland in *Alien Thunder* (d. Claude Fournier, 1973).

drama, giving a Canadian view of criminal life usually found only in American films.

Canadian Film Awards 1973

The CFA judging and presentation ceremony was moved from Toronto to Montreal in 1973 in order to represent other provinces. The ceremony, however, did not take place as a result of opposition from local film-makers who objected to money being spent on an awards procedure. The ceremony was abandoned, but awards were made: best feature film: *Slipstream;* best actress: Geneviève Bujold *(Kamouraska);* best actor: Jacques Godin *(OK la liberté);* Special Jury Prizes: Claude Jutra, Gilles Carle.

JE T'AIME   Jan. 1974
(I Love You)

Prod. co. Cinévideo-Télé-Capitale (Quebec); *rel.* Films Mutuels; *prod.* Claude Heroux; *dir./scen./ed.* Pierre Duceppe; *cam.* (Color) René Verzier; *music* Franck Dervieux, *Prem.* Le Cinéma Parisien, Montreal. 90 min.

Roles	Cast
Elisa Boussac	Jeanne Moreau
Martine Boussac	Roseline Hoffman
Marcellin	Lionel Villeneuve
Arthur Tremblay	Jean Duceppe
Jerome Demers	Jean-René Ouellet

Romantic but banal melodrama of torment and passion in a small Quebec village involving a woman from France, her daughter, and their lovers.

ALIEN THUNDER   Feb. 1974

Prod. co. Onyx Films; *rel.* Cinerama, Inc.; *prod.* Marie-José Raymond; *dir./cam.* (color) Claude Fournier; *scen.* George Malko; *ed.* Yves Langlois; *music* Georges Delerue. *Prem.* Capitol Theatre, Regina, Sask. 90 min. *Dist.* Ambassador Films.

Roles	Cast
Dan Candy	Donald Sutherland
Almighty Voice	Gordon Tootoosis
Sounding Sky	Chief Dan George
Malcolm Grant	Kevin McCarthy
Inspector Brisebois	Jean Duceppe
Emilie Grant	Francine Racette

This film is based on a true story in which a Cree Indian kills a North West Mounted Police sergeant. He is hunted for two years; the end brings tragedy for all those involved. An unusual, quiet, and engrossing frontier story, told in terms that place it far from the conventional American western.

Denise Filiatrault in *Il était une fois dans l'est (Once upon a Time in the East)* (d. André Brassard, 1974).

IL ETAIT UNE FOIS DANS L'EST   Feb. 1974
(Once upon a Time in the East)

Prod. co. Carle-Lamy; *rel.* Société Nouvelle de Cinématographie; *prod.* Pierre Lamy; *dir./scen.* Andre Brassard; *cam.* (color) Paul Van der Linden; *ed.* André Corriveau; *music* Jacques Perron. *Prem.* St. Denis Theatre, Montreal. 101 min. *Dist.* Lapointe Films.

Roles	Cast
Hélène	Denise Filiatrault
Pierrette	Michelle Rossignol
Lise Paquette	Frédérique Collin
Carmen	Sophie Clement
Sandra	André Montmorency
Bec-de-lièvre	Amulette Garneau
Maurice	Denis Drouin
Hossanna	Jean Archambault

Characters from plays written by Michel Tremblay, come together in the lively and sordid nightworld of Montreal East, where they have been formed by life into strange and desperate patterns of behavior. A good deal of truth, a knowing insight into hearts and minds, and some rousing performances make the sen-sational aspects of the activity depicted very real and touched with tragedy.

BINGO   March 1974

Prod. co./rel. New World Mutual Films; *prod.* Pierre David and Jean-Claude Lord; *dir./scen./ed.* Jean-Claude Lord; *cam.* (color) Claude Larue; *music* Michel Comte. *Prem.* Cinéma Le Parisien, Montreal. 116 min.

Roles	Cast
François	Rejean Guenette
Geneviève	Anne Marie Provencher
Fernand	Claude Michaud
Hélène	Alexandra Stewart
Pierre	Gilles Pelletier
Eva	Manda Parent
Madeleine	Janine Fluet
Eugene	Jean Duceppe

The most important film of 1974, this is a disturbing, dramatic fiction with documentary overtones set around the Front de Libération du Québec October

215

crisis in Montreal in which two young students are unwittingly involved and then destroyed by politics and big business. Under its deceptively lighthearted title (which refers to an aunt's mania for the game), this picture brings out the ugliest aspects of French-Canadian nationalism. At first a thoughtful study of the effect of a factory strike on a family, it soon divides the generations as it depicts the treachery of the establishment, both in the political and economic sense. Terrorism raises its ugly head, issues are exploited by individuals for their own gain, the guilty go free, and the innocent suffer. As the plotting of right-wing factions to seize power increases in force, so the tragedy of a society torn by indecision and despair reveals itself. Jean-Claude Lord has not since made a film of such power and purpose as this.

THE APPRENTICESHIP
OF DUDDY KRAVITZ

April 1974

Prod. co. International Cinemedia Centre; *exec. prod.* Gerald Schneider; *prod.* John Kemeny; *dir.* Ted Kotcheff; *scen.* Mordecai Richler, based on his novel of the same name, and adaptation by Lionel Chetwynd; *cam.* (color) Brian West; *ed.* Thom Noble; *music* Stanley Myers. *Prem.* Place-des-Arts, Montreal. 120 min. *Dist.* Astral Films.

Roles	*Cast*
Duddy	Richard Dreyfuss
Yvette	Micheline Lanctot
Max	Jack Warden
Virgil	Randy Quaid
Uncle Benjy	Joseph Wiseman
Friar	Denholm Elliott
Dingleman	Henry Ramer
Farber	Joe Silver
Grandfather	Zvee Scooler
Calder	Robert Goodier

Mordecai Richler's popular novel about a determined Jewish lad in Montreal who tries to get to the top by selling whatever and whomever he can, comes to the screen with its humanity, pathos, and good humor intact, but the use of five American actors in the lead roles tends to give the Montreal setting the flavor of New York's East Side.

BAR SALON

May 1974

Prod. co. Les Films André Forcier Inc.; *prod.* Jean Dansereau; *dir.* André Forcier; *scen.* André Forcier and Jacques Marcotte; *cam.* (b&w) François Gill and Claude Racine; *ed.* François Gill; *music* Michel

Richard Dreyfuss and Micheline Lanctôt in *The Apprenticeship of Duddy Kravitz* **(d. Ted Kotcheff, 1974).**

McLean. *Prem.* CGEP St. Laurent, Montreal. 84 min. *Dist.* New Cinema.

Cast: Guy L'Ecuyer, Jacques Marcotte, Madeleine Chartrand, Lucille Belair, Gelinas Fortin, Michele Dion.

An extraordinary, low-budget film about a corner pub in one of the impoverished areas of Montreal and its owner, the customers, their failings, and their bleak future. Mostly a hopeless lot, they are observed with a stark realism and a love for the "lower depths" of cinema expressionism.

ACTION: THE OCTOBER   Sept. 1974
CRISIS OF 1970

Documentary. *Prod. co./rel.* National Film Board; *prod.* Tom Daly, Normand Cloutier, and Robin Spry; *dir.* Robin Spry; *cam.* (b&w) various photographers; *ed.* Shelagh MacKenzie and Joan Henson. *Prem.* Stratford International Film Festival. 87 min.

A strong and gripping feature-length documentary that delves into the sources and rise of the separatist movement in Quebec, from the death of Duplessis to the October Crisis of 1970. Three-quarters of the film deals with the events in October that began with the kidnapping of James R. Cross. Photos and archival footage shot by the NFB during that period are used to supplement the footage shot by other groups. The protagonists involved in this drama are men named Trudeau, Bourassa, Levesque, Drapeau, Douglas, Lemieux, and others. Their speeches and explanations are interwoven with the kidnappings, the communiqués, the FLQ manifesto, the War Measures Act, the death of Pierre Laporte, the arrival of the Canadian army, the arrests and escapes, and the civil rights questions. The film ends at the end of 1970 with the arrest of the alleged killers of Pierre Laporte.

LES ORDRES (The Orders)   Sept. 1974

Prod. co. Les Productions Prisma; *rel.* Films Mutuels; *scen./ed./dir.* Michel Brault; *cam.* (b&w/color) Michel Brault, *asst.* Michel Bissonnette. *Prem.* at Cinema Place Ville Marie, Montreal. 107 min.

Roles	*Cast*
Clement Boudreau	Jean Lapointe
Marie Boudreau	Helen Loiselle
Richard Lavoie	Claude Gauthier
Claudette Dussault	Louise Forestier
Jean-Marie Beauchemin	Guy Provost

An affecting, dramatized account of the experiences of people taken to prison under the War Measures Act during the October crisis of 1970 in Montreal. Some were guilty, but many were innocent, caught in the dragnet that supposes all are guilty. The accumulation

A scene from *Action—The October Crisis of 1970* (d. Robin Spry, 1973).

of significant and human details conveys honestly and fairly the humiliation of innocent people, caught up in the backlash of a violent period of terrorist activity.

WHY ROCK THE BOAT?   Sept. 1974

Prod. co. National Film Board; *rel.* Columbia Pictures of Canada; *exec. prod.* James de B. Domville; *prod.* William Weintraub; *dir.* John Howe; *scen.* William Weintraub, based on his novel; *cam.* (color) Savas Kalogeras; *ed.* Marie-Helen Guillemin; *music/lyrics* John Howe. *Prem.* Avenue Theatre, Montreal. 111 min.

Roles	*Cast*
Harry Barnes	Stuart Gillard
Ronny Waldron	Ken James
Julia Martin	Tiiu Leek
Philip L. Butcher	Henry Beckman
Fred O'Neill	Budd Knapp
Herb Scannell	Sean Sullivan
Isobel Scannell	Patricia Gage
Señor Gomez	Ruben Moreno
Carmichael	Cec Linder
Club President	Henry Ramer
Benson	Barrie Baldaro
Hilda	Patricia Hamilton

Jean Lapointe in *Les Ordres* **(d. Michel Brault, 1974).**

Stuart Gillard and Ken James in *Why Rock the Boat?* **(d. John Howe, 1974).**

A fresh, gentle, and witty comedy about a young reporter who goes to work on a Montreal paper in the forties, only to lose his innocence and discover the facts of life. Based on the actual experiences of the writer, William Weintraub. Stuart Gillard is perfect in the leading role.

BLACK CHRISTMAS   Oct. 1974

Prod. co. Vision IV; *prod.* Robert Clark and Gerry Arbeid; *dir.* Robert Clark; *orig. scen.* Roy Moore; *cam.* (Technicolor) Reginald Morris; *ed.* Stan Cole; *music* Carl Zittrer. *Prem.* Imperial Theatre, Toronto. 98 min. *Dist.* Ambassador Films.

Roles	*Cast*
Jess	Olivia Hussey
Peter	Keir Dullea
Barb	Margot Kidder
Phyl	Andrea Martin
Mrs. Mac	Marian Waldman
Chris	Art Hindle
Clare Harrison	Lynne Griffin
Mr. Harrison	James Edmond
Nash	Douglas McGrath
Lt. Fuller	John Saxon

An abysmal horror film about an unspeakable "something" that terrorizes a college for girls over the Christmas season.

CHILD UNDER A LEAF   Oct. 1974

Prod. co. Potterton; *rel.* Les Films Mutuels; *prod.* Robert Baylis and Murray Shostak; *dir./scen./ed.* George Bloomfield; *cam.* (Eastmancolor) Donald Wilder; *music* Francis Lai. *Prem.* Towne Cinema, Toronto. 90 min.

Roles	*Cast*
Domino	Dyan Cannon
Joseph	Donald Pilon
Husband	Joseph Campanella

also Micheline Lanctot, Bud Knapp, Albert Waxman.

A foolish film about a married woman, her lover, their "love child," and her jealous and violent husband.

Other Films of 1974

The Inbreaker (d. George McCowan). Lower-bill emotional drama set in the Pacific coast deep-sea fishing trade.

Jacques Brel is Alive and Well (d. Denis Heroux). An unusual work from Mr. Heroux, who has filmed the musical play with flair and imagination.

Janis (d. Howard Alk). A documentary on the life of

Brenda Donohue in *Me* (d. John Palmer, 1974).

the rock singer, Janis Joplin.

The Keeper (d. Tom Drake). A comic horror with Christopher Lee.

Love at First Sight (d. Rex Bromfield). Young love notable only for the introduction to the screen of Dan Aykroyd.

The Man Who Skied Down Everest (d. F. R. Crawley). A documentary on the Japanese skier who spent more time walking up than skiing down. (Academy Award for Best Feature Length Documentary 1976.)

Me (d. John Palmer). Based on Martin Kinch's play about a violent relationship between a writer and his lovers.

The Melting Pot (d. Deke Miles). A documentary on the great Winnipeg flood.

Monkeys in the Attic (d. Morley Markson). A weird and overblown domestic imbroglio.

My Pleasure is My Business (d. Albert Waxman). Toronto welcomes the Happy Hooker, Xavier Hollander.

Mystery of the Million Dollar Hockey Puck (d. Jean Lafleur and Peter Svatek). Likable children's film.

125 Rooms of Comfort (d. Patrick Loubert) are in Grand Central Hotel in St. Thomas, Ontario, and the owner wants to sell it.

Only God Knows (d. Peter Pearson). Cheerful but strained attempt at a Canadian *Carry On* with Gordon Pinsent and Lawrence Dane.

La Pomme, La Queue . . . Et Les Pepins! (d. Claude Fournier). Sex comedy about an impotent lover.

Sally Fieldgood & Co. (d. Boon Collins). Set in British Columbia, this film was intended to be a robust comedy about a traveling lady of pleasure and the miners she visits.

A Star Is Lost (d. John Howe). A musical from the NFB that was lost before it began.

The Supreme Kid (d. Peter Bryant). A likable but overlong tale about present-day wanderers.

To Kill the King (d. George McCowan). Contrived Canadian–U.S. drama about the assassination of the American president.

Canadian Film Awards 1974

Following the collapse of the CFA in Montreal in 1973 due to dissent on the part of local film-makers, the CFA was not held in 1974.

GINA   Jan. 1975

Prod. co. Carle-Lamy; *rel.* Cinepix; *prod.* Pierre Lamy; *scen./ed./dir.* Denys Arcand; *cam.* (color) Alain Dostie; *music* Michel Pagliaro and Benny Barbara. *Prem.* Place Ville Marie, Montreal. 95 min.

Roles	*Cast*
Gina	Celine Lomez
Bob	Claude Blanchard
Dolores	Frédérique Collin
Assistant Cameraman	Serge Theriault
Director	Gabriel Arcand
Titel	Jocelyn Berube

also Andre Gagnon, Carol Faucher, Paule Baillargeon.

Based partly on his own experiences as a documentary film-maker, Denys Arcand has made an ironic study of a unit shooting a film about conditions in a strike-bound textile factory and of its involvement with a striptease girl. Told in violent and symbolic terms, it is a strangely disturbing and critical statement about individuals and their pursuits.

SUNDAY IN THE COUNTRY   March 1975

Prod. co. Impact-Quadrant; *rel.* Ambassador Films;

prod. David Perlmutter; *dir.* John Trent; *scen.* Robert Maxwell and John Trent, from a story by David Main; *cam.* (color) Marc Champion; *ed.* Tony Lower; *music* Paul Hoffert. *Prem.* Uptown 2, Toronto. 90 min.

Roles	*Cast*
Adam Smith	Ernest Borgnine
Leroy	Michael J. Pollard
Lucy	Hollis McLaren
Dinelli	Louis Zorich
Ackerman	Cec Linder
Luke	Vladimir Valenta
Sergeant	Al Waxman
Eddie	Tim Henry
Conway	Murray Westgate
Timmy Peterson	Ralph Endersby
Jennifer Logan	Sue Petrie
Policeman	Ratch Wallace
Highway Patrol	Mark Walker and Gary Reineke
Station Master	Eric Clavcring
Pastor	David Hughes
Radio Announcer	Carl Banas
Church goers	Franz Russell, Ruth Springford, Alan King, Laddie Dennis, Joan Hurley, Winnifred Springbett, Jonathan White, and Jim Barron.

Celine Lomez in *Gina* (d. Denys Arcand, 1979).

Monique Mercure and Louis Pelletier in *Les Vautours* (d. Jean-Claude Labrecque, 1975).

A contrived and bloody melodrama about a farmer and his terrible vengeance on three bank robbers. This film marked the beginning of Canada's pseudo-American film period (the setting is supposedly the U.S.) with American actors in the leading roles.

LES VAUTOURS (The Vultures)   March 1975

Prod. co. Films Jean-Claude Labrecque Inc.; *prod.* Louise Ranger; *dir./ed.* Jean-Claude Labrecque; *scen.* Robert Gurik, from an original idea by Jean-Claude Labrecque; *cam.* (color) Alain Dostie; *music* Dominique Tremblay. *Prem.* Dauphin Cinema, Quebec City. 91 min. *Dist.* Lapointe Films.

Cast: Gilbert Sicotte, Monique Mercure, Carmen Tremblay, Amulette Garneau.
also (in alphabetical order):
Gabriel Arcand, Paule Baillargeon, Jacques Bilodeau, Raymond Cloutier, Jean Duceppe, Robert Gravel, Georges Proulx, Rita Lafontaine, Roger Lebel, Nicole Leblanc, Guy L'Ecuyer, Gilbert Lepage, Claude Maher, Jean Mathieu, Gilles Pelletier, Denise Proulx, Anne-Marie Provencher, Philippe Robert, Yolande Roy, Jean-Pierre Saulnier.

A young man becomes an unwitting pawn in an artful political game played out during the corrupt regime of Premier Maurice Duplessis of Quebec; a shadowy and thoughtful film about human relationships and individual selfishness. (See *Les Années de Rêves,* page 263).

LIES MY FATHER TOLD ME   May 1975

Prod. co. Pentimento and Pentacle VIII; *rel.* Columbia (Astral Films in Canada); *prod.* Anthony Bedrich and Harry Gulkin; *dir.* Jan Kadar; *orig. story/scen.* Ted Allan; *cam.* (color) Paul Van Der Linden; *ed.* Edward Beyer and Richard Marks; *music* Sol Kaplan. *Prem.* Cinema Place Ville Marie, Montreal. 103 min.

Roles	Cast
Zaida	Yossi Yadin
Harry Herman	Len Birman
Annie Herman	Marilyn Lightstone
David	Jeffrey Lynas
Mr. Baumgarten	Ted Allan
Mrs. Tannenbaum	Barbara Chilcott
Mrs. Bondy	Mignon Elkins
Uncle Benny	Henry Ramer
Edna	Carole Lazare
Cleo	Paskal

A poor man's "fiddler without music" in which a young boy remembers his youth and grandfather in old

Len Birman and Marilyn Lightstone in *Lies My Father Told Me* (d. Jan Kadar, 1974).

Montreal. Overly sentimental and unevenly directed, it is nonetheless sensitive and intelligent.

SUDDEN FURY   May 1975

Prod. co. Film Can; *rel.* Ambassador; *prod.* Ben Caza; *scen./dir.* Brian Damude; *cam.* (Eastmancolor) James Kelly; *ed.* David Nicholson; *music* Matthew McCauley. At Cinema Canada market, Cannes Film Festival 1975. 95 min.

Roles	*Cast*
Fred	Dominic Hogan
Janet	Gay Rowan
Al	Dan Hennessy
Laura	Hollis McLaren
Dan	David Yorston
Polanski	Sean McCann
Gas Station Attendant	Eric Clavering

Set in the Ontario countryside during summertime, this effectively told, low-budget film concerns a wrought-up husband whose work is failing, whose wife is unfaithful, and who, on a car journey northwards, becomes thoroughly demented when she refuses to give him the money he asks for to buy land in a real estate scheme, which he hopes will restore him to the affluent society.

In the "American Tragedy" situation, an accident gives him the opportunity to leave his wife to die. A sympathetic young man comes along and attempts to save her. By the time this straightforward but ingenious tale has finished, in a climax worthy of Shakespeare, the innocent man is the murderer.

POUR LE MEILLEUR   Sept. 1975
ET POUR LE PIRE
(For Better, For Worse)

Prod. co. Carle-Lamy Productions Ltd.; *rel.* Cinepix; *prod.* Pierre Lamy; *scen./dir.* Claude Jutra; *cam.* (color) Alain Dostie; *ed.* Pascale Laverriere; *music* Pierre Brault. *Prem.* Stratford International Film Festival, Avon Theatre. 110 min.

Roles	*Cast*
Bernard	Claude Jutra
Helene	Monique Miller
Loulou	Monique Mercure
Johnny	Pierre Dufresne

A minor work from Claude Jutra, but nevertheless a deft, light, whimsical comedy about love and marriage, romance and reality, filmed with insight and imagination.

ELIZA'S HOROSCOPE   Sept. 1975

Prod./rel. O-Zali Films Inc.; *prod./dir./scen./ed.* Gordon Sheppard; *cam.* (Eastmancolor) Jean Boffety, Paul Van Der Linden, Michel Brault; *music* Elmo Peeler; *prem.* Stratford International Film Festival. 103 min. *Dist.* Bellevue Films. (Opened in Toronto and Montreal in 1976.)

Roles	Cast
Eliza	Elizabeth Moorman
Lila	Lila Kedrova
Tommy	Tommy Lee Jones
Mime	Pierre Byland
Marcel	Marcel Sabourin
Richard	Richard Manual

Eliza's Horoscope was shot in the summer of 1970. The original distributor, Warner Brothers, withdrew from the film when its budget went far in excess of the

Elizabeth Moorman in *Eliza's Horoscope* (d. Gordon Sheppard, 1975).

Monique Miller and Claude Jutra in *Pour le meilleur et pour le pire (For Better, For Worse)* (d. Claude Jutra, 1975).

original estimate. Work on the film proceeded in stops and starts for the next four years, which explains the use of three directors of photography. Heavily allegorical and densely symbolic, the often abstract events concern a young country girl who goes to Montreal to have a child. To find her true love, she consults with an ancient Chinese astrologer who reads her horoscope and predicts that she will meet the right man within the next ten days. The girl commences to make the predication come true in a confusing search, in which she meets characters as strange as herself.

LA TETE DE NORMANDE ST-ONGE   Oct. 1975
(The Head of Normande St.-Onge)

Prod. co./rel. Les Productions Carle–Lamy Ltd.; *dir.* Gilles Carle; *scen.* Gilles Carle and Ben Barzman; *cam.* (Eastmancolor) François Protat and Michel Brault; *ed.* Gilles Carle and Avdei Chriaeff; *music* Lewis Furey. *Prem.* La Parisien Cinema, Montreal. 105 min. *Dist.* Cinepix Ltd.

Roles	Cast
Normande	Carole Laure
Magician	Reynald Bouchard
Friend	Raymond Cloutier

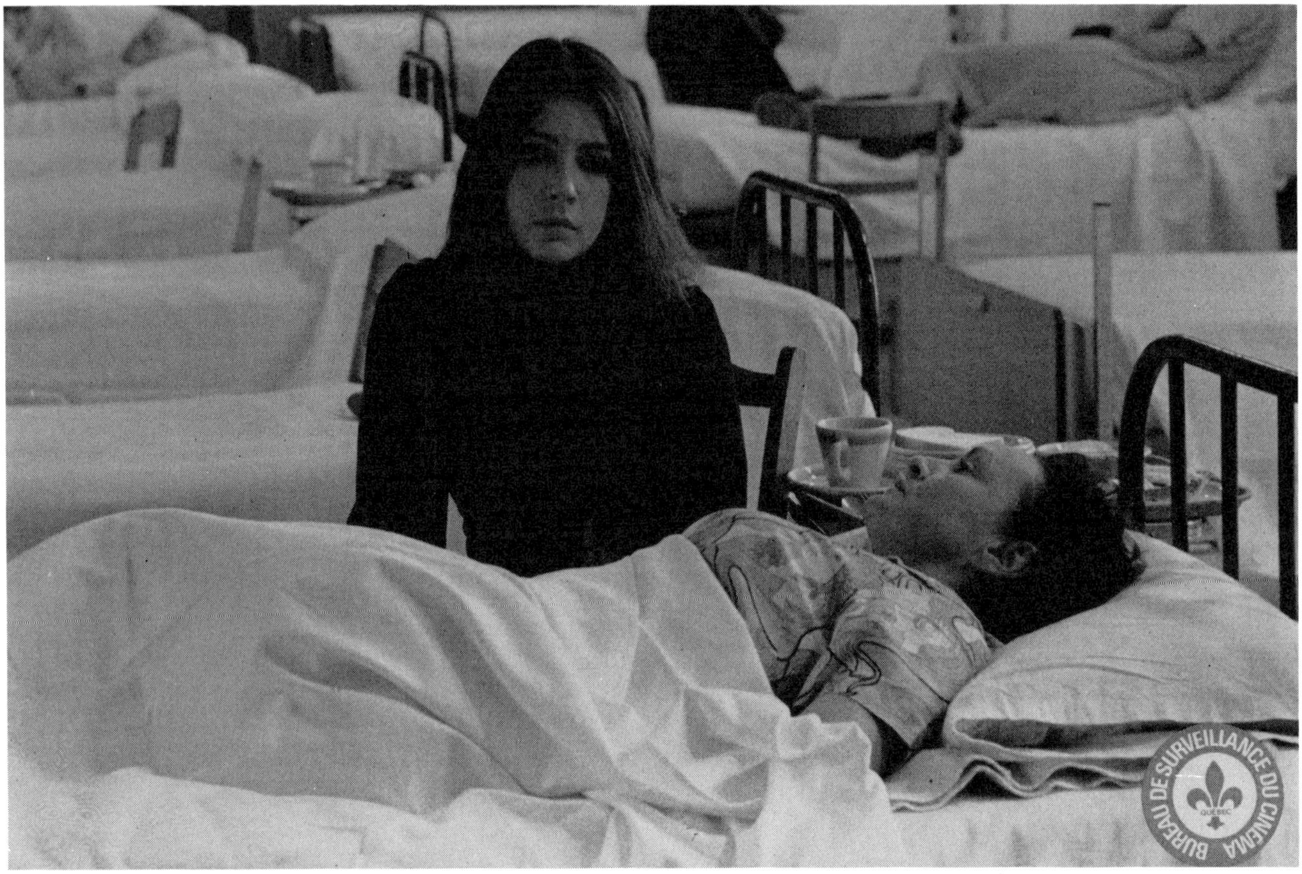

Carole Laure in *La Tête de Normande St-Onge (The Head of Normande St-Onge)* d. Gilles Carle, 1976).

Louise Cuerrier in *L'Amour blessé (Confidences de la nuit)* (d. Jean-Pierre Lefebvre, 1975).

Normande, a shopgirl, trying to understand the supposed insanity of her mother, falls victim to her own kind of mental aberrations. With the exception of the "dream sequences" (which represent Carle at his most extreme and are self-indulgent), this is a film of tenderness, humor, and sympathy, with fine backgrounds and character delineations.

Other Films of 1975

L'Amour Blessé (d. Jean-Pierre Lefebvre). A tedious evening with a lonely lady in her room listening to a talk show. The camera watches and the audience waits; the atmosphere and use of natural sounds, however, is quite striking.

The Clown Murders (d. Martyn Burke). A clownish attempt at being Agatha Christie.

Cold Journey (d. Martin Defalco). A poor film about a rich subject: the young American Indian who is taken away from his own world, partly educated in the white man's ways, only to find himself an alien in both societies.

It Seemed Like a Good Idea at the Time (d. John Trent). A modern Keystone Cops that is far from being a good idea at any time.

André Melançon in *Partis pour la gloire* (d. Clement Perron, 1975).

Mahoney's Last Stand (d. Harvey Hart). Alexis Kanner returns with his boring Ernie Game, set in the countryside.

The Mourning Suit (d. Leonard Yakir) Set against a Winnipeg background, this is a slow but often sincere tale of a Jewish tailor and his beliefs, contrasted with the negative outlook of a young man.

Mustang (d. Marcel Lefebvre). A lively and colorful tale about a small town and its annual rodeo and how the violence of the Old West permeates some of the participants.

The Parasite Murders (d. David Cronenberg). Another of the director's sleazy horrors.

Partis pour la gloire (d. Clement Perron). A disturbing film about the people of a small Quebec town who were not interested in World War II and wanted nothing to do with the army.

Recommendation for Mercy (d. Murray Markowitz). A true story of a crime of passion makes a tacky movie.

Running Time (d. Mort Ransen). An uncertain mixture of comedy and music involving an old lady and a group of young schoolboys.

Ti-Cul Tougas (d. Jean-Guy Noel). A minor romance about four different individuals looking for love.

And: two Children's Films: *Lions for Breakfast* (d. William Davidson) and *Wings in the Wilderness* (d. Dan Gibson), and three likable Quebec comedies: *Les Aventures d'une jeune veuve* (d. Roger Fournier), *Tout feu tout femme* (d. Gilles Richer), and *Les Beaux dimanches* (d. Richard Martin).

Canadian Film Awards 1975

Best feature film: *Les Ordres;* Film of the Year, *The Apprenticeship of Duddy Kravitz;* John Grierson Award: Pierre Juneau; best feature film (nonfiction): *Janis;* best documentary film over 30 minutes: *Cree Hunters of Mistassini;* best documentary film under 30 minutes: *At 99: A Portrait of Louise Tandy Murch;* best animated film: *The Owl Who Married a Goose;* best theatrical short film: *Along These Lines;* best TV drama: *A Bird in the House;* best director: Michel Brault *(Les Ordres);* best actress: Margot Kidder *(Black Christmas* and *A Quiet Day in Belfast);* best actor: Stuart Gillard *(Why Rock the Boat?);* best direction (nonfeature): Robin Spry *(Action* and *Face).* The Jury: Denis Heroux, Tadeusz Jaworski, Janine Manatis, Josef Skvorecky, Vaclav Taborsky.

BRETHREN   May 1976

Thomas Hauff in *Brethren* (d. Dennis Zahoruk, 1976).

James Naughton and Tedde Moore in *Second Wind* (d. Don Shebib, 1976).

Lawrence Benedict and Celine Lomez in _The Far Shore_ (d. Joyce Wieland, 1975).

Prod. co. Tundra and Clearwater Film Ltd.; _prod._ Chalmers Adams; _dir./scen./ed._ Dennis Zahoruk; _cam._ (color) David Ostriker; _music_ Michael Snook. _Prem._ Ontario Film Theatre, Toronto. 91 min. _Dist._ Canadian Filmmakers Distribution Centre.

Cast: Tom Hauff, Kenneth Welsh, Richard Fitzpatrick, Sandra Scott, Larry Reynolds, Candace O'Connor

A remarkable first feature by film school graduate Zahoruk, about three brothers who return to a small Ontario town to attend the funeral of their father. The various family stresses and resentments that come to light are treated and developed with considerable wit and ironic observation, with no lack of feeling or understanding of emotions involved.

SECOND WIND   May 1976

Prod. co. Olympic Films Inc.; _rel._ Ambassador Films; _prod._ James Margellos; _dir./ed._ Donald Shebib; _Scen._ Hal Ackerman; _cam._ (color) Reginald Morris; _music_ Hagood Hardy. _Prem._ Plaza II, Toronto. 93 min.

Roles	_Cast_
Roger	James Naughton
Linda	Lindsay Wagner

Pete	Kenneth Pogue
Paula	Tedde Moore
Frank	Tom Harvey
Howie	Louis Del Grande
Packard	Gerard Parkes
Simon˙	Jonathan Welsh
Graham	Cec Linder
Kevin	Alan Levson

A stylish film from Shebib, but one with little wind as we meet an American couple in Toronto whose marriage isn't working because the husband goes out running. Slight and superficial, with few questions answered.

THE FAR SHORE   Aug. 1976

Prod. co. Far Shore Inc., _rel._ New Cinema; _prod._ Joyce Wieland and Judy Steed; _exec. prod._ Pierre Lamy; _dir._ Joyce Wieland; _scen._ Brian Barney, from an original story by Wieland; _cam._ (color) Richard Leiterman; _ed._ George Appleby and Brian French; _music_ Douglas Pringle. _Prem._ National Arts Centre, Ottawa. 104 min.

Roles	_Cast_
Eulalia Turner	Celine Lomez
Tom McLeod	Frank Moore

Denholm Elliot and Hollis McLaren in *Partners* (d. Don Owen, 1976).

Ross Turner	Lawrence Benedict	Heather Grey	Hollis McLaren
Cluny	Sean McCann	Paul Howard	Michael Margotta
Mary McEwan	Charlotte Blunt	Philip Rudd	Lee Broker
Kate	Susan Petrie	Barbara	Judith Gault
Fiddler	Jean Carignan	Hayes	Robert Silverman
		Aunt Margot	Irene Mayeska

A well-meaning but simple and melodramatic story of a selfish husband, his misunderstood wife, and an idealistic painter. Lots of broding over love, life, and art, with an inappropriate score and stilted direction.

PARTNERS   Oct. 1976

Prod. co. Clearwater Films; *rel.* Astral Films of Canada; *prod.* Chalmers Adams and Don Owen; *dir.* Don Owen; *scen.* Norman Snider and Don Owen; *cam.* (color) Marc Champion; *ed.* George Appleby; *music* Murray McLaughlan. *Prem.* Imperial Theatre, Toronto. 97 min.

Roles	*Cast*
John Grey	Denholm Elliott

An uneven mixture of Old-World charm and modern merchandising in which an American multinational firm tries to take over an old-established, family-owned Canadian paper company. The younger members of the new and the old, American and Canadian, meet and fall in love. The American longs for tradition, the girl's father dies, and by now the story becomes much too cluttered to be convincing.

Other Films of 1976

Death Weekend (d. William Fruet). A shoddy tale of rape and violence in a country retreat.

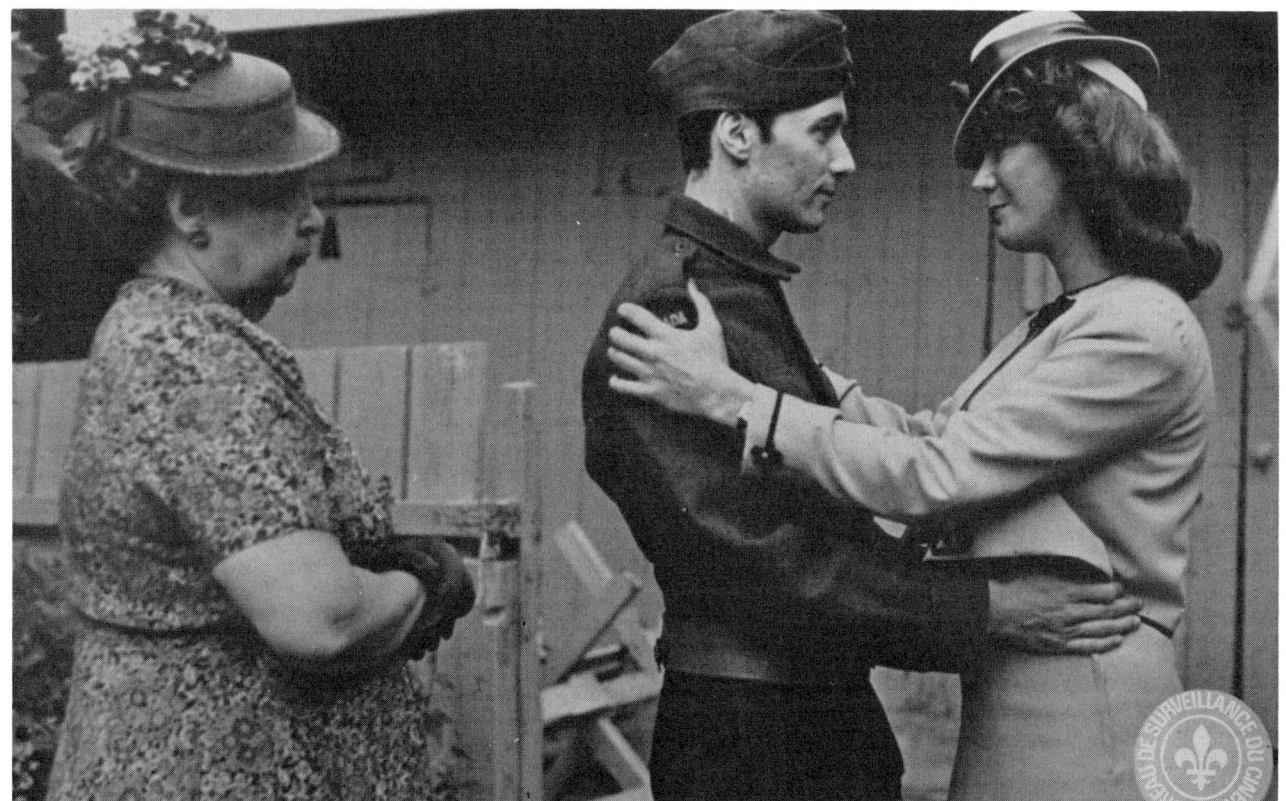

Juliette Huot and Denise Filiatrault in *Je suis loin de toi Mig-*
nonne **(d. Claude Fournier, 1976).**

Jacques Boulanger in *Parlez-nous d'amour* **(d. Jean-Claude**
Lord, 1976).

François Tasse and Denise Filiatrault in *Soleil se lève en retard*
(d. André Brassard, 1976).

Monique Mercure and Marcel Sabourin in *J. A. Martin, photo-*
graphe **(d. Jean Beaudin, 1977).**

A scene from *Why Shoot the Teacher* (d. Silvio Narizzano, 1977).

East End Hustle (d. Frank Vitale). More sleaze: prostitute stands up to her pimp.

L'Eau chaude l'eau frette (A Pacemaker and a Side-Car) (d. Andre Forcier). A dumpy, rowdy rooming house in Montreal and its shady inhabitants. Overdone and overstated.

Find The Lady (d. John Trent). Not worth looking for, a sequel to *It Seemed Like a Good Idea At the Time*.

Goldenrod (d. Harvey Hart). A rodeo rider in Calgary loses his confidence and his job after an injury and slips into depression. Striking performance from Donelly Rhodes, ably supported by Donald Pleasence.

Jacob Two Two Meets The Hooded Fang (d. Theodore Flicker). A children's film that fails due to heavy-handed treatment.

Je suis loin de toi Mignonne (d. Claude Fournier). Sentimental comedy romance set in Montreal during the Second World War in which couples meet and marry; done with charm and feeling.

The Little Girl Who Lives Down the Lane (d. Nicholas Gessner). Another in the growing number of pseudo-American films, this one a mystery with little to recommend it.

Parlez-nous d'amour (d. Jean-Claude Lord). Far-fetched comedy about a popular host of a TV show for women.

Rabid (d. David Cronenberg). A nasty business about a blood-sucking lady.

Ragtime Summer (d. Alan Bridges). A hot summer in 1921 in a quiet Ontario town is disrupted by the arrival of a new science teacher from England (David Warner); a slight story told with quiet conviction.

Rituals (d. Peter Carter). More violence in the countryside patterned after *Deliverance*.

Shadow of the Hawk (d. George McCowan). Silly story based on Indian mysticism.

Shoot (d. Harvey Hart). An even sillier story about American hunters who shoot each other as though they were opposing armies.

Le Soleil se lève en retard (d. André Brassard). A gentle description of a 30-year-old unmarried woman whose previous unhappy relationship with a man makes it difficult for her to love again.

A Sweeter Song (d. Allan Eastman). A pleasant and likable film about a sports photographer and his misadventures.

Ti-Mine, Bernie pis la gang (d. Marcel Carriere). A funny family comedy about get-rich-quick fantasies and winters in Florida.

Canadian Film Awards 1976

The awards in 1976 went to the following—best direction Harvey Hart: *(Goldenrod);* best actress: Marilyn Lightstone *(Lies My Father Told Me);* best actor: André Melancon *(Partis pour la gloire);* best documentary: *Volcano: An Inquiry into the Life and Death of Malcolm Lowry* (NFB) by Donald Brittain; best animated film: *The Street* (NFB) by Caroline Leaf; and best documentary short: *Cooperage* by Phillip Borsos; The John Grierson Award: Tom Daly, who has been with the NFB since 1941. The International Jury was discontinued in preference for a jury made up of representatives from guilds and craft unions.

J. A. MARTIN, PHOTOGRAPHE   Feb. 1977
(J. A. Martin, Photographer)

Prod. co./rel. National Film Board; *dir.* Jean Beaudin; *scen.* Jean Beaudin and Marcel Sabourin; *cam.* (Eastmancolor) Pierre Mignot; *ed.* Jean Beaudin; *music* Maurice Blackburn. *Prem.* Le Dauphin, Montreal. 101 min.

David Petersen in *Skip Tracer* (d. Zale Dalen, 1977).

Roles	Cast
J. A. Martin	Marcel Sabourin
Rose-Aimée	Monique Mercure
Mother	Marthe Thierry
Friend	Jean Lapointe
Woman	Mariette Duval

A quietly beautiful but emotionally uninvolving study of a pioneer photographer in turn-of-the-century Quebec, of his travels with his wife, and of her disenchantment with married life.

WHY SHOOT THE TEACHER   July 1977

Prod. co. Fraser Films and Lancer Telproductions; *rel.* Ambassador Films; *exec. prod.* Fil Fraser; *prod.* Lawrence Hertzog; *dir.* Silvio Narizzano; *scen.* James De-Felice, based on Max Braithwaite's book; *cam.* (color) Marc Champion; *ed.* Max Benedict, Stan Cole; *music* Ricky Hyslop. *Prem.* Britannia 6, Ottawa. 99 min.

Roles	Cast
Max Brown	Bud Cort
Alice Field	Samantha Eggar
Lyle Bishop	Chris Wiggins
Harris Montgomery	Gary Reineke
Dave McDougall	John Friesen
Bert Field	Michael J. Reynolds
Inspector Woods	Kenneth Griffith

An effective adaption of Max Braithwaite's humorous and episodic novel about a young teacher trying to cope with the loneliness of a Saskatchewan prairie school in winter, and the economic poverty of the Depression. Bud Cort is miscast, unfortunately, as the inexperienced young man.

SKIP TRACER   July 1977

Prod. co. Highlight Productions Ltd.; *prod.* Laara Dalen; *scen./ed./dir.* Zale Dalen; *cam.* (color) Ron Orieux; *music* J. Douglas Bodd. *Prem.* Varsity Theatre, Vancouver. 94 min. Dist. I.F.D.

Roles	Cast
John Collins	David Petersen
Brent Solverman	John Lazarus
Leo Gabrowski	Rudy Szabo
Sara Pettigrew	Sue Astley

A first feature by Zale Dalen of considerable force and power concerning a man who comes to despise himself for his work as a debt collector for a Vancouver agency.

LE VIEUX PAYS OU   Aug. 1977
RIMBAUD EST MORT
(The Old Country Where Rimbaud Died)

Prod. co./rel. Cinak-Filmoblic-INA; *dir.* Jean-Pierre Lefebvre; *scen.* Marielle Amiel and Jean-Pierre

A scene from *Le vieux pays où Rimbaud est mort (The Old Country Where Rimbaud Died)* (d. Jean-Pierre Lefebvre, 1977).

Jane Eastwood and Len Cariou in *One Man* (d. Robin Spry, 1976).

Allan Moyle, Craig Russell, and Hollis McLaren in *Outrageous* (d. Richard Benner, 1977).

Lefebvre; *cam.* (Eastmancolor) Guy Dufaux; *ed.* Marguerite Duparc; *music* Claude Fonfrede. *Prem.* Festival of Quebec, Quebec City. 113 min.

Roles	Cast
Abel	Marcel Sabourin
Anne	Anouk Ferjac
Jeanne	Myriam Boyer
Father	Roger Blin
Mother	Germaine Delbat
Husband	François Perrot
Brother	Mark Lesser

Jean-Pierre Lefebvre went to France to make this film, a statement about what a Quebecois feels on returning to the land of his ancestors. It is a visit of discovery, and the revelations are simple, charming, sometimes happy but often sad. It is really much too slight, but nonetheless the intent and the illusion are there.

ONE MAN   Sept. 1977

Prod. co./rel. National Film Board; *dir.* Robin Spry; *scen.* Robin Spry, Peter Pearson, and Peter Madden; *cam.* (Eastmancolor) Douglas Keifer; *ed.* John Kramer; *music* Ben Low. *Prem.* National Arts Centre, Ottawa. 88 min.

Roles	Cast
Jason Brady	Len Cariou
Alicia Brady	Jayne Eastwood
Marion Galbraith	Carol Lazare
Colin Angus Campbell	Barry Morse
Ernie Carrick	August Schellenberg
Ben Legault	Jean Lapointe
Rodney Porter	Sean Sullivan
Dr. Gendron	Terry Haig
Leo	Marc Legault
First Hood	Danny Freedman
Second Hood	Gilles Renaud
John, TV Announcer	Bob Girolami
Jaworski	Jacques Godin

A compelling and concerned drama in which a Montreal TV reporter tries to expose a factory owner for emitting dangerous pollutants causing the death of children, and then finds himself and his family threatened by corporate and political interests. Much of what it has to say later came true with the discovery of the contamination of the Love Canal in Niagara Falls, N.Y.

Gordon Pinsent and Brian Painchaud in *Who Has Seen the Wind* (d. Allan King, 1977).

OUTRAGEOUS!   Sept. 1977

Prod. co. Film Consortium of Canada, Inc.; *prod.* William Marshall and Hendrick J. Van der Kolk; *Scen./dir.* Richard Benner, based on a story from "Butterfly Ward" by Margaret Gibson; *cam.* (Eastmancolor) James B. Kelly; *ed.* George Appleby, *music* Paul Hoffert; *orig. lyrics* Brenda Hoffert. *Prem.* National Arts Centre, Ottawa. 100 min. *Dist.* New Cinema.

Roles	Cast
Robin Turner	Craig Russell
Liza Connors	Hollis McLaren
Perry	Richert Easley
Martin	Allan Moyle
Bob	David McIlwraith
Jason	Gerry Salzberg
Anne	Andrée Pelletier
Jo	Helen Shaver
Nurse Carr	Martha Gibson
Mrs. Connors	Helen Hughes
Dr. Beddoes	Jonah Royston
Stewart	Richard Moffatt
Hustler	David Woito
Jimmy	Rusty Ryan
Jackie Loren	Jackie Loren
Performer in Gold	Michael Daniels
Performer in Pink	Michel

Lively, human, and often moving account of the relationship between a female impersonator and a schizophrenic girl, told with humor and believability.

WHO HAS SEEN THE WIND   Nov. 1977

Prod. co. Souris River Films; *rel.* Astral Films; *exec. prod.* Pierre Lamy; *dir.* Allan King; *scen.* Patricia Watson, from the novel by W. O. Mitchell; *cam.* (color) Richard Leiterman; *ed.* Arla Saare; *music* Eldon Rathburn. *Prem.* Ontario Film Theatre, Toronto. 100 min.

Roles	Cast
Brian	Brian Painchaud
The Young Ben	Douglas Junor
Gerald O'Connal	Gordon Pinsent
Maggie	Chapelle Jaffe
The Ben	Jose Ferrer
Mrs. Abercrombie	Charmion King
Reverend Powelly	David Gardner
Miss MacDonald	Patricia Hamilton
Ruth Thompson	Helen Shaver
Digby	Tom Hauff

Sean   Gerard Parkes
Mrs. MacMurray   Nan Stewart

A difficult book to film about a boy's growing-up period on the Saskatchewan prairies during the Depression and his growing awareness of life and death, this film version is lovely, light, and lyrical, and beautifully acted by an understanding cast of players.

Other Films of 1977

L'Ange et la Femme (d. Gilles Carle). A heavy-handed piece of erotic and violent supernatural symbolism about an angel who takes possession of the body of a murdered woman. With Carole Laure and Lewis Furey.

Blood and Guts (d. Paul Lynch). A violent melodrama about wrestling, which may or may not be taking place in Canada.

Blood Relatives (d. Claude Chabrol). So far as Canadian horror films go, this is better than most but minor for Chabrol. With Donald Sutherland, Stephane Audran, Donald Pleasence, David Hemmings.

Cathy's Curse (d. Eddy Matalon). An eight-year-old girl activates forces from beyond the grave—enough to send everyone to theirs!

Deadly Harvest (d. Timothy Bond). The world is starving—a dreary bore.

The Disappearance (d. Stuart Cooper). A distinguished cast of British and Canadian actors led by Donald Sutherland fail to bring conviction to this slick, stylish thriller, an Anglo-Canadian coproduction.

Full Circle (d. Richard Lorraine). Another Anglo-Canadian film with Mia Farrow and Keir Dullea, a thriller set in a strange house with strange powers, altogether too strange for its own good.

Leopard in the Snow (d. Gerry O'Hara). Canada's favorite American actor at that time, Keir Dullea, leads a cast of British actors through a wretched Harlequin romance.

Panique (d. Jean-Claude Lord). Unbelievable and badly told story of a town that finds its water poisoned.

Power Play (d. Martyn Burke) (formerly *Coup D'-Etat*). A crass and unconvincing film about a revolution in a South American state, with Peter O'Toole, David Hemmings, and many others who probably wished they were not involved.

The Rubber Gun (d. Allan Moyle). A cooperative, self-indulgent, semibiographical study of a peculiar art dealer, played somewhat self-consciously by Stephen Lack.

The Third Walker (d. Teri McLuhan). Twins are separated by mistake at birth and grow up with different families in opposite social conditions—a somewhat murky situation that is not really of much interest. With Colleen Dewhurst, William Shatner, Monique Mercure, Frank Moore.

Three-Card Monte (d. Les Rose). An excellent first feature written, produced, and acted by Richard Gabourie, about a small-time swindler in Toronto who cares for a 12-year-old orphan boy.

Tomorrow Never Comes (d. Peter Collinson). A foolish coproduction with England about a policeman in a corrupt Canadian resort town, with Canada's favorite British actors at that time, Donald Pleasence and Oliver Reed.

The Uncanny (d. Denis Heroux). Yet another silly Anglo-Canadian coproduction with Peter Cushing and Ray Milland, about cats taking revenge on humans.

Welcome to Blood City (d. Peter Sasdy). The last of the coproductions with Britain—Keir Dullea in a horror that takes place in a western town.

Full-length documentaries: Aho, The Forest People (d. François Floquet); *Famille et Variations* (d. Mireille Dansereau); *Film of the XXI Olympiad* (d. Jean-Claude Labrecque); *Jules the Magnificent* (d. Michel Moreau); *Killers of the Wild* (d. Robert Ryan).

Television features: *Dreamspeaker* (d. Claude Jutra). An emotionally disturbed boy is befriended by Indians; *The Fighting Men* (d. Donald Shebib). Well-made, familiar service story made fresh and interesting by taking place in the Canadian armed forces.

Canadian Film Awards 1977

The awards in 1977 went to the following—best feature film: *J. A. Martin, Photographe* (Jean Beaudin); best documentary: *The Inquiry Film* (Jesse Nishihata); best documentary under sixty min.: *Greenpeace: Voyages to Save the Whales* (Michael Chechik, Ron Precious, Fred Easton); best animated film: *Spinnolio* (John Weldon); best theatrical short: *Spartree* (Phillip Borsos); best TV drama film: *Dreamspeaker* (Claude Jutra); best actress; Monique Mercure *(J. A. Martin, Photographe);* best actor: Len Cariou *(One Man);* best supporting actress: Carol Lazare *(One Man);* best supporting actor: Jean Lapointe *(One Man);* The Grierson Award: Fernand Dansereau; Special Jury Award for a first feature: Zale Dalen *(Skip Tracer).* The jury was made up of representatives from guilds and craft unions. (In 1978 the Canadian Film Awards ended. The Genie Awards took their place. See page 127).

Blackout (d. Eddy Matalon). Silly pseudo-American disaster film: the power fails in New York. With Jim Mitchum, Robert Carradine.

High Ballin' (d. Peter Carter). Another silly pseudo-American melodrama about violent truck drivers, with Peter Fonda, Jerry Reed.

I, Maureen (d. Janine Manatis). Slight but affecting story of a woman trapped in a difficult marriage, with Colleen Collins, Diane Bigelow.

I Miss You, Hugs and Kisses (d. Murray Markowitz). Tin-pot version of an actual murder case in which a wife is disposed of for the sake of a mistress and an insurance policy, with Donald Pilon, Elke Sommer.

In Praise of Older Women (d. George Kaczender). A trite soft-core sex film about a young Hungarian (sadly miscast in the acting of the American Tom Berenger) and his "adventures" with Karen Black, Susan Strasberg, and others.

Keiko (d. Claude Gagnon). A film in Japanese about Japan made by a *gaijin* (foreigner). Gagnon moved to Japan from Montreal and lived there for ten years, marrying Yuri Yoshimura, who became his co-producer. This intimate, low-budget, personal film concerns the place of women in Japanese society as seen through the life of Keiko and her discovery of love. Junko Wakashiba, Akiko Kitamura, Takuma Ikeuchi. (Opened in Montreal in 1979; in Toronto, 1983.)

Marie-Anne (d. Martin Walters). A simple yet telling story of the first white woman to travel to Fort Edmonton, played by Andrée Pelletier, and who, in her life to come, becomes the grandmother of Louis Riel.

Murder By Decree (d. Robert Clark). Poorly directed and complicated Sherlock Holmes story, but well played by Christopher Plummer and James Mason.

The Silent Partner (d. Daryl Duke). A gifted director gives assurance to this brutal and morally offensive depiction of a bank robbery, carried out in Toronto by such unlikely citizens as Elliott Gould and Susannah York. Christopher Plummer provides a Canadian voice.

Something Rotten (d. Harvey Frost). Indeed it is, as a queen misuses her power in a thriller played out by a central European monarchy, with Charlotte Blunt.

Two Solitudes (d. Lionel Chetwynd). An inexperienced director with a poorly cast American actor (Stacy Keach) makes a mockery of Hugh MacLen-

Gloria Carlin in *Two Solitudes* **(d. Lionel Chetwynd, 1978).**

Raymond Cloutier and Roger Blay in *Riel* **(d. George Bloomfield, 1979).**

nan's important novel about French-English relations in Quebec during the first World War.

Une Amie d'enfance (d. Francis Mankiewicz). A slight but perceptive story of two childhood friends who meet years later and find that life has changed them too much for them to find friendship again; with Pauline Martin and Pauline Lapointe.

Vie d'ange (d. Pierre Harel). A one-joke film that goes on much too long about two lovers who copulate and cannot come apart.

RIEL   April 1979

Prod. co. and *rel.* CBC and Green River; *prod.* John Trent; *dir.* George Bloomfield; *scen.* Roy Moore; *cam.* (color) Vic Sarin; *ed.* Myrtle Virgo; *music* William McCauley. *Prem.* Ontario Film Theatre, Toronto. 140 min.

Roles	*Cast*
Riel	Raymond Cloutier
Gabriel Dumont	Roger Blay
Sir John A. MacDonald	Christopher Plummer
Bishop Bourget	Jean-Louis Roux
Ritchot	Marcel Sabourin
Taylor	Arthur Hill
Barker	William Shatner
Crozier	Leslie Nielsen
MacTavish	Barry Morse
Dr. Schultz	Lloyd Bochner
Smith	Don Harron
Wolsley	John Neville
Dr. Roy	Claude Jutra
Ouellette	Don Francks
Nolin	Normand Chouinard
Middleton	Chris Wiggins

There is much to admire in this long description of the life of one of Canada's most debatable historical figures, but excessive length and confusion of characters and events leave a blurred and distorted portrait.

ECLAIR AU CHOCOLAT
(Chocolate Eclair)   May 1979

Prod. co. Films Mutuels; *rel.* Pierre David & Robert Menard Production for Les Productions Mutuelles Ltd. and Les Productions Videofilms Ltd.; *dir.* Jean-Claude Lord; *scen.* Lord and Jean Salvy, from novel by Jean Santacroce; *cam.* (color) Francois Protat; *ed.* Lord; *music* Richard Gregoire, on a theme by Diane Juster. *Prem.* Cannes Film Festival (Market). 105 min.

Roles	*Cast*
Marie-Louise Prenant	Lise Thouin
Petit-Pierre Prenant	Jean Belzil-Gascon

Lise Thouin and Jean Belzil-Gascon in *Eclair au chocolat* (d. Jean-Claude Lord, 1979).

Lucien Prenant   Jean-Louis Roux
William Sinclair   Colin Fox
Dominique   Danielle Panneton
Uncle   Aubert Pallascio
Robert   Olivier Fillion
Fabienne   Valerie Deltour

A sensitive, entirely natural child study about the young son of a single mother who loves his absent father through the stories she tells of him. But one day, the fantasy ends and the boy's world changes. A winning and perceptive work.

DRYING UP THE STREETS   Sept. 1979

Prod. co. and *rel.* CBC; *prod.* Ralph Thomas; *dir.* Robin Spry; *scen.* B. A. Cameron; *cam.* (color) Ken Gregg; *ed.* Myrtle Virgo. *Prem.* First shown on CBC-TV and at the Montreal Film Festival 1979. 90 min. *Cast:* Len Cariou, Don Francks, Calvin Butler, August Schellenberg, Jacques Hubert, Sarah Torgov, Jayne Eastwood, Frank Moore.

"They're drying up the streets" is a slang expression which means that police have stopped shipments of heroin from reaching street addicts. Among the tide of violent and often inaccurate films about drugs and the young people who use them, this film stands out as an honest, entirely believable story of an innocent young girl, up from the country, who gets caught in the web of Toronto's underworld of drug activity.

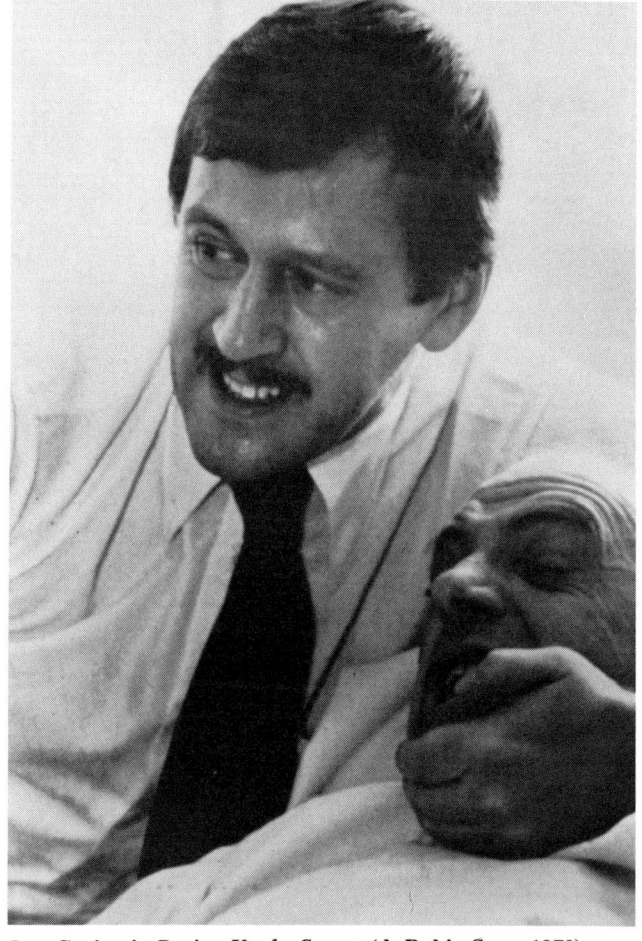

Len Cariou in *Drying Up the Streets* (d. Robin Spry, 1979).

The Brood (d. David Cronenberg). Another of this director's unpleasant horror films, with Oliver Reed, Samantha Eggar, Art Hindle.

Jigsaw (d. Claude Pinoteau). A France-Canada co-production in which Lino Ventura comes to Montreal to search for his son caught up in the drug trade and finds instead Angie Dickinson.

Meatballs (d. Ivan Reitman). Desperate comedy about summer camp antics, with no Canadian identification, supposedly American, in which foolish juveniles are treated in alternately cruel and sentimental terms. Bill Murray, Harvey Atkin, Kate Lynch. (Reitman left for Hollywood and later made *Ghostbusters,* among other mediocrities.)

Mondo Nude (d. Anthony Kramreither). A semidocumentary about Toronto's Miss Nude World contest, weakened by a lack of viewpoint.

Summer's Children (d. Julius Kohanyi). A first feature by a former short-film-maker showing considerable ability and appeal about a brother-and-sister love affair, discreet to the point of becoming tiring, with Tom Hauff, Paully Jardine, and Don Francks.

LES BONS DEBARRAS   Feb. 1980

Prod. co./rel. Les Productions Prisma; *dir.* Francis Mankiewicz; *scen.* Rejean Ducharme; *cam.* (Eastmancolor) Michel Brault; *ed.* André Corriveau; *music* Bernard Buisson. *Prem.* Berlin Film Festival 1980. 109 min.

Roles	*Cast*
Manon	Charlotte Laurier
Michelle	Marie Tifo
Guy	Germain Houde
Madame	Louise Marleau
Maurice	Gilbert Sicotte

Manon, thirteen, lives in a dilapidated house in an isolated village in Quebec's Laurentians, with her unwed mother and her mother's slightly simple brother. She is aware of the sadness of her poverty and lives by a fierce passion for her mother, for whom she will do anything. This unusual, powerful, yet tender study is compelling and honest, with its squalid background set against the natural beauty of the countryside. The use of the French, native to the region, is well caught and beautifully apt.

CORDELIA   Feb. 1980

Charlotte Laurier in *Les Bons Debarras (Good Riddance)* (d. Francis Mankiewicz, 1980).

A scene from *Cordelia* (d. Jean Beaudin, 1979).

Prod. co. National Film Board; *prod.* Jean-Marc Garand; *dir./ed.* Jean Beaudin; *scen.* Jean Beaudin and Marcel Sabourin from "La Lampe dans la Fenêtre" by Pauline Cadieux; *ed.* Jean Beaudin; *cam.* (color) Pierre Mignot; *music* Maurice Blackburn. *Prem.* Dauphin Cinema, Montreal. 118 min. *Dist.* La Corporation des Films Mutuels.

Roles	Cast
Cordelia Viau	Louise Portal
Samuel Parslow	Gaston Lepage
Isidore Poirier	Pierre Gobeil
M. Leduc	Gilbert Sicotte
Joseph Fortier	Raymond Cloutier
Judge Taschereau	Jean-Louis Roux
Hangman Radcliff	James Blendick
Jailer Groulx	Rolland Bedard

In his second film, the director of *J. A. Martin, Photographer,* turns to the true story of an unconventional young woman at the turn of the century in Quebec who was hanged for a murder she did not commit. Beautifully played by Louise Portal, in an otherwise somewhat slow and confined realization.

L'HOMME A TOUT FAIRE   March 1980
(The Handyman)

Prod. co. Corporation Image Ltée; *prod.* René Malo; *dir./scen.* Micheline Lanctot; *cam.* (color) André Gagnon; *ed.* Annik de Bellefeuille; *music* François Lanctot. *Prem.* Parisien Cinema, Montreal. 99 min. *Dist.* Dabara Films.

Andrée Pelletier and Jocelyn Berube in *The Handyman* (*L'Homme à tout faire*) **(d. Micheline Lanctot, 1979).**

Roles	Cast
Armand	Jocelyn Bérubé
Thérèse	Andrée Pelletier
Coque l'Oeil	Paul Dion
Bernard	Gilles Renaud
Georges	Marcel Sabourin

In her first film as a director, the talented actress Micheline Lanctot tells a charming story of an affluent and bored suburban housewife who breaks the heart of her amorous handyman. It is played with just the right touch of romance and longing, and is a delight from beginning to end.

L'AFFAIRE COFFIN   May 1980

Prod. co. Films Ciné Scène and Les Productions Videofilms; *rel.* Corporation des Films Mutuels; *prod.* Robert Menard; *dir.* Jean-Claude Labrecque; *cam.* (color) Pierre Mignot; *ed.* André Corriveau; *music* Anne Laubert. *Prem.* Cannes Film Festival 1980. 100 min.

Roles	Cast
Wilbert Coffin	August Schellenberg
Capitaine Forget	Yvon Dufour
Maureen Patterson	Micheline Lanctot
Ben Menard	Jean-Marie Lemieux
Alain Courtemanche	Gabriel Arcand
Chauffeur de taxi	Raymond Cloutier

This is a small-scale but dramatically effective re-telling of the 1953 murder of three American hunters in a Gaspé forest. It becomes a political issue, and Wilbert Coffin, from an Anglo-Protestant village, is hanged for the murder. There was no real proof that he was guilty.

FANTASTICA   May 1980

Prod. co. Les Productions du Verseau, Inc.; *prod.* Charlyne Ascaso; *dir.* Gilles Carle; *scen.* Gilles Carle and Oscar Paul; *cam.* (color) François Protat; *ed.* Hugues Darmois; *music* Lewis Furey. *Prem.* opened the Cannes Film Festival 1980. 110 min. *Dist.* Pan-Canadian.

Roles	Cast
Lorca	Carole Laure
Paul	Lewis Furey
Euclide Brown	Serge Reggiani
Johanne McPherson	Claudine Auger
Jim McPherson	John Vernon
Emma	Denise Filiatrault
Hector	Claude Blanchard
Georges	Donald Pilon

Donald Pilon, Claudine Auger, and John Vernon in *Fantastica* (d. Gilles Carle, 1980).

Jennifer Dale and Winston Rekert in *Suzanne* **(d. Robin Spry, 1980).**

Julien	Gilbert Sicotte
Pompier	Guy L'Ecuyer

With music and songs by Lewis Furey, this ambitious France-Canada coproduction (but set in Quebec) from the imaginative Gilles Carle falls short of what it was intended to be: a fantasy world of music and nature in loving harmony with its people. Carle's vision is not entirely realized and his story of traveling musicians and their concern for the environment seems implausible on any level. It is not without charm, however, and one responds to his concern and genuine feelings for life.

SUZANNE   Sept. 1980

Prod. co. RSL; *rel.* Ambassador Films; *prod.* Robert Lantos; *exec. prod.* Stephen J. Roth; *dir.* Robin Spry; *scen.* Robin Spry and Ronald Sutherland, based on the novel *Snow Lark* by Ronald Sutherland; *cam.* (color) Miklos Lente; *ed.* Firma Noveck; *music* François Cousineau, theme by Luc Plamondon and François Cousineau. *Prem.* Elgin Theatre, Toronto. 114 min.

Roles	*Cast*
Suzanne McDonald	Jennifer Dale
Nicky Callaghan	Winston Rekert
Georges Laflamme	Gabriel Arcand
Andrew McDonald	Ken Pogue
Yvette McDonald	Michelle Rossignol
Kathy	Marianne McIsaac
Jimmy	Michael Ironside
Marilyn	Gina Dick
Pierre	Pierre Curzi
Greg	Gordon Thompson
Brenda Callaghan	Helen Hughes
André	Adam Chase

Set against the background of the working-class world of Montreal during the early fifties, a young girl finds herself attracted to men, used and left by them, and finally marries the man she does not love to give a home and father to the child she carries by a petty criminal—her true but doomed lover. Robustly played and forcefully told, it is poignant without false emotions, compellingly directed, with an unforgettable performance by Winston Rekert.

Other Films of 1980

Au revoir, à Lundi (Goodbye, See You Monday) (d.

Maurice Dugowson). In this Canada-France coproduction set in Montreal, two women become involved in love affairs with married men. Their few pleasures are diminished by the disappointments they must suffer in the unequal relationships. This film is much superior to those that were being made then in North America about unconventional affairs and the changing patterns of love and marriage. Although the pace is somewhat slow, the treatment unimaginative, the situations and the talented cast give it a direct appeal and emotional depth.

L'Arrache-Coeur (Heartbreak) (d. Mireille Dansereau). A sensitively told story of the difficult love-hate relationship between a mother and her daughter, understandingly played by Louise Marleau and Françoise Faucher.

L'hiver bleu (Blue Winter) (d. André Blanchard). A fresh and likable portrait of two girls and their discovery of what it means to be grown up as they live through the long winter of unemployment and cold weather in the mining town of Abitibi; with Christiane Levesque, Nicole Scant.

Canada's American Films, 1980

"Stars and Stripes" pictures, defined as films that use Canadian towns for cities or unnamed places primarily in the U.S. and that employ mainly American actors, included in 1980 the following: *The Changeling* (see page 156, *Death Ship* (d. Alvin Rakoff), George Kennedy, Richard Crenna; *Dirty Tricks* (d. Alvin Rakoff), Elliott Gould, Kate Jackson; *Double Negative* (d. George Bloomfield), Susan Clark, Anthony Perkins; *Final Assignment* (d. Paul Almond), Geneviève Bujold, Michael York, Burgess Meredith; *The First Hello* (d. Harvey Hart), Timothy Bottoms; *Going for Broke* (formerly *Never Trust An Honest Thief*) (d. George McCowan), Orson Welles, Michael Murphy; *Head On* (d. Michael Grant), Sally Kellerman; *Highpoint* (d. Peter Carter), Richard Harris, Christopher Plummer, Beverly D'Angelo; *The Kidnapping of the President* (d. George Mendeluk), Hal Holbrook, Van Johnson, William Shatner, Ava Gardner; *The Last Chase* (d. Martyn Burke), Lee Majors, Burgess Meredith; *The Lucky Star* (d. Max Fischer), set in Amsterdam, Louise Fletcher, Rod Steiger; *Middle-Age Crazy* (d. John Trent), Bruce Dern, Ann-Margret; *Mr. Patman* (formerly *Midnight Madness*) (d. John Guillermin), James Coburn, Kate Nelligan; *Off Your Rocker* (d. Morley Markson), Milton Berle, Red Buttons, Dorothy Malone; *Title Shot* (d. Les Rose), Tony Curtis, Richard Gabourie; *Phobia* (d. John Hus-

A scene from *L'hiver bleu* (d. André Blanchard, 1979).

ton), Paul-Michael Glaser, Susan Hogan; *Prom Night* (d. Paul Lynch), Jamie Lee Curtis, Casey Stevens; *Scanners* (d. David Cronenberg), Jennifer O'Neill, Patrick McGoohan; *Circle of Two* (d. Jules Dassin), Richard Burton, Tatum O'Neal; *Improper Channels* (d. Eric Till), Alan Arkin; *Terror Train* (d. Roger Spottiswoode) Ben Johnson, Jamie Lee Curtis; *Tulips* (d. Rex Bromfield), Gabe Kaplan, Bernadette Peters; *Your Ticket is No Longer Valid* (d. George Kaczender), Richard Harris, Jeanne Moreau, George Peppard; *Silence of the North* (d. Allan King), Ellen Burstyn, Tom Skerrit; *Atlantic City* (d. Louis Malle), Burt Lancaster, Susan Sarandon; *Babe!* (d. Rafal Zielinski), Buddy Hackett, Yasmine Bleeth; *Crunch* (d. Mark Warren), John Vernon, Norman Fell; *Happy Birthday Gemini* (d. Richard Brenner), Madeline Kahn, Rita Moreno.

Many of the above films still had not been released by 1984. Three extremely odious films that were shown are *Nothing Personal* (d. George Bloomfield), Donald Sutherland, Suzanne Somers; *Hog Wild* (d. Les Rose), Michael Biehn, Patty D'Arbanville; and *Out of the Blue* (d. Dennis Hopper), Linda Manz, Dennis Hopper.

Full-Length Documentaries Made in 1980

Meat the Cleaver (Cinophrenic) (d. Joseph Sutherland). A study of violence that accompanies rock music.

Mondo Strip (d. Anthony Kramreither). The world's best strippers.

Plusiers Tombent en Amour (d. Guy Simoneau). Prostitution in Montreal.

Skating on Thin Ice (d. Bill Reid). The world of ice hockey.

La Vie de Couple (d. Diane Letourneau). The life of a married couple.

Anthony Burgess's Rome, the best of the Neilson-Ferns *Cities* TV series, is a film that leaps from the small screen to become a vivid work of movement and imagination, thanks to the splendid cinema mind of veteran documentary film-maker, Christopher Chapman. (Chapman is Canada's leading independent documentary film-maker, distinguished by his *A Place To Stand, Festival,* and his films on nature and the land.)

Films Shown on Television in 1980

Cries in the Night. William Fruet's somewhat empty, rustic tale of terror in an old house. Barry Morse, Kay Hawtrey. 103 min.

Parallels (d. Mark Schoenberg) is about a priest who feels he is losing touch with the church and its people. David Fox, Judith Mabey. 92 min.

The Intruder (d. David Eustace). Another small town, another evil stranger. 90 min.

Tanya's Island (d. Alfred Sole). On a tropical island, beauty feels sorry for the beast and King Kong finally "gets" the girl. 93 min.

Anatomy of a Horror (Deadline) (d. Mario Azzopardi). A highly acclaimed writer of horror films realizes that the true horror is in his own life. Stephen Young. 100 min.

Teddy (d. Lewis Lehman) A child's teddy bear brings about the demise of a small western town. 99 min.

South Pacific 1942 (d. Paul Donovan). An incompetent comedy about an incompetent submarine crew. Alan MacGillivray. 105 min.

LE NOEL DE MADAME BEAUCHAMP   Feb. 1981

Prod. co. Les Films 26; *prod.* Raphael Levy and Armand Moyal; *scen./ed./dir.* Raphael Levy; *cam.* (color) Magi Torruella. *Prem.* Cinematheque Quebecois, Montreal. 90 min. *Distr.* Armand Moyal & Associates.

Roles	*Cast*
Yvette Beauchamp	Yvette Thuot
the young Yvette	Danielle Schneider
Jean Deniaud	Jean Faubert
the tramp	Marc Legault
Jean's fiancée	Daniele Paradis

A simple yet warm and sympathetic study of a rich and generous older woman who falls in love with a younger and self-absorbed man, and must then face the consequences of her experience. Beautifully acted by Yvette Thuot and Jean Faubert.

CA PEUT PAS ETRE L'HIVER,   April 1981
ON N'A MEME PAS EU D'ETE
(It Can't Be Winter, We Haven't Had Summer Yet)

Prod. co. La Maison des Quatre; *rel.* J. A. Lapointe Films; *prod./scen./dir.* Louise Carré; *cam.* (color) Robert Vanherweghem; *ed.* André Theberge; *music* Marc O'Farrell. *Prem.* Cinematheque Quebecois, Montreal. 87 min.

Roles	*Cast*
Adele Marquis	Charlotte Boisjoli
Germain Lafond	Jacques Galipeau
Lise	Celine Lomez
Camille	Mireille Thibault
Jean-Pierre	Serge Belair

Somewhat along the same lines as *Madame Beauchamp,* this is a modest yet affecting study of a

Anne Létourneau and Gabriel Arcand in *Les Plouffe (The Piouffe Family)* (d. Gilles Carle, 1981).

newly widowed woman who suddenly realizes that she has given her life over to her selfish husband and her eight children, and decides to break away from family constraints and live her own life. A splendid and touching performance from Charlotte Boisjoli.

LES PLOUFFE (The Plouffe Family)   April 1981

Prod. co. International Cinema Corporation—Ciné London; *rel.* Ciné 360; *prod.* Justine Heroux; *exec. prod.* Denis Heroux and John Kemeny; *dir.* Gilles Carle; *scen.* Gilles Carle and Roger Lemelin, based on a novel by Roger Lemelin; *cam.* (color) François Protat; *ed.* Yves Langlois; *music* Stephane Venne. *Prem.* Cinema Capital, Quebec City. 255 min.

Roles	Cast
Théophile	Emile Genest
Josephine	Juliette Huot
Cécile	Denise Filiatrault
Ovide	Gabriel Arcand
Napoléon	Pierre Curzi
Guillaume	Serge Dupire
Denis Boucher	Rémi Laurent
Rita Toulouse	Anne Létourneau
Pastro Foibeche	Gerard Poirier

The ups and downs and sorrows and joys of a working-class family in Quebec City during the thirties and forties. Warm, witty, and nostalgic, it serves as a reminder to Quebecois of how far they have come since the time when attending church, listening to priests, having babies, and struggling against poverty seemed all that life was made of.

HEARTACHES   May 1981

Prod. co. Rising Star Films Inc.; *prod.* Pieter Kroonenburg, David J. Patterson, and Jerry Raibourn; *dir.* Donald Shebib; *scen.* Terence Heffernan; *cam.* (color) Vic Sarin; *ed.* Gerry Hambling and Peter Boita; *music* Simon Michael Martin. *Prem.* Star II, Cannes 1981. 93 min.

Roles	Cast
Rita Harris	Margot Kidder
Bonnie Howard	Annie Potts
Stanley Howard	Robert Carradine
Marcello Di Stassi	Winston Rekert
Mario Di Stassi	George Touliatos
Aldo	Guy Sanvido
Alvin	Arnie Achtman
Andy	Michael Zelniker
Doctor	Peggy Feury

Set against a "never-never" city in North America, a young and pregnant girl meets a brassy young woman, and the two go to work in a mattress factory. Life for one of the women has hope for a secure future, but for the other, it is a matter of catch as catch can, with all the inevitable disappointments. Beautifully shot, sensitively directed by Shebib, and engagingly played.

THE HOUNDS OF NOTRE DAME   May 1981

Prod. co. Pere Film Productions Ltd.; *prod.* Fil Fraser;, *dir.* Zale Dalen; *scen.* Ken Mitchell; *cam.* (color) Ron Orieux; *ed.* Tony Lower, *mus.* Maurice Marshall. *Prem.* Coronet Cinema, Regina, Sask. 95 min. *Dist.* Pan-Canadian Films.

Roles	*Cast*
Father Murray	Thomas Peacocke
Mother Therese	Frances Hyland
Archbishop Williams	Barry Morse
Tom Howard	Lawrence Reese
Lila Petrie	Lenore Zann
Ron Fryer	David Ferry
Bob Cormack	Phil Ridley

An affectionate and lively depiction of 36 hours in the life of legendary Father Athol Murray, founder of Notre Dame College in Regina, set on the post-Depression prairies with the clouds of war looming

Margot Kidder in *Heartaches* (d. Don Shebib, 1981).

Thomas Peacocke and Barry Morse in *The Hounds of Notre Dame* (d. Zale Dalen, 1980).

large over a poverty-stricken community.

TICKET TO HEAVEN   May 1981

Prod. co. Stalker Productions Inc.; *rel.* United Artists Classics; *prod.* Vivienne Leebosh; *dir.* R. L. Thomas; *scen.* R. L. Thomas and Anne Cameron, adapted from the novel *Moonwebs* by Josh Freed; *cam.* (color) Richard Leiterman; *ed.* Ron Wisman; *music* Micky Erbe and Maribeth Solomon. *Prem.* Star III, Cannes 1981. 109 min.

Roles	*Cast*
David Kappel	Nick Mancuso
Larry	Saul Rubinek
Ingrid	Meg Foster
Ruthie	Kim Cattrall
Linc Strunk	R. H. Thomson
Lisa	Jennifer Dale
Eric	Guy Boyd
Sarah	Dixie Seatle
Patrick	Robert Joy
Karl	Stephen Markle
Greg	Timothy Webber
Morley Kappel	Paul Soles
Mr. Stone	Harvey Atkin
Dr. Dryer	Patrick Brymer
Esther Kappel	Marcia Diamond
Danny	Michael Zelnicker

An interesting and outspoken first feature depicting the inside workings of a "religious" cult in San Francisco that attracts emotionally deprived youngsters and forces them into following its beliefs. The parents carry out a true-life kidnapping of their son in order to free him from clutches of the businessman who is making money at the expense of the followers.

SURFACING   Oct. 1981

Rel. Pan-Canadian; *prod.* Beryl Fox; *dir.* Claude Jutra; *scen.* Bernard Gordon, based on the novel by Margaret Atwood; *cam.* (color) Richard Leiterman; *ed.* Toni Trow; *music* Jean Cousineau and Ann Mortifee. *Prem.* Carlton Cineplex, Toronto. 88 min.

Roles	*Cast*
Joe	Joseph Bottoms
Kate	Kathleen Beller
David	R. H. Thomson

Saul Rubinek and Kim Cattrall in *Ticket to Heaven* (d. Ralph L. Thomas, 1981).

Margaret Dragu in *Surfacing* (d. Claude Jutra, 1981).

Anna	Margaret Dragu
Wayne	Michael Ironside
Rod	Larry Schwartz

Margaret Atwood's naturally Canadian novel is here turned into an American-looking film with two American actors who are out of place in a murky transposition of the original story. What should be intended as an examination into thoughts, feelings, and the innermost fears of human abstractionism becomes a meaningless, coarse, and sour depiction of a daughter's search in the northern backwoods for her missing father.

Other Films of 1981

Alligator Shoes. The first film of short-film-maker Clay Borris about two Acadian beer-swilling brothers in Toronto and the death of their young aunt.

Black Mirror (Haute Surveillance) (d. Pierre-Alain Jolivet). A France-Canada coproduction based on the novel by Jean Genet; a ludicrous, stylized study of women in prison.

By Design (d. Claude Jutra). Two wealthy dress designers who also happen to be lesbians decide to have a baby and inveigle a young photographer to be the father. Tedious, superficial, and unpleasant. Vancouver is passed off as an unnamed American city. Saul Rubinek, Sarah Botsford, Patty Duke Astin.

Ghostkeeper (d. James Makichuk). Three young people are marooned in a snowbound mansion ruled over by an old woman whose weird sons kill all strangers. A local Calgary film made quickly on a low budget, it is too slight, predictable, and poorly written to be acceptable.

Kelly (d. Christopher Chapman) in which Chapman, Canada's leading documentary film-maker, takes on his first feature and is defeated by an inane story in which a young and wealthy girl is tamed by the outdoor life—the outdoors in this case being Alberta passed off as Alaska!

Canada's American Films, 1981

The 1981 group of "Stars and Stripes" pictures included *By Design, Kelly* (see above), and *Tribute* (d. Bob Clark; Jack Lemmon in an overwrought performance as a New York publicity agent dying of cancer); *Bells* (d. Michael Anderson), Richard Chamberlain, John Houseman; *Chatwill's Verdict* (d. William Fruet), Henry Silva, Barbara Gordon; *Curtains* (d. Richard Ciupka), John Vernon, Samantha Eggar; *Firebird 2015 AD* (d. David Robertson), Darren McGavin, Doug McClure; *Hard Feelings* (d. Daryl Duke), Carl Marotte; *Harry Tracy, Desperado* (d. William A. Graham), Bruce Dern; *The Hot Touch* (d. Roger Vadim), Wayne Rogers, Marie-France Pisier, Melvyn Douglas, Samantha Eggar; *Incubus* (d. John Hough), John Cassavetes, John Ireland; *Melanie* (d. Rex Bromfield), Glynnis O'Conner, Paul Sorvino; *Misdeal* (d. John Trent), John Heard, Levon Helm; *My Bloody Valentine* (d. George Mihalka), Paul Kelman, Lori Hallier; *Threshold* (d. Richard Pearce), Donald Sutherland, John Marley; *Utilities* (d. Harvey Hart), Robert Hays, Brooke Adams, John Marley; *Happy Birthday to Me* (d. J. Lee Thompson), Melissa Sue Anderson; Glenn Ford; *Gas* (d. Les Rose), Donald Sutherland, Susan Anspach; *The Amateur* (d. Charles Jarrott), John Savage, Christopher Plummer, Marthe Keller.

Documentaries Made in 1981

Being Different (d. Harry Rasky). A study of people born physically deformed.

The Magic Show (d. Norman Campbell). A screen ver-

249

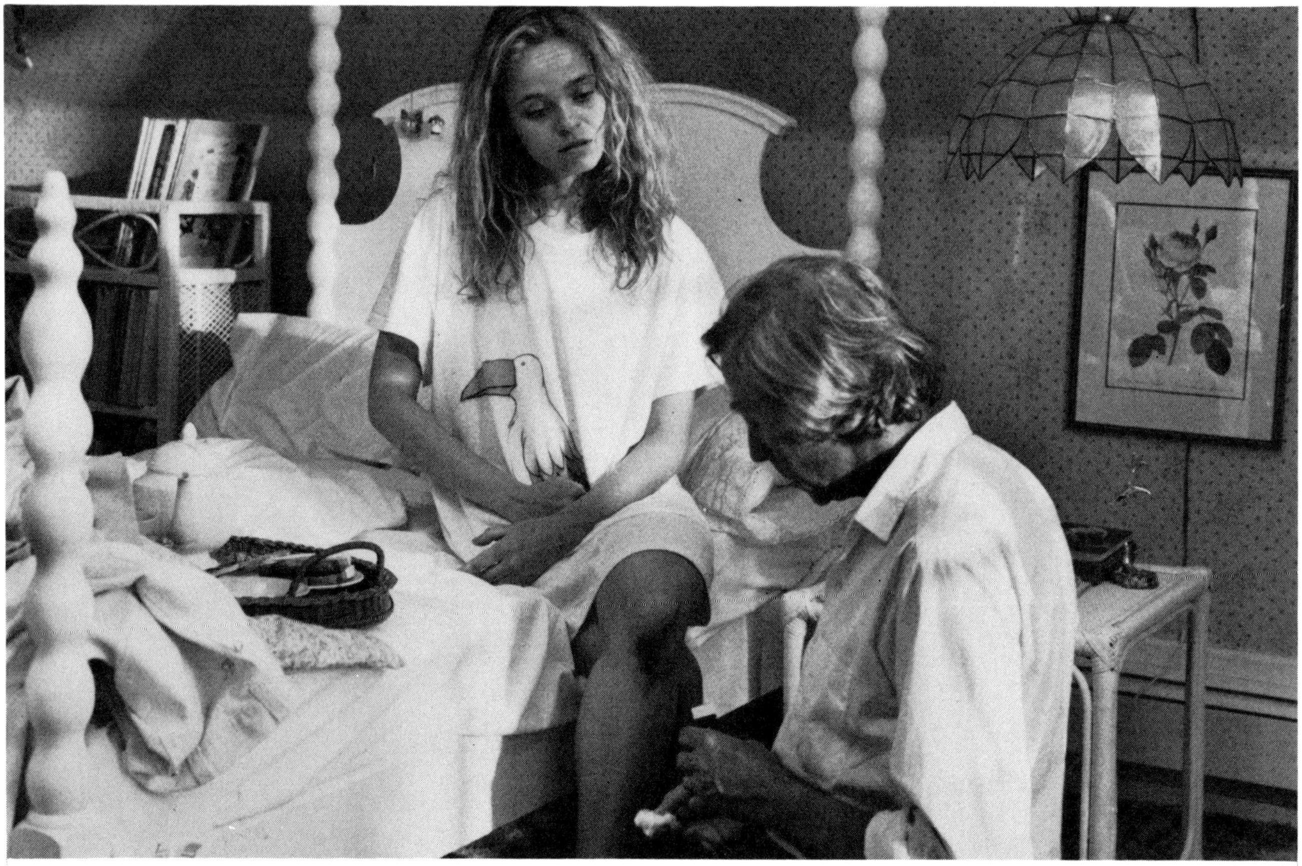

Les Beaux Souvenirs (d. Francis Mankiewicz, 1982).

Claudia Aubin and Pierre Curzi in *Les Fleurs sauvages (The Wild Flowers)* **(d. Jean-Pierre Lefebvre, 1982).**

sion of Doug Henning's spectacular stage presentation.

Some Do It for Money, Some Do It for Fun (d. Anthony Kay). Sex-oriented entertainment shows.

Innu-Asi (d. Arthur Lamothe). Another in the series portraying the life of the Montagnais Indian people.

The Dream Never Dies (d. William Johnson). A look at the Canadian Ski Team.

The Lover's Exile (d. Marty Gross). A faithful record of the Bunraku Theatrical Ensemble of Osaka, Japan, in Japanese with English subtitles.

Imagine the Sound (d. Ron Mann). Ninety minutes of conversation and music from jazz players Cecil Taylor, Bill Dixon, Art Davis, Paul Bley; nicely filmed, but the acceptance of the music depends on one's interpretation of jazz.

LES BEAUX SOUVENIRS   May 1982
(The Old Memories)

Prod. co. National Film Board of Canada—Lamy, Spencer et Compagnie Ltee; *rel.* NFB; *dir.* Francis Mankiewicz; *scen.* Rejean Ducharme; *cam.* (color) Georges Dufaux; *ed.* André Corriveau; *music* Jean Cousineau. *Prem.* Cannes Film Festival (Market). 113 min.

Roles	Cast
Marie	Monique Spaziani
Viviane	Julie Vincent
Papa	Paul Hebert
Rick	R. H. Thomson

A strange, brooding, yet compelling narrative, told in fragments that finally come together, about a young woman who returns to her family home outside Quebec City only to find that her father ignores her in favor of her sister, who has moved into her former bedroom and has removed all traces of their dead mother. Her sister is also possessed by an odd passion for her father. The past slowly reappears and the various pieces make up an absorbing family study.

LES FLEURS SAUVAGES   May 1982
(The Wild Flowers)

Prod. co. and rel. Cinak Ltee.; *prod.* Marguerite Duparc; *Scen./dir.* Jean-Pierre Lefebvre; *cam.* (color) Guy Dufaux; *ed.* Marguerite Duparc; *music* Raoul Duguay. *Prem.* Cannes Film Festival (Directors' Fortnight). 152 min.

Roles	Cast
Simone	Marthe Nadeau
Michele	Michele Magny
Pierre	Pierre Curzi
Eric	Eric Beausejour
Claudia	Claudia Aubin

Jouer sa vie (The Great Chess Movie) (1982; director Gilles Carle is shown).

251

Jackie Burroughs and Richard Farnsworth in *The Grey Fox* (d. Phillip Borsos, 1982).

A gentle, understanding, and perceptive look at family life observed during the summer when, for a week, the wife's mother comes on her annual visit to see her, the husband, and the two children. The little irritants, tensions, misunderstandings, the joys and delights are accurately told, together with the moments of happiness, the sadness of time passing, the sudden awareness at the end of the day of the need to find some meaning to those things in life that become increasingly unimportant. It is acted with perfect naturalism by the entire cast.

THE GREAT CHESS MOVIE   Aug. 1982
(Jouer sa vie)

Prod. co. the National Film Board in cooperation with Radio-Canada (CBC); *prod.* Hélène Verrier; *dir.* Gilles Carle and Camille Coudari; no writing credit; *cam.* (color) Pierre Letarte, Thomas Vamos; *ed.* Yves Leduc. *Prem.* Montreal Film Festival. 79 mins.

Cast: Anatoly Karpov, Victor Korchnoi, Bobby Fischer, Borris Spasky.

A witty and engaging documentary study of the great names of international chess. Like the principal pieces on the black-and-white board, they are ana-lyzed by the pawns, a group of grand masters. Fernando Arrabal goes deeper with a commentary that looks at the players' personal eccentricities, suggesting religious, sexual, and psychological motivations. Scenes from movies showing actors at the game are cleverly interspersed, making a witty and humorous compilation of a most unusual screen subject.

THE GREY FOX   Aug. 1982
Prod. co. Mercury Pictures; *prod.* Peter O'Brian; *dir.* Phillip Borsos; *scen.* John Hunter; *cam.* (color) Frank Tidy; *ed.* Ray Hall; *music* Michael Baker, The Chieftains; *Prem.* Taormina Film Festival. 92 min. *Dist.* United Artists Classics.

Roles	*Cast*
Bill Miner	Richard Farnsworth
Kate	Jackie Burroughs
Shorty	Wayne Robson
Jack	Ken Pogue
Fernie	Timothy Webber
Louis	David Petersen
Detective Seavey	Gary Reineke

A graceful, beautifully photographed, romanticized biography of Bill Miner, the American train robber who came to Canada at the turn of the century to ply his "trade," having been chased out of the United States. Gentle, intelligent, leisurely told, it is a refreshing glimpse into history set against the magnificent scenery of British Columbia.

BIG MEAT EATER   Nov. 1982

Prod. Laurence Keane for BDC Entertainment; *dir.* Chris Windsor; *scen.* Phil Savath, Keane, Windsor; *cam.* (color) Douglas MacKay; *ed.* Lilla Pederson, Keane, Windsor; *music* J. Douglas Dodd. *Prem.* Ridge Theatre, Vancouver. 77 min.

Roles	*Cast*
Bob Sanderson	George Dawson
Jan Wczinski	Andrew Gillies
Abdulla	Clarence "Big" Miller
Joseph Wczinski	Stephen Dimopoulos
Rosa Wczinski	Georgina Hegedos

On a modest budget of $150,000 the young filmmakers responsible for this musical-comedy-horror-farce joined forces at the Simon Fraser University Workshop in Vancouver to make it a reality. Apart from *Strange Brew,* which came a year later, filmmakers in this country have concentrated on realism, historical reconstruction, political drama, but very seldom on native humor. This film joins the few and strengthens the category considerably. It is so artless that it becomes entertaining, and the only mystery to the plot is in trying to find it. What little there is becomes further diffused by some delightful songs. It is about a mad butcher and his equally mad friends who become involved in most of the awful capers ever found in grade-B movies.

LA QUARANTAINE (The Forties)   Dec. 1982

Prod. co. National Film Board; *prod.* Jacques Vallée; *dir.* Anne-Claire Poirier; *scen.* Poirier and Marthe Blackburn; *cam.* (color) Michel Brault; *ed.* André Corriveau; *music* Joel Bienvenue. *Prem.* Odeon Theatre (Berri), Montreal. 105 min. *Dist.* Mutual Films.

Roles	*Cast*
Grosse Louise	Monique Mercure
Tarzan	Jacques Godin
Le King	Roger Blay
Helene	Luce Guilbeault
La Plume	Michele Rossignol
Françoise	Patricia Nolan
Babette	Louise Remy
Bo-Jean	Benoit Girard
Bilou	Pierre Theriault
Jacques	Pierre Gobeil
Peau-Dure	Aubert Pallascio

Ten childhood friends, now forty years older, agree

The ten friends in *La Quarantaine* (d. Anne-Claire Poirier, 1982).

to meet at one of their old haunts in a small town in Quebec to discover what has happened to them in the intervening years. It is a night of revealations; some have prospered, others have failed, some have found happiness, others have known tragedy. The film is carried out entirely by conversation, which ranges over the amusing and the dramatic; yet movement and change is always evident, with the whole skillfully held together by the marvelous ensemble acting, the direction, and the very real expression of feelings and emotions.

Other Films of 1982

Escape from Iran (The Canadian Caper) (d. Lamont Johnson). A hurried job of telling the true story of how the Canadian ambassador to Iran at the time of the revolution assisted American embassy officials in escaping from the country. Gordon Pinsent, R. H. Thomson, Chris Wiggins. *Prod.* Canamedia Productions Ltd., 96 min., color.

Humongous (d. Paul Lynch). Another version of the "dreadful something" hiding in the basement, this time in an old house on an island. Janet Julian, David Wallace, Janit Baldwin. *Prod.* Humongous Productions, 93 min., color.

Scandale (d. George Mihalka). Low-budget "quickie" made to cash in on the reputed use by the staff of the Quebec legislature of video equipment to make a porno picture. At first a funny spoof, it turns sour when hard-core pornography is introduced. Sophie Lorain, Alpha Boucher, Gilbert Comtois. *Prod.* RSL Films, 90 min., color.

Une Journée en Taxi (d. Robert Menard). Frustrating taxi ride through Montreal with a prisoner out on leave who is determined to kill the friend who betrayed him. Jean Yanne, Gilles Renaud. *Prod.* Videofilms Ltd. (a France-Canada coproduction), 90 min., color.

La Bête Lumineuse (d. Pierre Perrault). Known for his once human and understanding ethnographic studies, Perrault has lost his sense of objectivity in this dreary, unpleasant study of a group of "hunters" who escape from the city to enjoy themselves in the country. Nothing seems true or believable. Louis-Philippe Lecuyer and others. *Prod.* NFBC, 128 min., color.

Canadian-American Films of 1982

The Class of 1984 (d. Mark Lester). A thoroughly revolting picture cynically exploiting the issue of crime and violence in schools. Perry King, Merrie-Lynn Ross, Roddy McDowall, Timothy Van Patten.

Death Bite (d. William Fruet). A horror film about snakes. Peter Fonda, Oliver Reed.

Hank Williams: "The Show He Never Gave" (d. David Acomba). A musical in which Sneezy Waters portrays the memorable Hank Williams, with Dixie Seatle.

If You Could See What I Hear (d. Eric Till). Tiresome tale of the life of blind American singer Tom Sullivan. Marc Singer, R. H. Thomson.

Julie Darling (d. Paul Nicholas, shot mostly in Germany). Tired story of a teenage daughter who loves daddy and does in his second wife. Anthony Franciosa, Isabelle Mejias.

Kings and Desperate Men (d. Alexis Kanner). Confused and pretentious kidnap melodrama. Patrick McGoohan, Margaret Trudeau, Alexis Kanner.

Paradise (d. Stuart Gillard, shot in Israel). Feeble reworking of *The Blue Lagoon,* with a touch of the *Arabian Nights.* William Aames, Phoebe Cates.

Porky's (d. Bob Clark, shot in Florida). Gross sex comedy about students in the fifties. Kim Cattrall, Dan Monahan.

Rats (d. Robert Clouse). A silly horror film about giant rats, unconvincingly played by dachshunds! Sam Bloom, Sara Botsford.

Sneakers (d. Joseph L. Scanlon, shot in Florida). Two 13-year-old tennis players and the pressures on their lives. Susan Anton, Carling Bassett.

Visiting Hours (formerly *Fright*) (d. Jean-Claude Lord). Psychopath on the loose in a hospital; Lee Grant, William Shatner.

Cross Country (d. Paul Lynch), *Losin' It* (d. Curtis Hanson, formerly, *Tijuana*), *Porky's II; The Next Day* (d. Bob Clark), *Screwballs* (d. Rafal Zielinski). Four despicable projects: the first is an unremitting stream of rape, violence, and murder, with the remaining three being the usual witless, tasteless, vulgar excursions into what purports to be teenage sex frolics which debase their characters and audiences alike.

Also: *Videodrome* (d. David Cronenberg). An exceedingly unpleasant work in which the director digs himself even deeper into his pit of depravity with this pretentious exploration into technology gone wrong. James Woods, Deborah Harry. *Prod.* Filmplan, 90 min., color.

Documentaries Made in 1982

Poetry in Motion (d. Ron Mann). An efficiently made "record" film of more than two dozen characters (best not named) who call themselves poets and read and perform what they call poetry. It is difficult to know whether this is a serious film or a send-up. Nothing

Carole Laure and Nick Mancuso in *Maria Chapdelaine* (d. Gilles Carle, 1983).

much is in motion, and if this is poetry, it is better not to know it. *Prod.* Sphinx, 90 min., color.

The Kid Who Couldn't Miss (d. Paul Cowan). Based partly on the play with music, *Billy Bishop Goes to War,* this is a likable, revealing, and sympathetic study of Canada's flying hero of WWI, played by Eric Peterson, who appears (between scenes from newsreels and interviews) with people who knew Bishop. *Prod.* National Film Board, 80 min., color.

SIEGE   Jan. 1983

Prod. co. Salter Productions Ltd.; *prod.* Phillip M. Robinson; *dir.* Paul Donovan; *scen.* Donovan, based on an idea by Marc Vautour; *cam.* (Eastmancolor) Lester Krizsan; *ed.* Ian McBride; *music* Peter Jermyn, Drew King. *Prem.* Manila Film Centre. 83 min. *Dist.* Summa Vista (Canada), Manson International (overseas).

Roles	Cast
Horatio	Tom Nardini
Barbara	Brenda Bazinet
Cabe	Douglas Lennox
Chester	Darel Haney
Daniel	Terry-David Despres
Goose	Jeff Pustil
Patrick	Jack Blum
Steve	Keith Knight
Ian	Brad Wadden
Lloyd	Gary Dempster

A dishonest and violent melodrama set in Halifax, Nova Scotia, based on the 42-day police strike that took place there in 1982. The far-fetched events concern rowdies attacking a "gay" bar, leading to the intervention by another group called The New Order, resulting in carnage and destruction everywhere.

MARIA CHAPDELAINE   April 1983

Prod. co. Astral Film Production; *rel.* in collaboration with Radio Canada (Canadian Broadcasting Corp.) and La Societe nationale de programmes T.F.1 (France); *Exec. prod.* Harold Greenberg; *prod.* Murray Shostak, Robert Baylis; *dir.* Gilles Carle; *scen.* Carle, Guy Fournier, based on the novel by Louis Hemon; *cam.* (color) Pierre Mignot; *ed.* Avde Chiriaeff; *music*

Lewis Furey. *Prem.* Cinema Le Dauphin, Montreal. 108 min. *Dist.* Astral Films.

Roles	Cast
Maria Chapdelaine	Carole Laure
Francois Paradis	Nick Mancuso
Father Cordelier	Claude Rich
Laura Chapdelaine	Amulette Garneau
Samuel Chapdelaine	Yoland Guerard
Eutrope Gagnon	Pierre Curzi
Lorenzo Surprenant	Donald Lautrec
Marie-Ange	Marie Tifo

Louis Hemon's romantic and sentimental story of pioneer life in Quebec, first published in 1913, is here miscast, misconceived, and misbecoming—a subject for which Carle seems to have little sympathy or understanding. It has no sense of history, style, or unity.

(This is the third film version of the book. The first was made by Julien Duvivier in 1934 with Madeleine Renaud and Jean Gabin; the second by Marc Allegret in 1949 with Michele Morgan and Phillippe Lemaire.)

THE TERRY FOX STORY April 1983

Prod. co. Astral Film Production; *rel.* 20th Century–

Gordon Pinsent as Boyd in *The Life and Times of Edwin Alonzo Boyd* (d. Les Rose, 1983).

Fox (Canada) in cooperation with CTV Television (Canada) and HBO (U.S.); *prod.* Robert Cooper; *dir.* Ralph L. Thomas; *scen.* Edward Hume; *story* John and Rose Kastner; *cam.* (color) Richard Ciupka; *ed.* Ron Wisman; *music* Bill Conti. *Prem.* Odeon, Vancouver. 98 min.

Roles	Cast
Bill Vigars	Robert Duvall
Terry Fox	Eric Fryer
Doug Alward	Michael Zelniker
Darrell Fox	Chris Makepeace
Rika Noda	Rosalind Chao
Betty Fox	Elva Mai Hoover
Rolly Fox	Frank Adamson
Judith Fox	Marie McCann
Dr. Simon	R. H. Thomson
Dan Grey	Saul Rubinek
Gregg	Gary Darycott
Bob Cady	Matt Craven
Wilson	Chuck Shamata
Peg Leg	Patrick Watson

Terry Fox was a young Canadian who lost a leg to cancer, and, determined to make the most of his limited life, choose to run across Canada to raise money

Eric Fryer in *The Terry Fox Story* (d. Ralph L. Thomas, 1983).

for medical research. His heroic undertaking is shown here with a documentarylike realism, chronicled with honesty and insight.

THE LIFE AND TIMES   April 1983
OF EDWIN ALONZO BOYD

Prod. co. Poundmaker Productions Ltd. in association with CTV Network (Toronto); *prod.* Barry Pearson; *dir.* Les Rose; *scen.* Rose and Pearson; *cam.* (b&W & color) Edward Higginson; *ed.* Christopher Hutton; *music* Alex Pauk and Zina Louie. *Prem.* CTV. 97 min.

Roles	*Cast*
Edwin Alonzo Boyd	Gordon Pinsent
Doreen Boyd	Mary Ann McDonald
Willie "The Clown" Jackson	Jean-Marc Amyot
Lennie Jackson	Domenic Tudino
Steve Suchan	Jack Langhorn
Mary Mitchell	Karen Kennedy
Ann Jackson	Sharolyn Sparrow

An unusual and compelling documentary-drama that mixes actors with actual events and newsreel and staged photography in telling the life story of a notori-ous Toronto bank robber. Gordon Pinsent speaks the narration and also plays Edwin Boyd with a lively and fugitive sense.

RIEN QU'UN JEU (Just A Game)   May 1983

Prod. co./rel. Cine-Groupe; *prod.* Monique Messier, Yvon Michon, and Jacques Pettigrew; *dir.* Brigitte Sauriol; *scen.* Sauriol and Messier; *cam.* (color) Paul Van der Linden; *ed.* Marcel Pothier; *music* Yves Laferrière. *Prem.* Cannes Film Festival (Directors' Fortnight). 100 min.

Roles	*Cast*
Mychele	Marie Tifo
André	Raymond Cloutier
Catherine	Jennifer Grenier
Julie	Julie Mongeau

This is a remarkably observed, understated, and elo-quent study of the silent agony of a daughter forced into an incestuous relationship with her father. When she finally refuses to continue it, he turns his attention to his younger daughter. The wife makes matters worse by blaming the girls and excusing the father's behavior, in order to hide her own weaknesses. While

Jennifer Grenier and Julie Mongeau in *Rien qu'un jeu (Just a Game)* **(d. Brigitte Sauriol, 1983).**

Pierre Curzi in *Lucien Brouillard* (d. Bruno Carrière, 1983).

somewhat awkward in places, the whole is well acted, rings entirely true, and accurately reflects a growing situation in which the children are paying the price for their emotional suffering—the fathers rarely being brought to trial.

LUCIEN BROUILLARD   June 1983

Prod. co./rel. ACPAV; *prod.* René Gueissaz; *dir.* Bruno Carrière; *scen.* Carrière and Jacques Jacob; *cam.* (color) Pierre Mignot; *ed.* Michel Arcand. *Prem.* Sydney Film Festival. 88 min.

Roles	*Cast*
Lucien Brouillard	Pierre Curzi
Jacques Martineau	Roger Blay
Alice Tanguay	Marie Tifo
André Morin	Paul Savoie
Premier Provencher	Jean Duceppe

To the working-class people of a Montreal neighborhood, Lucien Brouillard is a hero and savior. Injustice, and political and legal trickery are the objects of his anger, and his attacks upon them, both verbal and physical, lead to prison. His savior, in turn, is a childhood friend from the same social background, who has become a lawyer and is set upon joining the ruling political party that Lucien so despises. Both a psychological thriller and a perceptive social drama, this unusual film, which is only thinly disguised when it comes to describing the Quebec social scene, is marred by a contrived assassination attempt and by the fact that the character of Lucien becomes so unlikeable that audiences are likely to lose patience with him.

BONHEUR D'OCCASION (The Tin Flute) July 1983

Prod. co. coproduction of Cine St-Henri Inc. with the National Film Board and the Canadian Broadcasting Corp; *rel.* Cine 360; *exec. prod.* Raymond, and Robert Verrall; *prod.* Marie-Jose Raymond; *dir.* Claude Fournier; *scen.* Fournier and Raymond; based on the novel by Gabrielle Roy; *add. writing* Anne Cameron; *cam.* (Eastmancolor) Claude Fournier; *ed.* Yves Langlois; *music* François Dompierre; *theme song.* Nancy Ward and Mouffe, sung by Diane Tell. *Prem.* Moscow Film Festival. 123 min. *Dist.* Spectrafilm.

Roles	*Cast*
Rose Anne Lacasse	Marilyn Lightstone
Florentine Lacasse	Mireille Deyglun
Azarius Lacasse	Michel Forget
Jean Levesque	Pierre Chagnon
Emmanuel Letourneau	Martin Neufeld
Yvonne Lacasse	Charlotte Laurier
Marguerite	Linda Sorgini

Based on Gabrielle Roy's popular novel, *Bonheur d'occasion (Second-Hand Happiness)*, published in 1945, the book was one of the first to depict life among the working-class people of Quebec. Times were hard, the Depression was ending, the Second World War was near. The family in this story goes through the familiar cycle of life and death, heartbreak and unemployment; the settings are drab but lively, the streets and buildings re-create the impression of the thirties. The author's theme of the erosion of human faith and values in the face of poverty and industrialization comes through with poignancy and purpose. Unfortunately, this cinema version seems inconsistent in the telling, the reason being that it was edited down to its present running time from a five-hour version for television. (Filmed in French and English.)

STRANGE BREW   August 1983

Prod. co./rel. MGM-UA; *prod.* Louis M. Silverstein; *dir.* Dave Thomas, Rick Moranis; *scen.* Thomas, Moranis, Steven de Jarnatt; *cam.* (color) Steven Poster; *ed.* Patrick McMahon; *music* Charles Fox. *Prem.* Uptown Theatre, Toronto. 90 min.

Roles	*Cast*
Doug McKenzie	Dave Thomas
Bob McKenzie	Rick Moranis
Brewmaster Smith	Max von Sydow
Claude Elsinore	Paul Dooley
Pam Elsinore	Lynne Griffin
Jean LaRose	Angus MacInnes

Also with: Douglas Campbell, Tom Harvey, Brian McConnachie, Len Doncheff, Jill Frappier, David Beard, Thick Wilson and Mel Blanc (voice of Mr. McKenzie).

This is such an innocuous concoction that it is hard to find fault with its lack of brillance or drive when it comes to adding up the laughs in this slight but entirely amiable comedy. More a romp than a revealation, it introduces to the screen the two Canadian "hosers" who became well known on the small screen, with a host of fellow comedians, in *SCTV.* They might have had a better film had their colleagues joined forces with them to tell this story of a mad brewer who plans to take over the world with his newly brewed and potent beer. The brothers, in their bumbling way, soon put an end to his ambitions. However, there is enough

Mireille Deyglun and Martin Neufeld in Bonheur d'occasion
(The Tin Flute) *(d. Claude Fournier, 1983).*

good humor to sustain the whole, and audiences abroad will be introduced for the first time to the big sociocultural Canadian joke in which hosers are identified by their liking for plaid clothing, toques, earmuffs, an infinite capacity for back bacon and beer, and the habit of ending every comment with the query "eh?" They have undoubtedly created a national characteristic, one that many Canadians would prefer to ignore.

RUNNING BRAVE   Sept. 1983

Prod. Ira Englander; *rel.* Buena Vista; *dir.* "D. S. Everett" (Donald Shebib); *scen.* Henry Bean and Shirley Hendryx; *cam.* (color) François Protat; *ed.* Tony Lower, Earle Herdan; *music* Mike Post. *Prem.* Hollywood Theatre, Toronto. 105 min.

Roles	*Cast*
Billy Mills	Robby Benson
Coach Easton	Pat Hingle
Pat Mills	Claudia Cron
Dennis	Jeff McCraken
Billy's father	August Schellenberg
Frank	Denis Lacroix
Eddie	Graham Greene
Catherine	Margo Kane

On October 14, 1964, in Tokyo, Japan, Lieutenant Billy Mills, an American Indian running for the U.S. Marine Corps, edged out world record holders, Ron Clarke of Australia and Mohamed Gammoudi of Tunisia, to win the Gold Medal in the 10,000-meter run. The race was regarded by many to be the most remarkable result in the history of the Olympic Games, and to this date, Mills remains the only American to have ever won that event. This is a Canadian film financed by the Ermineskin Band of Cree Indians who saw in it an attempt to depict Indian history in a positive light. It was filmed entirely in Alberta with Edmonton and Drumheller being used for the South Dakota reservation and the University of Kansas (actually the University of Alberta). The Commonwealth Stadium was used to re-create the famous race. The story strikes a commendable balance between sports and the social situation relating to the poverty and discrimination borne by the Indians; but many individuals question whether or not the $8 million spent by the Crees could not have been better used to improve the present-day way of life of Canada's Indians.

Dave Thomas and Rick Moranis as the McKenzie brothers in *Strange Brew* **(d. Thomas and Moranis, 1983).**

Brent Carver and Martha Henry in *The Wars* (d. Robin Phillips, 1983).

(Donald Everett Shebib did not agree with Ira Englander's final version and had his name removed from the credits.)

UPS AND DOWNS   Nov. 1983

Prod. co. Quest Film Production; *rel.* Astral Films; *prod./dir.* Paul Almond; *scen.* Almond and Lewis Evans; *cam.* (color) Peter Benison; *ed.* Yurij Luhovy; *music* Bo Harwood. *Prem.* Park Theatre, Vancouver. 97 min.

Roles	Cast
Arthur Holmes	Colin Skinner
Chip	Andrew Sabiston
Drifty	Gavin Brannon
Penelope	Leslie Hope
Sam	Margo Nesbit
Mouse	Alison Kemble
Emmie	Sandy Gauthier

Filmed in Vancouver by Paul Almond (*Isabel, Act of the Heart, Journey*) and written in part by him, this film seems to bear out the contention that the reason certain film-makers such as Almond have found refuge in obscure subjects is due in no small measure to their inability to tell a story in direct terms, thereby giving it meaning and character. This slight film concerning the daily lives of mostly spoiled children in a private school, replete with the usual pranks and put-ons, is pleasant and likable, but entirely lacking in identity, insight, and purpose.

THE WARS   Nov. 1983

Prod. co. Nielsen-Ferns International, the National Film Board, Polyphon Film-und-Fernseh, CFDC, Famous Players; *prod.* Richard Nielson; *dir.* Robin Phillips; *scen.* Timothy Findley, based on his novel; *cam.* (color) John Coquillon; *ed.* Tony Lower; *music* Glenn Gould. *Prem.* Odeon-Hyland Theatre, Toronto. 120 min. *Dist.* Spectrafilm.

Roles	Cast
Robert Ross	Brent Carver
Mrs. Ross	Martha Henry
Mr. Ross	William Hutt
Rowena Ross	Anne-Marie MacDonald
Miss Davenport	Jackie Burroughs
Captain Taffler	Jean Leclerc
Lady Barbara d'Orsey	Domini Blythe
Captain Leather	Alan Scarfe
Lady Emmeline	Margaret Tyzack
Nurse Turner	Barbara Budd

Guy L'Ecuyer and Michel Côté in *Au clair de la lune* (d. Andrè Forcier, 1983).

The first film of stage director Robin Phillips, this much fought over film (during production) comes· to the screen as a stilted, pretentious, and cumbersome portrayal of an upper-class Toronto family and their son who goes to the western front during WWI.

Other Films of 1983

Au Clair de la lune (Moonshine) (d. André Forcier). A sad and funny tale of a strange friendship between a former bowling champion (now a sandwich board man) and an albino, who spends his time in dreams. Abstract and illusionary, it is always thoughtful and lively. Guy L'Ecuyer, Michel Côté. *Prod.* Les Productions Albinie, 92 min., color.

Contrecoeur (d. Jean-Guy Noel). A whimsical piece about two wives going to visit their husbands, who travel by tanker-truck and become attached to the driver—with surprising results. A slight but charming glimpse of another side of Quebec society. Monique Mercure, Anouk Simard, Raymond Cloutier, Gilbert Sicotte. *Prod.* Les Productions Pierre Lamy, 95 min., color.

Latitude 55 (d. John Juliani and written in part by him). A two-character play on film that is intended to be a philosophical study of a strange encounter between a young woman, a cultural representative for Alberta, and a Polish potato farmer who might also be a mystic. The result is trying for all concerned. Andrée Pelletier, August Schellenberg. *Prod.* Savage God One, 100 min., color.

Dead Wrong (d. Len Kowalewich). A tedious and unconvincing adventure film about drug-smuggling from Colombia to Canada, wasting the talents of Winston Rekert, who is paired with Britt Ekland playing an undercover Mountie. *Prod.* Sounder Films, 93 min., color.

Les Doux Aveux (Sweet Lies and Tender Oaths) (d. Fernand Dansereau). This is a delightful four-part, two generations study of an eccentric grandmother who leaves the home of her nagging daughter, finds her own place to live, and meets an equally eccentric older man who becomes her friend. Héléne Loiselle, Marcel Sabourin, Geneviève Brassard, Gilbert Turp. *Prod.* Animage Inc., 92 min., color.

Larose, Pierrot et la luce (d. Claude Gagnon). Three friends decide to turn away from the daily grind and rebuild a house left to one of them by his grandmother. A gentle and likable film of personal discovery. Richard Niquette, Lou Matte, Louise Portal. *Prod.* Yoshimura-Gagnon Ltee., 105 min., color.

Les Yeux rouges or *Les Verites Accidentelles* (Red Eyes) (d. Yves Simoneau). For once, a police yarn from a Canadian point-of-view: a police officer in a Quebec city tracks down a voyeur known as "red eyes." A nifty, scary, and entirely probable tale. Marie Tifo, Jean-Marie Lemieux, Pierre Curzi, Raymond Bouchard. *Prod.* Le Loup Blanc Inc., 90 min., color.

Sonatine (d. Micheline Lanctot). Miss Lanctot's first film since the enjoyable *The Handyman* deals with two adolescent girls who try to escape from the indifference they encounter in their daily lives. A film of perception and understanding on a somewhat familiar theme. Pascale Bussières, Marcia Pilote, Kliment Demtchev, Pierre Fauteux. *Prod.* Corporation Image M&M Ltee., 90 min., color.

Canada's American Films, 1983

That the "film boom of Hollywood North" collapsed this year is well illustrated by the fact that only one "Stars and Stripes" film was released in 1983. This was the clumsy and sentimental *A Christmas Story,* directed by Bob (Porky's) Clark with Melinda Dillon and Darryl McGavin, about a boy who wants an airgun for Christmas. It has no charm and no genuine humor. Fortunately, by its very nature, it is unlikely to turn up on Christmases yet to come. *Nobody Makes Me Cry* (d. Lou Antonio), about two widows played by Elizabeth Taylor and Carol Burnett, for HBO; *Heavenly Bodies* (d. Lawrence Dane), a sex-musical set among the workout girls on a Chicago TV station; and *Draw* (d. Steven Stern), a wretched western with Kirk Douglas and James Coburn. Also: *Falcon's Gold* (d. Bob Schulz).

Coproductions: the enormously expensive cinema and television film, *Louisiana* (France-Canada) (d. Philippe de Broca), a threadbare tenth-rate version of *GWTW*, wasting the talents of Margot Kidder, Ian Charleston, Len Cariou, Raymond Pellegrin; and, with Israel: *Tell Me That You Love Me* (d. Tzipi Trope). A protracted and unreal story of a failed marriage set against affluent Tel-Aviv backgrounds. Among the players, Nick Mancuso, Andrée Pelletier, Kenneth Welsh, and others, can do little with their poorly written parts.

Carroll Ballard filmed Farley Mowat's *Never Cry Wolf* in northern Canada. As the book is a justly famous Canadian work in this country, the advertising for the film here referred to Canada, although the film itself never does. For the rest of the world, the advertising sets it in Alaska. Speaking of northern Canada, Norman Jewison made his American story, *Iceman,* there, directed by Fred Schepsi. Jewison's following film, *Agnes of God,* was filmed in Montreal and Guelph, Ontario.

Films Shown on Television in 1983

Ready for Slaughter (d. Allan King). A film about farmers going bankrupt. Gordon Pinsent. CBC.

Out of Sight, Out of Mind (d. Zale Dalen). A study of the treatment of the criminally insane. Robert Joy and Nicholas Campbell. CBC.

Reasonable Force (d. Peter Rowe). An indictment of racism against Indians in British Columbia. CBC.

Sons and Daughters (a series based on stories by Alice Munro, Earle Birney, Lucy Maud Montgomery, Adelle La Rouche, and Brian Doyle). CBC in cooperation with an enterprising new production company, Atlantis Films of Toronto.

Documentaries Made in 1983

Bix (d. Brigitte Berman). An overlong yet interesting collection of reminiscences by those friends and musicians who worked with Bix Beiderbecke, the jazz cornetist.

Falasha: Exile of the Black Jews (d. Jamie Boyd, Simcha Jacobovici). A well-intended but labored and confused study of the Falashas in Ethiopia and Israel.

Memoire battante (d. Arthur Lamothe). Another of this film-maker's long and talkative anthropological studies, here concerning the Indian people of the Montagnais Reservation in Quebec.

La Turlute des annees dures (d. Marguerite Duparc). Uses archive material to re-create the years between the wars in Quebec, with a sprinkling of everything including politics, religion, and song, as well as a reference to the rest of Canada now and then.

Pourquoi l'etrange monsieur Zolock s'interessait-il tant à la bande dessinée? (Why Is the Strange Mr. Zolock So Interested in Comic Strips?) (d. Nicole Boisvert). A lively and colorful look at the work of French-speaking cartoonists in France and Belgium.

Raymond Massey: Actor of the Century (d. Harry Rasky). While hardly the "actor of the century," Raymond Massey was a very distinguished player (born in Toronto), and this film is made very real and enjoyable by his recollections of work and friends during his long career on stage and in the cinema. He died shortly after this film was finished on July 29, 1983.

LES ANNEES DE REVES   May 1984
(Years of Dreams and Revolt)

Prod. co. Les Films Vision 4; *rel.* Les Films René Malo Inc.; *prod.* Claude Bonin; *dir.* Jean-Claude Labrecque; *scen.* Robert Gurik, Marie Laberge, based on a story by Labrecque; *cam.* (color) Alain Dostie; *ed.* François Labonte; *music* songs of the period. First shown at the Cannes Film Festival, (Directors' Fortnight). 96 min.

Roles	*Cast*
Claudette Pelletier	Anne-Marie Provencher
Louis Pelletier	Gilbert Sicotte
Aunt Yvette	Monique Mercure
Aunt Adele	Amulette Garneau
Aunt Marie	Carmen Tremblay
Armand, Member of the National Assembly	Roger Lebel
John	André Mathieu
John-John	John Wildman
Mathieu at 2½ years old	Alexandre Guertin-Aird
Mathieu at 5 years old	Guillaume Lemay-Thivierge

Jean-Claude Labrecque continues his social history of Quebec as seen through the eyes of a single family, which he began in *Les Vautours* in 1974. Unlike the first film, however, which was set mainly in a multi-room house with a dark and claustrophobic atmosphere, this picture goes out in the streets to capture the swirling unrest which followed the quiet "pre-revolutionary" period. Many of the family characters, including the three aunts, are back, and the whole is not lacking in passion and feeling, yet strangely it remains slight and superficial in spite of the creator's affinity with the period and the events set against it.

LE CRIME D'OVIDE PLOUFFE   May 1984
(The Crime of Ovide Plouffe)

Prod. co. Cine-Plouffe II Inc., with CBC; *prod.* Justine Heroux; *dir.* Denys Arcand; *scen.* Roger Lemelin, Denys Arcand; *cam.* (color) François Protat; *ed.* Monique Fortier; *music* Olivier Dassault. First shown at the Cannes Film Festival (Market). 105 min. *Dist.* Les Films René Malo Inc.

Roles	*Cast*
Ovide Plouffe	Gabriel Arcand
Rita Toulouse (Plouffe)	Anne Létourneau
Pacifique Berthet	Jean Carmet
Marie	Véronique Jannot
Maman Plouffe	Juliette Huot
Napoléon Plouffe	Pierre Curzi
Jeanne Plouffe	Louise Laparé
Cécile Plouffe	Denise Filiatrault
Guillaume Plouffe	Serge Dupire
Stan Labrie	Donald Pilon
Grand Avocat	Roger Lebel
Agent de Voyage	Dominique Michel
Jeune Avocat de la Défense	Marcel Leboeuf

The story of Ovide; his lusty wife, Rita; and his demure would-be mistress, Marie; this minichapter from a TV miniseries coproduced with France conveys very little of the social and historical details in the original book. Set in Quebec City during the early fifties it manages, however, to be consistently entertaining, affectionate, and funny as it tells of Ovide's troubles with his wife, his business, his family, friends, and mistress.

Prod. co. Cinak Ltd.; *prod.* Yves Rivard; *dir.* Jean-Pierre Lefebvre; *scen.* Lefebvre, Barbara Easto, Pierre Curzi, Mario Tifo; *cam.* (color) Guy Dufaux; *ed.* Barbara Easto; *music* Lefebvre. First shown at the Cannes Film Festival (A Certain Regard). 88 min. *Dist.* Astral Films.

Roles	Cast
Jean-Baptiste Beauregard	Pierre Curzi
Claire Louise	Marie Tifo
The Vendor	Marcel Sabourin

Think of "S," asks Jean-Pierre Lefebvre, as in "smile, satire, symbol, surrealism, sexuality . . ." One morning, the hero, Jean-Baptiste, is eagerly awaiting his girlfriend, Claire, an actress, who is returning that same evening to Montreal after shooting a TV commercial in Toronto. Jean-Baptiste has nothing special to do (besides contemplate the approach of his fortieth birthday), and he falls into a mood of introspection. His thoughts center on his relations with women, and so preoccupied he goes walking and in all innocence provokes a series of meetings and events. Before the day is over the coincidences multiply, reviving the fantasies of his childhood, his adolescence, his first marriage and divorce, until finally he is reunited with Claire and brought back to the present. Once again, Lefebvre takes an ordinary man and some commonplace thoughts and spins them into a likable and affecting revue that touches psychologically on the banality of life. Marie Tifo is delightful playing all the women he encounters.

DESERTERS   July 1984

Prod. co./rel. Exile Ltd.; *prod./dir./scen./ed.* Jack Darcus; *cam.* (color) Tony Westman; *music* Michael Conway Baker. *Prem.* Ridge Theatre, Vancouver. 95 min.

Roles	Cast
Sgt. Ulysses Hawley	Alan Scarfe
Noel Manufort	Dermot Hennelly
Peter	Jon Bryden
Val Manufort	Barbara March
Army Captain	Ty Haller

Jack Darcus's fourth film (*Great Coups of History* 1970, *Proxyhawks* 1972, *Wolfpen Principle* 1974) is, like its predecessors, dark and dreary and muddled in thought and resolution. Yet there are moments in this story of a brutal U.S. army sergeant chasing two deserters from the Vietnam war who have fled across the border into Canada that are compelling and true, and made even more persuasive by the excellent performances of Alan Scarfe (who made his first film appearance in Larry Kent's *Bitter Ash* in 1963) and Barbara March. Very much a filmed stage play set in a small dark house, it resembles a potted version of Tennessee Williams crossed with Terence Rattigan.

Prod. co. Zebra Films with the NFB; *prod.* Annette Cohen & Don Owen; *scen./dir.* Don Owen; *cam.* (color) Douglas Kiefer; *ed.* Peter Dale, David Nicholson; *music* Patricia Cullen and The Parachute Club. *Prem.* CinePlex, Toronto. 99 min. *Dist.* Pan-Canadian Films.

Roles	Cast
Izzy Marks	Isabelle Mejias
Jesse Fixit	Peter Spence
Peter Marks	Peter Kastner
Julie Marks	Julie Biggs
Carl	Chuck Shamata

Don Owen has gone back to the characters he made famous two decades ago in *Nobody Waved Goodbye*. Peter and Julie, eighteen years removed from their own troubled adolescence, married and now divorced, are disappointed with what has become of their lives and are at a loss to know how to cope with their seventeen-year-old daughter, who, filled with sullen resentment and angry rebellion, repeats in a uncertain and at times irritating way, the process by which young people try to find values to live by. The difference in period, however, dictates that their unrest is directed against nuclear weapons, unemployment, and political inaction, accompanied by the frenzied sounds of today's pop music. There are some very good individual scenes, but the whole seems to amount to sequences from television news and social studies.

Other Films of 1984

Bay Boy (d. Daniel Petrie). Mr. Petrie, after working in Hollywood for many years, returned to Nova Scotia to film this gentle and loving story of his boyhood days. Kiefer Sutherland, Leah Pinsent, Peter Donat, Liv Ullman, Isabelle Mejias. *Prod.* ICC, 110 min., color.

La Femme de l'hôtel (d. Lea Pool). A film of frosty beauty and introspective despair concerning a filmmaker and her encounter with an older woman. Paule Baillargeon, Louise Marleau, Marthe Turgeon. *Prod.* ACPAV, 88 min., color.

Freeloading (d. Joseph Sutherland). A trite comedy set in a TV studio about fools, cheats, and other assorted characters who fail to amuse or enlighten us. Richard Comar, Duke Edwards, Susan Hart. *Prod.* Freeloading Films, 90 min., color.

Gentle Sinners (d. Eric Till). This two-hour, made-for-CBC TV movie brings back to feature films the quiet and distinguished director, Eric Till, remembered for *A Fan's Notes* and *Hot Millions* (UK) among other films; here he brings to the screen with feeling and insight the novel by W. D. Valgardson about a seventeen-year-old boy who escapes from the stifling atmosphere of his childhood home to find freedom and love on his uncle's farm in Alberta. Ed McNamara, Christopher Earle, Kenneth Pogue, Jackie Burroughs. *Prod.* CBC, 120 min., color.

La Guerre des Tuques (The Dog Who Stopped the War) (d. Andre Melancon). A comedy-drama for children set in rural Quebec in which two warring groups of children spend their Christmas holidays trying to conquer a castle built of ice and snow. Charming and provocative. Cedric Plourde, Julien Elie. *Prod.* Rock Demers, 89 min., color.

Isaac Littlefeathers (d. Les Rose). An unlikely and contrived racial drama concerning an Indian and a Jewish schoolboy and their relations with the inhabitants of a small town in western Canada. Lou Jacobi, Scott Hylands, Tom Heaton, William Korbut, Lynda Mason-Green, Lorraine Behnan. *Prod.* Barry Pearson, 90 min., color.

Mario (d. Jean Beaudin). Based on Claude Jasmin's novel, *La Sablière,* and set in the Magdalen Islands, this is a beautifully filmed (Pierre Mignot) fable of two young brothers in which the innocence, affection, and fantasy in their lives lead to their destruction. Xavier Norman Petermann, Francis Reddy, Nathalie Chalifour, Jacques Goding, Marcel Sabourin. *Prod.* NFB, 97 min., color.

Next of Kin (d. Atom Egoyan). A stimulating first film by the director in which a repressed youth is taken to a family counselor for therapy and meets and goes to live with a cheerful Armenian family. In keeping with this electronic age, tape recorders and videos play a large part in the proceedings. Patrick Tierney, Berge Fazlian. *Prod.* Ego Film Arts, 72 min., color.

Reno and the Doc (d. Charles Dennis). Silly attempt at a screwball comedy set on the ski slopes of the Rocky Mountains. The accomplished Kenneth Welsh is wasted together with Henry Ramer and lovely Linda Griffiths. *Prod.* Ren-Doc Films, 90 min., color.

Surrogate (d. Don Carmody). An appalling sex-and-violence story wasting the talents of Carol Laure, Art Hindle, and Shannon Tweed. *Prod.* Cinepix, 90 min., color.

That's My Baby (d. Edie Yolles, John Bradshaw). A run-of-the mill comedy about male motherhood, nicely played by Timothy Webber, Sonja Smits, Lenore Zann, Frank Moore. *Prod.* Gemini Films, 100 min., color.

Thrillkill (d. Anthony Kramreither). A far-fetched video game of mystery and death, which leads its participants into a world of electronic murder. Robin Ward, Gina Massey, Frank Moore. *Prod.* Kramreither, 96 min., color.

Walls (d. Tom Shandel). A prison drama based on a true hostage incident in a British Columbia penitentiary in 1975, taken from a stage play, and given life and meaning by actors Winston Rekert, Alan Scarfe, and Andrée Pelletier. *Prod.* Jericho Films, 92 min., color.

Before filming *Le Jour "S . . .",* Jean-Pierre Lefebvre wrote, directed, photographed, and recorded the very personal 16mm *Au rythme de mon coeur* (To the Rhythm of My Heart) a semidocumentary that grew out of his trips across Canada and his visits to workshops and seminars, much of which is related to the death of his wife and collaborator, Marguerite Duparc.

Documentaries Made in 1984

And When They Shall Ask (d. John Morrow). History of the Russian Mennonites in Canada.

Le Dernier Glacier (d. Roger Frappier). The economic effect on the people of Shefferville, Quebec, after the mine closes down.

Hookers on Davie (d. Holly Dale and Janis Cole). A candid study of the lives of prostitutes in the city of Vancouver.

Pas fou comme on le pense (Not Crazy like You Think) (d. Jacqueline Levitin). A group of former psychiatric patients meets to discuss what happened to them and why.

Raoul Wallenberg: Buried Alive (d. David Harel). The story of a Swedish diplomat in Hungary during the Second World War and how he saved thousands of Jews from the Holocaust.

Rencontre avec une femme remarquable: Laure Gaudreault (d. Iolande Cadrin-Rossignol). A study of the life of Laure Gaudreault, journalist, teacher, and union organizer in Montreal during the thirties, and of her work for the women's movement.

National Film Board

The NFB continues to live in a state of uncertainty as it awaits the government's elusive and long-awaited "policy" on the film situation in this country with specific reference to the future role of the board. While the report is confidential, enough is known, it seems, to reassure the NFB that it will not be dismantled and turned into a film school, as the 1982 Royal Commission on the Arts recommended. François Macerola, the new commissioner, thinks the board will remain largely intact, with some of its activities reduced or altered. In the meantime, "Life goes on here," he said, "We're not waiting for the policy to make our day-to-day decisions." Of its more than fifty films produced in 1984, it received justified praise for its seven-part series, *War,* in which Gwynne Dyer examines the history and causes of war through the ages. It also won another Academy Award for Best Documentary Short with *Flamenco at 5:15,* an enchanting study of dancers in rehearsal. Three NFB films competed in Zagreb: *Mushrooms, Old Lady Trio-Xmas Tree,* and *A Piece of the Action.* Shown in the Information program were *The Old Lady's Camping Trip, The Awful Fate of Melpomenus Jones, Starlife,* and *The Real Inside.* Shown at the American Film Festival in New York were *Mary of Mile 18, Reflections on Suffering, Daisy: The Story of a Facelift,* and *Faces.* The Banff festival showed *La Journée d'un curé de campagne, La Bête lumineuse, Change of Heart,* and Norman McLaren's beautiful "adieu," *Narcissus,* being shown everywhere to great acclaim. In 1984, McLaren, then seventy, officially retired from the NFB. His contemporaries, Colin Low and Tom Daly, are still active with *Standing Alone,* a major work depicting a blood Indian living on a reservation in Alberta.

The Ontario Film Institute Award

This award for excellence is given annually to a filmmaker who best represents indigenous values in Canadian cinema.

1980   Christopher Chapman
1981   Terence Macartney-Filgate
1982   Gordon Pinsent
1983   Jean-Pierre Lefebvre
1984   Don Shebib

The Ontario Film Institute Award is a scientifically stylized approximation of the Zoetrope, a toy based on the principle of persistence of vision, invented by W. G. Horner of Bristol, England, in 1834, and one of the many inventions that paved the way for motion pictures. It was designed and manufactured at the Ontario Science Centre.

Addendum

Jacques et Novembre (d. François Bouvier and Jean Beaudry). This modest Quebec film is quite unusual in that it tells in semidocumentary fashion of the last months of a young man (portrayed by director Beau-dry) dying from cancer. An enthusiastic movie buff, he decides to make a film about his life, his friends, and his death. By no means a gloomy or heavy chronicle, it is filled with humor and sympathy. (Jean Beaudry, Carole Frechette, Marie Cantin.) Les Productions du Lundi Matin Inc. Berlin Film Festival, February 1985. 72 mins.

Joshua Then and Now (d. Ted Kotcheff). Working under impossible "international" pressures to make a $12 million feature and TV mini-series from Mordecai Richler's mordant novel about the misadventures of a sardonic author, Ted Kotcheff has made an alternately witty and strained film that is fine until Joshua grows up and becomes James Woods—who is unable to cope with the complex character. (James Woods, Gabrielle Lazure, Alan Arkin.) RSL Corp. Cannes Film Festival, May 1985. 117 mins.

Night Magic (d. Lewis Furey). A musical fantasy about a company of music hall singers and dancers, one of whom turns out to be an angel. Familiar consequences arise when it comes to matters of the heart. The music, which should carry the make-believe, is undistinguished and repetitive. (Nick Mancuso, Carole Laure, Stephane Audran.) RSL Corp. Cannes Film Festival, May 1985. 92 mins.

90 Days (d. Giles Walker). Supposedly a sequel to the same film-maker's *The Masculine Mystique* of 1984, two of the characters return: one to wed a mail-order Korean bride, often charming, the other to become a donor to a sperm bank, in doubtful taste. (Stefan Wodoslawsky, Christine Pak, Sam Grana.) NFB. Montreal Film Festival, August 1985. 100 mins.

My American Cousin (d. Sandy Wilson). Coming after several years of abominable teenage sex comedies from Canada and the U.S., this memoir of Sandy Wilson's youth in Vancouver during the 1950s when her cousin from California comes to spend the summer with her family is refreshing, funny, and nicely observed. (Margret Langrick, John Wildman, Richard Donat.) Independent Pictures. Toronto Film Festival, September 1985. 95 mins.

Bibliography

Books

Audley, Paul. *Canada's Cultural Industries.* Toronto: James Lorimer & Co., 1983.

Backhouse, Charles. *Canadian Government Motion Picture Bureau, 1917–1941.* Ottawa: Canadian Film Institute, 1974.

Bassett, John. *The Film Industry in Ontario.* Toronto: Ministry of Industry & Tourism, 1973.

Bastien, Jean-Pierre. *Quebec 75 Cinema.* Montreal: Cinémathèque Quebecois, 1975.

Beattie, Eleanor. *A Handbook of Canadian Films.* Toronto: Peter Martin Associates Ltd, 1977.

Belanger, Leon H. *Les Ouimetoscopes.* Montreal: VLB Editieur, 1978.

Berton, Pierre. *Hollywood's Canada.* Toronto: McClelland & Stewart Ltd., 1975.

Bossin, Hyman. *Stars of David.* Toronto: The Jewish Standard, 1956.

Branigan, Harry L. *Yesteryear Memories of a Man Called Branigan.* Guelph, 1981.

Browne, Colin. *Motion Picture Production in British Columbia: 1898–1940.* British Columbia: Province of British Columbia, 1979.

Cowie, Peter. *A Concise History of the Cinema.* 2 vols. New York: A. S. Barnes, 1971.

Crean, S. M. *Who's Afraid of Canadian Culture?* Toronto: General Publishing, 1976.

Dean, Malcolm. *Censored! Only in Canada.* Toronto: Virgo Press, 1981.

Dew, Desmond. *Let's Try It This Way.* New York: Vantage Press, Inc., 1983.

Drabinsky, Garth H. *Motion Pictures and the Arts in Canada: The Business and The Law.* Toronto: McGraw-Hill Ryerson Ltd., 1976.

Evans, Gary. *John Grierson and the National Film Board.* Toronto: University of Toronto Press, 1984.

Feldman, Seth, ed. *Take Two.* Toronto: Irwin Publishing Inc., 1984.

———, and Joyce Nelson, eds. *Canadian Film Reader.* New York: New York Zoetrope, 1977.

Fulford, Robert. *The Arts in Canada.* Toronto: Copp Clark Pub., 1977.

———. *Marshall Delaney at the Movies.* Toronto: Peter Martin Associates, 1974.

Gathercole, Sandra. *Canada: Film Policy Proposals.* Ottawa: Council of Canadian Filmmakers, 1975.

Gray, C. W. *Movies for the People.* Toronto: National Film Board, 1973.

Handling, Piers. *Canadian Feature Films 1964–1969.* Ottawa: Canadian Film Institute, 1976.

———, ed. *Self-Portrait.* Ottawa: Canadian Film Institute, 1980.

Hofsess, John. *Inner Views: Ten Canadian Film-Makers.* Toronto: McGraw-Hill Ryerson, 1975.

Hunnings, Neville March. *Film Censors and the Law.* London: George Allen & Unwin Ltd., 1967.

James, Jonathan. *The Canadian Writer's Guide.* Don Mills: Fitzhenry & Whiteside, 1976.

James, Rodney C. *Film As a National Art: NFB of Canada and the Film Board Idea.* New York: Arno Press, 1977.

Johnson, A. W. *Touchstone for the CBC.* Toronto: Canadian Broadcasting Corporation, 1977.

Jones, D. B. *Movies and Memoranda.* Ottawa: Deneau Publishers, 1981.

Kidd, J. R. *Survey of Film Services in Canada.* Toronto: Canadian Association for Adult Education, 1950.

Knelman, Martin. *This Is Where We Came In.* Toronto: McClelland & Stewart, 1977.

Lindsay, John C. *Turn Out the Stars before Leaving.* Toronto: Boston Hills Press, 1984.

Lyshyshyn, James. *National Film Board of Canada: A Brief History.* Toronto: National Film Board, 1976.

Marcorelles, Louis. *Living Cinema: New Directions in Contemporary Film-Making.* London: George Allen & Unwin Ltd., 1973.

Monk, Lorraine. *Between Friends/Entre Amis.* Ottawa: National Film Board, 1976.

Morris, Peter. *Canadian Feature Films: 1913–1964.* Pts. 1 and 2. Ottawa: Canadian Film Archives, 1965.

———. *Embattled Shadows, A History of Canadian Cinema 1895–1939.* Montreal: Queen's University Press, 1978.

———. *The Film Companion.* Toronto: Irwin Publishing Inc., 1984.

———. *The National Film Board of Canada: The War Years.* Ottawa: Canadian Film Institute, 1965.

Noguez, Dominique. *Essais sur le cinéma Quebecois.* Ottawa: Editions du Jour, 1970.

Norman, Agnes. *Film in Newfoundland and Labrador 1904–1980.* St. John's: Newfoundland Independent Film Makers Cooperative, 1981.

Ostry, Bernard. *The Cultural Connection.* Toronto: McClelland and Stewart Ltd., 1978.

Page, Jim. *Seeing Ourselves.* Toronto: National Film Board, 1979.

Paquet, André. *How to Make or Not to Make a Canadian Film.* Montreal: Cinémathèque Canadienne, 1967.

Pratley, Gerald. *Canada.* Encyclopedia Americana, 1968.

Quadrant Films. *How to Invest in Films & Not Find Your Money Gone with the Wind.* Toronto: Quadrant Films, 1970.

Richard, Valliere T. *Norman McLaren: Manipulator of Movement.* Newark: University of Delaware Press, 1982.

Robertson, G. D. *Motion Picture Industry in Canada.* Ottawa, 1931.

Rotha, Paul. *The Film Till Now.* London: Spring Books, 1967.

Rowland, Wade. *Making Connections.* Toronto: Gage, 1979.

Scott, Jay. *Midnight Matinees.* Toronto: Oxford University Press, 1985.

Spencer, Michael D. *Film Canada.* Montreal: C.F.D.C. 1977.

Stokes, Peter B. *A Report on the Motion Picture Distribution Industry in Canada.* Kingston: Queen's University Press, 1978.

———. *The Role of Government in the Feature Film Industry.* Toronto: Canadian Motion Picture Distributors Association, 1978.

Tadros, Jean-Pierre. *Le Cinéma au Québec: Bilan d'une industrie 1975.* Montreal: Editions Cinéma/Quebec, 1975.

———. *Quebec Film Industry Handbook 1979–1980.* Montreal: Editions Cinéma/Quebec, 1980.

Thompson, Patricia, ed. *Canadian Film Digest Yearbook.* Toronto: Nat Taylor 1971–84.

Topalovich, Maria. *The Canadian Film Awards (A Pictorial History).* Toronto: Stoddard Publishing Co., 1984.

Walsh, Michael. *The Canadian Movie Quiz Book.* Scarborough: Macmillan, 1970.

Periodicals/Miscellaneous

Being Ourselves, Seeing Ourselves. A Brief Submitted to the Federal Cultural Policy Review Committee. Montreal: National Film Board of Canada, 1981.

Bibliography of Canadian Cinema. Ottawa: Canadian Film Institute, 1973.

Big World–Small Format. Ottawa: Secretary of State, 1976.

Biographie des Réalisateurs de l'ONF. Montreal: National Film Board of Canada, 1955.

Bulletin. Ottawa: Canadian Film Institute, 1957–71 inclusive.

Cahiers des films. Montreal: Gouvernement du Quebec, 1979.

Canada & Co-productions: A Report on Canada's Participation in International Feature Film Co-productions and Their Impact on the Canadian Film Industry. Toronto: Council of Canadian Filmmakers, 1980.

Canadian Cinematography. Toronto, 1961–69 inclusive.

Canadian Federation of Film Societies. Toronto, 1956–76 inclusive.

Canadian Film Awards, International Jury Folders. Toronto, 1968–73 inclusive.

Canadian Film Digest. Toronto, 1971–74 inclusive.

Canadian Film Digest Yearbook. Toronto, 1971–84 inclusive.

Canadian Film News. Toronto, 1949–54 inclusive.

Canadian Film-TV Weekly. Toronto, 1968–70 inclusive.

Canadian Film-TV Weekly Yearbook. Toronto, 1951–71 inclusive.

Canadian Newsreel. Toronto, 1954–56 inclusive.

Cinema Canada. Montreal, 1972–84 inclusive.

Cinema Canada. Ottawa: Film Festival Bureau, 1980.

Cinema Quebec. Montreal, 1971–75 inclusive.

Copie Zéro. Montreal: Cinémathèque Quebecoise, 1979–84 inclusive.

The Critic. Toronto, 1950–52 inclusive.

Culture, Broadcasting and the Canadian Identity. A Brief Submitted to the Cultural Policy Review Committee. Toronto: Canadian Broadcasting Corporation, 1981.

Feature Film Financing Seminar. Canada: Motion Picture Institute of Canada, 1979.

Filebook. Toronto, 1957–72 inclusive.

Film Canadiana. Ottawa: Canadian Film Institute, 1969–82 inclusive.

The Film Industry in Canada: Report. Ottawa: Secretary of State, 1976.

Film Producers Guide, Canada. Ottawa: Canadian Film Archives, 1964.

Film Production Directory Ontario/Canada. Toronto: Ministry of Industry & Tourism, 1980–84 inclusive.

Get the Picture. Toronto: Ministry of Industry & Tourism, 1979.

Investigation into an Alleged Combine in the Motion Picture Industry in Canada. Ottawa: Department of Labor, 1931.

Motion Magazine. Toronto, 1973–78 inclusive.

Motion Picture & Television Production Locations. Alberta, 1981.

New Canadian Film. Montreal: Cinémathèque Quebecoise, 1969–78 inclusive.

Objectif. Montreal, 1960–67 inclusive.

Ontario, Canada Film Locations. Toronto: Ministry of Industry & Tourism, 1977.

Ontario Film Theatre Program Notes. Toronto, 1969–84 inclusive.

Panorama. Toronto: National Film Board of Canada, 1972–81 inclusive.

Pay TV in Canada. Toronto: Council of Canadian Filmmakers, 1980.

Pot Pourri. Montreal: National Film Board of Canada, 1968–77 inclusive.

A Rational National Defence. A Collection of Newspaper Articles. Ottawa: National Film Board of Canada, 1978.

Report of the Federal Cultural Policy Review Committee. Ottawa: Government of Canada, 1982.

A Report on the Distribution of Feature Films in Canada. Toronto: Canadian Motion Picture Distributors Association, 1978.

Vision. Toronto, 1955–58 inclusive.

Zoom. Toronto, 1962.

Index to the Films of NFB Producers and Directors

This is not a complete listing of all NFB films made since it began production. This compilation represents films currently in circulation and reflects the magnitude and diversity of the board's work.

P—Producer
D—Director

Gifted Ones, The (P)
Grierson (P)
Henry Larsen's Northwest Passages (P-D)
Judoka (P)
Lake for the Prairie, A (P)
Later Journeys of Vihjalmur Stefansson, The (P-D)
Legendary Judge, The (P)
Little Summermusik, A (P)
Lively Pond, The (P)
Log Drive (P)
Long Ways to Go (P)
Memories and Predictions (P-D)
Men Against the Ice (P-D)
Morning on the Liévre (P-D)
Music from Montréal (D)
Oceans of Science (P)
Once Upon a Prime Time (P)
Our Street Was Paved with Gold (P)
People of the Book, The (P)
Poisons, Pests and People (P)
River with a Problem (P)
Safe Clothing (D)
Salmon's Struggle for Survival, The (P)
Script to Screen (P)
Second Arctic Winter Games, The (P)
Stories of Tuktu series, The (13 films) (P)
Story of H. M. S. Shannon, The (P)
Sunny Munchy Crunchy Natural Food Shop, The (P)
Tomorrow is Too Late (P)
28° Above-Below (P)
Twenty-four Hours in Czechoslovakia (D)
World in a Marsh (P)

Ball, Ian

Continuum (D)

Balla, Nicholas

Adventure in Newfoundland (P)
Adventures (P)
Age of the Buffalo (P)
Algeria (P)
Atlantic Rescue (P)
Bear and the Mouse, The (P)
Can the Earth Provide? (P)
Canadian Wood Frame Houses (P)
Challenge to Mankind (P)
Clerk, The (P)
Columbia
David and Hazel: A Story in Communication (P)
Department Manager, The (P)
Global Struggle for Food, The (P)
Gone Curling (P)
Jamie—The Story of a Sibling (P)
Kind of Blades (P)
Life Line (P)
Man and His Resources (P)
Man on the Assembly Line, The (P)
More Milk for More People (P)
My Island Home (P)
Nahanni (P)
One Step at a Time (P)
People by the Billions (P)
Pony, The (P)
Queen's Plate, The (P)
Quest, The (P)

Rallye des neiges (P)
Rough Road to Freedom, The (P)
Shop Steward, The (P)
Skilled Worker, The (P)
Stowaway, The (P)
Stress (P)
Struggle for a Border series (9 films) (P)
Sun, Sand and Sea (P)
That Mouse (P)
To Each a Rightful Share (P)
Vice-President, The (P)
Voyageurs, The (P)
Water Dwellers, The (P)
Winter Rally (P)
Women on the March (P)
World of Three, The (P)
Yukon Old, Yukon New (P)

Ballantyne, Tanya

Merry-Go-Round, The (D)
Things I Cannot Change, The (D)

Bas, Joe

Play to Learn (D)

Bashford, Ron

House on the Prairie, A (D)

Battista, Franco

Laugh Lines—A Profile of Kaj Pindal (D)

Beaudet, Marc

All Stakes Are Down, No More Bets (P)
Beyond Curtains (P)
Catch, The (P)
Cold-Rodders (P)
Cries from Within (D)
Ice Birds (P)
Mon oncle Antoine (P)
Tomorrow Winter Comes (P)
"Troubbes" de Johnny, Les (P)
Two Years or More (P)
"Water, water, everywhere . . ." (P)
Yesterday—Today—The Netsilik Eskimo (P)

Beaudin, Jean

Dear Theo (D)
Games of the XXI Olympiad (D)
J. A. Martin, Photographer (D)
Par une belle nuit d'hiver (D)

Beaudry, Diane

Ballad to Cornwallis (Atlanticanada series) (D)
Just-A-Minute (2 parts) (P-D)
Maud Lewis: A World Without Shadows (D)
Threats (P)
Unbroken Line, The (D)
Unremarkable Birth, An (P-D)

Bédard, Jean

Cavendish Country (P-D)
Champions, The (D)
Day in the Night of Jonathan Mole, A (D)
Dionne Quintuplets, The (D-P)
Fields of Sacrifice (P-D)
Henry Ford's America (P-D)
His Worship, Mr. Montréal (D)
King of the Hill (D)
Ladies and Gentlemen . . . Mr. Leonard Cohen (D)
Memorandum (D)
Never a Backward Step (D)
Paperland—The Bureaucrat Observed (P-D)
Players, The (D)
Saul Alinsky Went to War (D)
Small is Beautiful: Impressions of Fritz Schumacher (D)
Starblanket (P-D)
Thunderbirds in China (P)
Trip Down Memory Lane, A (P)
Vacant Lot, The (P)
Van's Camp (D)
Volcano: An Inquiry into the Life and Death of Malcolm Lowry
 (P-D)

Brossard, Nicole

Some American Feminists (D)

Brousseau, Raymond

All Stakes Are Down, No More Bets (D)
As Usual (D)
Quebecois Rediscovered, A (D)

Brown, Janice H.

Agony of Jimmy Quinlan, The (D)
Lady from Grey County, The (D)

Browne, Colin

Strathyre (D)

Browning, Bob

Best Friends (D)

Brun, Michael

Count Down to '76 (D)
People Like You (D)
Where Have All the Farms Gone?

Bryant, Peter

Andy (D)

Budner, Gerald

A Is for Architecture (D)
Exeter (D)
Paul Kane Goes West (D)
World of David Milne, The (D)

Bulbulian, Maurice

Little Burgundy (D)
On the Tobacco Road (D)

Burstyn, Tom

Flash William (D)

Burwash, Cecily

Andy (P)
Invention of the Adolescent, The (P)
Mrs. Ryan's Drama Class (P)
Name of the Game Is Volleyball, The (P)
Sir! Sir! (P)
Summerhill (P)
This Land (P)

Burwash, Gordon

Ernie Game, The (P)
John A. Macdonald (The Impossible Idea) (D)
Portrait of the Artist (D)
Three Apprentices (D)
Three Country Boys (D)

Cameron, Douglas

Anywhere to Everywhere (D)
Forecast for Survival (D)
On Power Refueling (D)
To the Edge of the Universe (P)
To Make a Map (D)

Campbell, Austin

Age of the Buffalo (P-D)
Pipers and A' (D)

Campbell, Ken

Woodlot Management (D)

Campbell, Peter

Never a Dull Moment (D)

Canell, Marrin

Bookmaker's Progress (P)
Bow and Arrow (P)
Children Enfants Niños . . . (P)
Harmonium in California (P)
His Worship, Mr. Montréal (D)
Mother Tongue (P)
Paperland—The Bureaucrat Observed (P)
Song of the Paddle (P)
Solzhenitsyn's Children . . . are making a lot of noise in Paris (P)
Sweater, The (P)
Whistling Smith (D)

Canning, William

Angus (P)
Blades and Brass (P-D)
Christ is Risen (P-D)
Don't Knock the Ox (P)
Dowry, The (P)
En garde (P)
Flight in White (P-D)
Focus on Fingerprinting (P)
For You, Mr. Bell (P-D)

Get Wet (P-D)
Go with Us (P)
King of the Hill (P-D)
Lady and the Owl, The (P-D)
Niagara for Sale (P-D)
North (P)
Tale of Mail, A (P-D)
Temples of Time (P-D)
That's the Price (P)
To Track a Shadow (P)
Valley in a River (P)
War II—Total War (P-D)
Welcome to Smiths Falls (D)
We're Gonna Have Recess (P)

Capener, Richard

Fat Freedom (D)

Carle, Gilles

Machine Age, The (D)
Merry World of Léopold Z, The (D)
Olympic Swimmers (D)
Percé on the Rocks (D)
Rink, The (D)

Carney, James

Challenge of Change, The (D)
City Is, A (D)
Great Clean-up, The (D)
In One Day (D)
Search into White Space (D)
Sisters of the Space Age (D)
Where Do We Go from Here? (D)
World of One in Five, The (D)

Carrick, William

Ducks, of course (D)

Carrière, Marcel

Games of the XXI Olympiad (D)
Glimpses of China (D)
In Search of Medea (D)
Indian Speaks, The (D)
Moontrap, The (D)
Ping-pong (D)
Wrestling (D)

Caslor, Brad

Blowhard (D)

Chapman, Christopher

Persistent Seed, The (D)
Sense of Humus, A (D)

Charette, Yvon

26 Times in a Row (P)

Chatwin, Len

Community Action Theater on Tour (D)
Co-op Housing: Getting It Together (P)
Co-op Housing:
    The Best Move We Ever Made (P)
Cree Hunters of Mistassini (P)
Crowded Wilderness, A (P)
Do Your Thing (P)
Greenlanders, The (P)
Labrador North (P)
Memo from Fogo, A (P)
New Alchemists, The (P)
Our Land is Our Life (P)
Point (The):
    Community Legal Clinic (P)
Promises, Promises . . . (P)
Question of Television Violence, The (P)
Some People Have to Suffer (P)
Temiscaming, Québec (P)
That Gang of Hoodlums? (P)
Urban Transportation series (3 films) (P)
Working Mothers series (11 films) (P)

Cherry, Lawrence

Fighting Forest Fires with Hand Tools (D)
Fighting Forest Fires with Power Pumps (D)
Pony, The (D)

Clish, Stanley

Canada at War series (13 films) (P)
King of Blades (D)

Cloutier, Normand

Action: The October Crisis of 1970 (P)
Reaction:
    A Portrait of a Society in Crisis (P)

Coderre, Laurent

Fleurs de macadam, Les (The Asphalt Flowers) (D)
Metamorphoses (D)
Rencontre (D)
Rusting World (D)
Zikkaron (D)

Cohen, Sheldon

Bossa Bop (D)
Sweater, The (D)

Collier, Mike

Winter Survival (P-D)

Conant, Theodore

Child of the Future, The (P-D)
City under Pressure (D)

Condie, Richard

Getting Started (D)
Oh Sure (D)

Constant, Maurice

Changing Forest, The (D)

Costa, Italo

Waterloo Farmers (D)

Coté, Guy L.

Acadia, Acadia (P)
Azzel (D)
Beluga Days (P)
Both Sides of the Coin (D)
Cattle Ranch (D)
Dominga (D)
Essay on Science, An (D)
Fishermen (D)
Harvesting (P)
Marastoon—The Place Where One is Helped (D)
Mother-to-be (P)
Railroaders (D)
Roughnecks (D)
Wake Up, mes bons amis (P)
Waterdevil, The (P)

Courtois, Dorothy

About Conception and Contraception (P)
About Puberty and Reproduction (P)
About VD (P)
Amisk (P)
Bloodsugar (P)
Loops to Learn By (P)
Matrioska (P)
Mystery of Bay Bulls, The (P)
No Apple for Johnny (P)
Out of Silence (P)
Quiet Wave, A (P)
What Teacher Expects . . . (P)

Coutu, Jean

Plea for the Wanderer (D)

Cowan, Paul

Coaches (D)
Coming Back Alive (D)
Descent (D)
Going the Distance (D)
I'll go again (D)

Cowling, Barry

Change by Degrees (D)
Empty Harbours, Empty Dreams (P)
Fixed in Time—A Victorian Album (P)
New Denmark (P)
Seaweed Walk (D)

Cowling, Diane

(see Diane Beaudry Cowling)

Cox, Kirwan

Has Anybody Here Seen Canada? (P)

Crabtree, Grant

Saddlemaker, The (D)
Stowaway, The (D)
To the Edge of the Universe (D)

Crama, Nico

Co Hoedeman, Animator (D)
From the Ashes of War (P)
It Wasn't Easy (D)

Crawley, Pat

Accident (D)

Croullière, Monique

Shakti—"She is Vital Engergy" (D)

Curnick, David

Summer Center (D)

Daly, Tom

A is for Architecture (P)
Above the Horizon (P)
Accident (P)
Action: The October Crisis of 1970 (P)
Age of the Beaver(P)
Alberta Girls (P)
Anger after Death (P)
Antonio (P)
Arctic Outpost (P)
Atomic Juggernaut (P)
Back-breaking Leaf, The (P)
Bannerfilm (P)
Beware, Beware, My Beauty Fair (P)
Blood and Fire (P)
Burden They Carry, The (P)
Cars in Your Life, The (P)
Cattle Ranch (P)
Centaur (P)
Child series (5 films), (P)
Christmas Fantasy, A (P)
Christopher's Movie Matinee (P)
Circle of the Sun (P)
City of Gold (P)
City Out of Time (P)
Climates of North America, The (P)
Coaches (P)
Co Hoedeman, Animator (P)
Cold Pizza (P)
Coming Home (P)
Corral (P)
Cowboy and Indian (P)
Crafts series (4 films) (P)
Dance Class (P)
Danny and Nicky (P)
Days of Whiskey Gap, The (P)
Descent (P)
Downhill (P)
Easy Pill to Swallow, An (P)
Eskimo Artist—Kenojuak (P)
Espolio (P)
Essay on Science, An (P)
Face (P)
Falling from Ladders (P)

Dansereau, Fernand

Day after Day (P)
Françoise (P)
Golden Gloves (P)
Manouane River Lumberjacks (P)
Mission of Fear (D)
Moontrap, The (P)
Paul-Emile Borduas (P)
This is No Time for Romance (D)
Terra Nova (P)

Dansereau, Jean

Buy Low, Sell High (D)
Flyway North (D)
Joy of Winter, The (D)
Springboard to the Sun (D)

Davies, Bill

Contracting Out (D)
80 Goes to Sparta, The (D)
India Trip, The (D)
Jews of Winnipeg, The (D)
Little Summermusik, A (D)
Samsara (P-D)
Squarejohns (D)

De Bellefeuille, Daisy

Case of Eggs, A (P)
Script to Screen (P)
Star (P)

Defalco, Martin

Bird of Passage (D)
Charlie's Day (D)
Class Project: The Garbage Movie (P)
Cold Journey (D)
Don Messer:
   His Land and His Music (D)
Northern Fisherman (D)
Other Side of the Ledger, The (D)
Trawler Fisherman (D)
What in the World is Water? (D)

Delorme J. Claude

Script to Screen (D)

Desbiens, Francine

Little Men of Chromagnon, The (D)
Plage, La (P)
This is Me (P)

Devlin, Bernard

Case of Eggs, A (D)
David Thompson (The Great Mapmaker) (D)
End of the Nancy J, The (P-D)
Gold Seekers, The (P)
Louis-Hippolyte Lafontaine (P)
Matter of Survival, A (D)
Nature's Food Chain (P)
Promised Land, The (D)
Octopus Hunt (D)

Question of Identity, A (P)
Seniority versus Ability (D)
Striker (P)
Survival in the Bush (D)
Ti-Jean Goes Lumbering (P)
Visit, The (D)
Voyageurs, The (D)

Dew, Desmond

Aviators of Hudson Strait (P)
Bow and Arrow (P)
Count Down to '76 (P)
Descent (P)
Ethiopian Mosaic (P)
Forest under Siege (P)
Freshwater World (P)
Great White Bird, A (P)
In All Seasons (P)
Long View, The (P)
Matter of Fat, A (P)
No Way They Want to Slow Down (P)
One Man's Garden (P)
Operation G.A.T.E. (P)
Oshawa Kid, The (P)
People Like You (P)
Safe Escort (P)
Sisters of the Space Age (P)
Space Connection (P)
Sword of the Lord, The (P)
Ten-Tenths Ice (P)
To Make a Map (P)
Tugboat (P)

Dewar, Stephen

Where Are You Goin' Company Town? (D)

Dick, Ronald

Struggle for a Border series (9 films) (P-D)

Dolgoy, Mark

Give'em a Half Turn (D)
Priory, the Only Home I've Got (D)

Dolgoy, Reevan

Going the Distance (D)
Jablonski (D)
Promises, Promises . . .(D)

Domville, James De B.

Arctic IV (D)
Bargain Basement (P)
His Worship, Mr. Montréal (P)
Kaszuby (P)
New Gold for Alaska (P)
One Man (P)
Seven Shades of Pale (P)
Sub-Igloo (P-D)
Thunderbirds in China (P)
Volcano: An Inquiry into the Life and Death of Malcolm Lowry (P)

Doucet, Bob

What Do You Do?/What Are You Doing? (D)

Drew, Les

Energy Carol, The (D)
North Wind and the Sun, The (D)
Underground Movie, The (P-D)
What Do You Do?/What Are You Doing? (P)
What on Earth! (D)

Driessen, Paul

Air! (D)
Bleu perdu, Le (D)
Cat's Cradle (D)
Old Box, An (D)

Drouin, Jacques

Mindscape (D)

Duckworth, Martin

Accident (D)
Cell 16 (D)
Passing Through Sweden (D)
Temiscaming, Québec (D)
12,000 Men (D)
Wish, The (D)

Dufaux, Georges

At the End of My Days (D)
Caroline (D)
Cries from Within (D)
Games of the XXI Olympiad (D)
Going the Distance (D)
Multiple Man (D)
Precision (D)
Sudden Departure (D)
Two Years or More (D)

Dufresne, Jean-V

Backyard Theater (P)
LeDevoir (2 Parts) (D)
Une Job Steady . . . Un Bon Boss (P)

Duke, Daryl

David and Bert (D)

Dumesnil, Thérèse

Tomorrow Winter Comes (D)

Duncan, Robert

Agony of Jimmy Quinlan, The (D)
His Worship, Mr. Montréal (D)
Margaret Laurence, First Lady of Manawaka (D)
Point, The (D)
Volcano: An Inquiry into the Life and Death of Malcolm Lowry (P)

Dunn, Willie

Ballad of Crowfoot, The (D)

Other Side of the Ledger, The (D)

Durden, J. V.

Above the Timberline (D)
Butterflies, Beetles and Bugs (D)
Changing Forest, The (P)
Color of Life, The (P-D)
Embryonic Development of Fish, The (D)
Embryonic Development—The Chick (D)
Forest Tent Caterpillar, The (P-D)
Introducing Insects (D)
Maple Leaf, The (P-D)
Microscopic Fungi (D)
Spruce Bog, The (P)

Dyer, John

Two Dreams of a Nation: The Fortin Family of Quebec and
    Alberta (P)

Elkin, Ian

Chasing the Eclipse (D)
New Mayor, The (D)

Elliott, Floyd

Drinking (P)
Fight for Breath (A): Emphysema (P)

Elnécavé, Viviane

Eye (D)
Just a Little Love Song (D)
Notre jeunesse en auto-sport (Our Sports Car Days) (D)

Fajardo, Jorge

Steel Blues (D)

Fanning, David

Yes or No Jean-Guy Moreau (D)

Farley, T.

Lord Elgin (Voice of the People) (P)
Salute to Flight Series (3 films) (P)

Fedorenko, Eugene

Every Child (D)

Feeney, John

Christmas Fantasy, A (D)
Eskimo Artist—Kenojuak (D)
Living Stone, The (D)
Pangnirtung (D)
Sky (D)

Ferguson, Graeme

Question of Television Violence, The (D)

Fiddler, Gordon

Under Ground (D)

Fletcher, Trevor

Four-line Conics (D)

Foldès, Peter

Hunger (D)
Metadata (D)

Ford, Stephen

Continuing Past, The (D)
Life Line (D)

Forest, Léonard

Georges-P. Vanier (P)
Out of Silence (D)
Promised Land, The (P)
Sun Like Nowhere Else, A (D)
Ti-Jean in the Land of Iron (P)
Walls of Memory (D)

Forget, Robert

French World Comes to Québec, The (P)
Indian Memento (P)
Little Burgundy (P)
Multiple Man (P)
Sheer Sport (P)
Wow (P)

Fortier, Robert

End of a Summer Day (D)
Harmonium in California (D)
Mad Canadian, The (D)
Metal Workers (D)

Fougères, J.-P. Olivier

Azzel (P)
Dorminga (P)
Marastoon—The Place Where One is Helped (P)

Foulds, Hugh

Bear's Christmas, The (D)
Citizen Harold (D)
For Land's Sake (D)

Fournier, Claude

Wrestling (D)

Fox, Beryl

Doctor Woman: The Life and Times of Dr. Elizabeth Bagshaw (P)
Fields of Endless Day (P)
Heavy Horse Pull (P)
3 Track (P)

Fox, Raoul

Another Side of the Forest (D)

Kainai (D)

Frappier, Roger

Day in Forillon, A (P)
Day in Point Pelée, A (P)

Fraser, Donald

Earth and Mankind series (6 films) (D)

Fresco, Bob

Mudflats Living (D)

Frund, Jean-Louis

Great Blue Heron, The (D)

Gabori, Susan

New Romance: Aspects of Sexuality and Sexual Roles (D)

Gagné, Jacques

Scream From Silence, A (P)
Temps d'une vente, Le (D)

Gagnon, André-Marcel

Eli, Eli, lamma sabachtani? (D)

Gagnon, Lina

Beginnings (D)

Garand, Jean-Marc

At the End of My Days (P)
Before the Time Comes (P)
J. A. Martin, Photographer (P)
On the Tobacco Road (P)
Plea for the Wanderer (P)
Sun Like Nowhere Else, A (P)

Garceau, Raymond

In the Name of the Son (D)
Inventors of Thingumajigs (D)
Log Drive (D)
Pris au collet (D)
Thingumajigs (D)
Ti-Jean in the Land of Iron (D)
Waterdevil, The (D)

Gascon, Gilles

If at First . . . (D)
Piece of Cake, A (D)
Québec in Silence (D)

Gauvreau, Pierre

In the Name of the Son (P)
Once Upon a Hunt (P)

Geertsen, George

Men in the Park, The (D)
Prison (D)

Gervais, Suzanne

Beginnings (D)
Climates (D)
Cycle (D)
Plage, La (D)

Gibbard, Susan

Centaur (D)
Girls of Mountain Street (D)

Gillson, Denis

Who Were the Ones? (P)

Gillson, Malca

Alberta Girls (D)
Last Days of Living, The (D)
Musicanada (D)
War is Over, The (P)
You're Eating for Two (D)

Ginsberg, Donald

Four Teachers (D)
Long Way Back, The (D)
Political Dynamite (P)

Giraldeau, Jacques

Down Through the Years (D)
Element 3 (D)
Gold Seekers, The (D)
Québecois Rediscovered, A (D)
Shape of Things, The (D)
We Are All . . . Picasso! (D)

Glover, Guy

Angel (P)
Aucassin and Nicolette (P)
Bethune (P)
Buildings Already Begun, The (P)
Continuing Past, The (P)
Flight (P)
Fluxes (P)
Four Families (P)
Grievance, The (P)
History Makers, The (series of 17 films) (P)
Housewife, The (P)
Illegal Abortion (P)
Invention of the Adolescent, The (P)
Lewis Mumford on The City series (6 films) (P)
Marching the Colors (D)
Never a Backward Step (P)
Of Sport and Men (P)
Parliamentary Procedure (P)
Poets on Film, Nos. 1, 2 and 3 (P)
Promised Land, The (P)
Purse, The (P)
Québec as Seen by Cartier-Bresson, Le (P)
Quiet Racket, The (P)

Red Kite, The (P)
Searching Man, The (P)
Seniority versus Ability (P)
Street, The (P)
Summer We Moved to Elm Street, The (P)
Tax: The Outcome of Income (P)
Vaillancourt (P)

Glover, Rupert

Light Fantastick, The (D)

Godbout, Claude

Multiple Man (D)

Godbout, Jacques

Double Vision (D)
Fabienne (D)
Kid Sentiment (D)
Paul-Emile Bourduas (D)
People Might Laugh at Us (D)
"Troubbes" de Johnny, Les (D)
Vivre sa ville (D)
Yul 871 (D)

Goldsmith, Sidney

Animal Movie, The (P)
Canada: Landform Regions (P)
Continuum (P)
Development of a Fish Embryo (P)
Electronic Fish Finders (P-D)
Energy Carol, The (P)
Espolio (D)
Fields of Space (P-D)
Forecast for Survival (P)
Four-line Conics (P)
Fundamentals of Fish Spoilage (P-D)
Harness the Wind (D)
Perception of Orientation, The (P)
Physics of Underwater Sound (3 films) (P)
Riches of the Earth (D)
Satellites of the Sun (D)
Under the Rainbow (D)

Gosnell, Larry

Flower and the Hive, The (P)
Supermarkets and the Farmer (D)

Gosselin, Bernard

Beluga Days (D)
Catch, The (D)
César's Bark Canoe (D)
Joy of Winter, The (D)
Manhattan Odyssey, The (D)
Northwest Passage (D)
Skiff of Renald à Thomas, The (D)

Gough, Bill

Brothers Byrne, The (D)

Gould, John

282

Pikangikum (D)

Grana, Saverio

Citizen Sailor (P-D)
Diving Below Daylight (P-D)
Gulf Stream (P)
Insulation Story, The (D)
Porter's Magic Dreams (P)
SDL-1 Shakedown (P-D)

Greaves, William

Smoke and Weather (D)

Grégoire, Normand

Horizon (D)
Passage (D)
Series 4 (D)

Greene, Barbara

Crazy Quilt (D)
Listen, Listen, Listen (D)
Bella Bella (D)
'round and 'round (D)
Ruth and Harriett (D)

Greenwood, Trevor

Medium Is the Massage, You Know, The (D)

Grgic, Zlatko

Deep Threat (D)
Hot Stuff (D)
Who Are We? (D)

Groulx, Gilles

Golden Gloves (D)

Guilbeault, Luce

Some American Feminists (D)

Gulkin, Harry

Challenger: An Industrial Romance (P)

Haldane, Donald

Drylanders (D)
Gifted Ones, The (D)
Political Dynamite (D)

Hale, Jeff

Great Toy Robbery, The (D)

Haley, Ted

Dories (D)
Just One of the Boys, (D)

Hammond, Arthur

Easy Pill to Swallow, An (P)
Corporation series (7 films) (P-D)
Flora—Scenes from a Leadership Convention (P)
Healing (P)
I Hate to Lose (P)
It Wasn't Easy (P)
Journey to the End (P)
Last Days of Living, The (P)
Meditation in Motion (P)
Mighty Steam Calliope, The (P)
Mother Tongue (P)
Never a Backward Step (D)
North China Factory (P)
Reflections on a Leadership Convention (P)
Sami, Four Lands, One People, The (P)
Sami Herders (P)
Solzhenitsyn's Children . . . are making a lot of noise in Paris (P)
Song of the Paddle (P)
This Land (D)
Tigers and Teddy Bears (P)
Unbroken Line, The (P)

Hart, Roger

Challenger: An Industrial Romance (P)
Crowded Wilderness, A (P)
Encounter on Urban Environment (D)
Journeyman, The (D)
Labrador North (D)
Land—A New Priority, The (D)
Memo from Fogo, A (D)
Nearest Point Everywhere, The (D)
New Bargain, A (D)
Point (The): Community Legal Clinic (P)
Prince Edward Island Development Plan, The (2 films) (D)
Promises, Promises . . . (P)
Threads (D)
Wuxing People's Commune (P)

Hébert, Marc

Ice Birds (D)
Sheer Sport (D)

Hébert, Pierre

Around Perception (D)
Catuor (P)
Cycle (P)
Des ensembles (P)
Little Men of Chromagnon, The (P)
On Hop—Hop Op (D)
Opus 3 (D)
Piece of Cake, A (D)
Population Explosion (D)
Santa Claus Is Coming Tonight (D)

Heczko, Zina

Laughlines—A Profile of Kaj Pindal (D)
Pictures Out of My Life (D)

Hénaut, Dorothy Todd

Horse Drawn Magic (D)
New Alchemists, The (D)
Sun, Wind and Wood (D)

Temiscaming, Québec (P)
VTR Saint-Jacques (D)

Henderson, Anne

". . . And They Lived Happily Ever After" (D)
Right Candidate for Rosedale, The (D)
Threads (D)

Henson, Joan

Bing Bang Boom (D)
Dance Class (D)
First Born (D)
Improv (D)
One Hand Clapping (D)
Origami (D)
Standing Buffalo (D)
Three Guesses (D)

Herman, André

Kaszuby (D)

Héroux, Claude

French World Comes to Québec, The (P)

Hewitson, Walford

Atomic Juggernaut (P)
Blindness (P)
First Aid for Aircrew (D)
Juggernaut (P)
Lacrosse (P)
Learning Lacrosse (2 parts) (P)
North Pacific (P)
Pollution Front Line (P-D)
Steeltown (P)
Twenty-four Hours in Czechoslovakia (P)
Waiting for Caroline (P)

Hicks, Israel

Striker (P)

Hinton, Christopher

Blowhard (D)

Hoedeman, Co

Continental Drift (D)
Lumaaq: An Eskimo legend (D)
Man and the Giant (The): An Eskimo Legend (D)
Matrioska (D)
Oddball (D)
Owl and the Lemming, The (D)
Owl and the Raven, The (D)
Sand Castle, The (D)
Tchou-tchou (D)
Treasure of the Grotoceans, The (D)

Holdway, Les

Wandering Spirit Survival School (D)

Hollander, Peter

Azzel (P)
Dominga (P)
Marastoon: The Place Where One is Helped (P)

Hopkins, Don

Black Ice (P)
Doctor Woman: The Life and Times of Dr. Eizabeth Bagshaw (P)
Drinking (P)
Emergency Blood Transfusion (D)
Fight for Breath, Emphysema, A (P)
Heavy Horse Pull (P)
Holstein (P)
Hot Wheels (P)
Lost Pharoah: The Search for Akhenat, The (P)
Nishnawabe-Aski—The People and the Land (P)
Pictures from the 1930s (P)
Shutdown (P)
Simpler Life, A (P)
Smokers' Lungs (P)
Sons of Haji Omar (P)
S.P.L.A.S.H. (P)
3 Track (P)
Tree Power (P)
Wandering Spirit Survival School (P)
Wintersong (P)

Howe, John

Canadians Can Dance (P-D)
David and Hazel: A Story in Communication (D)
Do Not Fold, Staple, Spindle or Mutilate (D)
Ducks, of course (D)
Georges-Etienne Cartier (D)
Gone Curling (D)
Head Men, The (D)
Jamie—The Story of a Sibling (D)
Long Ways to Go (D)
Lord Durham (D)
Mathematics at Your Fingertips (D)
North of 60 East (D)
Portrait of the Artist (D)
Queen's Plate, The (D)
Robert Baldwin (A Matter of Principle) (D)
Star (D)
Strangers at the Door (D)
Three Grandmothers (D)
Wedding Day (D)
Where Mrs. Whalley Lives (P)
Why I Sing (D)
Why Rock the Boat ? (D)
Yukon Old, Yukon New (D)

Howells, Barrie

Activator One (P)
Admittance, The (P)
Baby This Is for You (P)
Ballad of Crowfoot, The (P)
Best Damn Fiddler from Calabogie to Kaladar, The (P)
Biosphere, The (P)
Bookmaker's Progress (P)
Bow and Arrow (P)
Bye Bye Blues (P)
Chairs for Lovers (P-D)
Children Enfants Ninos (P)

City Is, A (P)
Co Hoedeman Animator (P)
Community Action Theater on Tour (P)
Death of a Legend (P)
Development Without Tears (P)
Encounter at Kwacha House—Halifax (P)
Encounter with Saul Alinsky (2 parts) (P)
Exploding Cities (P)
From the Ashes of War (P)
Growing Dollars (P)
Half—Half—Three-quarters—Full (P)
Halifax Neighborhood Center Project (P)
Harmonium in California (P)
Last Days of Living, The (P)
Laurette (P)
Little by Little—Upgrading Barrio Escopa (P)
Meet the Martins (P)
More Than Just the Trees (P)
Mrs. Case (P)
Nearest Point to Everywhere, The (P)
No Fitting Habitat (P)
North China Commune (P)
North China Factory (P)
Organizing for Power: The Alinsky Approach series (P)
Paperland—The Bureaucrat Observed (P)
Ports Canada (P)
PowWow at Duck Lake (P)
Prince Edward Island Development Plan, The (Parts 1 and 2) (P)
Saul Alinsky Went to War (P)
Search into White Space (P)
Seventh Step to Freedom, The (P)
Small is Beautiful: Impressions of Fritz Schumacher (D)
Some Call It Progress (P)
Summer Center (P)
Trafficopter (P-D)
Unbroken Line, The (P)
Viking Visitors to North America (P)
Water: The Hazardous Necessity (P)
Whistling Smith (P)
Wilf (P)
Wuxing People's Commune (P)
Yes or No Jean-Guy Moreau (P)

Hughes, David

Indian Dialogue (D)

Humble, Robert

Child series (5 films) (D)

Hutton, Joan

Spring and Fall of Nina Polanski, The (D)

Huycke, Susan

First Born (P)

Hyde, Laurence

City Limits (P-D)
Family House (P-D)
Stories of Tuktu series, The (13 films) (D)
Tugboat (D)

Ianzelo, Tony

Alberta Girls (D)
Antonio (D)
Bate's Car: Sweet as a Nut (D)
Blackwood (D)
Cree Hunters of Mistassini (D)
Cree Way (D)
Don't Knock the Ox (D)
Goodbye Sousa (D)
Here Is Canada (D)
High Grass Circus (D)
Little Big Top (D)
Mighty Steam Calliope, The (D)
Musicanada (D)
North China Commune (D)
North China Factory (D)
Our Land is Our Life (D)
Viking Visitors to North America (D)
Whales Are Waiting, The (D)
Wuxing People's Commune (D)

Jackson, Douglas

Art of Eating, The (P-D)
Blake (P)
Crafts of My Province (D)
Danny and Nicky (P-D)
Gastronomie, La (D)
Heatwave Lasted Four Days, The (P-D)
Huntsman, The (P-D)
Lacrosse (P-D)
Learning Lacrosse (2 parts) (P-D)
Norman Jewison, Filmmaker (P-D)
Sloane Affair, The (P-D)
Wheat (P)
Why Men Rape (P-D)

Jackson, Stanley

Boat That Ian Built, The (P)
Children Learn from Filmstrips (D)
Cornet at Night (D)
Depressive States (2 parts) (D)
Feelings of Depression (D)
First Steps (P)
Folie à deux (D)
Manic State (D)
Organic Reaction Type—Senile (D)
Paranoid Conditions (D)
Profile of a Problem Drinker (D)
Quest, The (D)
Shyness (D)
Stigma (D)
Vacant Lot, The (P)

James, Blake

Prairie Album (D)
Through a Broken Pane (D)

Jensen, Lasse

New Denmark (P)

Jobin, Claude

Horizon (D)

Jobin, Victor

Down Through the Years (P)
Golden Gloves (P)
Gold Seekers, The (P)
Hors d'oeuvre (P)
Manouane River Lumberjacks (P)
Promised Land, The (P)
They Called It Fireproof (P)

Jodoin, René

About Flowers (P)
Among Fish (P)
Balablok (P)
Bronswik Affair, The (P)
Canadian Shield (The): Saguenay Region (P)
Child in His Country, A (P)
Contemporary Songs of French Canada (series of 6 films) (P)
Dance Squared (D)
Dans la vie (P)
Glaciation (P)
Horizon (P)
Horsing Around (P)
Hunger (P)
Introduction to Jet Engines, An (D)
Monsieur Pointu (P)
Nébule (P)
Notes on a Triangle (D)
Oddball (P)
Passage (P)
Series 4 (P)
Spheres (D)
Tree is a Living Thing, A (P)
Wind (P)

Johnson, George

Caravaners (D)
Horse Drawn Magic (P)

Jones, Kirk

Changing City, The (D)
Crafts of My Province (D)
Painting a Province (D)

Jones, Peter

Augusta (P)
Baymen, The (P)
Bear's Christmas, The (P)
Behind the Masks (P)
Boy Next Door, The (P)
Canada at War series (13 films) (P)
Changing City, The (P)
Comet at Night (P)
Crafts of My Province (P)
David and Bert (P)
Day in the Night of Jonathan Mole, A (P)
Drylanders (P)
Ducks, of Course (P)
Egypte (P)
Estuary (P)
Everybody's Prejudiced (P)
Figure Skating (P)
Fire in Town (P)
Fisherman's Fall (P)

For Land's Sake (P)
Harrison's Yukon (P)
Helicopter Canada (P)
He's Not the Walking Kind (P)
Images: Stone: B.C. (P)
Jablonski (P)
Joey (P)
Learn to Ski (P)
Man Who Chooses the Bush (P)
Mental Patients' Association (P)
Mudflats Living (P)
Negotiating a New Canadian Constitution (P)
New Channels for Sockeye (P-D)
No Big Money (P)
Painting a Province (P)
Play to Learn (P)
Pleasure Faire (P)
Prairie—Passing Through (P)
Quo Vadis, Mrs. Lumb? (P)
Salmon People (P)
Settlement of the Western Plains (P)
Soccer (P)
Strathyre (P)
Supermarkets and the Farmer (P)
Three Farmers (P)
Trail Ride (P)
TV Sale (P)
Waterfowl—A Resource in Danger (P)
We Call Them Killers (P)

Jovanovic, Bané

DNA (P-D)
Question of Immunity (P-D)
Sea, The (D)
28° Above—Below (P-D)

Jovanovic, S.

Oceans of Science (D)
Tomorrow Is Too Late (D)

Jutra, Claude

Devil's Toy, The (D)
Knowing to Learn (D)
Mon oncle Antoine (D)
Wow (D)
Wrestling (D)

Kaczender, George

City Scene (D)
Don't Let the Angels Fall (D)
Game, The (D)
Little White Crimes (D)
Phoebe (D)
Sabre and Foil (D)
World of Three, The (D)
You're No Good (D)

Kasma, Jacques

Ghosts of a River (D)

Katadotis, Peter

Agony of Jimmy Quinlan, The (P)
Biosphere, The (P)
Champions, The (P)
Class Project: The Garbage Movie (P)
Cree Way (P)
Cycling: Still The Greatest (P)
Dionne Quintuplets, The (P)
Diving: No Place for Cowards (P)
Fiddlers of James Bay, The (P)
Inheritance, The (P)
Insulation Story, The (P)
John Raftery Amateur Boxer (P)
Monica Goermann—Gymnast (P)
More Than just the Trees (P)
My Floating World—Miyuki Tanobe (P)
Mystery of Bay Bulls, The (P)
Nearest Point to Everywhere, The (P)
No Day of Rest (P)
Occupational Health series (P)
Our Health Is not for Sale (P)
Paper Wheat (P)
Small is Beautiful: Impressions of Fritz Schumacher (P)
Some People Have to Suffer (P)
Two Dreams of a Nation (P)
Wages of Work, The (P)
Who Will I Sentence Now? (P)

Kellar, Steven

John Raftery Amateur Boxer (D)
Monica Goermann Gymnast (D)

Kelly, Ron

Quo Vadis, Mrs. Lumb? (D)
Valley in a River (D)
Waiting for Caroline (D)

Kemeny, John

Bethune (P)
Circle, The (P)
Don't Let the Angels Fall (P)
Encounter at Kwacha House—Halifax (P)
Encounter with Saul Alinsky (2 parts) (P)
Game, The (P)
Halifax Neighborhood Center Project (P)
Henry Larsen (P)
Indian Dialogue (P)
Indian Relocation: Elliot Lake (P)
Ladies and Gentleman . . . Mr. Leonard Cohen (P)
Level 4350 (P)
Lonely Boy (P)
Long Haul Men, The (P)
Memorandum (P)
Miner (P)
No Reason to Stay (P)
Pikangikum (P)
Place for Everything, A (P)
PowWow at Duck Lake (P)
Real Story of Radar, The (P)
Ride for Your Life (P)
Sabre and Foil (P)
Saul Alinsky Went to War (P)
Stefansson: The Arctic Prophet (P)
Things I Cannot Change, The (P)
Three Apprentices (D)

Three Fishermen (D)
Trawler Fishermen (P)
Unemployment: Voices from the Line (P)
Untouched and Pure (P)
You're No Good (P)

Kendall, Anthony

Lost Pharoah, The Search for Akhenaten, The (P-D)

Kennedy, Grant

Crowded Wilderness, A (D)
Point (The): Community Legal Clinic (D)

Kent, Anthony

Viking Visitors to North America (D)

Kent, Larry

Cold Pizza (D)
Saskatchewan—45° Below (D)

Ketchum, Nick

Fields of Endless Day (P)

Kiefer, Douglas

Oceans of Science (D)
Ready When You Are (D)
Small is Beautiful: Impressions of Fritz Schumacher (D)
Tomorrow Is Too Late (D)

King, Roberta

Heavy Horse Pull (D)

Kish, Albert

Bekevar Jubilee (D)
Freeze-in (P)
Hold the Ketchup (D)
The Image Makers
Los Canadienses (D)
Louisbourg (D)
Our Street Was Paved with Gold (D)
Paper Wheat (D)
Ports Canada (D)
This Is a Photograph (D)
Time Piece (D)

Klein, Bonnie Sherr

Citizens' Medicine (P-D)
Encounter at Kwacha House-Halifax (D)
Encounter with Saul Alinsky (2 parts) (D)
Harmonie (P-D)
Little Burgundy (D)
Not a Love Story: A Film About Pornography (D-P)
Organizing for Power: The Alinsky Approach (5 films) (D)
Patricia's Moving Picture (D)
Pow Wow at Duck Lake (D)
Right Candidate for Rosedale, The (D-P)
VTR St. Jacques (D)
Working Chance, A (P-D)

Klein, Judith

Catuor (D)
Modulations (D)
Sports Challenge (D)

Koenig, Joseph

Bird of Passage (P)
Bing Bang Boom (P)
Change in the Maritimes (P)
Change in the Western Mountains (P)
Changing Wheat Belt, The (P-D)
Christopher's Movie Matinée (P)
Climates of North America, The (D)
Continental Drift (P)
Cosmic Zoom (P)
Cruise, The (P)
DNA (P)
Energy and Matter (P)
Ever-changing Lowlands, The (P)
Flowers on a One-way Street (P)
Half-masted Schooner, The (P)
Hymn (P)
If at First . . . (P)
Imperial Sunset (P)
Jet Pilot (D)
Mathematics at Your Fingertips (P)
Matrioska (P)
Medium Is the Massage, You Know, The (P)
Origins of Weather, The (D)
Pardonnez-moi, Mr. Karsh (P)
Place for Everything, A (P)
Question of Immunity (P)
Real Story of Radar, The (D)
Rise and Fall of the Great Lakes, The (P)
Saskatchewan—45° Below (P)
Search for Learning, A (P)
Tiny Terrors, The (D)
Underground Movie, The (P)
Unstructured for a Summer (P)
What Is Life? (P)
What Is the Big Complaint (P)
What Teacher Expects . . .(P)
You Don't Back Down (P)

Koenig, Wolf

About Puberty and Reproduction (P)
About VD (P)
Amisk (P)
Anywhere to Everywhere (P)
Aucassin and Nicolette (P)
Back-breaking Leaf, The (P)
Best Friends (P)
Blood and Fire (P)
Bossa Bop (P)
Cars in Your Life, The (P)
Christmas at Moose Factory (P)
City of Gold (D)
Coldspring Project, The (P)
Coming Back Alive (P-D)
Days of Whisky Gap, The (P)
Deep Threat (P)
Drag, The (P)
Enemy Alien (P)
Energy Carol, The (P)

Exeter (P)
Extinction of the Dinosaurs (P)
Face of the Earth (P)
Family That Dwelt Apart, The (P)
Festival in Puerto Rico (D)
Forecast for Survival (P)
Glen Gould (2 films) (P-D)
Great Toy Robbery, The (P)
Hard Rider (P)
Hecklers, The (P)
Hot Stuff (P)
Hottest Show on Earth, The (P)
House That Jack Built, The (P)
Housewife, The (P)
Icarus (P)
Innocent Door, The (P)
King Size (P)
Lady Fishbourne's Complete Guide to Better Table Manners (P)
Light Fantastik, The (P)
Lion and the Mouse, The (P)
Man: The Polluter (P)
Natsik Hunting (P)
No Apple for Johnny (P)
Pictures Out of My Life (P)
Poets on Film (P)
Population Explosion (P)
Prairie—Passing Through (P)
Prison (P)
Propaganda Message (P)
Satellites of the Sun (P)
Sikusilarmiut (P)
Spinnolio (P)
Standing Buffalo (P)
Steeltown (D)
Stravinsky (D)
Street, The (P)
Sur le pont d'Avignon (D)
Tax: The Outcome of Income (P)
Ten—The Magic Number (P)
Through a Broken Pane (P)
Tickets, s.v.p. (P)
Tilt (P)
Token Gesture, A (P)
To See or Not to See (P)
What Do You Do?/What Are You Doing? (P)
What on Earth! (P)
Who Are We? (P)

Kramer, John

Has Anybody Here Seen Canada? (D)
Inheritance, The (D)

Krepakevich, Jerry D.

Agriculture Canada (D)
Blowhard (P)
Bush Pilot: Reflections on a Canadian Myth (P)
Chasing the Eclipse (P)
Getting Started (P)
Give'em a Half Turn (P)
House on the Prairie, A (P)
How Things Have Changed (D)
I've Never Walked the Steppes (D)
Loved, Honoured, Bruised (P)
McIntyre Block, The (P)
Oh Sure (P)

Tudor King (P)
Wings of Time, The (P)

Kreps, Bonnie

No Life for a Woman (P-D)

Krizsan, Les

Insulation Story, The (D)
Medoonak the Stormmaker (D)

Kroeker, Allan

Pedlar, The (D)
Tudor King (D)

Kroitor, Roman

Above the Horizon (P-D)
Acting Class (P)
Back Alley Blue (P)
Back-breaking Leaf, The (P)
Bargain Basement (P)
Baymen, The (P)
Bravery in the Field (P)
Bekevar Jubilee (P)
Blood and Fire (P)
Breakdown (P)
Cars in Your Life, the (P)
Challenger: An Industrial Romance (P)
Coming Back Alive (P-D)
Days of Whiskey Gap, The (P)
Festival in Puerto Rico (D)
Flora—Scenes from a Leadership Convention (P)
For Gentlemen Only (P)
Glen Gould (2 films) (P-D)
Happiness is Loving Your Teacher (P)
Henry Ford's America (P)
Hold the Ketchup (P)
Hutterites, The (P)
In the Labyrinth (D)
I Wasn't Scared (P)
Legault's Place (P)
Listen Listen Listen (P)
Little White Crimes (P)
Living Machine, The (D)
Lonely Boy (D)
Margaret Laurence, First Lady of Manawaka (P)
Nobody Waved Good-bye (P)
Northern Composition (P)
One Man (P)
Paul Tomkowicz: Street-railway Switchman (D)
Population Explosion (P)
Propaganda Message (P)
Red Dress, The (P)
Revolution's Orphans (P)
Sail Away (P)
So Long to Run (P)
Stravinsky (P-D)
Striker (P)
Twice Upon A Time (P)
Why Men Rape (D)
Universe (D)
Voice of the Fugitive (P)

Labrecque, Jean-Claude

Feux Follets (D)
Games of the XXI Olympiad (D)
60 Cycles (D)

Labrosse, Jean-Michel

Duel-Duo (D)

Lachapelle, Jean-Pierre

Oceans of Science (D)

Ladouceur, Jean-Paul

Sur le pont d'Avignon (D)

Lafleur, Jean

Beware, Beware, My Beauty Fair (D)

Laing, John

Flash William (D)

Lalonde, Bernard

Once Upon a Hunt (P)

L'Amare, Pierre

Adelaide Village (P-D)
11 Steps to Survival (P-D)
Struggle for a Border series (9 films) (D)

Lamb, Derek

Afterlife (P)
Bead Game (P)
Continuum (P)
Every Child (P)
Fat Freedom (P)
Harness the Wind (P)
Hottest Show on Earth, The (P)
I Know an Old Lady Who Swallowed a Fly (D)
Interview (P)
Lady Fishbourne's Complete Guide to Better Table Manners (P)
Laughlines—A Portrait of Kaj Pindal (P)
Magic Flute, The (P)
National Scream, The (P)
Special Delivery (P)
Spinnolio (P)
Sufi Tale, A (P)
Sweater, The (P)
This is an Emergency (P)
This Is Your Museum Speaking (P)
What the Hell is Going On Up There? (P-D)
Why Me? (P-D)

Lambart, Evelyn

Fine Feathers (D)
Hoarder, The (D)
Impossible Map, The (D)
Mr. Frog Went A-Courting (D)
Lion and the Mouse, The (D)
Paradise Lost (D)
Rythmie (P)

North Wind and the Sun, The (D)

Licastro, Joe

Drinking (D)
Emergency Blood Transfusion (D)
Fight for Breath (A): Emphysema Smokers' Lungs (D)

Littleton, James

Celtic Spirits (D)
Tree Power (P-D)

Long, Jack

Hometown, The (P)
Images Stone B.C. (D)
Man Who Digs For Fish, The (D)

Longpré, Bernard

Branch et Branch (D)
Carrousel (D)
Dimensions (D)
Monsieur Pointu (D)
Nébule (D)
Tête en fleurs (Marie) (D)

Low, Ben

Wintersong (D)

Low, Colin

A is for Architecture (P)
Age of the Beaver (D)
Alberta Girls (P)
Another Side of the Forest (P)
Arctic IV (P)
Bate's Car: Sweet As a Nut (P)
Bill Loosely's Heat Pump (P)
Biosphere, The (P)
Boat that Ian Built, The (P)
Cell 16 (P)
Child series (4 films) (P)
Christ is Risen (P)
Circle of the Sun (D)
City of Gold (D)
City Out of Time (D)
Coaches (P)
Coming Home (P)
Corral (D)
Crafts series (4 films) (P)
Cree Hunters of Mistassini (P)
Days of Whiskey Gap, The (D)
Descent (P)
Earthware (P)
First Born (P)
First Steps (P)
Forest under Siege (P)
Forest Watchers, The (P)
Freshwater World (P)
God Help the Man Who Would Part with His Land (P)
Gold (D)
Great White Bird, A (P)
Great Clean-up, The (P)
Greenlanders, The (P)

Have I Ever Lied to You Before (P)
Here is Canada (P)
High Grass Circus (P)
Hinchinbrook Diary (P)
Hors d'oeuvre (P)
Hutterites, The (D)
I Am an Old Tree (P)
I Don't Think It's Meant for Us . . .(P)
I Know an Old Lady Who Swallowed a Fly (P)
In all Seasons (P)
In Praise of Hands (P)
In Search of the Bowhead Whale (P)
Jack Rabbit (P)
Jolifou Inn, the (D)
Kainai (P)
King of the Hill (P)
Lady and the Owl, The (P)
Land—A New Priority, The (P)
Little Big Top (P)
Log House (P)
Los Canadienses (P)
Lumsden (P)
Memo from Fogo, A (P)
Metal Workers, The (P)
Musicanada (P)
My Financial Career (P)
Nell and Fred (P)
New Alchemists, The (P)
New Romance: Aspects of Sexuality and Sexual Roles (P)
Newfoundland Project series (P)
Niagara for Sale (P)
One Little Indian (P)
Operation G.A.T.E. (P)
Other World, The (P)
Our Land is Our Life (P)
Path of the Paddle series (4 films) (P)
Peep Show, The (P)
Pinto for the Prince, A (D)
Potatoes (P)
Question of Television Violence, The (P)
Ride, The (P)
River (P)
Rock-a-bye (P)
Romance of Transportation in Canada, The (D)
Running Time (P)
Sananguagat: Inuit Masterworks (P)
Sea, The (P)
Sense of Humus, A (P)
Sense of Place, A (P)
Sisters of the Space Age (P)
Sub-Igloo (P)
Sword of the Lord, The (P)
That Gang of Hoodlums? (P)
Threads (P)
Time Piece (P)
21-87 (P)
Universe (D)
Waiting for Fidel (P)
Waterloo Farmers (P)
Wax and Wool (P)
We Can't Stand Still Can We? (P)
Whales Are Waiting, The (P)
Winds of Fogo, The (D)
World of David Milne, The (P)
You're Eating for Two (P)

Low, Stephen

Challenger: An Industrial Romance (P-D)

Lower, Bob

Bush Pilot: Reflections on a Canadian Myth (D)
House on the Prairie, A (D)
McIntyre Block, The (D)
New Mayor, the (D)

Macartney-Filgate, Terence

Back-breaking Leaf, The (D)
Blood and Fire (D)
Cars in Your Life, The (D)
Fields of Endless Day (D)
Labrador: Land out of Time (D-P)
This is an Emergency (D)
Up Against the System (D)
Young Social Worker Speaks Her Mind, A (D)

Macaulay, Eunice

Special Delivery (D)

MacDonald, Douglas

Drinking (P)
Mother of Many Children (P)
Pictures from the 1930s (P)
Simpler Life, A (P)
Sons of Haji Omar (P)

Mackay, Bruce

Half-masted Schooner, The (D)
Northern Composition (D-P)
Pearly Yeats, The (D)
Sail Away (P-D)
Still in One Piece Anyway (D)

Mackenzie, Shelagh

Fixed in Time—A Victoria Album (D)
Unstructured for a Summer (D)

MacLeod, Alec

First Steps (D)

MacLeon, Paul

Farming of Fish, The (D)

MacNeill, Ian

Four Families (P)
Lewis Mumford on The City series (6 films) (P)
Rosewood Daydream, A (P-D)
Stress (D)

Mahoney, Mike

Dores (D)
Just One of the Boys (D)

Makosinski, Art

Those Wild Wild Mushrooms (D)

Mallette, Yvon

Boomsville (D)
Family that Dwelt Apart, The (D)

Mankiewicz, Francis

Day in Point Pelée, A (D)
Once Upon a Hunt (D)

Marchiori, Carlos

Drag, The (D)

Marsh, D'Arcy

Indian Relocation: Elliot Lake (D)

Martell, Jan-Marie

Pretend You're Wearing a Barrel (D)

Martin, Kent

Eastern Graphic (D)
Empty Harbours, Empty Dreams (D)
Family of Labrador, A (D)
Moses Coady (D)

Martin, Marcel

Columbia, The (P)
Devil's Toy, The (P)
Down Through the Years (P)
Harvesting (P)
Knowing to Learn (P)
Shape of Things, The (P)
Sudden Departure (P)
Walls of Memory (P)

Mason, Bill

Blake (D)
Cry of the Wild (D)
Coming Back Alive (D)
Death of a Legend (D)
Face of the Earth (D)
In Search of the Bowhead Whale (D)
Paddle to the Sea (D)
Path of the Paddle series (4 films) (D)
Rise and Fall of the Great Lakes, The (D)
Song of the Paddle (D)
Wolf Pack (D)

Matzkuhn, Bettina

Hometown, The (D)

May, Derek

Angel (D)
Film for Max, A (D)
McBus (D)
Mother Tongue (D)
Niagara Falls (D)

Pandora (D)
Pictures from the 1930s (P-D)
Sananguagat: Inuit Masterworks (D)

Mazur, Derek

New Mayor, The (P-D)

McCaw, Peter

Azzel (P)
Dominga (P)

McCready, Kenneth

Among Fish (D)
Bill Loosley's Heat Pump (D)
Glaciation (D)
Innocent Door, The (D)
We Can't Stand Still Can We? (D)

McCurdy, Mark

Doctor Woman: The Life and Times of Dr. Elizabeth Bagshaw (D)

McDonnell, Fergus

Back into the Sun (D)
Cars in Your Life, The (D)

McGowan, Sharon

Rosanna: Portrait of an Immigrant Woman(D)

McGregor, Julie

Token Gesture, A (P)

McKay, Jim

Stanley Takes a Trip (P)
Teeth Are to Keep (D)

McKennirey, Michael

Art of the Possible, The (P)
Atonement (D)
Beyond Kicks (P)
Conquered Dream, The (P)
Eastern Graphic (D)
Flash William (P)
Flora: Scenes from a Leadership Convention (P)
From the Ashes of War (D)
Great White Bird, A (D)
Harmonie (P)
Has Anybody Here Seen Canada? (P)
Healing (P)
I Don't Have to Work That Big (D)
I'll Go Again (P)
Journey to the End (P)
Keepers of Wildlife (D)
Little Big Top (P)
Long View, The (D)
New Mayor, The (P)
People of the Seal (2 films) (P)
Sons of Haji Omar (P)
Unbroken Line, The (P)

Welcome to Smith Falls (P)

McLaren, Ian

Adieu Alouette series (12 films) (P)
Atlantic Canada series (12 films) (P)
Art of Eating, The (P)
Baby this is for You (P)
Ballad to Cornwallis (P)
Bella Bella (P)
Boo Hoo (P)
Brothers Byrne, The (P)
Change by Degrees (P)
Crazy Quilt (P)
David and Bert (P)
Eastern Graphic (P)
Hecklers, The (D-P)
Journeymen, The (P)
Medoonak the Stormmaker (P)
Pacific Canada series (8 films) (P)
Pen-Hi Grad (P)
Ready When You Are (P)
Scoggie (P)
Slow Hello, A (P)
Soccer (P)
Still in One Piece Anyway (P)
This Riel Business (P-D)
Une Job Steady . . . Un Bon Boss (P-D)
We Sing More than We Cry (P)
We're Here to Stay (P-D)
Where You Goin' Company Town? (P)
Whistling Smith (P)
World is Round, The (P-D)

McLaren, Norman

À la pointe de la plume
Alouette
Around Is Around
Ballet Adagio
Blinkity Blank
Boogie-Doodle
Boucles
Camera Makes Whoopee
Canon
Caprice en couleurs
C'est l'aviron
Chairy Tale, A
Défense de Madrid, La
Discours de bienvenue de Norman McLaren
Dollar Dance
Écran d'épingles, L'
Étoiles et bandes
Fiddle-de-dee
Five for Four
Hen Hop
Hoppity Pop
Il était une chaise
Là-haut sur ces montagnes
Lignes horizontales
Lignes verticales
Little Phantasy on a 19th-Century Painting, A
Love on the Wing
Mail Early
Mail Early for Christmas
Merle, Le
Mosaïque

Munro, Grant

Animal Movie, The (D)
Animated Motion (P-D) (with Norman McLaren)
Boo Hoo (D)
Canon (D)
Christmas Cracker (D)
Eye Hears, The Ear Sees, The (P)
My Financial Career (D)
Neighbours (D)
Tour en l'air (P-D)
Toys (P-D)
Two Bagatelles (D)

Nachtigall, Dieter

Red Dress, The (P)

Nance, Margit

Post Partum Depression (D)

Nason, Kent

Tracker (D)

Nelson, Barrie

Propaganda Message (D)
Ten—The Magic Number (D)

Newman, David

Our Health Is Not for Sale (D)
Occupational Health series (D)
Sons of Haji Omar (D)
Who Will I Sentence now? (D)

Newman, Sydney

Story of Peter and the Potter, The (P)

Nichol, Robert

Do Your Thing (D)
Fisherman's Fall (D)
Mac's Mill (D)
November (P-D)
Perception—Structure or Flow (P-D)
Striker (D)
That Gang of Hoodlums? (P-D)
Wheat (D)
Wilf (D)

Nilsson, Eric M.

Place for Everything, A (D)

Nirenberg, Les

Québécoise, La (D)

Notkin, Richard

Autobiographical by A. M. Klein (D)

Noyes, Elliot, Jr.

Alphabet (D)
In a Box (D)

Nutter, Christopher

Garden (D)

Obomsawin, Alanis

Amisk (P-D)
Christmas at Moose Factory (D)
Mother of Many Children (P-D)

O'Connor, Hugh

Above the Horizon (P-D)
Above the Timberline (P)
Edge of the Barrens, The (P)
Ethiopian Mosaic (P)
Face of the High Arctic, The (P)
In the Labyrinth (D)
Life in the Woodlot (P)
Microscopic Fungi (P)
Paul-Emile Borduas (P)
Persistent Seed, The (P)
Snow (P)
Trout Stream (P)

Ofield, Jack

People at Dipper (D)

Olivier, Suzanne

Des ensembles (D)

Orieux, Ron

Fort Good Hope (D)

Ossei, John K.

Ananse's Farm (D)

Overing, Claudia

Beyond the Naked Eye (D)
Congenital Broncho-oesophageal Fistula in an Adult (D)
Mechanical Knee, The (D)
Other World, The (D)

Owen, Don

Cowboy and Indian (D)
Ernie Game, The (D)
Further Glimpse of Joey, A (D)
High Steel (D)
Holstein (D)
Ladies and Gentlemen . . . Mr. Leonard Cohen (D)
Nobody Waved Goodbye (D)
Notes for a Film about Donna and Gail (D)
Runner (D)
You Don't Back Down (D)

Page, Ken

28° Above—Below (D)

Palardy, Jean

Correlieu (D)
Ti-Jean Goes Lumbering (D)

Paré, Laurence

Matter of Life, A (P)

Parker, Graham

Each Day That Comes (D)
Joey (D)
Perception of Orientation, The (D)
Power of Matter, The (D)
River with a Problem (D)
Squarejohns (P)
Where Mrs. Whalley Lives (D)

Parent, Jacques

Perception of Orientation, The (D)
Physics: An Interactive Approach (D)

Parker, Morton

Angkor, the Lost City (D)
Blindness (D)
Charles Tupper (The Big Man) (D)
Clerk, The (D)
Department Manager, The (D)
Dues and the Union (P)
General Foreman, The (P-D)
John Cabot (A Man of the Renaissance) (D)
Man on the Assembly Line, The (D)
Parliamentary Procedure (D)
Red Kite, The (D)
Shop Steward, The (D)
Skilled Worker, The (D)
Vice-President, The (D)

Parks, Wo Ted

To Make a Map (D)

Parsons, Bruce

Price of Fire, The (D)

Patel, Ishu

About Puberty and Reproduction (D)
About VD (D)
Afterlife (D)
Bead Game (D)
How Death Came to Earth (D)
Perspectrum (D)

Patton, Richard

Mental Patients' Association (D)

Patenaude, Michel

Light Fantastick, The (D)

Paterson, Kris

Mudflats Living (D)
Pleasure Flaire (D)

Patry, Pierre

Françoise (D)
Ghosts of a River (D)
Louis-Hippolyte Lafontaine (D)

Payne, Gordon

Negotiating a New Canadian Constitution (D)

Pearson, Ann

Patricia's Moving Picture (P)

Pearson, George

Atonement (P)
Beyond Kicks (P)
Challenge of Change, The (P)
Charlie's Day (P)
Cold Journey (D)
Conquered Dream, The (P)
Corporation series (7 films) (P)
Don Messer: His Land and His Music (P)
End of a Summer Day (P)
Goodbye Sousa (P)
Here Is Canada (P)
In One Day (P)
India Trip, The (P)
Keepers of Wildlife (P)
Mighty Steam Calliope, The (P)
Northern Fisherman (P)
Other Side of the Ledger, The (P)
People of the Seal (2 films) (P)
Running Time (P)
Quiet Wave, A (P)
Rock-a-bye (P)
Search into White Space (P)
Small Smoke at Blaze Creek (P)
Station 10 (P)
Tour en l'air (P)
Unplanned, The (P)
What in the World Is Water? (P)

Pearson, Peter

Best Damn Fiddler from Calabogie to Kaladar, The (D)
Dowry, The (D)
Saul Alinsky Went to War (D)

Pedersen, Jon

John Hooper's Way with Wood (D)
Tara's Mulch Garden (D)
Those Wild Wild Mushrooms (P)

Perles, Barry

Quiet Wave, A (D)

Perlman, Janet

Lady Fishbourne's Guide to Better Table Manners (D)
Why Me? (D-P)

Perrault, Pierre

Acadia, Acadia (D)
Beluga Days (D)
Moontrap, The (D)
Wake Up, mes bons amis (D)

Perron, Clément

Caroline (D)
Day after Day (D)
Georges-P Vanier (D)
Jusqu'au coeur (P)
Kid Sentiment (P)
Multiple Man (P)
Tattoo 67 (P)
We Are All . . . Picasso! (P)

Pettigrew, Margaret

Patricia's Moving Picture (P)
Recontre (P)
Right Candidate for Rosedale, The (P)
Rusting World (P)
Sea Dream (P)
Sun, Wind and Wood (P)

Pettigrew, William

Biosphere, The (D)
Bow and Arrow (D)
Buildings Already Begun, The (D)
Epilogue (D)
Kurelek (D)
Meet the Martins (P-D)
180 Is Max (D)
Oskee Wee Wee (D)
Special Place, A (D)

Phillips, Dale

Boomer (D)

Piché, René

In the Land Where the Sun Sets (P)

Pindal, Kaj

Caninabis (Junkie Dog) (D)
Horsing Around (D)
King Size (D)
Peep Show, The (D)
What on Earth! (D)

Pinney, Christopher

Beluga Baby (P)
Some People Have to Suffer (P-D)

Poirier, Anne-Claire

Before the Time Comes (P-D)
Mother-to-be (D)
Scream from Silence, A (P-D)
Shakti—"She Is Vital Energy" (P)
They Called Us: "Les Filles du Roy" (P-D)

Pojar, Bretislav

Balablok (D)
To See or Not to See (D)

Pollard, Brian

Islanders, The (D)
They All Can Work (D)

Portugais, Louis

About Pellan (D)
Algeria (D)
Correlieu (P)

Potterton, Gerald

My Financial Career (D)
Quiet Racket, The (D)
Railrodder, The (D)
Ride, The (D)

Poulin, Denis

Beyond Curtains (D)

Poulin, Hugues

Devoir, Le (2 parts) (D)

Poulsson, Andreas

Log House (D)
New Denmark (D)

Radford, Tom

Boomer (P)
China Mission: The Chester Ronning Story (D)
Every Saturday Night (D)
Fores's and Vladimir Krajina, The (D)
Happily Unmarried (P)
Keephills (P)
Man Who Chooses the Bush (D)
Slow Hello, A (D)
Wings of Time, The (D)
Wood Mountain Poems (P)

Ralph, John

At Long Last (D)
Offshore (D)

Ransen, Mort

Christopher's Movie Matinée (D)
Circle, The (D)
Falling from Ladders (D)
Inner Man, The (D)
Jacky Visits the Zoo (D)
No Reason to Stay (D)
Running Time (D)
Untouched and Pure (D)
You Are on Indian Land (D)

Rasmussen, Lorna

Happily Unmarried (P)

Raxlen, Ritchard

Anger after Death (D)
Bloodsugar (D)
Earthware (P-D)
Hinchinbrook Diary (D)
If He Is Devoured, I Win (D)
Legend (D)
Metalworkers (P)
Mirage (D)
Sky Is Blue, The (D)

Raxlen, Sarah

Gore Road (D)

Raymond, Peter

Art of the Possible, The (D)
Asivagtiin (The Hunters) (P)
Coldspring Project, The (P)
Flora—Scenes from a Leadership Convention (D)
Forest Watchers, The (D)
History on the Run: The Media and the '79 Election (P-D)
Innocent Door, The (P)
Lumsden (D)
Natsik Hunting (P)
Qilaluganiatut (Whale Hunting) (P)
Reflections on a Leadership Convention (D)
River (D)
Sikusilarmiut (P-D)

Razutis, Al

Egypte (D)

Redbird, Duke

Charley Squash Goes to Town (D)

Reeve, Josef

Flight (D)
Hard Rider (D)
Imperial Sunset (D)
Judoka (D)
North (D)
Pillar of Wisdom (D)
Poen (D)

Reígnier, Michel

Below Zero (P-D)
Indian Memento (D)
Tattoo 67 (D)

Reid, Bill

Back Alley Blue (D)
Coming Home (D)
Occupation (P-D)

Reid, Edmund

Family Camping (D)
More Milk for More People (D)

Reid, Ernest

Adventure in Newfoundland (P-D)
Aircraft in Forest Fire Control (P)
Boy Next Door, The (P-D)
Enduring Wilderness, The (P)
Figure Skating (P-D)
In All Seasons (D)
Learn to Ski (P-D)
Ski (P-D)
Space Connection (D)
Three Farmers (P-D)
Trail Ride (P-D)

Reniger, Lotte

Aucassin and Nocolette (D)

Reljic, Shelah

Harrison's Yukon (D)
He's Not the Walking Kind (P)
Mental Patients' Association (P)
Pretend You're Wearing a Barrel (P)
Rosanna: Portrait of an Immigrant Woman (P)
Salmon People (P)
Sauk-Ai (P)
She's a Railroader (P)
Soccer (D)

Remerowski, Ted

Mystery of Bay Bulls, The (D)

Rennick, Don

End of a Summer Day (P)
Prison (P)

Richardson, Boyce

Cree Hunters of Mistassini (D)
North China Commune (D)
North China Factory (D)
Occupational Health series (D)
Our Health Is Not for Sale (D)
Our Land Is Our Life (D)
Two Dreams of a Nation (D)
Who will I Sentence Now? (D)
Wuxing People's Commune (P)

Rigolo, Dino

Teeth Are to Keep (D)

Riley, Simon

History on the Run: The Media and the '79 Election (P)

Robertson, Strowan

Another Side of the Forest (D)

Schon, Jeffery

This is an Emergency (P)

Schuurman, Hubert

Greenlanders, The (D)
Sami, Four Lands, One People, The (D)
Sami Herders (D)

Scott, Cynthia

Listen Listen Listen (P)
Scoggie (D)
Some Natives of Churchill (D)
Ungrateful Land, The (D)
West series (12 films) (P-D)

Scott, Michael

Angus (D)
Boomer (P)
Bush Pilot: Reflections on a Canadian Myth (P)
Chasing the Eclipse (P)
China Mission: The Chester Ronning Story (P)
For Gentlemen Only (D)
Getting Started (P)
Give'em a Half Turn (P)
Keephills (P)
Loved, Honoured and Bruised (P)
McIntyre Block (P)
Never a Dull Moment (P)
New Mayor, The (P)
Oh Sure (P)
One Man (P)
Priory the Only Home I've Got (P)
The Red Dress (D)
Small Smoke at Blaze Creek (D)
Station 10 (D)
That's the Price (D)
They're Putting Us Off the Map (D)
Tudor King (P)
We're Gonna Have Recess (D)
Whistling Smith (D)

Séguillon, François

About Pellan (P)
Alegria (P)
Beyond the Naked Eye (P)
Both Sides of the Coin (P)
Bronze (P)
Congenital Broncho-oesophageal Fistula in an Adult (P)
Cries from Within (P)
Cross-country Skiing (P)
Eli, Eli, iamma sabachtani? (P)
Glimpses of China (P)
Manhattan Odyssey, The (P)
Modulo (P)
Northwest Passage (P)
Ping-pong (P)
Québec in Silence (P)
Ratopolis (P)
Saint-Urbain in Troyes (P)
Tomorrow Winter Comes (P)
What Are You Running For? (P)

Semotuk, Lydia

China Mission: The Chester Ronning Story (P)

Sens, Al

Twitch, The (D)

Shaffer, Beverly

Children of Canada series (7 films) (D)
Going the Distance (D)

Schaffer, Rita

Appointment, The (P)

Shandel, Tom

Behind the Masks (D)
Community Action Theater on Tour (D)
Lotomania (D)
We Call Them Killers (D)

Shannon, Kathleen

Children of Canada series (7 films) (P)
Co-op Housing: Getting It Together (P)
Co-op Housing: The Best Move We Ever Made (P)
Goldwood (D)
I Don't Think It's Meant For Us . . . (D)
Maud Lewis: A World Without Shadows (P)
Lady from Grey County, The (P)
Prairie Album (P)
Rencontre (P)
Rusting World (P)
Some American Feminists (P)
Sun, Wind and Wood (P)
Town Mouse and the Country Mouse, The (P)
Unremarkable Birth, An (P)
Working Chance, A (P)
Working Mothers series (11 films) (D)

Shapely, Rosemarie

Coming Back Alive (D)
Pearson Building, The (D)

Shatalow, Peter

Black Ice (D)

Shebib, Donald

Satan's Choice (D)
Search for Learning, A (D)

Shere, Ken

Wings of Time, The (P)

Shon, Jeffrey

Hottest Show on Earth, The (P)

Singer, Christa

Sense of Family, A (P)

Singer, Gail

Loved, Honoured and Bruised (D)

Sky, Laura

Co-op Housing: Getting it Together (D)
Co-op Housing: The Best Move We Ever Made (D)
Shutdown (P)

Smith, John N.

Acting Class (P-D)
Bargain Basement (D)
Bella Bella (P)
Case of Eggs, A (P)
Happiness is Loving Your Teacher (D)
Heatwave Lasted Four Days, The (P)
Journeyman, The (D)
New Boys, The (D)
Nishnawabe-Aski—The People and the Land (P)
No Day of Rest (D)
Ready When You Are (P-D)
Revolution's Orphans (D)
Star (P)
We Sing More than We Cry (D)
West series (12 films) (P)

Smith, Lynn

This Is Your Museum Speaking (D)

Soul, Veronika

Tax: The Outcome of Income (D)

Spak, Harvey

Wood Mountain Poems (D)

Sparling, Gordon

Water Dwellers, The (D)

Spencer, Michael

Angotee (P)
Arctic Saga (P)
Birds of Canada No. 6 (P)

Spiller, Frank

Canada in World War One (P)
Canada: Landform Regions (P)
City under Pressure (P)
Dance Squared (P)
Forest Region of Canada (P)
Introduction to Jet Engines, An (P)

Spotton, John

Activator One (D)
Buster Keaton Rides Again (D)
Forest, The (D)
Have I Ever Lied to You Before? (D)
Meet The Martins (P)
Memorandum (D)

Never a Backward Step (D)
Pinto for the Prince, A (D)

Springbett, David

Black Ice (P)
Sense of Family, A (P)
Shutdown (P)

Spry, Robin

Action: The October Crisis of 1970 (P-D)
Change in the Maritimes (D)
Downhill (P-D)
Face (P-D)
Flowers on a One-way Street (D)
Illegal Abortion (D)
Level 4350 (D)
Miner (D)
One Man (D)
Prologue (P-D)
Reaction: A Portrait of a Society in Crisis (P-D)
Ride for Your Life (D)

Squire, Ronald

Heavy Horse Pull (D)

Stear, Donald

Tale of Mail, A (D)

Steinhouse, Stephan

My Floating World—Miyuki Tanobi (D)

Stone, Noel

Columbia, The (D)

Stoney, George C.

God Help the Man Who Would Part with His Land (D)
I Don't Think It's Meant for Us . . . (P)
Little Burgundy (P)
Mrs. Case (P)
Nell and Fred (P)
Occupation (P)
Prince Edward Island Development Plan, The (2 films) (P)
These Are My People (P)
Up Against the System (P)
VTR St. Jacques (P)
You Are on Indian Land (P)
Young Social Worker Speaks Her Mind, A (P)

Stutz, Roland

Taxi (D)

Suèr, Henk

Co Hoedeman Animator (P)
From the Ashes of War (P)

Svatek, Peter

Beware, Beware, My Beauty Fair (D)

Swinden, Richard

A One/Two/Many/World (D)

Symansky, Adam

Inheritance, The (P)
Wages of Work, The (P)

Tasker, Rex

Atlanticanada series (12 films) (P)
Baymen, The (D)
Bus (A)—For Us (D)
Cancer in Women (P)
Celtic Spirits (P)
Don Breaks Out (P-D)
Dories (P)
Empty Harbours, Empty Dreams (P)
Encounter at Kwacha House—Halifax (D)
Family of Labrador, A (P)
Farming of Fish, The (P)
Fixed in Time—A Victorian Album (P)
Gros Morne: A Matter of Time (P)
Halifax Music Part I: General Music Program
Halifax Music Part II: Instrumental Program
Halifax Neighborhood Centre Project (D)
Islanders, The (P)
John Hooper's Way With Wood (P)
Just One of the Boys (P)
Labrador Hospital (P)
Last Corvette, The (P)
Loops to Learn By (D)
Margaree People (P)
Moses Coady (P)
New Denmark (P)
North Pacific (D)
Oshawa Kid, The (P-D)
Porter's Magic Dreams (P)
Queen (The), the Chef and the President (D)
Regina Telebus (D)
Seaweed Walk (P)
Steeltown (D)
Tara's Mulch Garden (P)
They All Can Work (P)
Tracker (P)
12,000 Men (P)
Wealth from the Sea (P)
Where Do We Go from Here? (P)
White Ship, The (P)

Taylor, Gilbert

3 Track (P-D)

Taylor, Herb

Forest Regions of Canada (D)

Taylor, John

Augusta (P)
Baby This Is for You (D)
Bear's Christmas, The (P)
Behind the Masks (P)
Beluga Baby (P)
Canaries to Clydesdales (P)
Caravaners (P)

Egypte (P)
Estuary (P)
Every Saturday Night (P)
For Land's sake (P)
For Good Hope (P)
Great Grand Mother (P)
Harrison's Yukon (P)
Horse Drawn Magic (P)
Lotomania (P)
Man Who Digs for Fish (P)
Mental Patients' Association (P)
Nails (P)
Negotiating a New Canadian Constitution (P)
No Big Money (P)
Prairie—Passing Through (P)
Rosanna: Portrait of an Immigrant Woman (P)
Sauk-Ai (P)
Slow Hello, A (P)
Strathyre (P)
TV Sale (P)
Twitch, The (P)
Winter Survival (P)

Théberge, André

Dernière neige, La (D)
Matter of Life, A (D)
Un fait accompli (D)

Thérien, Gilles

Ratopolis (D)
Two Years or More (D)

Thomas, Gayle

It's Snow (D)
Magic Flute, The (D)
Sufi Tale, A (D)

Thomas-d'Hoste, Michel

Hiroko Ikoko (D)

Thomson, Andy

Agony of Jimmy Quinlan, The (D)
Angus (D)
Blackwood (D)
Boat that Ian Built, The (D)
En garde (D)
Forests and Vladimir Krajina, The (P)
Fort Who?
Go With Us (D)
Insulation Story, The (P)
Journey to the Edge (D)
My Floating World—Miyuki Tanobe (P)
No Act of God (P)
No Day of Rest (P)
Occupational Health series (P)
Our Health Is not for Sale (P)
Telecommunications: Behind the Scenes (D)
Unplanned, The (D)
Whales are Waiting, The (D)
Who Will I Sentence Now? (P)

Thurling, Peter

Breakdown (D)

Todd, Richard

Nell and Fred (D)
Sunny Munchy Crunchy Natural Food Shop, The (D)

Toole, Gary

Beyond Kicks (D)
Cycling: Still the Greatest (D)
Diving: No Place for Cowards (D)
Mac's Mill (P)
More Than Just the Trees (D)
Northern Composition (D)
Potatoes (P)
Sense of Humus, A (P)
Waterloo Farmers (P)

Torrance, Jennifer

Post Partum Depression (P)

Tranter, Barbara

She's a Railroader (D)

Trecartin, F. Whitman

Dories (P)
Duty Free (D)
Freeze-in (D)
Gros Morne: A Matter of Time (D-P)
Halifax Music Part I: General Music Program (D)
Halifax Music Part II: Instrumental Program (D)
Insulation Story, The (D)
Moses Coady (D)
Those Wild Wild Mushrooms (P)

True, Cy

Last Corvette, The (D)
Wealth from the Sea (D)

Tunis, Ron

Animal Movie, The (D)
House That Jack Built, The (D)
This is Me (D)
Wind (D)

Tunstell, Douglas

Women on the March (D)

Turcot, Lise

Wandering Spirit Survival School (P)

Vaitiekunas, Vincent

Tree Is a Living Thing, A (D)

Valenta, Vladimir

Back Alley Blue (P)
Breakdown (P)
For Gentlemen Only (P)

Happiness is Loving Your Teacher (P)
I Wasn't Scared (P)
One Man (P)
Teach Me to Dance (P)
So Long to Run (P)

Vallée, Jacques

If Not . . . (D)

Vecchione, Judith

Yes or No Jean-Guy Moreau (P)

Verrall, David

Laughlines—A Portrait of Kaj Pindal (P)
Pearson Building, The (P)
National Scream, The (P-D)
Sweater, The (P)
This Your Museum Speaking (P)

Verrall, Robert

A Is for Architecture (D)
Alphabet (P)
Around Perception (P)
Bear's Christmas, The (P)
Best Friends (P)
Bloodsugar (P)
Boomsville (P)
Christmas at Moose Factory (P)
Citizen Harold (P)
Cosmic Zoom (P)
Doodle Film (P)
Drag, The (P)
11 Steps to Survival (P)
Energy and Matter (D)
Face of the Earth (P)
Going the Distance (P)
Goldwood (P)
Gore Road (P)
Great Toy Robbery, The (P)
Half-masted Schooner, The (P)
Hot Stuff (P)
In a Box (P)
Interview (P)
King Size (P)
Kurelek (P)
Little Red Riding Hood (P)
Loops to Learn By (P)
Man: The Polluter (P)
Men in the Park, The (P)
No Apples for Johnny (P)
North Wind and the Sun, The (P)
180 Is Max (P)
Origami (P)
Out of Silence (P)
Paul Kane Goes West (P)
Pikangikum (P)
Propaganda Message (P)
Sky is Blue, The (P)
Tax Is Not a Four-Letter Word (P)
Tickets, s.v.p. (P)
Tilt (P)
To See or Not to See (P)
Undergrouond Movie, The (P)

Valley of the Moon (P)
What is Life? (P)
What on Earth! (P)

Viljoen, Tina

Children Enfants Ninos (D)
Development With Tears (D)
Exploding Cities (D)
Growing Dollars (D)
Little by Little—Upgrading Barrio Escopa (D)
No Fitting Habitat (D)
Some Call it Progress (D)
Water the Hazardous Necessity (D)
Yes or No Jean-Guy Moreau (P)

Virgo, Don

Operation G.A.T.E. (D)
Safe Escort (D)
Ten-Tenths Ice (D)
Tomorrow Is Too Late (D)

Voizard, Marc

My Floating World—Miyuki Tanobe (D)

Walczewski, J.

New Romance: Aspects of Sexuality and Sexual Roles (D)

Walker, Giles

Bravery in the Field (D)
Descent (D)
Down to the Sea (P-D)
Freshwater World (D)
I wasn't Scared (P)
No Way They Want to Slow down (D)
Sword of the Lord, The (D)
Twice Upon a Time (D)

Wargon Allan

Lismer (D)

Warny, Clorinda

Beginnings (D)
Egg, The (D)
Happiness Is (D)

Watson, Patricia

Admittance, The (D)
Invention of the Adolescent, The (D)
Purse, The (D)
Summer We Moved to Elm Street, The (D)

Webber, Ron

Valley of the Moon (D)

Weintraub, William

Aviators of Hudson Strait, The (D)
Bekevar Jubilee (P)

Between Two Wars Series (3 films) (P)
Challenge for the Church (D)
Hold the Ketchcup (P)
I've Never Walked the Steppes (P)
Kaszuby (P)
Margaret Laurence, First Lady of Manawaka (P)
Matter of Fat, A (D)
Point, The (P)
Seven Shades of Pale (P)
Turn of the Century (P)
Walls Come Tumbling Down, The (D)
Why Rock the Boat?

Weldon, John

No Apple for Johnny (D)
Special Delivery (D)
Spinnolio (D)

Westcott, Margaret

Eve Lambart (P-D)
Lady from Grey County, The (P)
Some American Feminists (D)

Westman, Tony

Beluga Baby (D)
Going the Distance (D)
Salmon People (D)
Sauk-Ai (D)

Wheeler, Anne

Augusta (D)
Happily Unmarried (P-D)
Never a Dull Moment (P)
Priory, the Only Home I've Got (P)
Teach me to Dance (D)

White, Don

Estuary (D)

White, Doug

No Big Money (D)

Wilder, Donald

Legendary Judge, The (D)
Nahanni (D)
Rallye des neiges (D)

Wilkinson, Douglas

Angotee (D)
How to Build an Igloo (D)

Wilson, Christopher

Wandering Spirit Survival School (D)

Wilson, David

Wages of Work, The (D)

Wilson, Phyllis

Nishnawabe-Aski—The People and the Land (D)

Wilson, Sandra

He's Not the Walking Kind (D)
Pen-Hi Grad (D)

Wilson, Tim

Boy Meets Band (P)
Canada in World War One (P)
Chairmaker and the Boys, The (P)
Saddlemaker, The (P)
Tiny Terrors, The (P)

Winkler, Donald

Bookmaker's Progress (D)
Bannerfilm (D)
Crafts series (4 films) (D)
Doodle Film (D)
In Praise of Hands (D)
One Man's Garden (D)
Travel Log (D)

Wodoslawsky, Stefan

Bravery in the Field (P)
Twice Upon a Time (P)

Worobey, Don

Bear's Christmas, The (P)

Egypte (P)
Flashpoint (P)
Images Stone B.C. (D)
TV Sale (P)

Wright, Paul

Champions, The (P)
Dionne Quintuplets, The (P)
Henry Ford's America (P)
Paperland—The Bureaucrat Observed (P)

Wright, Cheryl

Cancer in Women (D)

Yoshida, Yuki

Children of Canada Series (7 films) (P)

Zannis, Mark

Class Project: The Garbage Movie (P)
Cree Way
Fiddlers of James Bay, The (P)
Inheritance, The (P)
Two Dreams of a Nation: The Fortin Family of Quebec and
    Alberta (P)
Unemployment: Voices from the Line (P)

Zolov, Jack

In Our Own Way (D)

Index

Page references in italics indicate illustrations.

307

Hemmings, David, 122, 236
Hemon, Louis, 39, 150, 255
Hénaut, Dorothy Todd, 283, 284
Henderson, Anne, 134, 284
Hendryx, Shirley, 260
Hen Hop, 26
Henley, Ted, 203
Hennelly, Dermot, 264
Hennessy, Dan, 222
Hennessy, Mary Lou, 162
Henning, Doug, 251
Henry, Martha, 149, 261
Henry, Tim, 220
Henry, Yves, 163
Henry Moore, 101
Henson, Joan, 217, 284
Hepburn, Premier Mitchell, 33, 45
Heppel, Sylvie, 194
Hepworth, Cecil, 56, 57
Herbert, John, 200
Herdan, Earle, 260
Here's to Harry's Grandfather, 102
Here Will I Nest, 38
Herman, André, 284
Hermant Building, Toronto, 78
Heron, Frank, 162
Héroux, Claude, 214, 284
Héroux, Denis, 90, 94, 174, 193, 197, 200, 210, 219, 225, 236, 246
Héroux, Herman, 284
Héroux, Justine, 246, 263
Hershey, Barbara, 125
Hersholt, Jean, 39
Hertzog, Lawrence, 232
Hewgill, Roland, 170
Hewitson, Walford, 187, 284
Hicks, Israel, 284
Higginson, Edward, 257
High, 100, 190
High Ballin', 122, 237
High Grass Circus, 122
Highlight Productions Ltd., 232
Highpoint, 244
High Tide at Noon, 171
Hilkman, Bert, 172
Hill, Arthur, 191, 238
Hill, Percy, 18
Hill, Robert, 35, 179
Hiller, Arthur, 148
Hindle, Art, 200, 219, 240, 265
Hingle, Pat, 153, 260
Hinton, Christopher, 284
Hired Gun (The Devil's Spawn), 89, 171
His Destiny, 33
Hiver bleu, L' (Blue Winter), 128, 244, *24*
Hobson, Valerie, 37
Hoedeman, Co., 122, 284
Hoffert, Brenda, 235
Hoffert, Paul, 183, 184, 220, 235
Hoffman, Guy, 168
Hoffman, Roseline, 214
Hogan, Dominic, 222
Hogan, Susan, 245
Hog Wild, 245
Holbrook, Hal, 244
Holden, Jackie, 210
Holdway, Les, 284
Holland brothers, 17
Hollander, Peter, 284
Hollander, Xavier, 219
Hollywood: and Hye Bossin, 77; Canadian references in movies of, 84; entertainment films of, 58, 59; and film acquisition, 20; and film rentals, 83; films of shown in Canada, 47;

mass appeal of, 14; power and influence of, 13, 58, 59; studios of, 135
"Hollywood North," 144, 145
"Hollywood's Canada," 39
Holmes, Edward (Ed), 170, 172
Holmes, Sherlock, 237
Holography, 119
Holt, Sir Herbert, 20
Home Box Office, 140, 256, 262
Home Feeling: Struggle for a Community, 144
Homer, 105
Homme à tout faire, L' (The Handyman), 241, *241*
Homme et le froid, L' (Below Zero), 102
Homme et son péché, Un (A Man and His Sin), 82, 163, *164*
Hood, Alan, 170
Hookers on Davie, 265
Hoover, Elva Mai, 256
Hope, Leslie, 261
Hopkins, Don, 284
Hopper, Dennis, 245
Horner, Harry, 178
Horner, W. G., 266
Hot Touch, The, 249
Houchen, Claudette, 188
Houde, Germain, 240
Hough, John, 249
Houle, Camil, 182
Hounds of Notre Dame, The, 132, 133, 247, *247*
House, Eric, 170, 196
Houseman, John, 249
House of Light, The (La Chambre Blanche), 194, 195
Howard, Leslie, 75
Howard, Richard, 170
Howard, Sandy, 127
Howay, Robert, 179, 187
Howe, C. D., 83, 84
Howe, John, 100, 217, 220, 284
Howells, Barrie, 187, 284, 285
Hubert, Jacques, 239
Hudson, Rochelle, 87, 161
Hudson's Bay, 75
Huffman, Linda, 199
Hughes, David, 220, 285
Hughes, Helen, 235, 243
Hugh MacLellan: Portrait of a Writer, 148
Human Journal, The, 200
Humble, Robert (Bob), 166, 180, 285
Hume, Edward, 140, 256
Humongous, 254
Humongous Productions, 254
Hunnicut, Gayle, 125
Hunter, Ian, 39
Hunter, John, 252
Hunter, John Clifford, 212
Huntingdon, Louise, 34
Huot, Juliette, 163, 167, 177, 179, 246, 263
Hurd, Mitzi, 179
Hurley, Joan, 220
Huron Indians, 94
Hurricans de Ville-Emard, Les, 196
Hurst, Brian Desmond, 101
Hussey, Olivia, 219
Huston, John, 244
Huston, Walter, 13
Hutt, William, 170, 261
Hutterites, The, 66
Hutton, Christopher, 257
Hutton, Joan, 285
Huycke, Susan, 285
Hyde, Laurence, 285
Hyland, Edward, 161

Hyland, Frances, 92, 176, 204, 247
Hylands, Scott, 209, 265
Hyslop, Ricky, 232

Ianzelo, Tony, 122, 285
IATSE, 18
ICC. *See* International Cinema Corporation
Iceman, 262
Ichikawa, Kon, 101
IFD. *See* International Film Distributors
If You Could Read My Mind, 2
If You Could See What I Hear, 254
If You Love This Planet, 143, *147*
Ikeuchi, Takuma, 237
Ile-aux-Coudres, 92
Il était une fois dans l'est (Once Upon a Time in the East), 215, *215*
Il était une guerre, 90
I'll Find a Way, 122
Il ne faut pas mourir pour ça (Don't Let It Kill You), 100, 190
I Love You (Je t'aime), 214
Image Makers, The, 40
Imagine the Sound, 251
I, Maureen, 122, 237
Imbault, Rita, 179
I'm going to Get You Elliott Boy, 200
I Miss You, Hugs and Kisses, 122, 237
Immortal Scoundrel, The (Etienne Brulé, gibier de potence), 167
Impact-Quadrant, 220
Imperial Theatre, Toronto, 53
Improper Channels, 245
INA, 232
In a Box, 92
Inbreaker, The, 219
Incredible Journey, The, 174
Incubus, 249
Independent distributors, 21
Independent film-makers, 16
Independent Pictures, 266
Initiation, L', 197
Innu Asi, 128, 251
In Praise of Older Women, 237
Inquiry Film, The, 236
In Search of Farley Mowat, 136
Inside Out, 200
Intent to Kill, 171
International Cinema Corporation (ICC), 246
International Cinemedia Centre, 216
International Critics' Award, 134
International Film Distributors (IFD), 21, 170, 171, 173, 232
International films, 127
Intertitles, 14
In the Enemy's Power, 24
Intruder, The, 245
Invaders, The, 75
Ipcress File, The, 87
Ireland, Ian, 191, 192
Ireland, John, 125, 249
Iron Curtain, The, 76, 77
Ironside, Michael, 243, 249
Irwin, Arthur, 63, 64, 71
Irwin, May, 18
Isaac Littlefeathers, 265
Isabel, 100, 101, 189, *189*
Ishimoto, 176
It Can't Be Winter, We Haven't Had Summer Yet (Ça peut pas être l'hiver, on n'a même pas eu d'été), 245
It Happened in Canada, 172
It Is Necessary to Be Among the Peoples of

320

327

330